Titles available from boyd & fraser

BASIC Programming

Applesoft BASIC Fundamentals and Style
BASIC Fundamentals and Style
Complete BASIC for the Short Course
Structured BASIC Fundamentals and Style for the IBM® PC and Compatibles
Structured Microsoft BASIC: Essentials for Business
Structuring Programs in Microsoft BASIC

COBOL Programming

Advanced Structured COBOL: Batch and Interactive
COBOL: Structured Programming Techniques for Solving Problems
Comprehensive Structured COBOL
Fundamentals of Structured COBOL

Database

A Guide to SQL
Database Systems: Management and Design

Computer Information Systems

Applications Software Programming with Fourth-Generation Languages
Business Data Communications and Networks
Expert Systems for Business: Concepts and Applications
Fundamentals of Systems Analysis with Application Design
Investment Management: Decision Support and Expert Systems
Learning Computer Programming: Structured Logic Algorithms, and Flowcharting
Office Automation: An Information Systems Approach

Microcomputer Applications

An Introduction to Desktop Publishing
dBASE III PLUS® Programming
DOS: Complete and Simplified
Introduction to Computers and Microcomputer Applications
Macintosh Productivity Tools
Mastering and Using Lotus 1-2-3®, Release 3
Mastering and Using Lotus 1-2-3®, Version 2.2
Mastering and Using WordPerfect® 5.0 and 5.1
Mastering Lotus 1-2-3®
Microcomputer Applications: A Practical Approach
Microcomputer Applications: Using Small Systems Software, Second Edition
Microcomputer Database Management Using dBASE III PLUS®
Microcomputer Database Management Using dBASE IV®
Microcomputer Database Management Using R:BASE System V®
Microcomputer Productivity Tools
Microcomputer Systems Management and Applications
PC-DOS®/MS-DOS® Simplified, Second Edition
Using Enable®: An Introduction to Integrated Software

Shelly and Cashman Titles

Computer Concepts with Microcomputer Applications (Lotus 1-2-3® and VP-Planner Plus® versions)
Computer Concepts
Essential Computer Concepts
Learning to Use WordPerfect®, Lotus 1-2-3®, and dBASE III PLUS®
Learning to Use WordPerfect®, VP-Planner Plus®, and dBASE III PLUS®
Learning to Use WordPerfect®
Learning to Use Lotus 1-2-3®
Learning to Use VP-Planner Plus®
Learning to Use dBASE III PLUS®
Computer Fundamentals with Application Software
Learning to Use SuperCalc®3, dBASE III®, and WordStar® 3.3: An Introduction
Learning to Use SuperCalc®3: An Introduction
Learning to Use dBASE III®: An Introduction
Learning to Use WordStar® 3.3: An Introduction
BASIC Programming for the IBM Personal Computer
Structured COBOL: Pseudocode Edition
Structured COBOL: Flowchart Edition
RPG II, RPG III, & RPG/400

Order information on page vi.

Mastering and Using LOTUS 1-2-3®
Release 2.2

H. Albert Napier

Rice University and
Napier & Judd, Inc.

Philip J. Judd

Napier & Judd, Inc.

boyd & fraser publishing company

Credits:

Publisher: Tom Walker
Acquisitions Editor: James H. Edwards
Editor: Donna Villanucci
Director of Production: Becky Herrington
Manufacturing Director: Dean Sherman
Cover Design/Illustration: Becky Herrington

This book was produced using Manuscript®

© 1990 by boyd & fraser publishing
A Division of South-Western Publishing Company
Boston, MA 02116

Manufactured in the United States of America

Lotus and 1-2-3 are registered trademarks of Lotus Development Corporation.
dBASE III, dBASE III PLUS and dBASE IV are registered trademarks of Ashton-Tate.
IBM PC is a registered trademark of International Business Machines.
R:BASE System V is a registered trademark of Microrim, Inc.
Paradox 3.0 is a registered trademark of Borland International.
Allways and Allways, The Spreadsheet Publisher are trademarks of Funk Software, Inc.
Lotus Manuscript and Manuscript are registered trademarks of Lotus Development Corporation.

Library of Congress Cataloging-in-Publication Data

```
Napier, H. Albert.
    Mastering Lotus 1-2-3 : version 2.2. / H. Albert Napier, Philip J.
  Judd.
      p.   cm.
    ISBN 0-87835-462-X
    1. Lotus 1-2-3 (Computer program)  2. Electronic spreadsheets.
  3. Business--Data processing.  I. Judd, Philip J.  II. Title.
  III. Title: Mastering Lotus one-two-three.
  HF5548.4.L67N363   1990
  005.36'9--dc20                                        89-17394
                                                            CIP
```

5 6 7 8 9 10 Ki 4 3 2

Dedication

This book is dedicated to our families for their loving support and patience.

Liz, J.B. and Lanham

Valerie, Michelle, Jacob and Heather

ORDER INFORMATION AND FACULTY SUPPORT INFORMATION

For the quickest service, refer to the map below for the South-Western Regional Office serving your area.

1 ORDER INFORMATION
5101 Madison Road
Cincinnati, OH 45227-1490
General Telephone–513-527-6945
Telephone: 1-800-543-8440
FAX: 513-527-6979
Telex: 214371

FACULTY SUPPORT INFORMATION
5101 Madison Road
Cincinnati, OH 45227-1490
General Telephone–513-527-6950
Telephone: 1-800-543-8444

Alabama	Massachusetts	Pennsylvania
Connecticut	Michigan (Lower)**	Rhode Island
Delaware	Mississippi	South Carolina
Florida	New Hampshire	Tennessee
Georgia	New Jersey	Vermont
Indiana*	New York	Virginia
Kentucky	North Carolina	West Virginia
Maine	Ohio	District of Columbia
Maryland		

*Except for ZIP Code Areas 463, 464. These areas contact Region 2 Office.
**Except for the Upper Peninsula. This area contacts Region 2 Office.

2 ORDER INFORMATION and FACULTY SUPPORT INFORMATION
355 Conde Street
West Chicago, IL 60185
General Telephone–312-231-6000
Telephone: 1-800-543-7972

Illinois	Minnesota	North Dakota
Indiana*	Missouri	South Dakota
Iowa	Nebraska	Wisconsin
Michigan (Upper)**		

*Only for ZIP Code Areas 463, 464. Other areas contact Region 1 office.
**Only for Upper Peninsula. Other areas contact Region 1 office.

3 ORDER INFORMATION
13800 Senlac Drive
Suite 100
Dallas, TX 75234
General Telephone–214-241-8541
Telephone: 1-800-543-7972

FACULTY SUPPORT INFORMATION
5101 Madison Road
Cincinnati, OH 45227-1490
General Telephone–513-527-6950
Telephone: 1-800-543-8444

Arkansas	Louisiana	Texas
Colorado	New Mexico	Wyoming
Kansas	Oklahoma	

4 ORDER INFORMATION and FACULTY SUPPORT INFORMATION
6185 Industrial Way
Livermore, CA 94550
General Telephone–415-449-2280
Telephone: 1-800-543-7972

Alaska	Idaho	Oregon
Arizona	Montana	Utah
California	Nevada	Washington
Hawaii		

BRIEF CONTENTS

CONTENTS

Chapter Two
Creating and Printing a Spreadsheet   35

Chapter Three
Useful Lotus Commands   121

Chapter Four
Creating and Printing Graphs

Chapter Five
Creating and Using a Template 245

Chapter Eight
Special Functions in Lotus 1-2-3

Chapter Ten
Advanced Macro Commands and Examples

Appendix A
Lotus 1-2-3 Command Trees 569

Appendix B
Summary of Commands Covered in This Book 577

PREFACE

■INTRODUCTION

Today, there are literally millions of people using personal computers. One of the most popular uses of personal computers, sometimes referred to as microcomputers, is for creating spreadsheets. A spreadsheet is typically completed on what are called "columnar pad" sheets of paper. Spreadsheets are used extensively in accounting, financial analysis and many other business planning and decision situations.

■OBJECTIVES OF THIS BOOK

This book was developed specifically for an introductory course on personal computers or spreadsheet analysis that utilizes IBM PCs or compatible hardware on which Lotus 1-2-3 can be used. The objectives of this book are as follows:

- To acquaint users with the process of using personal computers to solve spreadsheet analysis type problems.

- To provide a working knowledge of the basic and advanced capabilities of 1-2-3.

- To encourage the use of good problem-solving techniques for situations in which spreadsheet solutions are appropriate.

- To permit learning through examples using an exercise-oriented approach.

- To provide users with an excellent reference source to advance in their knowledge of 1-2-3.

■LEVEL OF INSTRUCTION

This book is designed to introduce the beginning, intermediate and advanced capabilities available in Lotus 1-2-3. It is pedagogically designed. First, the basic skills needed to create a spreadsheet are discussed. Subsequent chapters build on previously presented concepts and developed skills. A variety of practical examples provide an understanding of how Lotus 1-2-3 can be used. The book assumes the user has little or no experience with Lotus 1-2-3 or personal computers. However, individuals with some previous experience can also advance their knowledge of 1-2-3. The book is characterized by its continuity, simplicity and practicality. This book does not replace the Lotus 1-2-3 reference manual that accompanies the software package. Used in conjunction with the reference manual, this book will provide the user with a complete understanding of the capabilities of Lotus 1-2-3.

■ AUTHORS' EXPERIENCE

The authors have worked with personal computers since they were introduced. More than 20,000 people have participated in personal computer seminars for which the authors have been responsible for providing instruction. Insights from this experience are implicit throughout the book. In addition, the authors have more than 34 years of combined experience in teaching and consulting in the field of information systems and data processing.

■ LOTUS AUTHORIZED TRAINING COMPANY

The authors' consulting company, Napier & Judd, Inc., is a Lotus Authorized Training Company. The company's training materials, instructors and facilities have been evaluated and approved by Lotus Development Corporation. Only a small number of companies in the United States and Canada have been designated as a Lotus Authorized Training Company. This book is based on materials that have been used in the company's training activities in which more than 12,000 participants have been trained on Lotus 1-2-3.

■ DISTINGUISHING FEATURES

The distinguishing features of this book include the following:

Research-Based Material

The design of the book is based on how experienced 1-2-3 users actually utilize the software. Napier, Batsell, Lane and Guadagno at Rice University completed a study of 40 experienced 1-2-3 users from eight large organizations and determined the set of commands used most often by the individuals. The users studied had an average of 2.5 years experience and worked in a variety of corporations and governmental agencies.

The research indicates that 27 commands accounted for 85 percent of the commands issued by the experienced individuals. The materials in this book have been carefully planned to provide extensive coverage of these 27 most frequently used commands.

Proven Materials

This book is based on proven materials that have been used in college and university classes as well as training seminars. More than 12,000 individuals have learned to use 1-2-3 utilizing materials on which this book is based. For example, the authors have been responsible for training more than 4,000 members of the Texas Society of CPAs employing materials from this book.

Featuring Lotus 1-2-3 Release 2.2

This book features Lotus 1-2-3 Release 2.2.

Comprehensive Coverage

Major topics represented are: creating and printing worksheets and graphs; templates; combining and consolidating worksheets; linking spreadsheets in different files; database management; special functions; macros; and improving the appearance of spreadsheets and graphs using Allways.

Learning through Examples

The book is designed for learning through examples rather than learning a series of comma'
The materials are built around a series of example problems. Commands are learned fc
example, then reinforced. New commands are learned on subsequent examples. The e7
problems are logically related and integrated throughout the book.

Step-by-Step Instructions and Screen Illustrations

All examples include step-by-step instructions. Screen illustrations are used
assist the user while learning 1-2-3.

Extensive Exercises

At the end of each chapter, there are exercises that provide comprehe'
topics introduced in the chapter.

Graphics

One of the most powerful options available in 1-2-3 is graph'
business analysis and presentations. The user learns how to cr
bar, XY, and pie graphs.

Combining Information Between Worksheets

Many spreadsheet applications require movement of data from one worksheet to another or the combining of data from several worksheets into one worksheet. The process of using templates to create such "detail" worksheets and then combining information into a "summary" worksheet are covered. A method for linking worksheets in different files through the use of formulas is also presented.

Templates

Most experienced users of 1-2-3 make extensive use of templates. This book covers the process of building and using templates.

Database Capabilities

While 1-2-3 is not a database management system, it does have many database-like commands that can be applied to data in a worksheet. For example, the topics: how to sort data, complete queries on information in a worksheet, fill spreadsheets with sequences of data, create tables for decision-making purposes and create frequency distributions are shown.

Macros

With experience in using 1-2-3, the use of macros increases. Much of the power of 1-2-3 is really available to users of macros. This book introduces the process of building and using macros both at the simple and advanced levels. A method for automatically recording macro instruction is included.

Emphasis on Business and Organizational Problem Solving

The book includes many example problems that are similar to spreadsheets that may be encountered in a business or other type of organization.

What You Should Know

Each chapter includes a list of key concepts that emphasize what should be learned in the chapter.

RGANIZATION/FLEXIBILITY

The book is organized in a manner that takes the user through the fundamentals of Lotus 1-2-3 and then builds on the solid foundation to cover more advanced subjects. The book is useful for college courses, training classes, individual learning and as a reference manual.

In Chapter 1, the Lotus 1-2-3 package is described and explained. Typical applications are presented. The process of loading the software package is explained. The various parts of the 1-2-3 worksheet screen are detailed along with methods to move around the screen. The structure of the menu system is described, and the meaning of the function keys is summarized.

Chapter 2 contains a step-by-step process for creating, building and printing a spreadsheet. Operations included are: entering labels, numbers and formulas; copying numbers, formulas and labels; widening columns; inserting rows; entering headings; selecting formats for numeric data; saving and retrieving a spreadsheet; correcting for rounding errors, and more. A method for completing "What-if" analysis is illustrated.

Chapter 3 covers a variety of useful Lotus 1-2-3 commands. Some of the topics covered include: holding a cell constant in a formula; protecting cells; erasing the contents of cells; correcting errors; various file commands; percent formatting; hiding and displaying columns; label prefixes; moving cell contents; creating a page break for printing purposes; using borders and headers and footers; and printing options. Other topics represented are: creating and deleting range names; recalculation of a worksheet; searching and replacing data; checking the status of a worksheet; using the system command; freezing titles; using the Undo command; widening multiple columns; creating and clearing windows; inserting and deleting columns and rows; and suppressing zero values from appearing.

Numerous types of graphs can be prepared using 1-2-3. In Chapter 4, graphics capabilities are covered, including bar graph, line graph, stacked-bar graph, pie graph and XY graph. Other topics discussed are group graphing and printing a graph.

In Chapter 5, the process for building and using **template** worksheets is discussed. A template is a worksheet that is constructed and saved as a "shell" for the creation of worksheets at a later time containing the same formulas and/or text.

Many practical applications of spreadsheets require that information be combined from one or more spreadsheets into one or more other spreadsheets. The process for consolidating information from one or several worksheets into a summary worksheet is illustrated in Chapter 6. The method for linking worksheets in different files is also covered.

While 1-2-3 does not provide all the capabilities of a database management system, many database-like operations can be applied to data in a worksheet. Chapter 7 includes a discussion of sorting data and completing a query. Other topics include: filling cells with data, creating data tables that can be used in decision-making situations and creating and graphing a frequency distribution.

There are many pre-programmed functions available in Lotus 1-2-3. In Chapter 8, most of the special functions available in 1-2-3 such as functions for statistical analysis, financial analysis, date and time data, logical analysis, database operations, mathematical computations, special analyses such as lookup table calculations and string functions are discussed and illustrated.

In many situations, the same steps are applied to the development of a worksheet each time it is used. For example, an organization may summarize the budget expenditures of three departments into one worksheet. In 1-2-3, a macro can be developed that instructs the computer to repeat the steps automatically rather than have the user enter the set of steps each time the spreadsheets are summarized. An introduction to the process of creating and using macros appears in Chapter 9. A method for recording macro keystrokes is discussed and illustrated. The concept of using a macro library file for storing macros that are used in many types of applications is presented.

Advanced macro commands and examples of using the commands are described in Chapter 10. Some types of macros illustrated are: sorting data, restricting data entry to specific cells, automatically executing macros, interactive macros, changing program flow and looping, and using subroutines. User-designed menus are also created.

Lotus 1-2-3 Release 2.2 includes the add-in software package Allways, The Spreadsheet Publisher. Allways allows the user to prepare presentation-quality documents using spreadsheets and graphs. The use of Allways is illustrated in Chapter 11.

Appendices A and B contain menu tree diagrams and a brief summary of the commands covered in the book. The answers to the odd-number exercises are in Appendix C.

■ ACKNOWLEDGEMENTS

We would like to thank and express our appreciation to the many fine and talented individuals who have contributed to the completion of this book. We have been fortunate to have a group of reviewers whose constructive comments have been helpful in completing the book. Special thanks go to: Nancy Haney, Oakton Community College and PCT Professional Micro-computer Consulting/Training; Louis Fuxan, Delgado Community College; Barbara Vrana, Oklahoma City Community College; Mark Griffin, Davenport College of Business; and Tom Lightner, University of Colorado.

No book is possible without the motivation and support of an editorial staff. Therefore, we wish to acknowledge with great appreciation the following people at Boyd & Fraser: Tom Walker, vice-president and publisher, for the opportunity to write this book and for his constant encouragement; Jim Edwards and Donna Villanucci, for their keen assistance in the editing process; and the production staff for support in completing the book.

We appreciate the assistance provided by Marla McBryde, Arlene Waterman, Dan Jurden, Nancy Onarheim, Lori Ruzicka, Donna Kainer, Darlene Funderburke and Linda Rice of Napier & Judd, Inc. in the preparation of the initial drafts of the book.

Houston, Texas   H. Albert Napier
September, 1989   Philip J. Judd

CHAPTER ONE

GETTING STARTED WITH LOTUS 1-2-3

Chapter Overview
What Is Lotus 1-2-3?
Typical Applications
Hardware Requirements
Software Requirements
Loading the Lotus 1-2-3 Software Package
The Lotus 1-2-3 Worksheet Screen

    Row Numbers
    Column Letters
    Cell
    Cell Pointer
    Current Cell
    Cell Address
    Control Panel
    Mode Indicator
    Status Indicator
    Date and Time Indicators

Moving Around the Spreadsheet

    Using the Pointer-Movement Keys to Move the Cell Pointer
    Using the (PgDn) and (PgUp) Keys to Move the Cell Pointer
    Using the Tab Key to Move the Cell Pointer
    Using the (GoTo) Key (the (F5) Function Key) to Move the Cell Pointer
    Using the (Home) Key to Move the Cell Pointer
    Using the (End) Key in Combination with Other Keys to Move the Cell Pointer

Lotus 1-2-3 Menu Structure

    Using the Menu Structure
    Alternative Method for Using the Menu Structure

Overview of the Function Keys
Exiting Lotus 1-2-3
Summary
Key Concepts

OBJECTIVES

In this chapter, you will learn to:

- Load the Lotus 1-2-3 program into the computer
- Identify the basic features of the 1-2-3 worksheet screen
- Move the cell pointer around the worksheet
- Use the 1-2-3 menu
- Identify the use of the function keys in Lotus 1-2-3
- Exit Lotus 1-2-3

■ CHAPTER OVERVIEW

This book assumes that you have little or no knowledge of Lotus 1-2-3. In this chapter, you are introduced to the capabilities of 1-2-3 and typical applications. The hardware requirements for using 1-2-3 and the process for loading the software into a personal computer are explained. The basic items that appear on the worksheet screen are discussed. The process of moving around the 1-2-3 worksheet is defined. The process of entering information into a spreadsheet is introduced. The Lotus 1-2-3 menu structure is explained and illustrated. Finally, an overview of the special functions associated with the function keys is presented.

■ WHAT IS LOTUS 1-2-3?

Lotus 1-2-3 is an integrated software package. The term integrated means that Lotus has more than one basic capability. Lotus 1-2-3 can be used for creating spreadsheets (also referred to as worksheets), creating graphs, and manipulating information within and between spreadsheets. In this book, it is assumed that you are using Lotus 1-2-3 Release 2.2. However, if you are using an earlier version of Lotus 1-2-3, much of the material presented in this book is still applicable.

An example of a worksheet appears in Figure 1-1. In the next chapter, you are shown how to create and print this spreadsheet. Figure 1-2 is a graph that includes some information from the worksheet in Figure 1-1.

```
A1: [W19]                                                           READY

              A           B        C        D        E        F
1                                 ABC COMPANY
2                                   BUDGET
3
4
5                         QTR1     QTR2     QTR3     QTR4    YR TOTAL
6
7    SALES              $60,000  $61,200  $62,424  $63,672 $247,296
8
9    EXPENSES
10      SALARIES         35,000   35,500   36,200   37,000  143,700
11      RENT              9,000    9,000    9,000    9,000   36,000
12      TELEPHONE         1,000    1,050    1,103    1,158    4,311
13      OFFICE SUPPLIES     750      800      850      900    3,300
14      MISCELLANEOUS     1,000    1,030    1,061    1,093    4,184
15                      -----------------------------------------------
16      TOTAL EXPENSES   46,750   47,380   48,214   49,151  191,495
17                      -----------------------------------------------
18   GROSS PROFIT       $13,250  $13,820  $14,210  $14,521  $55,801
19                      ===============================================
20

                         UNDO
```

Figure 1-1

Up to six items such as SALES can appear on a graph. Graphs other than bar charts can be developed.

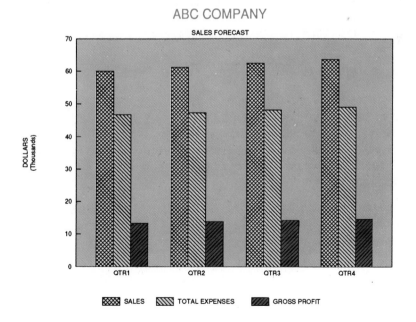

Figure 1-2

Lotus 1-2-3 can also be used to perform operations on a file. For example, information in a worksheet can be sorted by various criteria. Figure 1-3 is a worksheet that has information on salaries for a group of individuals that is not sorted in any particular order.

```
A1: [W11]                                                              READY

            A          B         C       D        E        F        G        H
1                                    ABC COMPANY
2                                    SALARY BUDGET
3
4
5    LAST NAME  FIRST NAME  DIV.    QTR1     QTR2     QTR3     QTR4     TOTAL
6    SPROUT     AL           3      5,950    5,950    6,450    6,450    24,800
7    LYLIE      SUSAN        1      7,800    7,800    7,800    8,580    31,980
8    CHIN       TOMMY        2      5,000    5,000    5,200    5,200    20,400
9    JOHNSON    ERNEST       1      8,000    8,000    8,800    8,800    33,600
10   VALETTI    GEORGE       3      5,900    5,900    6,300    6,300    24,400
11   ARMOUR     CYNTHIA      2      5,200    5,200    5,400    5,400    21,200
12   JONES      NINA         3      6,750    6,750    6,750    7,450    27,700
13                                  --------  --------  --------  --------  --------
14   TOTAL                          44,600   44,600   46,700   48,180   184,080
15
16
17
18
19
20
                            UNDO
```

Figure 1-3

Sometimes it is desirable to sort the information in a particular order. In Figure 1-4, the data that appears in Figure 1-3 has been sorted in ascending order by division number.

```
A1: [W11]                                                              READY

            A          B         C       D        E        F        G        H
1                                    ABC COMPANY
2                                    SALARY BUDGET
3
4
5    LAST NAME  FIRST NAME  DIV.    QTR1     QTR2     QTR3     QTR4     TOTAL
6    JOHNSON    ERNEST       1      8,000    8,000    8,800    8,800    33,600
7    LYLIE      SUSAN        1      7,800    7,800    7,800    8,580    31,980
8    ARMOUR     CYNTHIA      2      5,200    5,200    5,400    5,400    21,200
9    CHIN       TOMMY        2      5,000    5,000    5,200    5,200    20,400
10   SPROUT     AL           3      5,950    5,950    6,450    6,450    24,800
11   VALETTI    GEORGE       3      5,900    5,900    6,300    6,300    24,400
12   JONES      NINA         3      6,750    6,750    6,750    7,450    27,700
13                                  --------  --------  --------  --------  --------
14   TOTAL                          44,600   44,600   46,700   48,180   184,080
15
16
17
18
19
20
                            UNDO
```

Figure 1-4

■ TYPICAL APPLICATIONS

Lotus 1-2-3 is used in many organizations as well as for personal use. Some examples of Lotus 1-2-3 applications include:

Advertising expense forecast
Balance sheet forecasts
Budgets
Cash flow analysis
Checkbook balancing
Depreciation schedules
Household expenses
Income statement forecasts
Income tax projections
Income tax records
Inventory forecasting
Job bids and costing
Sports analysis
Stock portfolio analysis and records

■ HARDWARE REQUIREMENTS

To use Lotus 1-2-3 Release 2.2, you must have a microcomputer with a minimum of 320 kilobytes of random access memory (RAM). A hard disk is not required, but is useful. Your computer should have at least one floppy disk drive. A monochrome or color monitor can be used with Lotus 1-2-3. A color monitor is particularly useful if you want to see better quality graphics.

A printer is also necessary. A dot matrix printer provides the capability of printing spreadsheets as well as graphs. Most laser printers provide a full range of graphics printing capabilities. If high quality graphics are desired, a plotter is necessary.

Blank diskettes that have been appropriately formatted are also needed. These diskettes can be used to store spreadsheets and graphs on files to be used at a later time.

■ SOFTWARE REQUIREMENTS

The Lotus 1-2-3 diskettes on which the software is stored are needed. The software package includes several diskettes. The DOS system software disk is also needed. To install the 1-2-3 software on your personal computer, see the Lotus 1-2-3 reference manual that came with your software.

■ LOADING THE LOTUS 1-2-3 SOFTWARE PACKAGE

Before you attempt to load Lotus 1-2-3 into the memory of the microcomputer, all connections need to be checked. Make sure the monitor and printer are properly installed. The power cord should be connected to an appropriate electric outlet.

Turn on   the computer

Assuming that 1-2-3 Release 2.2 is installed in the directory 123R2 on the C drive, use the following steps to load the software.

Type   cd\123R2   (to change to directory 123R2)

Press   ⏎

Type   Lotus

Press   ⏎

In many situations, you may have a menu from which to select Release 2.2 or some other process for invoking the use of 1-2-3 Release 2.2. In a few seconds your screen will look like Figure 1-5.

```
1-2-3  PrintGraph  Translate  Install  Exit
Use 1-2-3

                    1-2-3 Access System
                    Copyright  1986, 1989
                 Lotus Development Corporation
                      All Rights Reserved
                         Release 2.2

The Access system lets you choose 1-2-3, PrintGraph, the Translate utility,
and the Install program, from the menu at the top of this screen.  If
you're using a two-diskette system, the Access system may prompt you to
change disks.  Follow the instructions below to start a program.

o  Use → or ← to move the menu pointer (the highlighted rectangle
   at the top of the screen) to the program you want to use.

o  Press ENTER to start the program.

You can also start a program by typing the first character of its name.

Press HELP (F1) for more information.
```

Figure 1-5

The menu at the top of the screen has the choices of 1-2-3, PrintGraph, Translate, Install and Exit. Notice that the characters 1-2-3 are highlighted with a rectangle that is referred to as a pointer. Below 1-2-3 appears the message "Use 1-2-3." This indicates that the Lotus 1-2-3 program will be entered if the 1-2-3 option is selected from the menu.

To select the "Use 1-2-3" option:

Press   ⏎

A message with copyright and licensing information then appears on the screen. A blank worksheet like the one in Figure 1-6 will appear on your screen in another few seconds.

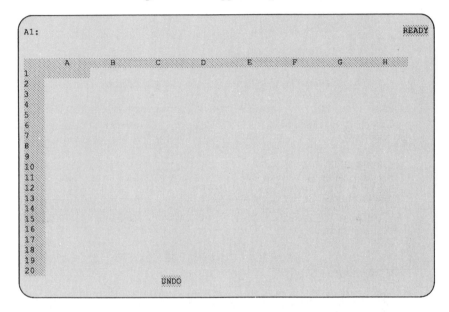

Figure 1-6

■ THE LOTUS 1-2-3 WORKSHEET SCREEN

Figure 1-6 is the standard form of the initial **worksheet** used by Lotus when it is loaded. In some situations, a worksheet is referred to as a **spreadsheet**. The terms **worksheet** and **spreadsheet** are used interchangeably in this book. A worksheet is a grid-like structure consisting of rows and columns.

Figure 1-7 is a worksheet screen after the main menu of Lotus 1-2-3 has been placed on the screen.

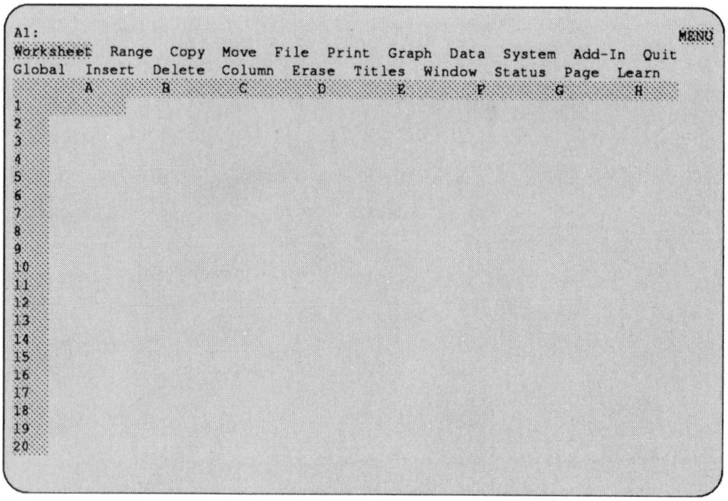

Figure 1-7

In this section various items that appear on the worksheet screen in Figure 1-7 are discussed.

Row Numbers

On the left border of the worksheet on the screen is a set of numbers called **row numbers**. Note that there are 20 rows appearing on the screen. There are a total of 8,192 rows available in the worksheet.

Column Letters

Across the top border of the worksheet on the screen is the set of letters A through H. These are the **column letters**. There are 256 columns in the worksheet. The columns are identified with the letters A through Z, AA through AZ, BA through BZ and so forth until the letter IV is reached.

Cell

A **cell** is the area on a worksheet that occurs at the intersection of a column and a row. Data is stored in a cell. A1 refers to the cell in the worksheet that is located at the intersection of column A and row 1. Initially, each cell is set to display 9 characters.

Cell Pointer

Notice on the screen that cell A1 is highlighted by a rectangular form. The item highlighting cell A1 is called the **cell pointer**. The cell pointer can be moved from cell to cell in the worksheet. Whenever information is input to the worksheet, it is placed in the cell highlighted by the cell pointer.

Current Cell

The **current cell** is highlighted by the cell pointer. The next data entry or operation affects this cell.

Cell Address

The location of a cell is called the **cell address**. A cell address is defined by a column letter followed by a row number. For example B2 is the cell address for the cell that occurs at the intersection of column B and row 2 in the worksheet.

Control Panel

Above the worksheet at the top of the screen is an area called the **control panel**. The control panel consists of three lines. The first line has the cell address for the current cell and the contents of the cell. Notice the cell address at the top left side of the screen. Assuming you have a blank worksheet and the cell pointer is in cell A1, then the cell address area on the first line of the control panel contains A1: and there will be blank spaces immediately to the right. Nothing appears to the right of A1:, because no data has been entered in the cell.

The second line of the control panel displays the current data when the contents of a cell are being created or edited. It is also used to display the Lotus 1-2-3 menus when the / key is pressed.

The third line of the control panel is used to display either a submenu or a one line description of the command item currently highlighted on the second line of the control panel.

Mode Indicator

The **mode indicator** appears at the top right corner of the first line in the control panel area of the worksheet. It indicates the current operating mode. For example, it may say READY indicating that 1-2-3 is ready for you to input information or create a formula. If it says MENU, then a menu appears on the screen and you can make a selection from the menu.

Status Indicator

The **status indicator** specifies the condition of certain keys or of the program. For example, if the [CapsLock] key is pressed the characters CAPS will appear in the right corner below the worksheet indicating that all alphabetic characters subsequently used are automatically capitalized. To remove the CAPS specification, you need only to press the `CapsLock` key again and the CAPS indicator no longer appears on the screen.

Date and Time Indicators

At the bottom left side of the screen the **date** and **time** indicators appear. Assuming the current date and time have been entered properly, the current date and time should appear. Lotus 1-2-3 has an option that allows you to suppress the date and time indicator from view.

■ MOVING AROUND THE SPREADSHEET

As mentioned earlier in this chapter, the cell pointer is the highlighted rectangle on the screen that indicates the location on the worksheet. The cell address of the cell pointer's location always appears in the top left corner of the screen. In this section, methods to move the cell pointer around the worksheet are discussed and illustrated.

Using the Pointer-Movement Keys to Move the Cell Pointer

The cursor movement keys, which are the basic keys used to move the cell pointer from cell to cell on the worksheet, are located on the right side of the keyboard (see Figure 1-8). The cursor movement keys are placed on the numeric keypad (sometimes called "the ten key") and/or they may be in a separate location as depicted in Figure 1-8. In Lotus 1-2-3 Release 2.2, these keys are referred to as the pointer-movement keys.

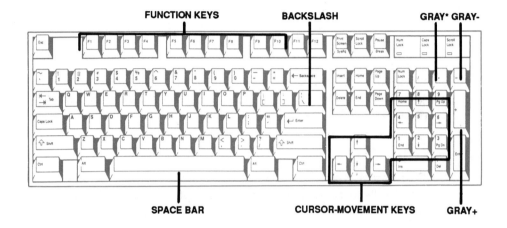

Figure 1-8

To illustrate the use of the pointer-movement keys:

Locate   the pointer-movement keys

Press   ⊕ key seven times

As shown in Figure 1-9, the cell pointer is now in cell H1. This fact is indicated on the first line of the control panel. The process of moving around the screen is sometimes called *scrolling*.

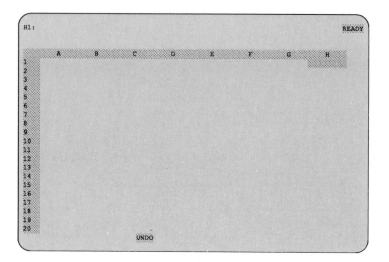

Figure 1-9

To move the cell pointer to cell I1:

Press   ⊕ key one time

As illustrated in Figure 1-10, the cell pointer has been moved to column I and column A has disappeared. 1-2-3 can only display a total of 72 characters across the screen and no portion of a column is displayed unless the entire column can be shown on the screen.

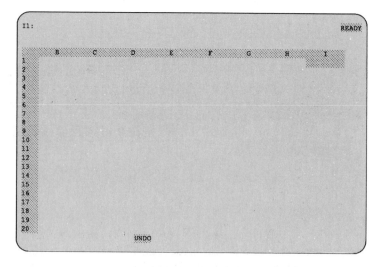

Figure 1-10

To move to cell A1:

Locate   the ⊕ key

Press   ⊕ key eight times until the cell pointer
               appears in cell A1

If the ⊕ key is pressed too many times, a "beep" sound will be heard indicating that you are trying to move to the left of column A. Anytime the "beep" sound occurs, it denotes that you are trying to perform some type of operation that is not permitted at that point.

To move the cell pointer rapidly:

Locate   the ⊕ key

Press   ⊕ key and hold it down

After the cell pointer has moved down 20 or 30 rows, stop depressing the ⊕ key. To return the cell pointer to cell A1:

Locate   the ⊕ key

Press   ⊕ key until the cell pointer
               appears in cell A1

A "beep" sound may be heard if the ⊕ key has been depressed after reaching cell A1.

Using the (PgDn) and (PgUp) Keys to Move the Cell Pointer

The cell pointer can be moved up and down one screen at a time using the (PgUp) and (PgDn) keys. (PgDn) stands for *Page Down* and (PgUp) means *Page Up*. These keys permit you to move the cell pointer up and down the screen 20 rows at a time. Note that on many keyboards there are Page Down and Page Up keys as well as the (PgDn) and (PgUp) keys. They can be used interchangeably.

To use the (PgDn) key:

Locate   the (PgDn) key

Press   (PgDn)

Assuming that the cell pointer was in cell A1 prior to pressing the (PgDn) key, then the cell pointer is now in cell A21. See Figure 1-11. If the cell pointer was not in cell A1, then the cell pointer has now moved 20 rows down in the worksheet from the cell it was in prior to pressing the (PgDn) key.

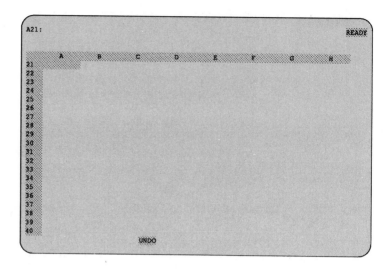

Figure 1-11

To use the (PgUp) key:

> **Locate** the (PgUp) key
>
> **Press** (PgUp)

Assuming that the cell pointer was in cell A21 prior to pressing the (PgUp) key, the cell pointer should now be in cell A1. If the cell pointer was not in cell A21, then the cell pointer is now 20 rows up in the worksheet.

Using the Tab Key to Move the Cell Pointer

The cell pointer can be moved to the right or left one screen at a time using the ⭢ (tab) key.

To move the cell pointer one screen to the right:

> **Make** sure the cell pointer is in cell A1
>
> **Locate** the ⭢ key (it is usually to the left of the letter Q)
>
> **Press** ⭢

As illustrated in Figure 1-12, the cell pointer has been moved to the right one screen and now appears in cell I1.

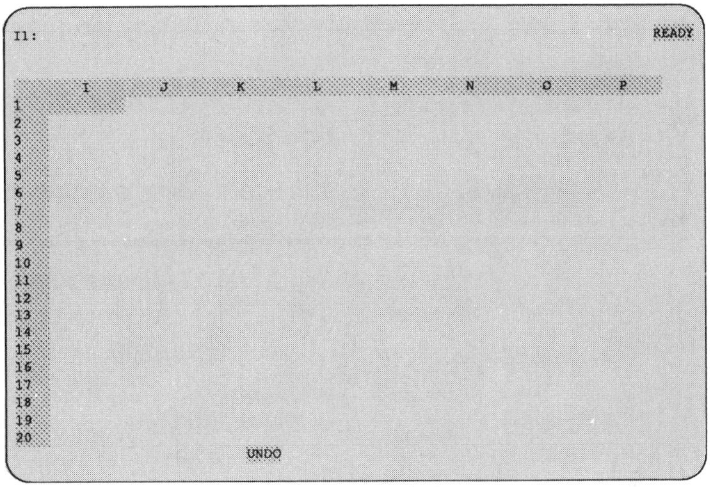

Figure 1-12

To move the cell pointer one screen to the left:

Make sure the cell pointer is in cell I1

Locate the ⟶ key

Depress a Shift key

Press ⟶

The cell pointer has been moved to cell A1 or one screen to the left. The shift key is marked with the word Shift. There are two shift keys on a keyboard.

Another way to move the cell pointer one screen to the right or left is:

Make sure the cell pointer is in cell A1

Depress the Ctrl key

Press →

The cell pointer should now be in cell I1. To return to cell A1:

Depress the Ctrl key

Press ←

Using the ⌊GoTo⌋ Key (the ⌊F5⌋ Function Key) to Move the Cell Pointer

Sometimes it is necessary to move the cell pointer to a particular cell in the worksheet. For example, to move the cursor to cell IV8192:

Make   sure the cell pointer is in cell A1

Locate   the ⌊F5⌋ function key (the ⌊F5⌋ key is
                usually at the top of keyboard or on the left side of
                the keyboard)

Press   ⌊F5⌋

As displayed in Figure 1-13, the screen now has a message in the control panel prompting you to enter the cell address desired.

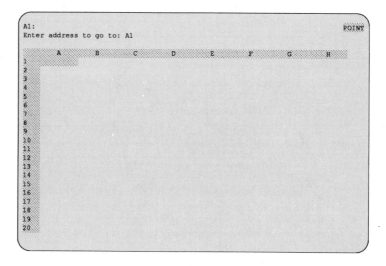

Figure 1-13

Type   IV8192

Note that lowercase or uppercase letters can be used when you type the cell address.

Press   ⏎

Figure 1-14 depicts the entering of cell address IV8192.

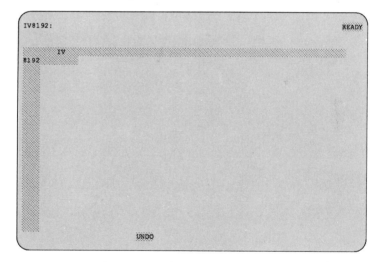

```
A1:                                                            EDIT
Enter address to go to: IV8192

          A        B        C        D        E        F        G        H
1
2
3
4
5
6
7
8
9
10
11
12
13
14
15
16
17
18
19
20
```

Figure 1-14

As illustrated in Figure 1-15, the cell pointer is now in cell IV8192.

```
IV8192:                                                        READY

              IV
8192




                              UNDO
```

Figure 1-15

Cell IV8192 is the cell in the bottom right corner of the worksheet. In other words, column IV is the last column in the worksheet and row 8,192 is the last row in the worksheet.

Using the Home Key to Move the Cell Pointer

The cell pointer can be moved to the top left corner of the worksheet by pressing the (Home) key. To demonstrate the use of the (Home) key:

Locate   the (Home) key

Press   (Home)

The cell pointer is now in cell A1.

Using the End Key in Combination with Other Keys to Move the Cell Pointer

Assume the cell pointer is in a blank cell. If the (End) key is pressed followed by a pointer-movement key, the cell pointer will be moved to the first nonblank cell in the direction of the pointer-movement key. If a nonblank cell does not exist in the selected direction, the cell pointer will move to the last cell in the selected direction. When the cell pointer is in a nonblank cell and the above action is repeated, then the cell pointer will be moved to the last nonblank cell in the direction selected. If nonblank cells do not exist in the selected direction, the cell pointer will be moved to the last cell in the selected direction.

If the (End) key is pressed followed by pressing the (Home) key, then the cell pointer is moved to the last cell in the worksheet which is defined by the last column and row that have a nonblank entry.

Note that the word END appears at the bottom of the screen when the (End) key is pressed. If you decide not to press a pointer-movement key after pressing the (End) key, the END indicator can be removed from the screen by pressing the (End) key again. The END indicator automatically disappears when a pointer-movement key is pressed.

■ LOTUS 1-2-3 MENU STRUCTURE

Earlier in this chapter, the menu structure was mentioned. In this section, the menu structure is discussed and defined.

To display the main 1-2-3 menu:

Press   /

The main 1-2-3 menu is now on the screen. Notice the word MENU now appears as the mode indicator. See Figure 1-16.

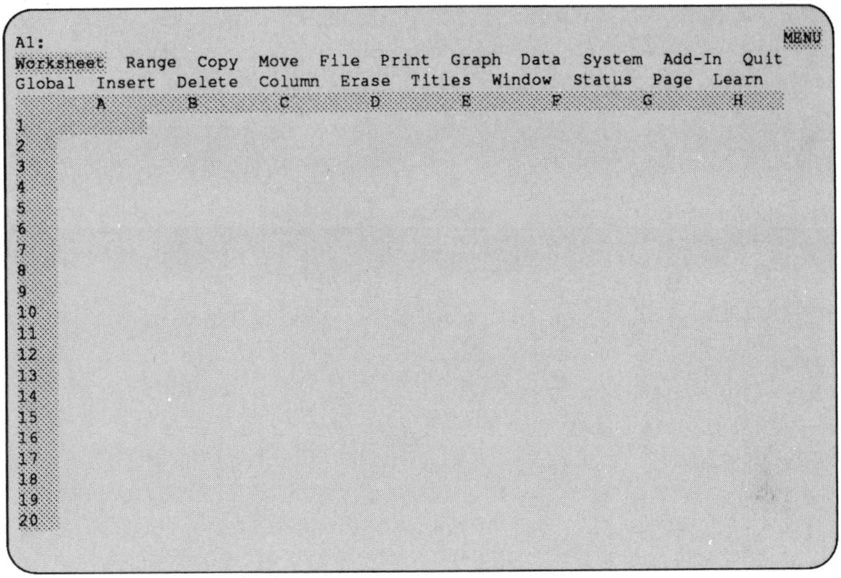

Figure 1-16

The menu appears on the second line of the control panel. The Worksheet option on the menu is highlighted. The submenu that will be used if the Worksheet option is selected appears on the third line of the control panel.

Other options on the main menu include Range, Copy, Move, File, Print, Graph, Data, System, Add-In and Quit. The options are used to perform a variety of operations on a worksheet. Many of these operations are presented in the remainder of this book.

To remove the Main menu from the screen:

Press   Esc

Esc stands for escape. It can be used to "back up" one level in the menu structure. In this situation, since the main menu is displayed on the screen, the main menu will disappear.

Using the Menu Structure

To illustrate the use of the menu structure, you will enter information in cell A1 and then erase the worksheet.

To specify some information to be entered in cell A1:

Make   sure the cell pointer is in cell A1

Type   Lotus

The word Lotus now appears on the second line of the control panel. Notice that when the first character is typed, the word LABEL appears in the mode indicator specifying that a label is being entered. See Figure 1-17.

Figure 1-17

To enter the information in cell A1:

Press   ⏎

The word Lotus is now shown in cell A1. See Figure 1-18.

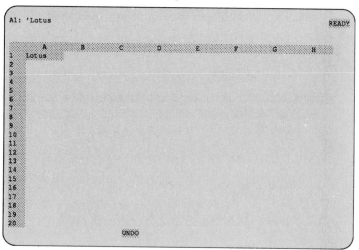

Figure 1-18

Note that all labels are *left justified* in a cell. In other words, the characters begin at the leftmost position in the cell. When a number is entered, the mode indicator says VALUE and the number is *right justified* in the cell when the ⏎ key is pressed; that is, the number appears in the rightmost portion of the cell. Notice that the characters '**Lotus** are visible next to the cell address A1: on the first line in the control panel. The ' is the symbol that means label in 1-2-3 and **Lotus** is the information stored in cell A1.

To erase the entire worksheet:

Press   /

At this point the main menu appears on the screen as shown in Figure 1-19. The menu structure works by moving the menu pointer to the desired menu option and pressing the ⏎ key.

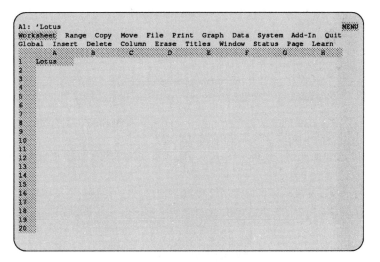

Figure 1-19

The menu pointer is a rectangular shape that is similar to the cell pointer. It is used to highlight options on the menu. Since Worksheet is the option desired, the menu pointer does not need to be moved and the ⏎ key can be pressed.

Press   ⏎

The submenu that previously appeared on the third line of the control panel is now shown on the second line of the control panel and becomes the menu that is in use. See Figure 1-20. Note that the menu pointer is on the word Global.

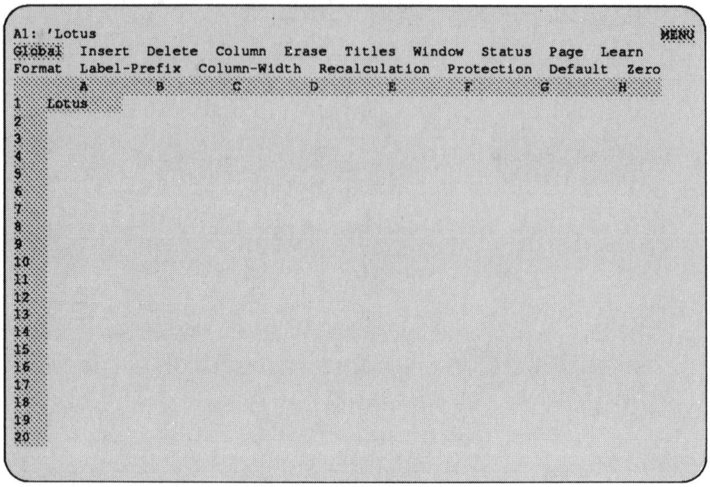

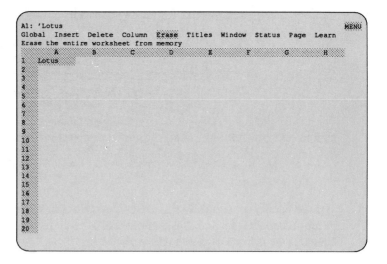

Figure 1-20

The next step in the process of erasing the worksheet on the screen is to move the menu pointer to the Erase menu option. See Figure 1-21.

To move the menu pointer to the Erase option:

Press   ➔ until the menu pointer is on the
                 word Erase

Figure 1-21

To complete the process of erasing the worksheet:

Press ⏎

Figure 1-22 illustrates that 1-2-3 gives you the option of making sure it is desirable to erase the worksheet. If the ⏎ is pressed while the No option is highlighted, then 1-2-3 returns to the READY mode and the worksheet is not erased.

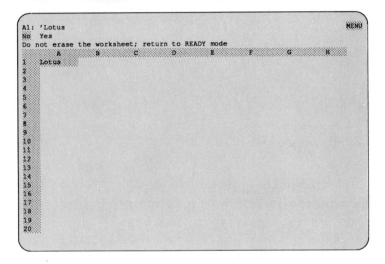

Figure 1-22

The final steps in the process for erasing the worksheet are:

Press → to move the menu pointer to the word Yes. Notice the explanation of the option on the third line of the control panel indicates the worksheet will be erased if the Yes menu option is selected.

Press ⏎

Your screen should have a blank worksheet on it and should look like Figure 1-23.

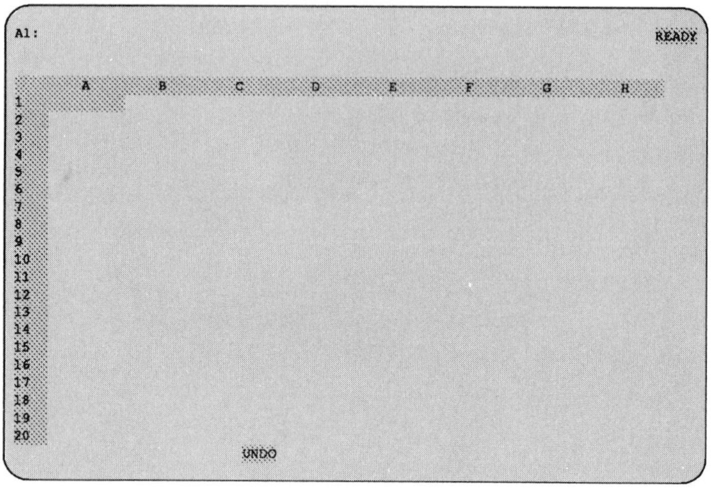

Figure 1-23

Alternative Method for Using the Menu Structure

The standard way of using the menu structure was explained in the previous section. Recall that when a menu is on the screen, to select a particular menu option, you must move the menu pointer to the appropriate menu option and press the ⏎ key. In this section, an alternative approach for using the menu structure is presented.

To illustrate the alternative method, the process for erasing a worksheet is repeated. To place the word Lotus in cell A1:

Make sure the cell pointer is in cell A1

Type Lotus

Press ⏎

Your screen should now look like Figure 1-24.

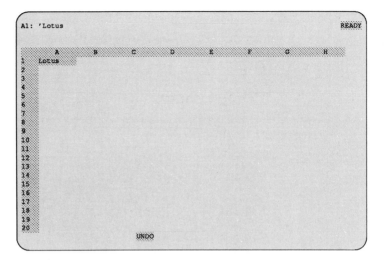

Figure 1-24

To begin the process of erasing the screen:

Press   /

The slash key is sometimes referred to as the **command key** because the initial set of command options appears as the main menu. The screen should now look like Figure 1-25.

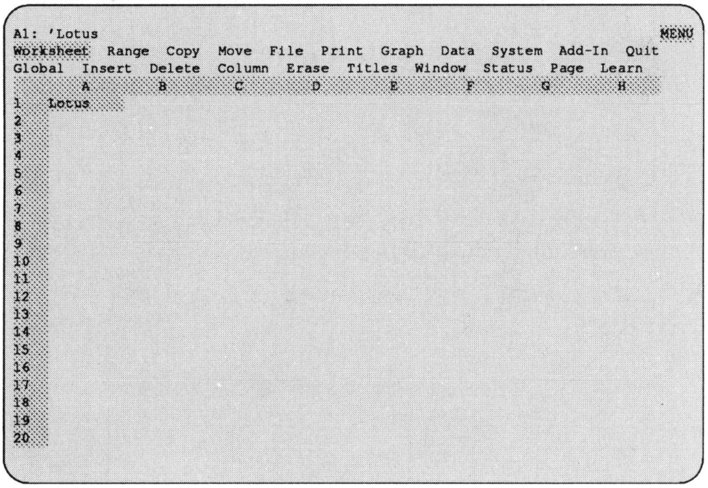

Figure 1-25

Look at the words on the main menu. Notice that none of the words start with the same first character. Rather than move the menu pointer to the desired menu option, you can press the letter on the keyboard corresponding to the first letter of the word in the menu. To illustrate the use of the first letter:

Select   Worksheet

by typing a **W**. The letter **W** activates the Worksheet option on the main menu. The screen should now look like Figure 1-26.

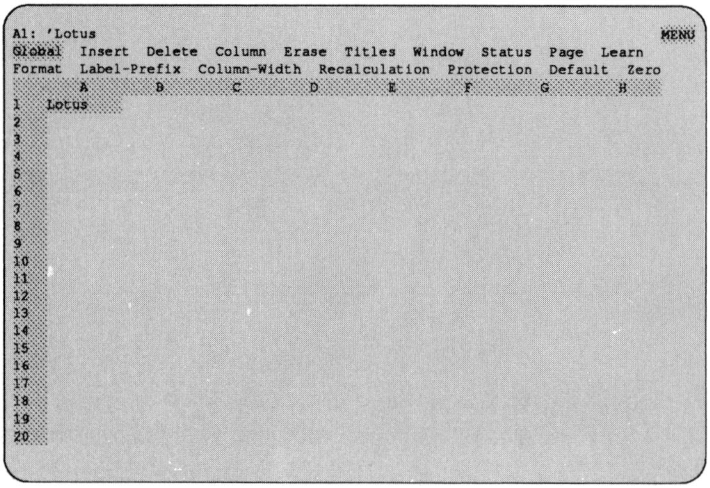

Figure 1-26

To select the menu option to erase the worksheet:

Select   Erase

by typing the letter **E** to indicate that you desire to select the Erase option on the menu. Your screen should now look like Figure 1-27.

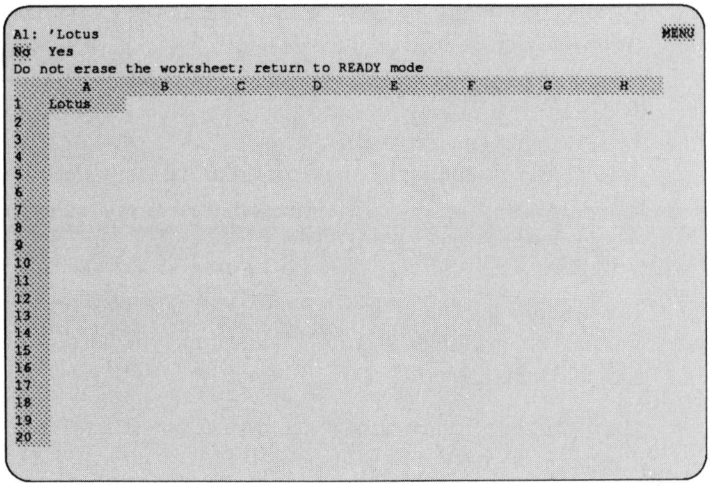

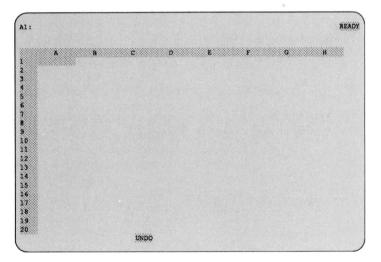

Figure 1-27

To select the menu option Yes, and then complete the process for erasing the worksheet:

Select   Yes

By typing **Y**, you indicate that the worksheet does in fact need to be erased. A blank screen like the one in Figure 1-28 should now appear on your screen.

Figure 1-28

In this book, the alternative method for using the menu structure is utilized in the illustrations. This approach saves time in the creation of worksheets. Initially, it may be advantageous for you to move the menu pointer to the appropriate menu option and then press the ⏎ key. Once you are comfortable with the way the menus are structured, then the use of first letters for selecting menu options can be used. After Lotus 1-2-3 is used for a short while, most individuals use the first letter approach for selecting menu options.

■ OVERVIEW OF THE FUNCTION KEYS

The function keys have been "programmed" in Lotus 1-2-3 to perform specific operations. One of these operations is the GOTO function, associated with the F5 key, that was presented earlier in this chapter.

The 1-2-3 Help System allows you to access an on-line reference for 1-2-3 features on your screen. To access the Help System:

Press   F1

A Help screen appears. To get assistance on specific topics, choose one of the menu options listed on the screen. Use the arrow keys to move the pointer to the desired option. When the desired option is highlighted, press the ⏎ key. To leave the Help System and return to the spreadsheet currently in use:

Press   Esc

Many of the function keys will be used in subsequent chapters. A brief description of the operations programmed for the function keys follows.

F1:	**Help**	Display Help screens that are available in Lotus 1-2-3
F2:	**Edit**	Switch to / from EDIT mode for current entry
F3:	**Name**	Display menu of names depending on what command is being used
F4:	**Abs**	Make / Unmake cell address "absolute"
F5:	**GoTo**	Move cell pointer to a particular cell in the worksheet
F6:	**Window**	Move cell pointer when "windows" appear on the screen
F7:	**Query**	Repeat most recent Data Query operation
F8:	**Table**	Repeat most recent Data Table operation
F9:	**Calc**	Recalculate worksheet values
F10:	**Graph**	Draw graph on screen using the most recent graph specifications

Alt F1:	**Compose**	Used in conjunction with keystrokes to input characters that are not on the standard keyboard
Alt F2:	**Step**	Turn STEP mode on or off
Alt F3:	**Run**	Select a macro to process
Alt F4:	**UNDO**	Cancels any changes made since 1-2-3 was last in READY mode
Alt F5:	**LEARN**	Turn LEARN mode on or off.
Alt F7:	**APP 1**	Start an available add-in application assigned to the key
Alt F8:	**APP 2**	Start an available add-in application assigned to the key
Alt F9:	**APP 3**	Start an available add-in application assigned to the key
Alt F10:	**APP 4**	Display menu of available add-in applications, or start an available add-in application assigned to the key.

■EXITING LOTUS 1-2-3

When it is desirable to exit Lotus 1-2-3, perform the following set of operations:

Press	/
Select	Quit
Select	Yes

You may need to select Yes twice if you have not saved the current worksheet.

| **Select** | Exit |

You should now have an appropriate prompt on the screen.

SUMMARY

In this chapter, an overview of Lotus 1-2-3 was presented. Lotus 1-2-3 is often used for business, government, and personal applications. Microcomputer hardware is required to process Lotus 1-2-3. Lotus 1-2-3 can be executed on IBM or IBM-compatible PCs. The actual Lotus 1-2-3 software is on a set of diskettes. The software can be loaded into the main memory by reading from a hard disk or from floppy disks. The key items on the worksheet screen are the row numbers, column letters, cells, cell pointer, current cell, cell address, control panel, mode indicator, status indicator, date indicator and time indicator. The cell pointer can be moved around the worksheet by using the arrow keys, the (PgDn) and (PgUp) keys, the ⊖ key and the (F5) function key. Lotus 1-2-3 has a set of menus containing various operations that can be applied to a worksheet. There are two ways to use the menu structure in 1-2-3. There is a set of function keys (F1 through F10) that are preprogrammed in Lotus 1-2-3 to perform specific operations such as moving to a specific cell in a worksheet.

KEY CONCEPTS

Cell	Hardware Requirements for 1-2-3
Cell Address	Help F1 Key
Cell Pointer	Menu
Column Letters	Menu Structure
Command Key	Mode Indicator
Control Panel	Pointer-movement Keys
Current Cell	Row Numbers
Date Indicator	Software Requirements for 1-2-3
End Indicator	Status Indicator
Escape Key	Time Indicator
Function Keys	Worksheet
GoTo F5 Key	Worksheet Erase

CHAPTER ONE
EXERCISE 1

INSTRUCTIONS: Answer the following questions in the space provided.

1. Define the following terms:

   a. Row Numbers _Numbers for each line on page (Horisonal) 1 - 20 etc._

   b. Column Letters _Letters for A - Z etc. vertical_

   c. Cell _Block - such a ____ = B1_

   d. Cell Pointer _Rectangular shaded area_

   e. Current Cell _Where cell pointer is located on screen_

   f. Cell Address _See "C" above has # & letter_

   g. Control Panel _Tells where cell is now - where cell is going   Left-Top_

   h. Mode Indicator _Ready - wait etc. Right Top_

   i. Status Indicator _Caps - Nums etc. middle-Right Lower_

   j. Time Indicator _Time document made Lower left_

   k. Date Indicator _Date   "   "   Lower left_

2. Describe the standard way of using the 1-2-3 menu structure.

   Highlight choice with cursor by moving to proper one with arrow and pressing enter

3.   Describe the alternative method of using the 1-2-3 menu structure.

Use the first letter of choice

4.   Describe the purpose of using the function keys F1 through F10.

To do certain things— Such as File Save— Puncuate— etc.

CHAPTER ONE
EXERCISE 2

INSTRUCTIONS: Identify the circled and enclosed items on the worksheet in Figure 1-29.

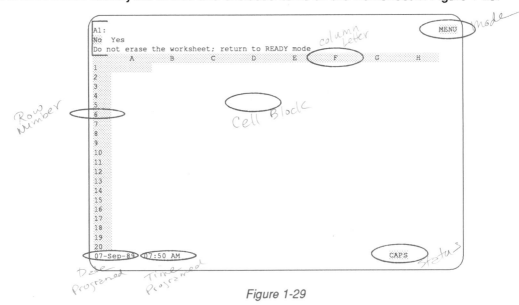

Figure 1-29

CHAPTER ONE
EXERCISE 3

INSTRUCTIONS: 1. Create the worksheet displayed in Figure 1-30.

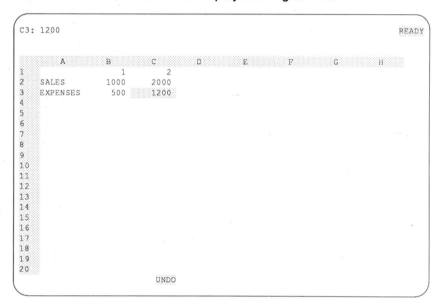

Figure 1-30

2. Erase the worksheet using the standard method.

CHAPTER ONE
EXERCISE 4

INSTRUCTIONS: 1.   Create the worksheet displayed in Figure 1-31.

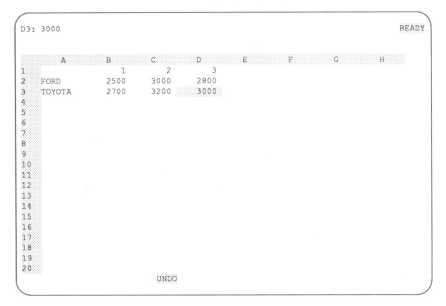

Figure 1-31

2.   Erase the worksheet using the alternate method.

CHAPTER TWO

CREATING AND PRINTING A SPREADSHEET

OBJECTIVES

In this chapter, you will learn to:

- Create, print, and save a spreadsheet
- Prevent rounding errors
- Print the cell formulas used to create the spreadsheet
- Use different numeric formats
- Make a backup of the spreadsheet file

■ CHAPTER OVERVIEW

One of the difficulties facing you as a beginning Lotus 1-2-3 user in learning to create a spreadsheet is how to begin! Chapter 2 cites an example problem and provides a step-by-step procedure on how to solve the problem with a Lotus 1-2-3 spreadsheet. While guiding you through the process for building the spreadsheet, the exercise provides information about 1-2-3 capabilities at the time you need them. After the spreadsheet is created, you can complete subsequent exercises for printing and storing the spreadsheet on a disk.

Additional exercises address typical problems you may have as a beginning user: how to solve rounding problems, how to print the cell formulas used in the spreadsheet, how to change the numeric display of the spreadsheet, and how to make a backup copy of the spreadsheet.

■EXAMPLE PROBLEM

The spreadsheet you create in this chapter will project sales for the last three quarters of a year based upon data from the first quarter. The information from the first quarter and the projections are as follows:

	1st Quarter	Projected Increase Per Quarter
Sales	$60,000	2%
Salaries	35,000	(given below)
Rent	9,000	(constant for all periods)
Telephone	1,000	5%
Office Supplies	750	$50
Miscellaneous	1,000	3%

The salary amounts for the quarters are as follows: $35,000; $35,500; $36,200; $37,000.

To complete the problem cited above, a common procedure for creating a spreadsheet using 1-2-3 will be followed. The procedure you will use is outlined below:

Creating Labels for the Spreadsheet

Correcting Errors

Expanding the Width of a Column

Entering Numbers, Formulas, and Copying Information in a Spreadsheet

Selecting a Format for the Data

Inserting Blank Rows for Headings

Entering Headings

Inserting Blank Rows within a Spreadsheet

Entering Underlines and Double Underlines

The completed spreadsheet is displayed in Figure 2-1.

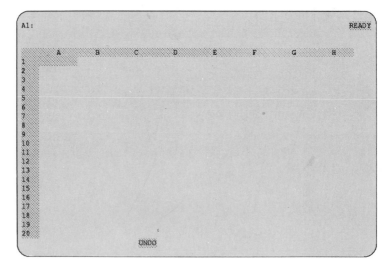

```
A1: [W18]                                                         READY

              A          B        C        D        E        F       G
 1                              ABC COMPANY
 2                                BUDGET
 3
 4
 5                        QTR1     QTR2     QTR3     QTR4   YR TOTAL
 6
 7    SALES             60,000   61,200   62,424   63,672  247,296
 8
 9    EXPENSES
10      SALARIES        35,000   35,500   36,200   37,000  143,700
11      RENT             9,000    9,000    9,000    9,000   36,000
12      TELEPHONE        1,000    1,050    1,103    1,158    4,311
13      OFFICE SUPPLIES    750      800      850      900    3,300
14      MISCELLANEOUS    1,000    1,030    1,061    1,093    4,184
15                     ---------------------------------------------
16      TOTAL EXPENSES  46,750   47,380   48,214   49,151  191,495
17                     ---------------------------------------------
18    GROSS PROFIT      13,250   13,820   14,210   14,521   55,801
19                     =============================================
20
                           UNDO                            CAPS
```

Figure 2-1

■ BUILDING THE SPREADSHEET

It is assumed that the microcomputer is turned on and that Lotus 1-2-3 has been loaded. A blank spreadsheet should be displayed on your screen such as the one in Figure 2-2.

```
A1:                                                              READY

         A       B       C       D       E       F       G       H
 1
 2
 3
 4
 5
 6
 7
 8
 9
10
11
12
13
14
15
16
17
18
19
20
                           UNDO
```

Figure 2-2

If your screen needs to be erased:

Press	/
Select	Worksheet
Select	Erase
Select	Yes

Creating Labels for the Spreadsheet

The term **label** refers to nonnumeric data. Note that numbers can be made into labels if they are not needed in computations (refer to the section on label prefixes in Chapter Three). Labels will be entered beginning in cell A1 to describe the contents of each row. Rows will be inserted later for the worksheet titles and headings.

To make all the labels appear in capital letters, make sure that the CAPS indicator appears at the bottom of the screen. If the Caps Lock key needs to be activated:

Press　　Caps Lock

CAPS should appear at the lower right corner of the screen. All of the alphabetic characters typed will be capital letters. (To turn the CAPS indicator off, tap the Caps Lock key again to "toggle" the indicator off).

The cell pointer should be in cell A1. If it is not, use the pointer- movement keys to move the cell pointer to cell A1.

Enter the labels in column A. The first label is SALES. To enter the label SALES in cell A1:

Type　　SALES

At the upper right corner of the screen, the mode indicator message changes from READY to LABEL. When data is first entered, the 1-2-3 program looks at the first character and judges the entry to be either a LABEL or a VALUE. Since the first character of SALES is nonnumeric, the entry will be considered a label. Never precede numbers that will be used in computation with spaces or other nonnumeric characters because 1-2-3 will interpret the entry as a label.

To enter the label SALES:

Press   ⏎

SALES has been entered in cell A1. The mode indicator changes back to READY.

To input the label EXPENSES in cell A2:

Move   the cell pointer to cell A2

Type   EXPENSES

Press   ⏎

To input the label SALARIES in cell A3:

Move   the cell pointer to cell A3

To indent the label:

Press   the space bar twice

Type   SALARIES

Pressing the space bar is an easy way to indent labels. Note that from this point on, the instructions utilize a "short-cut" for entering labels. Instead of pressing the ⏎ key, press the ⬇ key to enter a label and move to the next cell.

Press   ⬇

With one keystroke, the label SALARIES has been entered and the cell pointer has been moved to the next cell.

The cell pointer should now be in cell A4. To enter the next label:

Press   the space bar twice

Type   RENT

Press   ⬇

The cell pointer should now be in cell A5. To enter the next label:

Press   the space bar twice

Type   TELEPHONE

Press   ⬇

The cell pointer should now be in cell A6. To enter the next label:

> **Press**   the space bar twice
>
> **Type**   OFFICE SUPPLIES
>
> **Press**   ⊕

The cell pointer should now be in cell A7. To enter the next label:

> **Press**   the space bar twice
>
> **Type**   MISCELLANEOUS
>
> **Press**   ⊕

The cell pointer should now be in cell A8. To enter the next label:

> **Press**   the space bar four times
>
> **Type**   TOTAL EXPENSES
>
> **Press**   ⊕

The cell pointer should now be in cell A9. To enter the next label:

> **Type**   GROSS PROFIT
>
> **Press**   ⊖

The ⊕ key did not have to be pressed since GROSS PROFIT is the last label on the spreadsheet. The worksheet should look like Figure 2-3. If corrections need to be made, refer to the next section.

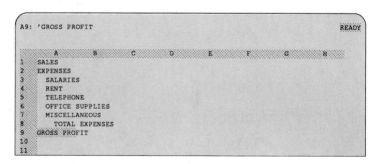

Figure 2-3

Correcting Errors

If an entry has been misspelled:

Move   the cell pointer to the cell displaying the error

Type   the entry correctly

Press

Refer to Figure 2-4 to see an example. In Figure 2-4, the word EXPENSES in cell A2 is spelled EXPANSES. To correct the error, move the cell pointer to cell A2, type EXPENSES, and press ⏎. The error is replaced with the correction.

REPLACING AN INCORRECT ENTRY
Move the cell pointer to the cell containing the error and type the desired entry . . .

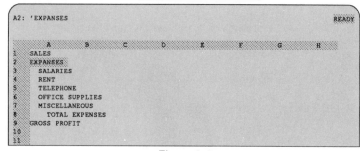

Figure 2-4
Part 1

then press ⏎ after typing the correction to replace the previous entry (EXPANSES is changed to EXPENSES in cell A2).

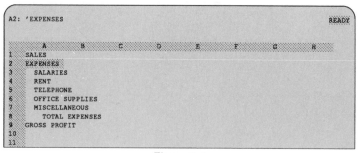

Figure 2-4
Part 2

The Esc key can be used to cancel data entered in the control panel if the ⏎ key has not yet been pressed. The Esc key may also be used to exit from a 1-2-3 menu. An alternative to pressing the Esc key several times (for example, to exit several levels of menus) is to hold down the Ctrl key and press the Break key.

If other errors have been made, clear the screen and begin the exercise again. If necessary, refer to the previous chapter for the instructions to clear a screen. Additional ways to correct errors are discussed in Chapter 3.

Expanding the Width of a Column

Several labels extend into column B. To enter data in column B but still see all of the labels in column A, you must widen column A. To widen column A:

Move   the cell pointer to the longest label in the column

In this example, move the cell pointer to cell A8, which has the indented label TOTAL EXPENSES.

Access the Lotus 1-2-3 menu and select the menu options for expanding a column.

Press   /

Select   Worksheet

Select   Column

Select   Set-Width

Press   → until the entire label is highlighted by the cell pointer

In the control panel, the message "Enter column width (1..240): 18" should be displayed as shown in Figure 2-5.

```
A8: [W18] '    TOTAL EXPENSES                                        POINT
Enter column width (1..240): 18

            A              B       C       D       E       F       G
1   SALES
2   EXPENSES
3      SALARIES              '
4      RENT
5      TELEPHONE
6      OFFICE SUPPLIES
7      MISCELLANEOUS
8         TOTAL EXPENSES
9   GROSS PROFIT
10
11
```

Figure 2-5

When the entire label is highlighted:

Press   ⏎

The column width of column A is now 18 characters (refer to Figure 2-6). Column B has *shifted* to the right and column H no longer appears on the screen, because column A occupies more screen space. Note that when the prompt "Enter column width (1..240):" appears, you do not have to highlight the desired width, but rather you can type the desired column width (such as 18) and press ⏎. The column width can be set from 1 character to 240 characters.

When the cell pointer is in any cell in column A, the control panel will display [W18], indicating that a column width of 18 has been set for the column. See Figure 2-6.

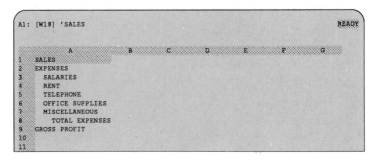

Figure 2-6

Entering the Assumptions

To enter the labels for the ASSUMPTIONS:

> **Move**   the cell pointer to cell A11
>
> **Type**   GROWTH RATE
>
> **Press**   ⬇

The cell pointer is in cell A12. To enter the next label:

> **Type**   ASSUMPTIONS
>
> **Press**   ⬇ twice

The cell pointer is in cell A14. To enter the next label:

> **Type**   SALES
>
> **Press**   ⬇

The cell pointer is in cell A15. To enter the next label:

Type   TELEPHONE

Press   ⊡

The cell pointer is in cell A16. To enter the next label:

Type   OFFICE SUPPLIES

Press   ⊡

The cell pointer is in cell A17. To enter the next label:

Type   MISCELLANEOUS

Press   ⏎

The screen should look like Figure 2-7.

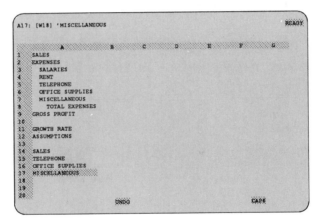

Figure 2-7

To input the assumed SALES growth rate for Quarters 2, 3 and 4 in columns C, D and E:

Move   the cell pointer to C14

Type   1.02

Because 1.02 is numeric, it is interpreted by Lotus 1-2-3 as a **value**. The mode indicator at the upper right corner of the screen displays the word VALUE. To enter the number:

Press   ⊡→

The cell pointer is in cell D14. Notice that the ⊡← key did not have to be pressed. Pressing the ⊡→ key after typing 1.02 did two things: entered 1.02 and moved the cell pointer to cell D14.

Type   1.02

Press   ⊡→

With the cell pointer in cell E14:

Type   1.02

Press   ⊡←

The SALES rate is not placed in column B because the rate is not needed for the first quarter.

Move   the cell pointer to cell C15

To input the TELEPHONE, OFFICE SUPPLIES and MISCELLANEOUS expense rates for Quarter 2:

Type   1.05

Press   ⊡↓

The cell pointer is in cell C16.

Type   50

Press   ⊡↓

The cell pointer is in cell C17.

Type   1.03

Press   ⊡←

You will enter the remaining growth rates for TELEPHONE, OFFICE SUPPLIES and MISCELLANEOUS expenses using a more efficient process in the next section. Your screen should appear as Figure 2-8.

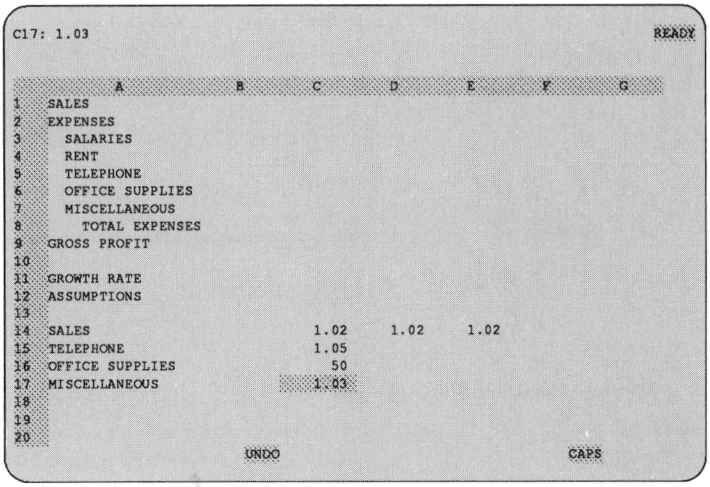

```
C17: 1.03                                                          READY

         A           B         C         D         E       F       G
 1   SALES
 2   EXPENSES
 3      SALARIES
 4      RENT
 5      TELEPHONE
 6      OFFICE SUPPLIES
 7      MISCELLANEOUS
 8         TOTAL EXPENSES
 9   GROSS PROFIT
10
11   GROWTH RATE
12   ASSUMPTIONS
13
14   SALES                    1.02      1.02      1.02
15   TELEPHONE                1.05
16   OFFICE SUPPLIES            50
17   MISCELLANEOUS            1.03
18
19
20
                        UNDO                               CAPS
```

Figure 2-8

Entering Numbers, Formulas and Copying Information in a Spreadsheet[1]

To enter the SALES amount for the first quarter:

Move the cell pointer to cell B1

Type 60000

Press ⏎

The formula for the second quarter of SALES multiplies the SALES amount in the first quarter by 1.02 to show a 2% projected increase. First place the cell pointer in the cell where the formula will be entered.

Move the cell pointer to cell C1

---

[1] See the section at the end of this chapter for more information on using formulas in Lotus 1-2-3.

Begin typing the formula:

Type   +

Move   the cell pointer to cell B1 (First Quarter SALES)

Type   *

The asterisk (*) is the symbol for multiplication.

Move   the cell pointer to cell C14

Press   ⏎

The number 61200 should now appear in cell C1. With cell C1 highlighted, look at the control panel at the upper left corner of the screen. The formula +B1*C14 should be displayed. This is the formula used to compute the number 61200 (refer to Figure 2-9). A formula can be typed directly into a cell. For example, by typing +B1*C14 with the cell pointer in cell C1 and pressing the ⏎ key, you would obtain the same result. It is *best* to point to the cells when creating a formula, because you tend to make fewer errors in specifying the formula.

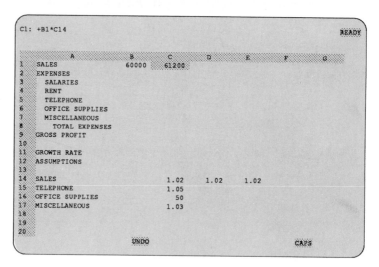

Figure 2-9

The formulas in Lotus 1-2-3 are based upon **relative cell location**. For example, the formula in cell C1, +B1*C14, is interpreted by Lotus 1-2-3 as "multiply the contents of the cell immediately to the left of the formula location by the number appearing 13 cells below the formula location." The SALES for Quarters 3 and 4 are also projected to increase from the previous quarter (the previous cell) by 2 percent. Therefore, the formula +B1*C14 can be **copied** to cells D1 and E1 and adjusted to +C1*D14 and +D1*E14, respectively.

The cell pointer should be highlighting cell C1. If not, move the cell pointer to cell C1.

Press /

Select Copy

The Copy command consists of two prompts. One prompt requires you to indicate which cells are to be copied. An easy way to do this is to highlight the cells to copy and press the ⏎ key. When the ⏎ key is pressed, another prompt requires you to specify the area to which the cell or cells will be copied. When the ⏎ key is pressed after the second prompt, the Copy command is completed.

The first prompt asks for the "range to copy FROM." Make sure that the cell or cells to copy are highlighted. Since C1 is the cell to copy and it is already highlighted:

Press ⏎

The second prompt asks for the "range to copy TO."

Move the cell pointer to cell D1

Type . (the period key)

Notice that "D1" (in the control panel) changes to "D1..D1" when the period key is pressed. The period key **anchors** the cell pointer so that more than one cell can be highlighted at a time. In this example, the cell pointer is **anchored** at cell D1 so that it can be **stretched** to cell E1.

Move the cell pointer to cell E1

Press ⏎

The formula in cell C1 has now been copied to cells D1 and E1 (Quarters 3 and 4). Refer to Parts 1 through 5 of Figure 2-10.

USING THE COPY COMMAND - RANGE TO COPY FROM
Step 1 of Copy Procedure: Highlight the cell(s) to copy and press ⏎.

```
C1: +B1*C14                                                    POINT
Enter range to copy FROM: C1..C1


             A          B          C          D          E          F          G
 1  SALES            60000      61200
 2  EXPENSES
 3    SALARIES
 4    RENT
 5    TELEPHONE
 6    OFFICE SUPPLIES
 7    MISCELLANEOUS
 8      TOTAL EXPENSES
 9  GROSS PROFIT
10
11  GROWTH RATE
12  ASSUMPTIONS
13
14  SALES                       1.02       1.02       1.02
15  TELEPHONE                    1.05
16  OFFICE SUPPLIES               50
17  MISCELLANEOUS                1.03
18
19
20
                                                              CAPS
```

Figure 2-10
Part 1

USING THE COPY PROCEDURE - RANGE TO COPY TO
Step 2 of Copy Procedure: Highlight the first cell to which the cell(s) will be copied.

```
D1:                                                           POINT
Enter range to copy TO: D1


             A          B          C          D          E          F          G
 1  SALES            60000      61200
 2  EXPENSES
 3    SALARIES
 4    RENT
 5    TELEPHONE
 6    OFFICE SUPPLIES
 7    MISCELLANEOUS
 8      TOTAL EXPENSES
 9  GROSS PROFIT
10
11  GROWTH RATE
12  ASSUMPTIONS
13
14  SALES                       1.02       1.02       1.02
15  TELEPHONE                    1.05
16  OFFICE SUPPLIES               50
17  MISCELLANEOUS                1.03
18
19
20
                                                              CAPS
```

Figure 2-10
Part 2

Step 3 of Copy Procedure: When copying to more than one cell, press the period key to **anchor** the cell pointer.

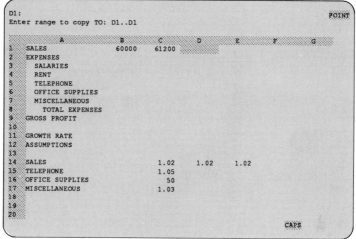

```
D1:                                                                  POINT
Enter range to copy TO: D1..D1

                A            B        C        D        E        F        G
1    SALES                 60000    61200
2    EXPENSES
3      SALARIES
4      RENT
5      TELEPHONE
6      OFFICE SUPPLIES
7      MISCELLANEOUS
8        TOTAL EXPENSES
9    GROSS PROFIT
10
11   GROWTH RATE
12   ASSUMPTIONS
13
14   SALES                          1.02     1.02     1.02
15   TELEPHONE                       1.05
16   OFFICE SUPPLIES                   50
17   MISCELLANEOUS                   1.03
18
19
20
                                                              CAPS
```

Figure 2-10
Part 3

Step 4 of Copy Procedure: **Stretch** the cell pointer from its anchored position to the rest of the area to which the cell will be copied.

```
E1:                                                                  POINT
Enter range to copy TO: D1..E1

                A            B        C        D        E        F        G
1    SALES                 60000    61200
2    EXPENSES
3      SALARIES
4      RENT
5      TELEPHONE
6      OFFICE SUPPLIES
7      MISCELLANEOUS
8        TOTAL EXPENSES
9    GROSS PROFIT
10
11   GROWTH RATE
12   ASSUMPTIONS
13
14   SALES                          1.02     1.02     1.02
15   TELEPHONE                       1.05
16   OFFICE SUPPLIES                   50
17   MISCELLANEOUS                   1.03
18
19
20
                                                              CAPS
```

Figure 2-10
Part 4

Step 5 of Copy Procedure: Press ⏎ to copy the desired cell(s) and complete the Copy Procedure.

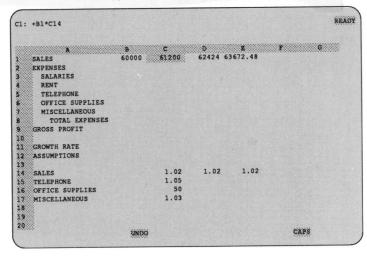

C1: +B1*C14   READY

	A	B	C	D	E	F	G
1	SALES	60000	61200	62424	63672.48		
2	EXPENSES						
3	SALARIES						
4	RENT						
5	TELEPHONE						
6	OFFICE SUPPLIES						
7	MISCELLANEOUS						
8	TOTAL EXPENSES						
9	GROSS PROFIT						
10							
11	GROWTH RATE						
12	ASSUMPTIONS						
13							
14	SALES		1.02	1.02	1.02		
15	TELEPHONE		1.05				
16	OFFICE SUPPLIES		50				
17	MISCELLANEOUS		1.03				
18							
19							
20							

                              UNDO   CAPS

Figure 2-10
Part 5

To copy the rates for TELEPHONE, OFFICE SUPPLIES and MISCELLANEOUS expense categories from Quarter 2 to Quarter 3 and Quarter 4:

Move   the cell pointer to cell C15

Press   /

Select   Copy

When prompted for the range to copy FROM:

Move   the cell pointer to C17

The period did not have to be pressed, because 1-2-3 automatically anchors the cell pointer at its current position when prompting for the "range to copy FROM." In this example the cell pointer is anchored at cell C15 and is **stretched** to highlight cells C15 through C17.

Press   ⏎

When prompted for the range to copy TO:

Move   the cell pointer to cell D15

Type   .

The period anchors the cell pointer ursor at cell D15.

Move   the cell pointer to cell E17

Press ↵

The expense growth rates have now been copied and your screen should look like Figure 2-11 Part 3.

COPYING MULTIPLE CELLS TO A RANGE

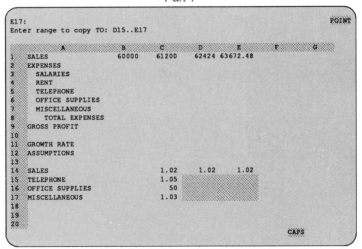

```
C17: 1.03                                                           POINT
Enter range to copy FROM: C15..C17

             A            B         C         D         E       F       G
1  SALES              60000     61200     62424 63672.48
2  EXPENSES
3    SALARIES
4    RENT
5    TELEPHONE
6    OFFICE SUPPLIES
7    MISCELLANEOUS
8       TOTAL EXPENSES
9  GROSS PROFIT
10
11 GROWTH RATE
12 ASSUMPTIONS
13
14 SALES                         1.02      1.02      1.02
15 TELEPHONE                     1.05
16 OFFICE SUPPLIES                 50
17 MISCELLANEOUS                 1.03
18
19
20                                                              CAPS
```

Figure 2-11
Part 1

```
E17:                                                               POINT
Enter range to copy TO: D15..E17

             A            B         C         D         E       F       G
1  SALES              60000     61200     62424 63672.48
2  EXPENSES
3    SALARIES
4    RENT
5    TELEPHONE
6    OFFICE SUPPLIES
7    MISCELLANEOUS
8       TOTAL EXPENSES
9  GROSS PROFIT
10
11 GROWTH RATE
12 ASSUMPTIONS
13
14 SALES                         1.02      1.02      1.02
15 TELEPHONE                     1.05
16 OFFICE SUPPLIES                 50
17 MISCELLANEOUS                 1.03
18
19
20                                                              CAPS
```

Figure 2-11
Part 2

```
C15: 1.05                                                    READY

           A           B        C        D        E       F      G
 1   SALES           60000    61200    62424  63672.48
 2   EXPENSES
 3       SALARIES
 4       RENT
 5       TELEPHONE
 6       OFFICE SUPPLIES
 7       MISCELLANEOUS
 8          TOTAL EXPENSES
 9   GROSS PROFIT
10
11   GROWTH RATE
12   ASSUMPTIONS
13
14   SALES                     1.02     1.02     1.02
15   TELEPHONE                 1.05     1.05     1.05
16   OFFICE SUPPLIES             50       50       50
17   MISCELLANEOUS             1.03     1.03     1.03
18
19
20
                              UNDO                      CAPS
```

Figure 2-11
Part 3

To input the data for SALARIES:

Move   the cell pointer to cell B3

Make sure that the cell pointer is in the *third* row.

Type   35000 (First Quarter SALARIES)

Press   ⊕

The cell pointer is now on cell C3.

To enter the salary amounts for Quarters 2, 3 and 4:

Type   35500 (Second Quarter SALARIES)

Press   ⊕

Type   36200 (Third Quarter SALARIES)

Press   ⊕

Type   37000 (Fourth Quarter SALARIES)

Press   ⏎

Your screen should look like Figure 2-12.

```
E3:  37000                                                              READY

                  A             B       C        D        E        F       G
  1    SALES                  60000    61200   62424  63672.48
  2    EXPENSES
  3        SALARIES           35000    35500   36200    37000
  4        RENT
  5        TELEPHONE
  6        OFFICE SUPPLIES
  7        MISCELLANEOUS
  8           TOTAL EXPENSES
  9    GROSS PROFIT
 10
 11    GROWTH RATE
 12    ASSUMPTIONS
 13
 14    SALES                           1.02    1.02     1.02
 15    TELEPHONE                       1.05    1.05     1.05
 16    OFFICE SUPPLIES                   50      50       50
 17    MISCELLANEOUS                   1.03    1.03     1.03
 18
 19
 20
                              UNDO                               CAPS
```

Figure 2-12

To input the data for RENT:

Move	the cell pointer to cell B4
Type	9000
Press	⏎

You can use the Copy command to copy the 9000 from Quarter 1 to Quarters 2, 3 and 4. The cell pointer should be in cell B4. To copy the amount:

Press	/
Select	Copy

When prompted for the range to copy FROM, note that the cell pointer is highlighting cell B4, which is the cell to copy. To indicate that B4 is the cell to copy:

Press	⏎

When prompted for the range to copy TO:

Move	the cell pointer to cell C4
Type	.

Move   the cell pointer to cell E4

Press   ⏎

The number 9000 should now be copied to Quarters 2, 3 and 4. Your screen should look like Figure 2-13.

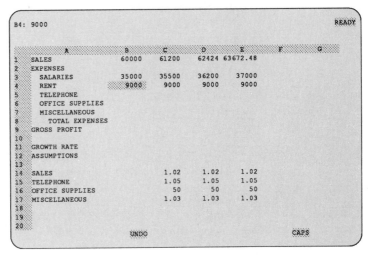

Figure 2-13

To input the data for TELEPHONE expenses for the first quarter:

Move   the cell pointer to cell B5

Type   1000

Press   ⏎

You can enter the following formula to indicate that TELEPHONE expenses will increase by 5 percent for the remaining quarters:

Move   the cell pointer to cell C5

Type   +

Move   the cell pointer to cell B5 (TELEPHONE expense for Quarter 1)

Type   *

Move   the cell pointer to cell C15 (GROWTH RATE factor for TELEPHONE expense)

Press ↵

The number 1050 should appear in cell C5. The formula +B5*C15 should be displayed in the control panel and your screen should look like Figure 2-14. The formulas for Quarters 3 and 4 will be completed later in this section.

```
C5:  +B5*C15                                                            READY

                    A           B        C        D        E        F        G
 1   SALES                    60000    61200    62424  63672.48
 2   EXPENSES
 3      SALARIES              35000    35500    36200    37000
 4      RENT                   9000     9000     9000     9000
 5      TELEPHONE              1000     1050
 6      OFFICE SUPPLIES
 7      MISCELLANEOUS
 8         TOTAL EXPENSES
 9   GROSS PROFIT
10
11   GROWTH RATE
12   ASSUMPTIONS
13
14   SALES                              1.02     1.02     1.02
15   TELEPHONE                          1.05     1.05     1.05
16   OFFICE SUPPLIES                      50       50       50
17   MISCELLANEOUS                      1.03     1.03     1.03
18
19
20
                            UNDO                             CAPS
```

Figure 2-14

To input the data for OFFICE SUPPLIES expenses for the first quarter:

Move	the cell pointer to cell B6
Type	750
Press	↵

OFFICE SUPPLIES expenses increase by $50 for the remaining quarters. To enter the appropriate formula:

Move	the cell pointer to cell C6
Type	+
Move	the cell pointer to cell B6
Type	+
Move	the cell pointer to C16

Press ⏎

The number 800 appears in cell C6. The formula +B6+C16 is now displayed in the control panel. Your screen should look like Figure 2-15. The formulas for Quarters 3 and 4 are completed later in this exercise.

```
C6: +B6+C16                                                          READY

          A              B          C          D          E          F          G
 1   SALES            60000      61200      62424   63672.48
 2   EXPENSES
 3       SALARIES     35000      35500      36200      37000
 4       RENT          9000       9000       9000       9000
 5       TELEPHONE     1000       1050
 6       OFFICE SUPPLIES  750       800
 7       MISCELLANEOUS
 8          TOTAL EXPENSES
 9   GROSS PROFIT
10
11   GROWTH RATE
12   ASSUMPTIONS
13
14   SALES                        1.02       1.02       1.02
15   TELEPHONE                    1.05       1.05       1.05
16   OFFICE SUPPLIES                50         50         50
17   MISCELLANEOUS                1.03       1.03       1.03
18
19
20
                          UNDO                                    CAPS
```

Figure 2-15

To input the data for MISCELLANEOUS expenses for the first quarter:

Move the cell pointer to cell B7

Type 1000

Press ⏎

To enter the formula that indicates MISCELLANEOUS expenses are to increase by 3%:

Move the cell pointer to cell C7

Type +

Move the cell pointer to cell B7

Type *

Move the cell pointer to cell C17

Press ⏎

The number 1030 now appears in cell C7. The formula +B7*C17 is displayed in the control panel and your screen should look like Figure 2-16.

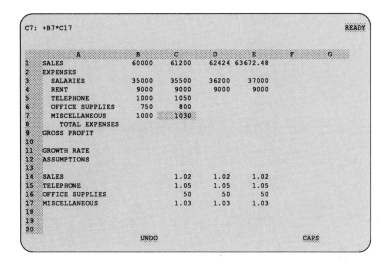

Figure 2-16

To copy the formulas for TELEPHONE, OFFICE SUPPLIES and MISCELLANEOUS expenses to Quarters 3 and 4:

Move the cell pointer to cell C5 (the formula for projecting TELEPHONE expenses)

Press /

Select Copy

When prompted for the range to copy FROM:

Move the cell pointer to cell C7 (the formula for projecting MISCELLANEOUS expenses)

The period key did not have to be pressed because 1-2-3 automatically anchors the cell pointer at its current position when prompting for the "range to copy FROM." In this example, the cell pointer is anchored at cell C5 and is **stretched** to highlight cells C5 through C7.

Press ⏎

When prompted for the range to copy TO:

Move   the cell pointer to cell D5

Type   .

Pressing the period key anchors the cell pointer at cell D5.

Move   the cell pointer to cell E7

The screen currently displays a highlighted rectangle that covers cells D5 through E7.

Press   ⏎

The formulas in cells C5 through C7 that project TELEPHONE, OFFICE SUPPLIES and MISCELLANEOUS expenses have been copied to cells D5 through E7. Your screen should look like Figure 2-17.

```
C5: +B5*C15                                                    READY

              A           B         C         D        E        F        G
  1  SALES               60000     61200   62424 63672.48
  2  EXPENSES
  3     SALARIES         35000     35500    36200    37000
  4     RENT              9000      9000     9000     9000
  5     TELEPHONE         1000      1050   1102.5 1157.625
  6     OFFICE SUPPLIES    750       800      850      900
  7     MISCELLANEOUS     1000      1030   1060.9 1092.727
  8        TOTAL EXPENSES
  9  GROSS PROFIT
 10
 11  GROWTH RATE
 12  ASSUMPTIONS
 13
 14  SALES                         1.02     1.02     1.02
 15  TELEPHONE                     1.05     1.05     1.05
 16  OFFICE SUPPLIES                 50       50       50
 17  MISCELLANEOUS                 1.03     1.03     1.03
 18
 19
 20
                            UNDO                            CAPS
```

Figure 2-17

You now need to sum the quarterly values for the various items to obtain the TOTAL EXPENSES for the first quarter. Lotus 1-2-3 has a special function that makes it easy to sum the expense values. The general format for the SUM function is:

@SUM(first cell..last cell)

Note that a range of cells is specified within the set of parentheses. By placing the @ character prior to the word SUM, you have indicated that you want to use the special function @SUM. The many other special functions available in 1-2-3 are discussed in Chapter 8.

To enter the @SUM function for calculating TOTAL EXPENSES for the first quarter:

Move   the cell pointer to cell B8

Type   @SUM(

Move   the cell pointer to cell B3 (the first item in column B
             to total, which is SALARIES)

Type   .

The period key anchors the cell pointer in cell B3.

Move   the cell pointer to cell B7

Type   )

Press   ⏎

The number 46750 should appear in cell B8. The formula @SUM(B3..B7) is displayed in the control panel, and your screen should look like Figure 2-18.

```
B8:  @SUM(B3..B7)                                                    READY

            A             B          C         D        E        F        G
 1   SALES            60000      61200     62424 63672.48
 2   EXPENSES
 3     SALARIES       35000      35500     36200    37000
 4     RENT            9000       9000      9000     9000
 5     TELEPHONE       1000       1050    1102.5 1157.625
 6     OFFICE SUPPLIES  750        800       850      900
 7     MISCELLANEOUS   1000       1030    1060.9 1092.727
 8        TOTAL EXPENSES  46750
 9   GROSS PROFIT
10
11   GROWTH RATE
12   ASSUMPTIONS
13
14   SALES                       1.02      1.02     1.02
15   TELEPHONE                    1.05      1.05     1.05
16   OFFICE SUPPLIES               50        50       50
17   MISCELLANEOUS                1.03      1.03     1.03
18
19
20
                         UNDO                              CAPS
```

Figure 2-18

To compute GROSS PROFIT, you must create a formula which subtracts TOTAL EXPENSES from SALES.

Move   the cell pointer to cell B9

Type   +

Move   the cell pointer to cell B1 (SALES)

Type   -

Move   the cell pointer to cell B8 (TOTAL EXPENSES)

Press   ⏎

The number 13250 should appear in cell B9. The formula +B1-B8 is displayed in the control panel.

You can use the Copy command to copy the formulas for computing TOTAL EXPENSES and GROSS PROFIT to the remaining three quarters.

Move   the cell pointer to cell B8 (TOTAL EXPENSES)

Press   /

Select   Copy

When prompted for the range to copy FROM:

Move   the cell pointer to cell B9 (GROSS PROFIT)

The copy FROM range should highlight cells B8 and B9.

Press   ⏎

When prompted for the range to copy TO:

Move   the cell pointer to cell C8

Type   .

Move   the cell pointer to cell E9

A highlighted rectangle covers cells C8 through E9.

Press   ⏎

Your screen should look like Figure 2-19.

```
B8:  @SUM(B3..B7)                                                    READY

                A         B        C         D         E        F       G
 1   SALES              60000    61200     62424  63672.48
 2   EXPENSES
 3     SALARIES         35000    35500     36200     37000
 4     RENT              9000     9000      9000      9000
 5     TELEPHONE         1000     1050    1102.5  1157.625
 6     OFFICE SUPPLIES    750      800       850       900
 7     MISCELLANEOUS     1000     1030    1060.9  1092.727
 8       TOTAL EXPENSES  46750    47380   48213.4  49150.35
 9   GROSS PROFIT       13250    13820   14210.6  14522.12
10
11   GROWTH RATE
12   ASSUMPTIONS
13
14   SALES                       1.02      1.02      1.02
15   TELEPHONE                   1.05      1.05      1.05
16   OFFICE SUPPLIES               50        50        50
17   MISCELLANEOUS               1.03      1.03      1.03
18
19
20
                        UNDO                              CAPS
```

Figure 2-19

To compute the total SALES for the year:

Move	the cell pointer to cell F1
Type	@SUM(
Move	the cell pointer to cell B1
Type	.
Move	the cell pointer to cell E1
Type	)
Press	⏎

The number 247296.4 appears in cell F1. The formula @SUM(B1..E1) appears in the control panel.

To copy the @SUM(B1..E1) formula to the appropriate rows below the SALES row:

| **Press** | / |
| **Select** | Copy |

When prompted for the range to copy FROM:

Press ⏎

Since F1 was already highlighted, the cell pointer did not have to be moved.

When prompted for the range to copy TO:

Move the cell pointer to cell F3

Type .

Move the cell pointer to cell F9

Press ⏎

The formula @SUM(B1..E1) has been copied from cells F1 to cells F3 through F9. Your screen should look like Figure 2-20.

```
F1: @SUM(B1..E1)                                                    READY

            A          B       C       D         E          F         G
 1   SALES           60000   61200   62424 63672.48 247296.4
 2   EXPENSES
 3      SALARIES     35000   35500   36200   37000    143700
 4      RENT          9000    9000    9000    9000     36000
 5      TELEPHONE     1000    1050  1102.5 1157.625 4310.125
 6      OFFICE SUPPLIES 750    800     850     900      3300
 7      MISCELLANEOUS 1000    1030  1060.9 1092.727 4183.627
 8         TOTAL EXPENSES 46750 47380 48213.4 49150.35 191493.7
 9   GROSS PROFIT    13250   13820 14210.6 14522.12 55802.72
10
11   GROWTH RATE
12   ASSUMPTIONS
13
14   SALES                    1.02    1.02    1.02
15   TELEPHONE                1.05    1.05    1.05
16   OFFICE SUPPLIES            50      50      50
17   MISCELLANEOUS            1.03    1.03    1.03
18
19
20
                        UNDO                            CAPS
```

Figure 2-20

To choose a numeric format (commas, dollar signs, the number of decimal places and so forth) for the worksheet:

Press /

Select Worksheet

Select Global

Select   Format

Notice that the Global settings now appear on your screen. See Figure 2-21.

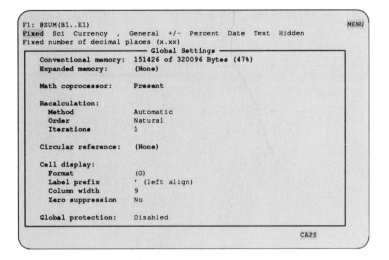

```
F1: @SUM(B1..E1)                                                        MENU
Fixed  Sci  Currency  ,  General  +/-  Percent  Date  Text  Hidden
Fixed number of decimal places (x.xx)
                            Global Settings
    Conventional memory:    151426 of 320096 Bytes (47%)
    Expanded memory:        (None)

    Math coprocessor:       Present

    Recalculation:
      Method                Automatic
      Order                 Natural
      Iterations            1

    Circular reference:     (None)

    Cell display:
      Format                (G)
      Label prefix          ' (left align)
      Column width          9
      Zero suppression      No

    Global protection:      Disabled


                                                            CAPS
```

Figure 2-21

You will now change the global format from **G** (General) to , (Comma).

Select   , (for comma)

Global means that the format chosen will be used as the default for the spreadsheet, unless another numeric format is specified. The , represents the comma format.

When prompted for the number of decimal places:

Type   0

Press   ⏎

Be sure to type the number "zero" and not the letter "O". Your screen should look like Figure 2-22.

Note the settings for memory and math coprocessor may be different on your computer.

```
F1: @SUM(B1..E1)                                                        READY

         A              B        C        D        E        F          G
 1  SALES            60,000   61,200   62,424   63,672  247,296
 2  EXPENSES
 3     SALARIES      35,000   35,500   36,200   37,000  143,700
 4     RENT           9,000    9,000    9,000    9,000   36,000
 5     TELEPHONE      1,000    1,050    1,103    1,158    4,310
 6     OFFICE SUPPLIES  750      800      850      900    3,300
 7     MISCELLANEOUS  1,000    1,030    1,061    1,093    4,184
 8        TOTAL EXPENSES 46,750 47,380  48,213   49,150  191,494
 9  GROSS PROFIT     13,250   13,820   14,211   14,522   55,803
10
11  GROWTH RATE
12  ASSUMPTIONS
13
14  SALES                        1        1        1
15  TELEPHONE                    1        1        1
16  OFFICE SUPPLIES             50       50       50
17  MISCELLANEOUS                1        1        1
18
19
20
                          UNDO                             CAPS
```

Figure 2-22

Notice that the various expense rates no longer have decimal numbers on the screen, because the previous format command indicated that the format for all numbers does not include any characters to the right of the decimal point.

To have the proper format for the growth rate assumption values, you must format a range of cells using the **Range Format Fixed** command sequence.

Move	the cell pointer to cell C14
Press	/
Select	Range
Select	Format
Select	Fixed
Press	⏎ to accept 2 decimal places
Move	the cell pointer to cell E17 to highlight the range of cells to format
Press	⏎

Your screen should look like Figure 2-23.

```
C14: (F2) 1.02                                                    READY

              A          B        C        D        E        F        G
1   SALES            60,000   61,200   62,424   63,672  247,296
2   EXPENSES
3     SALARIES       35,000   35,500   36,200   37,000  143,700
4     RENT            9,000    9,000    9,000    9,000   36,000
5     TELEPHONE       1,000    1,050    1,103    1,158    4,310
6     OFFICE SUPPLIES   750      800      850      900    3,300
7     MISCELLANEOUS   1,000    1,030    1,061    1,093    4,184
8        TOTAL EXPENSES 46,750  47,380   48,213   49,150  191,494
9   GROSS PROFIT     13,250   13,820   14,211   14,522   55,803
10
11  GROWTH RATE
12  ASSUMPTIONS
13
14  SALES                      1.02     1.02     1.02
15  TELEPHONE                  1.05     1.05     1.05
16  OFFICE SUPPLIES           50.00    50.00    50.00
17  MISCELLANEOUS              1.03     1.03     1.03
18
19
20
                        UNDO                              CAPS
```

Figure 2-23

Notice that rounding errors occur (e.g., SALES of 247,296 minus TOTAL EXPENSES of 191,494 should equal 55,802 rather than 55,803). The rounding error occurred because the numbers are *formatted* to *show* 0 decimal places on your screen, but the *values* in the cells are not truly *rounded* to 0 decimal places. Rounding errors are resolved later in this chapter.

Inserting Blank Rows for a Title and Column Headings

To insert six blank rows at the top of the spreadsheet:

Move   the cell pointer to cell A1

Press   /

Select Worksheet

Select Insert

Select Row

When prompted for the insert range:

Move   the cell pointer to cell A6

The period key did not have to be pressed because the **Worksheet Insert Row** command automatically anchors the cell pointer at its current position. The insert range is from rows A1 through A6, or rows 1 through 6. Note that the entire row does not have to be highlighted. Also notice that the cell pointer does not have to be in column A to insert rows; it can be in any column.

Press   ⏎

Your screen should look like Figure 2-24.

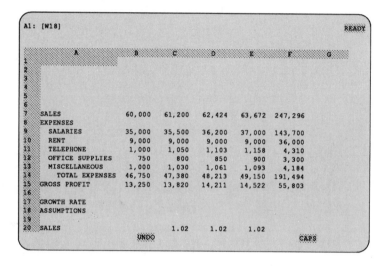

Figure 2-24

The worksheet formulas and values remain correct and are *adjusted* to the new location. For example, the formula for Quarter 2's SALES have been changed from +B1*C14 to +B7*C20 in cell C7.

Entering the Spreadsheet Title and Column Headings

When entering the spreadsheet title lines, you must determine where the spreadsheet title will be centered correctly. To input the first title line for this example:

Move   the cell pointer to cell C1

Press   the space bar five times

Type   ABC COMPANY

Press   ⏎

To enter the second title line:

Move	the cell pointer to cell C2
Press	the space bar seven times
Type	BUDGET
Press	⏎

To enter the column heading for the first quarter:

Move	the cell pointer to cell B5
Type	^QTR1
Press	⏎

The ^ mark causes the labels to be **centered** within the column; a **double quote mark** before the heading would cause the labels to be **right-justified** or **right-aligned** in the cell.

To enter the column headings for the last three quarters:

Press	→
Type	^QTR2
Press	→
Type	^QTR3
Press	→
Type	^QTR4
Press	→

To enter the column heading for the total column:

Type	^YR TOTAL
Press	⏎

Your screen should look like Figure 2-25.

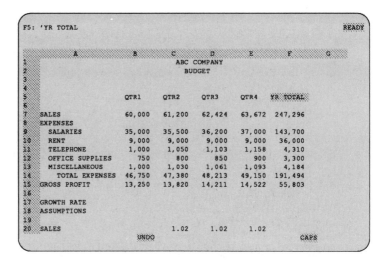

Figure 2-25

Inserting Blank Rows in a Spreadsheet

To insert a blank row between SALES and EXPENSES:

Move	the cell pointer to cell A8 (EXPENSES)
Press	/
Select	Worksheet
Select	Insert
Select	Row

When prompted for the row to insert:

Press	⏎

Since the cell pointer was already highlighting cell A8, pressing the ⏎ key at this point caused one row to be inserted at row 8. Your screen should look like Figure 2-26.

```
A8: [W18]                                                              READY

                A           B       C       D       E       F       G
 1                                ABC COMPANY
 2                                  BUDGET
 3
 4
 5                              QTR1    QTR2    QTR3    QTR4   YR TOTAL
 6
 7      SALES                 60,000  61,200  62,424  63,672  247,296
 8
 9      EXPENSES
10         SALARIES           35,000  35,500  36,200  37,000  143,700
11         RENT                9,000   9,000   9,000   9,000   36,000
12         TELEPHONE           1,000   1,050   1,103   1,158    4,310
13         OFFICE SUPPLIES       750     800     850     900    3,300
14         MISCELLANEOUS       1,000   1,030   1,061   1,093    4,184
15            TOTAL EXPENSES  46,750  47,380  48,213  49,150  191,494
16      GROSS PROFIT          13,250  13,820  14,211  14,522   55,803
17
18      GROWTH RATE
19      ASSUMPTIONS
20
                             UNDO                             CAPS
```

Figure 2-26

To insert a blank row between MISCELLANEOUS and TOTAL EXPENSES:

Move	the cell pointer to cell A15 (TOTAL EXPENSES)
Press	/
Select	Worksheet
Select	Insert
Select	Row

When prompted for the row to insert:

Press	⏎

Pressing the ⏎ key at this point causes one row to be inserted at row 15.

To insert a blank row between TOTAL EXPENSES and GROSS PROFIT:

Move	the cell pointer to cell A17 (GROSS PROFIT)

To illustrate that a blank row can be inserted when the cell pointer is in another column other than column A:

Move	the cell pointer to cell C17

Press	/
Select	Worksheet
Select	Insert
Select	Row

When prompted for the row to insert:

Press	⏎

Pressing the ⏎ key at this point caused one row to be inserted at row 17. Your screen should look like Figure 2-27.

```
C17:                                                                  READY

            A          B        C        D        E        F        G
1                             ABC COMPANY
2                               BUDGET
3
4
5                           QTR1     QTR2     QTR3     QTR4    YR TOTAL
6
7     SALES               60,000   61,200   62,424   63,672   247,296
8
9     EXPENSES
10      SALARIES          35,000   35,500   36,200   37,000   143,700
11      RENT               9,000    9,000    9,000    9,000    36,000
12      TELEPHONE          1,000    1,050    1,103    1,158     4,310
13      OFFICE SUPPLIES      750      800      850      900     3,300
14      MISCELLANEOUS      1,000    1,030    1,061    1,093     4,184
15
16      TOTAL EXPENSES    46,750   47,380   48,213   49,150   191,494
17
18    GROSS PROFIT        13,250   13,820   14,211   14,522    55,803
19
20    GROWTH RATE
                             UNDO                              CAPS
```

Figure 2-27

Entering Underlines and Double Underlines

To input subtotal underlines for the TOTAL EXPENSES:

Move	the cell pointer to cell B15
Type	\
Type	-
Press	⏎

By pressing \ once and then a minus sign or dash, a subtotal line has been created. The \ indicates you desire to fill a cell with whatever character(s) follows the \.

To copy the subtotal underlines to the rest of the current row:

Press   /

Select   Copy

When prompted for the range to copy FROM:

Press   ⏎

By pressing the ⏎ key, cell B15 is indicated as the cell to copy.

When prompted for the range to copy TO:

Move   the cell pointer to cell C15

Type   .

Move   the cell pointer to cell F15

Press   ⏎

Your screen should look like Figure 2-28.

```
B15: \-                                                          READY

            A           B       C       D        E        F        G
  1                          ABC COMPANY
  2                            BUDGET
  3
  4
  5                        QTR1    QTR2    QTR3    QTR4   YR TOTAL
  6
  7   SALES              60,000  61,200  62,424  63,672  247,296
  8
  9   EXPENSES
 10     SALARIES         35,000  35,500  36,200  37,000  143,700
 11     RENT              9,000   9,000   9,000   9,000   36,000
 12     TELEPHONE         1,000   1,050   1,103   1,158    4,310
 13     OFFICE SUPPLIES     750     800     850     900    3,300
 14     MISCELLANEOUS     1,000   1,030   1,061   1,093    4,184
 15                      ------- ------------------------------
 16       TOTAL EXPENSES 46,750  47,380  48,213  49,150  191,494
 17
 18   GROSS PROFIT       13,250  13,820  14,211  14,522   55,803
 19
 20   GROWTH RATE
                           UNDO                             CAPS
```

Figure 2-28

To copy row 15's subtotal underlines to row 17, make sure the cell pointer is in cell B15 and then:

Press   /

Select   Copy

When prompted for the range to copy FROM:

Move   the cell pointer to cell F15

Cells B15 through F15 should now be highlighted.

Press   ⏎

When prompted for the range to copy TO:

Move   the cell pointer to cell B17

Press   ⏎

Notice that to copy a range of cells, it is not necessary to highlight the entire area to which the cells are to be copied.

To input the double underlines in cell B19:

Move   the cell pointer to cell B19

Type   \

Type   =

Press   ⏎

To copy the double underlines to the rest of row 19:

Press   /

Select   Copy

When prompted for the range to copy FROM:

Press   ⏎

By pressing the ⏎ key, cell B19 is indicated as the cell to copy.

When prompted for the range to copy TO:

Move   the cell pointer to cell C19

Type   .

Move   the cell pointer to cell F19

Press   ⏎

Your screen should look like Figure 2-29.

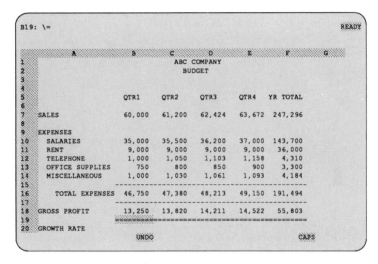

B19: \=   READY

	A	B	C	D	E	F	G
1			ABC COMPANY				
2			BUDGET				
3							
4							
5		QTR1	QTR2	QTR3	QTR4	YR TOTAL	
6							
7	SALES	60,000	61,200	62,424	63,672	247,296	
8							
9	EXPENSES						
10	SALARIES	35,000	35,500	36,200	37,000	143,700	
11	RENT	9,000	9,000	9,000	9,000	36,000	
12	TELEPHONE	1,000	1,050	1,103	1,158	4,310	
13	OFFICE SUPPLIES	750	800	850	900	3,300	
14	MISCELLANEOUS	1,000	1,030	1,061	1,093	4,184	
15		-----	-----	-----	-----	-----	
16	TOTAL EXPENSES	46,750	47,380	48,213	49,150	191,494	
17		-----	-----	-----	-----	-----	
18	GROSS PROFIT	13,250	13,820	14,211	14,522	55,803	
19							
20	GROWTH RATE						

UNDO   CAPS

Figure 2-29

To place two blank lines between the row with the double underlines and the ASSUMPTIONS:

Move   the cell pointer to cell A20

Press   /

Select   Worksheet

Select   Insert

Select   Row

Press   ⬇ one time

Press   ⏎

Your screen should look like Figure 2-30.

```
A20: [W18]                                                                    READY

            A           B          C          D          E          F          G
 1                                          ABC COMPANY
 2                                            BUDGET
 3
 4
 5                       QTR1       QTR2       QTR3       QTR4    YR TOTAL
 6
 7    SALES            60,000     61,200     62,424     63,672    247,296
 8
 9    EXPENSES
10      SALARIES       35,000     35,500     36,200     37,000    143,700
11      RENT            9,000      9,000      9,000      9,000     36,000
12      TELEPHONE       1,000      1,050      1,103      1,158      4,310
13      OFFICE SUPPLIES   750        800        850        900      3,300
14      MISCELLANEOUS   1,000      1,030      1,061      1,093      4,184
15                   ------------------------------------------------------
16      TOTAL EXPENSES 46,750     47,380     48,213     49,150    191,494
17                   ------------------------------------------------------
18    GROSS PROFIT     13,250     13,820     14,211     14,522     55,803
19                   ======================================================
20

                                    UNDO                                  CAPS
```

Figure 2-30

■SAVING AND NAMING THE SPREADSHEET

Pressing the [Home] key prior to saving a spreadsheet to a file is an optional step. If the [Home] key is pressed, the file will be saved with the cell pointer located in cell A1. When the file is later retrieved, the cell pointer will appear in cell A1.

Press	/
Select	File
Select	Save

When prompted for the file name:

Type	BUDGET
Press	←

File names can be a maximum of eight characters long. Acceptable characters are letters of the alphabet, numbers, and the underline (_) character. (The underline character takes up one space; it cannot be used to underline other characters in the file name). Do not include **spaces** or **periods** in the file name. The file named BUDGET contains the spreadsheet that was created.

Note that you may set up 1-2-3 to save files on a different disk or directory other than the one on which 1-2-3 is installed. In this book, you only need to save worksheets to a file when you are instructed to do so.

■CORRECTING THE ROUNDING ERROR

The worksheet that was just completed did not **foot** or balance correctly. The result in the YR TOTAL column is shown below:

Sales	247,296
-Total Expenses	191,494
Gross Profit	55,803 (does not foot correctly)

When multiplication, division, or exponents are used in a formula, the @ROUND function can be used to round a number to a specified number of decimal places. Otherwise, 1-2-3 uses the "hidden" decimal places in computation, resulting in rounding errors. The @ROUND function will be explained in more detail later in this chapter. For now, the following steps can be used for rounding the appropriate formulas where necessary in this example.

Note that you should *immediately* use the @ROUND function when creating formulas rather than going back to edit them. This example was done differently to show the results of *not* using the @ROUND function.

The three sets of formulas for SALES, TELEPHONE and MISCELLANEOUS expenses need to be edited to use the @ROUND function because the three lines contain multiplication.

Note that the only way rounding errors can occur in a spreadsheet is through multiplying, dividing, exponentiation or through the use of special functions such as the square root.

The @ROUND function's format is as follows:

```
@ROUND(number or formula,number of digits to round to)
```

SALES will be the first formula to be edited. The formula is +B7*C25 for the SALES projection for the Second Quarter. To round the SALES projection to 0 decimal places:

Move	the cell pointer to cell C7
Type	@ROUND (
Move	the cell pointer to cell B7
Type	*
Move	the cell pointer to cell C25
Type	,

To indicate zero decimal places:

Type	0
Type	)
Press	⏎

The formula @ROUND(B7*C25,0) is now in cell C7. The formula "B7*C25" is rounded to 0 decimal places. Your screen should look like Figure 2-31.

```
C7: @ROUND(B7*C25,0)                                                        READY


              A            B          C          D          E          F          G
 1                                ABC  COMPANY
 2                                    BUDGET
 3
 4
 5                         QTR1       QTR2       QTR3       QTR4     YR TOTAL
 6
 7   SALES                60,000     61,200     62,424     63,672    247,296
 8
 9   EXPENSES
10      SALARIES          35,000     35,500     36,200     37,000    143,700
11      RENT               9,000      9,000      9,000      9,000     36,000
12      TELEPHONE          1,000      1,050      1,103      1,158      4,310
13      OFFICE SUPPLIES      750        800        850        900      3,300
14      MISCELLANEOUS      1,000      1,030      1,061      1,093      4,184
15                        ------------------------------------------------
16      TOTAL EXPENSES    46,750     47,380     48,213     49,150    191,494
17                        ------------------------------------------------
18   GROSS PROFIT         13,250     13,820     14,211     14,522     55,803
19                        ================================================
20
                               UNDO                                 CAPS
```

Figure 2-31

To copy the rounded formula to the remaining quarters:

Press	/
Select	Copy

When prompted for the range to copy FROM:

Press	⏎

By pressing the ⏎ key, C7 was selected as the cell to copy.

When prompted for the range to copy TO:

Move	the cell pointer to cell D7

Type .

Move the cell pointer to cell E7

Press ⏎

The projections for SALES are now rounded to 0 decimal places.

The second set of formulas you need to round is for TELEPHONE expenses. The formula for TELEPHONE expenses in the Second Quarter is +B12*C26. To round the TELEPHONE expenses to 0 decimal places:

Move the cell pointer to cell C12

Rather than retyping the formula, use a shortcut to edit the current formula.

Press the F2 key

The F2 function key is often referred to as the "Edit" key when using 1-2-3.

Press the ← key until the cell pointer is under the + sign at the front of the formula—an alternative is to press the Home key to move to the beginning of the formula

Type @ROUND (

Press the Del key one time to delete the + sign if desired

Press the → key to move the cell pointer to the end of the formula—an alternative is to press the End key to move to the end of the formula

Type ,0)

Press ⏎

The formula @ROUND(B12*C26,0) is now in cell C12.

To copy the formula to the remaining quarters:

Press /

Select Copy

When prompted for the range to copy FROM:

Press   ⏎

By pressing the ⏎ key, you selected cell C12 as the cell to copy.

When prompted for the range to copy TO:

Move   the cell pointer to cell D12

Type   .

Move   the cell pointer to cell E12

Press   ⏎

TELEPHONE expenses are now rounded to 0 decimal places.

The next set of formulas to be rounded is for MISCELLANEOUS expenses. The formula for MISCELLANEOUS expenses in the second quarter is +B14*C28. To round the MISCELLANEOUS expenses to 0 decimal places:

Move   the cell pointer to cell C14

Press   F2 to edit the formula in cell C14

Press   Home to move to the beginning of the formula

Type   @ROUND (

Press   Del one time to delete the + sign if desired

Press   End to move to the end of a formula

Type   ,0)

Press   ⏎

The rounded formula @ROUND(B14*C28,0) is now in cell C14.

To copy the rounded formula to the remaining quarters:

Press   /

Select   Copy

When prompted for the range to copy FROM:

Press   ⏎

By pressing the ⏎ key, you selected cell C14 as the cell to copy.

When prompted for the range to copy TO:

Move   the cell pointer to cell D14

Type   .

Move   the cell pointer to cell E14

Press   ↵

The projections for MISCELLANEOUS expenses are rounded to 0 decimal places. The rounding error in the worksheet has been corrected. The corrected results in the YR TOTAL column are shown below:

Sales	247,296
-Total Expenses	191,495
Gross Profit	55,801

Your screen should look like Figure 2-32.

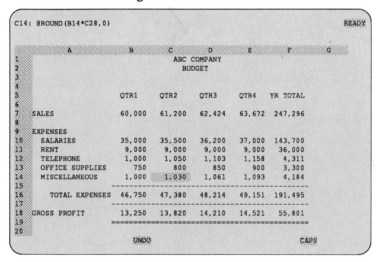

Figure 2-32

■IDENTIFYING THE SPREADSHEET PREPARER AND DATE THE SPREADSHEET IS CREATED

When a spreadsheet is used in an organization, it is useful to know who prepared the spreadsheet and the date on which it was prepared. One useful place to put the name of the spreadsheet preparer and date is just below the completed spreadsheet.

To indicate who created the BUDGET spreadsheet:

Move	the cell pointer to cell A31
Type	Prepared by
Type	Your name or initials
Press	⏎

To enter the current date on the spreadsheet:

Move	the cell pointer to cell A32
Type	@NOW
Press	⏎

Note that a number appears. The number represents the number of days that have passed since December 31, 1899. To format the date so that it is in an appropriate form:

Press	/
Select	Range
Select	Format
Select	Date
Type	1 (to select the first format option)
Press	⏎

Your name and the current date should now appear in cells A31 and A32. Your screen should look similar to Figure 2-33. Whenever you use the spreadsheet on your computer, the current date will always appear.

```
A32: (D1) [W18] @NOW                                              READY

              A            B        C        D        E        F       G
13    OFFICE SUPPLIES     750      800      850      900    3,300
14    MISCELLANEOUS     1,000    1,030    1,061    1,093    4,184
15                      -------------------------------------------
16    TOTAL EXPENSES   46,750   47,380   48,214   49,151  191,495
17                      -------------------------------------------
18  GROSS PROFIT        13,250   13,820   14,210   14,521   55,801
19                      ===========================================
20
21
22  GROWTH RATE
23  ASSUMPTIONS
24
25  SALES                        1.02     1.02     1.02
26  TELEPHONE                    1.05     1.05     1.05
27  OFFICE SUPPLIES             50.00    50.00    50.00
28  MISCELLANEOUS                1.03     1.03     1.03
29
30
31  Prepared by H. Al Napier
32         06-Sep-89
                         UNDO                            CAPS
```

Figure 2-33

There are several ways to place the date on a spreadsheet. These options and various uses of date functions such as @NOW are discussed in more detail in Chapter 8.

■SAVING AND REPLACING A SPREADSHEET

The spreadsheet previously created was saved before the rounding errors were corrected. In order to save the changes to the spreadsheet, you must save it to the disk again.

To replace the BUDGET spreadsheet file that was previously saved:

Press   Home

Pressing the Home key is optional.

Press   /

Select   File

Select   Save

When prompted for the file name, the name for the file that is currently on the screen should appear. In this example, BUDGET appears. To keep the file name as BUDGET:

Press ⏎

Since the file BUDGET already exists on the disk, a prompt appears requesting whether to cancel the Save command, replace the BUDGET file with the version in memory, or create a backup file named BUDGET.BAK from the previously saved file on the disk and also save the file that is currently in memory as BUDGET.WK1.

When prompted whether to Cancel, **R**eplace, or **B**ackup:

Select Replace

The previously saved version of BUDGET has now been replaced with the updated version that is currently displayed on the screen.

■RETRIEVING A SPREADSHEET

First, clear the screen before beginning the exercise. To clear the screen:

Press /

Select Worksheet

Select Erase

Select Yes

Clearing the screen is not necessary before retrieving a spreadsheet because the screen will be erased automatically when retrieving a spreadsheet file. Note that Worksheet Erase Yes did **not** erase the file BUDGET from the disk where it was previously saved. The Worksheet Erase Yes command only erases the spreadsheet from main **memory** so that the screen is cleared. The file BUDGET can still be retrieved from the disk. This action was taken to clarify the steps below.

To retrieve the file BUDGET:

Press /

Select File

Select Retrieve

When prompted for the file to retrieve:

Type BUDGET

Press ⏎

An alternative to typing the file name is to press the ⊞ key and use the pointer-movement keys to highlight the desired file with the pointer. Since BUDGET is the only file on the disk, it is already highlighted. Once the desired file is highlighted, press the ⟵ key to retrieve the file. Another alternative is to press the ➡ key until the desired file is highlighted; then press the ⟵ key.

The spreadsheet BUDGET is visible on your screen. It is now possible to make revisions or print it. Any changes are made *only* to the screen, not to the file on the disk. To save any changes to the file BUDGET, go through the process of saving and replacing the file that was presented in the previous section. To save revisions as a completely separate file, save the file, but type a different file name.

■ PREPARING THE PRINTER AND PRINTING THE SPREADSHEET

The spreadsheet is complete and the rounding errors have been corrected. The following steps outline how to print the results.

Prepare the Printer for Use

If you are using a dot matrix printer and the paper needs to be aligned, perform the following step before turning on the printer:

Turn   the cylinder that moves the paper so the paper perforation is directly above the print head and ribbon

For many printers, the gears can be damaged if the cylinder is manually turned while the motor is running. If you are using a laser printer, the above step is not required.

Before printing:

Check   to see that the printer is connected to the computer

Turn   on the printer

Your printer should now be on.

Printing the Spreadsheet

To specify the range to print:

Press	/
Select	Print
Select	Printer

Notice the Print Settings now appear on your screen. See Figure 2-34.

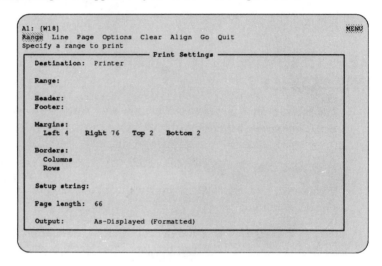

```
A1: [W18]                                                               MENU
Range Line Page Options Clear Align Go Quit
Specify a range to print
                              ─── Print Settings ───
    Destination:  Printer

    Range:

    Header:
    Footer:

    Margins:
      Left 4     Right 76    Top 2    Bottom 2

    Borders:
      Columns
      Rows

    Setup string:

    Page length:  66

    Output:        As-Displayed (Formatted)
```

Figure 2-34

You will now specify the setting for the range of cells you desire to print.

Select	Range

When prompted for the print range:

Move	the cell pointer to cell A1 (if the cell pointer is not already there)
Type	.
Move	the cell pointer to cell F32

The entire worksheet is now highlighted.

Press	⏎

To begin printing the range:

Select   Align

Select   Go

The printer should begin to print your spreadsheet.

Note that the Align command sets a 1-2-3 counter to 0 (top of page) before it begins to print. This command is especially useful when the paper has been readjusted in the printer or the printer has been reloaded.

To eject the page from the printer:

Select   Page

The page is ejected and the printer moves to the top of the next page. 1-2-3 counts the number of lines you printed (32 in this case), and subtracts the number of lines printed from the number that can be printed on a page. The difference is the number of lines that the printhead needs to be moved to reach the top of the next page. The number of lines that can be printed on a page varies from the default of 66 lines for some printers. To change the number of lines per page, use the **Print Printer Options Pg-Length** command. For many printers, an additional page needs to be ejected so that the paper remains aligned properly in the printer.

To eject a second page:

Select   Page

Tear   the perforation to remove the printed page
            (not necessary if you are using a laser printer)

To leave the Print menu:

Select   Quit

The printout should appear similar to the printout in Figure 2-35. If the printout is satisfactory, resave the spreadsheet so that the print setting will be saved with the spreadsheet. Save and replace the spreadsheet on file BUDGET using the **File Save Replace** command sequence.

```
                        ABC COMPANY
                          BUDGET


                QTR1     QTR2     QTR3     QTR4    YR TOTAL

    SALES       60,000   61,200   62,424   63,672   247,296

    EXPENSES
      SALARIES  35,000   35,500   36,200   37,000   143,700
      RENT       9,000    9,000    9,000    9,000    36,000
      TELEPHONE  1,000    1,050    1,103    1,158     4,311
      OFFICE SUPPLIES 750   800     850      900      3,300
      MISCELLANEOUS 1,000  1,030   1,061    1,093     4,184
                  ------------------------------------------
      TOTAL EXPENSES 46,750 47,380 48,214  49,151   191,495
                  ------------------------------------------
    GROSS PROFIT 13,250   13,820   14,210   14,521   55,801
                  ==========================================


    GROWTH RATE
    ASSUMPTIONS

    SALES                  1.02     1.02     1.02
    TELEPHONE              1.05     1.05     1.05
    OFFICE SUPPLIES      50.00    50.00    50.00
    MISCELLANEOUS          1.03     1.03     1.03
```

Figure 2-35

■PRINTING THE CELL FORMULAS OF A SPREADSHEET

At times you may want to see the cell formulas which comprise a spreadsheet. To print the cell formulas used to create the spreadsheet BUDGET, follow the steps below. It is assumed that BUDGET is currently in memory and that the Print Range for BUDGET has previously been set.

Press	/
Select	Print
Select	Printer
Select	Options
Select	Other
Select	Cell-Formulas
Select	Quit
Select	Align
Select	Go

Assuming that the print range has been set previously, the printer will print the contents of each nonblank cell.

To eject the printout when it is complete, and also to eject a second page (if necessary) to keep the paper aligned in the printer:

Select	Page
Select	Page *omit for exercise*

The printout should look like Figure 2-36 Parts 1 and 2.

```
C1: '      ABC COMPANY
C2: '         BUDGET
B5: ^QTR1
C5: ^QTR2
D5: ^QTR3
E5: ^QTR4
F5: 'YR TOTAL
A7: [W18] 'SALES
B7: (,0) 60000
C7: (,0) @ROUND(B7*C25,0)
D7: (,0) @ROUND(C7*D25,0)
E7: (,0) @ROUND(D7*E25,0)
F7: (,0) @SUM(B7..E7)
A9: [W18] 'EXPENSES
A10: [W18] '  SALARIES
B10: 35000
C10: 35500
D10: 36200
E10: 37000
F10: @SUM(B10..E10)
A11: [W18] '  RENT
B11: 9000
C11: 9000
D11: 9000
E11: 9000
F11: @SUM(B11..E11)
A12: [W18] '  TELEPHONE
B12: 1000
C12: @ROUND(B12*C26,0)
D12: @ROUND(C12*D26,0)
E12: @ROUND(D12*E26,0)
F12: @SUM(B12..E12)
A13: [W18] '  OFFICE SUPPLIES
B13: 750
C13: +B13+C27
D13: +C13+D27
E13: +D13+E27
F13: @SUM(B13..E13)
A14: [W18] '  MISCELLANEOUS
B14: 1000
C14: @ROUND(B14*C28,0)
D14: @ROUND(C14*D28,0)
E14: @ROUND(D14*E28,0)
F14: @SUM(B14..E14)
B15: \-
C15: \-
D15: \-
E15: \-
F15: \-
A16: [W18] '   TOTAL EXPENSES
B16: @SUM(B10..B14)
C16: @SUM(C10..C14)
D16: @SUM(D10..D14)
E16: @SUM(E10..E14)
F16: @SUM(B16..E16)
```

Figure 2-36
Part 1

```
B17: \-
C17: \-
D17: \-
E17: \-
F17: \-
A18: [W18] 'GROSS PROFIT
B18: (,0) +B7-B16
C18: (,0) +C7-C16
D18: (,0) +D7-D16
E18: (,0) +E7-E16
F18: (,0) @SUM(B18..E18)
B19: \=
C19: \=
D19: \=
E19: \=
F19: \=
A22: [W18] 'GROWTH RATE
A23: [W18] 'ASSUMPTIONS
A25: [W18] 'SALES
C25: (F2) 1.02
D25: (F2) 1.02
E25: (F2) 1.02
A26: [W18] 'TELEPHONE
C26: (F2) 1.05
D26: (F2) 1.05
E26: (F2) 1.05
A27: [W18] 'OFFICE SUPPLIES
C27: (F2) 50
D27: (F2) 50
E27: (F2) 50
A28: [W18] 'MISCELLANEOUS
C28: (F2) 1.03
D28: (F2) 1.03
E28: (F2) 1.03
A31: [W18] 'Prepared by H. Al Napier
A32: (D1) [W18] @NOW
```

Figure 2-36
Part 2

To return the print settings back to their previous setting (i.e., so when Go is selected, the spreadsheet will be printed rather than the cell formulas):

Select	Options
Select	Other
Select	As-Displayed

To leave the current menu:

Select	Quit

To leave the Print menu:

Select	Quit

The print settings have now been returned to their previous setting.

■ PRINTING THE CELL FORMULAS OF A SPREADSHEET IN TABULAR FORM

To display cell formulas exactly where they appear on the spreadsheet BUDGET requires changing the format of the spreadsheet. Before changing the format to see the cell formulas, make sure the file has been saved to the disk in the desired numeric format. In this way, the "final version" of the spreadsheet is safely saved on the disk and can be retrieved for later use.

To change the format of the spreadsheet to see the cell formulas:

Press	/
Select	Worksheet
Select	Global
Select	Format
Select	Text

The formulas are now displayed on the spreadsheet itself. However, some cell formulas are not fully displayed because the column width is not wide enough to accommodate them. For example, column F is not large enough to fully display the @SUM formulas. In row 16, the @SUM command is not displayed fully. Your screen should look like Figure 2-37.

```
A1: [W18]                                                          READY

                    A           B       C         D       E        F       G
 1                                    ABC COMPANY
 2                                     BUDGET
 3
 4
 5                            QTR1    QTR2      QTR3    QTR4    YR TOTAL
 6
 7   SALES                   60000  @ROUND(B  @ROUND(C  @ROUND(D  @SUM(B7.
 8
 9   EXPENSES
10      SALARIES             35000    35500     36200    37000  @SUM(B10
11      RENT                  9000     9000      9000     9000  @SUM(B11
12      TELEPHONE             1000  @ROUND(B  @ROUND(C  @ROUND(D  @SUM(B12
13      OFFICE SUPPLIES        750  +B13+C27  +C13+D27  +D13+E27  @SUM(B13
14      MISCELLANEOUS         1000  @ROUND(B  @ROUND(C  @ROUND(D  @SUM(B14
15                          -------------------------------------------
16       TOTAL EXPENSES@SUM(B10  @SUM(C10  @SUM(D10  @SUM(E10  @SUM(B16
17                          -------------------------------------------
18   GROSS PROFIT           +B7-B16  +C7-C16  +D7-D16  +E7-E16  @SUM(B18
19                          ===========================================
20
                             UNDO                                  CAPS
```

Figure 2-37

For this example, widen column F in order to view the full formula. The only other formulas not fully displayed in columns B through E are the @SUM functions in row 16 used to compute TOTAL EXPENSES and the formulas in which you entered the @ROUND function. For this example, only column F will be altered to fully display the formulas.

To widen column F:

Move	the cell pointer to cell F1 (or any other cell in column F)
Press	/
Select	Worksheet
Select	Column
Select	Set-Width

When prompted for the column width:

Press	the ➡ key until the formulas are fully displayed

In this example, the column width should be 15 characters wide. To accept 15 as the column width:

Press ⏎

The entire formula for each cell in column F is now displayed.

To print the cells in tabular form:

Press /

Select Print

Select Printer

Select Align

Select Go

The print range did not need to be specified because it was specified earlier.

To eject the printout and, if necessary, a second page to keep the paper properly aligned in the printer:

Select Page

Select Page

To exit the print menu:

Select Quit

The printout should look like Figure 2-38.

```
                              ABC COMPANY
                                BUDGET


                    QTR1      QTR2     QTR3     QTR4    YR TOTAL

     SALES          60000  @ROUND(B @ROUND(C @ROUND(D @SUM(B7..E7)


     EXPENSES
       SALARIES     35000     35500    36200     37000 @SUM(B10..E10)
       RENT          9000      9000     9000      9000 @SUM(B11..E11)
       TELEPHONE     1000  @ROUND(B @ROUND(C @ROUND(D @SUM(B12..E12)
       OFFICE SUPPLIES 750 +B13+C27 +C13+D27 +D13+E27 @SUM(B13..E13)
       MISCELLANEOUS 1000  @ROUND(B @ROUND(C @ROUND(D @SUM(B14..E14)
                    -------------------------------------------------
       TOTAL EXPENSES@SUM(B10 @SUM(C10 @SUM(D10 @SUM(E10 @SUM(B16..E16)
                    -------------------------------------------------
     GROSS PROFIT   +B7-B16  +C7-C16  +D7-D16  +E7-E16 @SUM(B18..E18)
                    =================================================



     GROWTH RATE
     ASSUMPTIONS

     SALES                    1.02      1.02     1.02
     TELEPHONE                1.05      1.05     1.05
     OFFICE SUPPLIES         50.00     50.00    50.00
     MISCELLANEOUS            1.03      1.03     1.03
```

Figure 2-38

To return the format to its original setting:

Press	/
Select	Worksheet
Select	Global
Select	Format
Select	,

When prompted for the number of decimal places:

Type	0
Press	⏎

Column F needs to be reset so that it once again has a column width of 9. To return column F to its original column width, make sure the cell pointer is within column F.

Press	/
Select	Worksheet
Select	Column
Select	Reset-Width

The width for column F is returned to the default size of 9 characters. Your screen should look like Figure 2-39.

```
F7: @SUM(B7..E7)                                                    READY

             A          B        C        D        E        F        G
  1                              ABC COMPANY
  2                                BUDGET
  3
  4
  5                      QTR1     QTR2     QTR3     QTR4    YR TOTAL
  6
  7   SALES            60,000   61,200   62,424   63,672   247,296
  8
  9   EXPENSES
 10     SALARIES       35,000   35,500   36,200   37,000   143,700
 11     RENT            9,000    9,000    9,000    9,000    36,000
 12     TELEPHONE       1,000    1,050    1,103    1,158     4,311
 13     OFFICE SUPPLIES   750      800      850      900     3,300
 14     MISCELLANEOUS   1,000    1,030    1,061    1,093     4,184
 15                    ------------------------------------------
 16       TOTAL EXPENSES 46,750   47,380   48,214   49,151  191,495
 17                    ------------------------------------------
 18   GROSS PROFIT     13,250   13,820   14,210   14,521    55,801
 19                    ==========================================
 20
                         UNDO                              CAPS
```

Figure 2-39

■CHANGING THE FONT USED IN PRINTING

In some situations, it may be desirable to change the print font used when a spreadsheet is printed. You can change the fonts and the appearance of a worksheet using the Allways add-in software package. See Chapter 11 for instructions on using Allways.

■USING ANOTHER FORMAT SPECIFICATION FOR THE SPREADSHEET

When building the spreadsheet BUDGET, you chose the numeric format Worksheet Global Format , 0 to display numbers with commas and no decimal places. The exercises in this section demonstrate how to use some of the other available format specifications.

Setting the Entire Spreadsheet with Dollar Signs

It is assumed that the BUDGET spreadsheet is displayed on your screen. If not, retrieve the file BUDGET before continuing and make sure your screen looks like Figure 2-39.

To change the numeric format in BUDGET so that dollar signs are added and two decimal places are shown, use the Currency format.

Press	/
Select	Worksheet
Select	Global
Select	Format
Select	Currency

When prompted for the number of decimal places:

Press   ↵

By pressing the ↵ key, the default of two decimal places is accepted. Notice that asterisks fill the majority of the spreadsheet instead of numbers. Due to the addition of a dollar sign, a period, and two decimal places to each cell containing a value or formula, **the columns are no longer wide enough to display many of the cells** in currency format. Sometimes asterisks may appear in only one or two cells in a column rather than throughout the entire worksheet. The columns need to be widened for you to see the contents of the cell(s) containing asterisks (refer to Figure 2-40). Make sure your cell pointer is in cell F1.

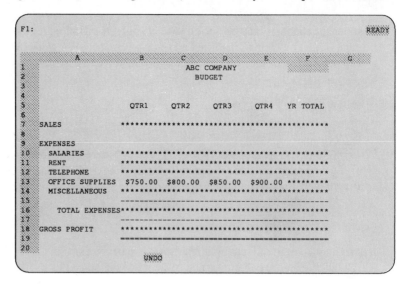

Figure 2-40

To widen the columns so that the numbers are visible:

Press   /

Select	Worksheet
Select	Global
Select	Column-Width
Press	the ⊕ key until the numbers can be seen in their entirety
Press	⏎

The column width should be set to 12 characters. Due to the column width change, column A scrolls off the screen. After pressing the [Home] key, your screen should look like Figure 2-41.

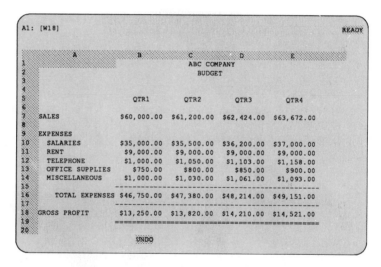

Figure 2-41

When the global column width is set, any columns that have been set individually using the Worksheet Column Set-Width command are *not* affected. This is the reason that the width of column A did not change.

Using More Than One Numeric Format in a Spreadsheet

In this exercise, you alter the BUDGET spreadsheet so that only the top and bottom rows of the spreadsheet display dollar signs.

It is assumed that the original BUDGET spreadsheet is displayed on the screen. If not, retrieve the file BUDGET before continuing and make sure it looks like Figure 2-39.

The BUDGET spreadsheet's format was set by **Worksheet Global Format , 0** which displays all numbers in the spreadsheet with commas and no decimal places. For the majority of the spreadsheet, this format is appropriate. However, another command is needed to change the top and bottom rows of the spreadsheet to show dollar signs.

To change the numeric format of the top row in BUDGET:

Press	/
Select	Range
Select	Format
Select	Currency

When prompted for the number of decimal places:

Type	0
Press	⏎

When prompted for the range to format:

Press	Esc

The **Range Format** command automatically **anchors** the cell pointer at its current position with the period key. To release the cell pointer from its anchored position, press the Esc key.

The first range to format is the top row of numbers of the BUDGET spreadsheet.

Move	the cell pointer to cell B7
Type	.
Move	the cell pointer to cell F7
Press	⏎

Cells B7 through F7 now have dollar signs.

To change the numeric format of the bottom row of numbers in BUDGET:

Move	the cell pointer to cell B18

Moving to the first cell of the range to format will eliminate the need to press the Esc key when prompted to highlight the range to format.

Press	/

Select	Range
Select	Format
Select	Currency

When prompted for the number of decimal places:

Type	0
Press	⏎

When prompted for the range to format:

Move	the cell pointer to cell F18
Press	⏎

Since the cell pointer was at cell B18, moving the cell pointer to cell F18 highlighted cells B18 through F18, which now display dollar signs. Your screen should look like Figure 2-42.

```
B18:  (C0)  +B7-B16                                              READY


                A           B         C         D        E        F        G
 1                                  ABC COMPANY
 2                                    BUDGET
 3
 4
 5                          QTR1      QTR2      QTR3     QTR4    YR TOTAL
 6
 7   SALES                $60,000   $61,200   $62,424  $63,672  $247,296
 8
 9   EXPENSES
10     SALARIES            35,000    35,500    36,200   37,000  143,700
11     RENT                 9,000     9,000     9,000    9,000   36,000
12     TELEPHONE            1,000     1,050     1,103    1,158    4,311
13     OFFICE SUPPLIES        750       800       850      900    3,300
14     MISCELLANEOUS        1,000     1,030     1,061    1,093    4,184
15                        --------------------------------------------------
16       TOTAL EXPENSES   46,750    47,380    48,214   49,151  191,495
17                        --------------------------------------------------
18   GROSS PROFIT        $13,250   $13,820   $14,210  $14,521  $55,801
19                        ==================================================
20

                           UNDO
```

Figure 2-42

The dollar signs in the Currency format do not align with each other in a column; the dollar signs are placed flush to the formatted number. If the dollar signs need to be aligned, it is not appropriate to use the Currency format. Instead, one-character columns must be inserted before each column of values and the dollar sign "$" must be typed manually. The dollar sign must be entered with a label prefix such as the apostrophe (e.g., '$).

Comparing Worksheet Global Format to Range Format

The Worksheet Global Format command sequence is used to set the format of how *most* of the numbers in the spreadsheet are to be displayed. The Range Format command sequence is used to set the format of **specified ranges** of numbers in the spreadsheet.

In the BUDGET worksheet, most of the worksheet was set to display commas; therefore, the Worksheet Global Format command sequence was used. The Range Format could have been used, but the former command sequence is faster. Two specified ranges, the top and bottom row of numbers, of the BUDGET worksheet were set to display dollar signs; therefore, the Range Format command sequence was used.

With the cell pointer in cell B18, look at the information in the control panel. "(C0)" is displayed, indicating that the Currency format with **0** decimal places was chosen with **Range Format**. All cells formatted with the Range Format command will display a similar message in the control panel when highlighted by the cell pointer. No format specification appears in the control panel for cells when the Worksheet Global Format command is used.

■ USING THE ROUNDING OPTION

As demonstrated in the BUDGET spreadsheet, rounding errors may occur in spreadsheets that have growth rates or percentages. To prevent this problem, use the @ROUND function whenever a formula includes multiplication, division, or exponents. The format for the @ROUND function is as follows:

```
@ROUND(formula,number of digits to round to)
```

Both the formula and the number of digits to round to must be specified.

In the BUDGET worksheet, the original formula for the Fourth Quarter of SALES was:

```
+D7*E25
```

The value of the computation was:

```
63672.48
```

Later, when the Worksheet Global Format command sequence was used to format the numbers to display commas and 0 decimal places, the number was formatted to *appear* as:

```
63,672
```

The number *appeared* as 63,672 but the *value used in computation* was still 63672.48. The use of this number can result in a rounding error.

To truly round the number, use the @ROUND function. The formula above must be entered as:

```
@ROUND(+D7*E25,0)
```

A summary of the differences are below:

Formula	Value	Global Format Appears as Comma 0	Number Used in Computation
+D7*E25	63672.48	63,672	63672.48
@ROUND (+D7*1.02,0)	63672	63,672	63672

The @ROUND function may not remove rounding errors properly for all situations (e.g., percentages). It may be necessary to "plug" a number to get the desired results.

■ MAKING A BACKUP OF A SPREADSHEET FILE

In 1-2-3 you can make a backup worksheet file on the disk with the File Save Backup command sequence. You can also place the worksheet on a separate diskette to create a backup file.

To make a backup file on the same disk on which your active files reside:

Press /

Select File

Select Save

Press ⏎

When prompted to Cancel, Replace or Backup:

Select Backup

A BAK file has been created.

When you use the **Backup** menu option again for the BUDGET file. 1-2-3 changes the file extension of the file on the disk from WK1 to BAK and saves the active version of the file as BUDGET.WK1.

To see that a BAK file has been created:

Press   /

Select   File

Select   List

Select   Other

BUDGET.BAK now appears on the list of files with BUDGET.WK1. To continue to the next exercise:

Press   ⏎

To save the BUDGET worksheet on a separate diskette in drive A, you first need to insert a formatted disk in drive A. Then you can save the worksheet using the following instructions:

Press   /

Select   File

Select   Save

Press   Esc three times

By pressing the Esc key three times, you clear the current directory and file name from the control panel.

Type   A:BUDGET

Press   ⏎

You now have saved a copy of BUDGET on the diskette in drive A that can be used in case you have a problem with your hard disk. Note that the extension WK1 file has been used. The WK1 extension will always be used except when you select the **Backup** menu option mentioned earlier in this section.

■CHANGING THE ASSUMPTIONS TO COMPLETE A "WHAT-IF" ANALYSIS

One of the advantages of using 1-2-3 is the ability to change some of the ASSUMPTIONS and see the impact of the changes on the other values in the worksheet. For example, suppose you show your supervisor the BUDGET spreadsheet results. Your supervisor may then ask some "what-if" questions and ask you to complete some further analysis.

Assume that you are asked to determine the impact on GROSS PROFIT if the growth rates for SALES are 5%, 9% and 6% in the Quarters 2 through 4 respectively.

To enter the new growth rates for SALES:

Move	the cell pointer to cell C25
Type	1.05
Press	⊕
Type	1.09
Press	⊕
Type	1.06
Press	⊕

Your worksheet is recalculated to reflect the new growth rates each time you change one of them. You can now see the new values for GROSS PROFIT that were computed using the new ASSUMPTIONS. If desired, you can change some of the other ASSUMPTIONS. Your screen should now look like Figure 2-43 if you made no additional changes.

```
E25: (F2) 1.06                                                      READY

                  A          B        C        D        E        F       G
 6
 7   SALES               $60,000  $63,000  $68,670  $72,790 $264,460
 8
 9   EXPENSES
10      SALARIES          35,000   35,500   36,200   37,000  143,700
11      RENT               9,000    9,000    9,000    9,000   36,000
12      TELEPHONE          1,000    1,050    1,103    1,158    4,311
13      OFFICE SUPPLIES      750      800      850      900    3,300
14      MISCELLANEOUS      1,000    1,030    1,061    1,093    4,184
15                      ---------------------------------------------
16      TOTAL EXPENSES    46,750   47,380   48,214   49,151  191,495
17                      ---------------------------------------------
18   GROSS PROFIT        $13,250  $15,620  $20,456  $23,639  $72,965
19                      =============================================
20
21
22   GROWTH RATE
23   ASSUMPTIONS
24
25   SALES                          1.05     1.09     1.06
                         UNDO                                    CAPS
```

Figure 2-43

■USING FORMULAS IN LOTUS 1-2-3

Lotus 1-2-3 allows the use of formulas to indicate operations such as addition and subtraction. The types of formulas and the order in which operations occur in formulas are discussed in this section.

Types of Formulas

The three types of formulas that can be entered into a cell in 1-2-3 are arithmetic, text, and logical.

Arithmetic Formulas

Arithmetic formulas are used to compute numeric values using arithmetic operators. For example, if the cell formula +A3-10 appears in B5, then the value 10 is subtracted from the number appearing in cell A3 and the result will appear in cell B5.

Text Formulas

Text formulas are used to calculate labels using the text operator (&). For example, if the text formula +C5&"EXPENSES" appears in cell K7, then the label that results from combining the label in cell C5 with EXPENSES will appear in cell K7.

Logical Formulas

Logical formulas are used to compare values in two or more cells using logical operators. A logical formula calculates a value of 0 (meaning false) or 1 (meaning true). For example, if the formula +C3<=25000 appears in cell D3, then the value 0 will appear in cell D3 whenever the value in cell C3 is greater than 25,000. A value of 1 will appear in cell D3 if the value in cell C3 is less than or equal to 25,000.

Operators and Order of Precedence

1-2-3 uses various operators in formulas to indicate arithmetic operations. Listed below are the mathematical operators allowed in 1-2-3. The operators are listed in the order of precedence by which operations are completed.

Operator	Definition
^	Exponentiation
- +	Negative, Positive
* /	Multiplication, Division
+ -	Addition, Subtraction

The operators that appear higher on the list are evaluated prior to operators that are lower on the list.

Exponentiation is the highest level operator. For example, if the arithmetic formula 10+5^2 is used for cell A5, then the result that appears in cell A5 is 35 (10 + 5 squared) not 225 (15 raised to the power of two).

Lotus 1-2-3 can tell the difference between a + or - sign that means a positive or negative number as opposed to the + or - sign meaning addition or subtraction. For example, if the formula 10/-5+10 appears in cell B8, then the result that appears in the cell is 8 (-2+10) not 2 (10/5).

Multiplication and division operators are evaluated before addition and subtraction operators. For example, if cell C8 contains the formula 7-3/2, the value that appears in cell C8 is 5.5 (7-(3/2)) not 2 ((7-3)/2).

The order of precedence can be overridden using sets of parentheses. If more than one set of parentheses is included in a formula, then the order of execution begins with the innermost set of parentheses and proceeds to the outermost set of parentheses. For example, suppose the formula ((10/2) + 3) * 4 is used for cell E1; the result appearing in cell E1 is 32.

SUMMARY

Creating spreadsheets is faster and more effective using a spreadsheet software package such as Lotus 1-2-3. Creating formulas and values that can be copied, inserting and deleting entire rows and columns with menu commands, and saving the file for easy editing are just a few advantages of the Lotus 1-2-3 spreadsheet software package.

KEY CONCEPTS

Assumptions	Print Printer Options
@NOW	Print Printer Options Other As-Displayed
@ROUND	Print Printer Options Other Cell-Formulas
@SUM	Print Printer Range
Centering labels	Range Format Currency
Copy	Range Format Fixed
Ctrl-Break	Relative cell location
Esc	Replacing a spreadsheet file
File Retrieve	Saving a worksheet
File Save	Value
Font	Worksheet Column Reset-Width
Format	Worksheet Column Set-Width
Formula	Worksheet Global Column-Width
Label	Worksheet Global Format
Print Printer Align Go	Worksheet Insert Row

CHAPTER TWO
EXERCISE 1

INSTRUCTIONS: Circle T if the statement is true and F if the statement is false.

T F
1. One way to correct incorrect data is to move to the incorrect data's cell, retype the data correctly, and press the ⏎ key to enter the correction.

T F
2. The formula SUM(A..A7) will add the data in cells A1 through A7.

T **F**
3. To round a number to two decimal places, you use the **Range Format** command.

T F
4. The **Worksheet Erase Yes** command sequence erases the worksheet currently in use from main memory.

T F
5. A print range must be specified before a spreadsheet can be printed.

T F
6. The "@" character must precede special functions such as the SUM and ROUND functions.

T **F**
7. Lotus 1-2-3 will automatically save changes that are made to a spreadsheet file.

T F
8. The **File Retrieve** command is used to look at a previously saved file.

T **F**
9. "BUDGET 1" is an acceptable file name.

T **F**
10. The letter "X" is the symbol for multiplication when using Lotus 1-2-3.

T **F**
11. Fonts cannot be changed.

CHAPTER TWO
EXERCISE 2

INSTRUCTIONS: Explain a typical situation when the following keystrokes or Lotus 1-2-3 commands are used.

Problem 1:   / File Save

Problem 2:   / Worksheet Insert Row

Problem 3:   +B1*1.09

Problem 4:   / Worksheet Global Column-Width

Problem 5:   / Worksheet Column Set-Width

Problem 6:   / Worksheet Erase Yes

Problem 7:   / Print Printer Range

Problem 8:   / Print Printer Align Go

Problem 9:   F2

Problem 10:   +B7-B6

Problem 11:   @ROUND (+B7*B8,0)

Problem 12:   @SUM(B1..B25)

Problem 13:   / Worksheet Global Format , 2

Problem 14:   / Range Format Currency 2

Problem 15:   / File Retrieve

Problem 16:   / Copy

Problem 17:   / Range Format Fixed 2

Problem 18:   / File Save Replace

CHAPTER TWO
EXERCISE 3
Correcting a Spreadsheet

INSTRUCTIONS: The following example illustrates a common error. Follow the instructions below to create the error and answer the questions.

Clear the screen (use the **Worksheet Erase Yes** command).

In cell A1, type 52 and press ↵.
In cell A2, type 30 and press ↵.
In cell A3, type A1-A2 and press ↵.

Your screen should look like Figure 2-44.

Figure 2-44

1. What caused the error in cell A3?

2. How can the error be corrected?

CHAPTER TWO
EXERCISE 4
Correcting a Spreadsheet

INSTRUCTIONS: The following example illustrates a common error. Follow the instructions below to create the error and answer the questions.

Clear the screen (use the **Worksheet Erase Yes** command).

In cell A1, type 52 and press ⏎.
In cell A2, press the space bar one time. Type 30 and press ⏎.
In cell A3, type +A1-A2 and press ⏎.

The screen should look like Figure 2-45.

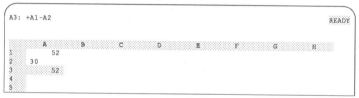

A3: +A1-A2   READY

	A	B	C	D	E	F	G	H
1	52							
2	30							
3	52							
4								
5								

Figure 2-45

1. What caused the error in computing A1-A2?

2. How can the error be corrected?

CHAPTER TWO
EXERCISE 5
Correcting a Spreadsheet

INSTRUCTIONS: The following example illustrates a common error. Use the instructions below to create the error and answer the questions.

Clear the screen (use the **Worksheet Erase Y**es command).

In cell A1, type 52 and press ⏎.
In cell A2, type 30 and press ⏎.
In cell A3, type +A1 and press ⏎. Then type -A2 and press ⏎.

The screen should look like Figure 2-46.

Figure 2-46

1. What caused the error in computing A1-A2?

2. How can the error be corrected?

CHAPTER TWO
EXERCISE 6
Creating a Spreadsheet

INSTRUCTIONS: Create the spreadsheet below. It will be used for exercises in other chapters. The following spreadsheet consists of straight data entry (no formulas). Save the file under the name UNIT-PROD (for Unit Production). Print the spreadsheet.

The spreadsheet should look like Figure 2-47.

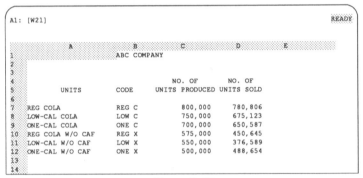

Figure 2-47

CHAPTER TWO
EXERCISE 7
Creating a Spreadsheet

INSTRUCTIONS: Create the spreadsheet below. It will be used for an exercise in a later chapter. The following spreadsheet consists of straight data entry except for the SUM formula in cell C15. Save the file under the name SALES. Format only cells C8 through C13 and C15. Print the spreadsheet.

The spreadsheet should look like Figure 2-48.

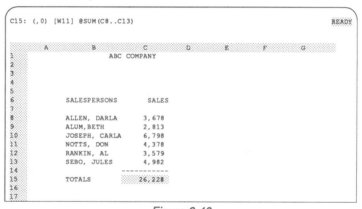

```
C15: (,0) [W11] @SUM(C8..C13)                                    READY


        A          B          C         D       E       F       G
  1                        ABC COMPANY
  2
  3
  4
  5
  6             SALESPERSONS      SALES
  7
  8             ALLEN, DARLA      3,678
  9             ALUM,BETH         2,813
 10             JOSEPH, CARLA     6,798
 11             NOTTS, DON        4,378
 12             RANKIN, AL        3,579
 13             SEBO, JULES       4,982
 14                             -----------
 15             TOTALS            26,228
 16
 17
```

Figure 2-48

CHAPTER TWO
EXERCISE 8
Creating a Spreadsheet

INSTRUCTIONS: Create and print the spreadsheet below.

REVENUE is 25,000 in YEAR 1 and projected to increase by 6 percent for years 2 through 5. EXPENSES are 9,500 in YEAR 1 and projected to be 25 percent of REVENUE in YEARS 2 through 5.   PROFIT BEFORE TAX is REVENUE minus EXPENSES. TAXES are 40 percent of PROFIT BEFORE TAX. PROFIT AFTER TAX is PROFIT BEFORE TAX less TAXES. Place your name and the current date on the spreadsheet. Save the file under the name PRACTICE. This file will be used in an exercise in a subsequent chapter.

Before placing your name and the current date on your worksheet, the screen should look like Figure 2-49.

```
C5:  @ROUND(B5*(1+C14),0)                                                    READY

              A            B         C        D        E        F        G
 1                              PROJECTED PROFITS
 2
 3                          YEAR 1   YEAR 2   YEAR 3   YEAR 4   YEAR 5    TOTAL
 4
 5  REVENUE               25,000   26,500   28,090   29,775   31,562  140,927
 6  EXPENSES               9,500    6,625    7,023    7,444    7,891   38,483
 7                        ------------------------------------------------------
 8  PROFIT BEFORE TAX     15,500   19,875   21,067   22,331   23,671  102,444
 9  TAXES                  6,200    7,950    8,427    8,932    9,468   40,978
10                        ------------------------------------------------------
11  PROFIT AFTER TAX       9,300   11,925   12,640   13,399   14,203   61,466
12                        ======================================================
13  ASSUMPTIONS
14  REVENUE GROWTH RATE               6%       6%       6%       6%
15  EXPENSE RATE                     25%      25%      25%      25%
16  TAX RATE                40%      40%      40%      40%      40%
17
18
19
20
                            UNDO
```

Figure 2-49

CHAPTER TWO
EXERCISE 9
Editing a Spreadsheet

INSTRUCTIONS: Retrieve the file BUDGET. Edit BUDGET using the instructions below. Use Figure 2-50 as a guide. Note that the file created will be entitled BUDGET2 and will be needed for an exercise in a later chapter.

1. Expand the worksheet to include projections through YEAR 10. Insert six columns (F-K) between QTR4 and YR TOTAL using the **Worksheet Insert Column** command sequence. Rename the headings QTR1 through QTR4 with the headings YEAR 1 through YEAR 4 and continue the headings through YEAR 10.Copy the growth rate information to YEARS 5 through 10.Copy the formulas, values, subtotal lines, and total lines from YEAR 4 (E7..E19) to YEAR 5 through YEAR 10 (F7..K19).

2. Change the sums under YR TOTAL to reflect the additional years. Change the formula in cell L7 from @SUM(B7..E7) to @SUM(B7..K7). Copy the formula in cell L7 to cells L10..L18. Replace the result of copying the @SUM formula in cells L15 and L17 (which now display zeroes) with subtotal lines.

3. Use the **Move** command to move the titles ABC COMPANY and BUDGET to column F. The titles will be centered on the new spreadsheet.

4. Save the spreadsheet, being sure to name the new spreadsheet BUDGET2. BUDGET and BUDGET2 are two separate files on the disk. The final result should look like Figure 2-50 (the entire spreadsheet will not be entirely visible on the screen at one time).

```
                                                    ABC COMPANY
                                                      BUDGET


                     YEAR 1   YEAR 2   YEAR 3   YEAR 4   YEAR 5   YEAR 6

   SALES            $60,000  $61,200  $62,424  $63,672  $64,945  $66,244

   EXPENSES
     SALARIES        35,000   35,500   36,200   37,000   37,000   37,000
     RENT             9,000    9,000    9,000    9,000    9,000    9,000
     TELEPHONE        1,000    1,050    1,103    1,158    1,216    1,277
     OFFICE SUPPLIES    750      800      850      900      950    1,000
     MISCELLANEOUS    1,000    1,030    1,061    1,093    1,126    1,160
                    -----------------------------------------------------
      TOTAL EXPENSES 46,750   47,380   48,214   49,151   49,292   49,437
                    -----------------------------------------------------
   GROSS PROFIT     $13,250  $13,820  $14,210  $14,521  $15,653  $16,807
                    =====================================================


   GROWTH RATE
   ASSUMPTIONS

   SALES                       1.02     1.02     1.02     1.02     1.02
   TELEPHONE                   1.05     1.05     1.05     1.05     1.05
   OFFICE SUPPLIES            50.00    50.00    50.00    50.00    50.00
   MISCELLANEOUS               1.03     1.03     1.03     1.03     1.03
```

Figure 2-50
Part 1

```
YEAR 7   YEAR 8   YEAR 9   YEAR 10 YR TOTAL

$67,569  $68,920  $70,298  $71,704 $656,976


  37,000   37,000   37,000   37,000 $365,700
   9,000    9,000    9,000    9,000  $90,000
   1,341    1,408    1,478    1,552  $12,583
   1,050    1,100    1,150    1,200   $9,750
   1,195    1,231    1,268    1,306  $11,470
  ------------------------------------------
  49,586   49,739   49,896   50,058 $489,503
  ------------------------------------------
 $17,983  $19,181  $20,402  $21,646 $167,473
 ==========================================




   1.02     1.02     1.02     1.02
   1.05     1.05     1.05     1.05
  50.00    50.00    50.00    50.00
   1.03     1.03     1.03     1.03
```

Figure 2-50
Part 2

CHAPTER TWO
EXERCISE 10

INSTRUCTIONS: Work the following set of problems using the information provided to make sure you understand the order of precedence in the calculation of formulas. Assume that cell A1=3, cell B2=4 and cell C4=8.

	Formula	Order of Evaluation	Answer
a.	+C4-B2*2	8-(4*2)	0
b.	+B2-A1-C4/B2	4-3-(8/4)	-1
c.	+B2-(A1-C4)/B2	4-((3-8)/4)	5.25
d.	+A1/-3+3	(3/-3)+3	2
e.	+A1-4*C4/B2^2	3-((4*8)/4^2)	1
f.	(A1-4)*C4/B2^2	(3-4)*(8/4^2)	-0.5
g.	+A1*B2/C4-10/2	((3*4)/8-(10/2))	-3.5

CHAPTER THREE

USEFUL LOTUS COMMANDS

OBJECTIVES

In this chapter you will learn to:

- Keep a cell address constant in a formula
- Protect cells
- Erase cells
- Correct cell errors
- Use various file commands
- Use the percent format
- Hide columns from view
- Change location of data in a cell
- Move cell contents
- Create page breaks
- Print borders, headers and footers

- Create range names and tables
- Control the recalculation of a spreadsheet
- Search and replace data
- Check status of a worksheet
- Use the system command
- Keep titles on the screen
- Undo a previous entry
- Widen multiple columns
- Create windows
- Insert and delete columns and rows

■ CHAPTER OVERVIEW

Chapter 2 provided general procedures for building spreadsheets. Chapter 3 describes a variety of Lotus 1-2-3 commands that are often indispensable when creating and maintaining spreadsheets. For example, one exercise demonstrates how to use the Worksheet Titles command so that column headings and row labels do not scroll off of the screen when you move the cell pointer around on a large spreadsheet.

■ ABSOLUTE AND RELATIVE CELL ADDRESSES

Use the file SALES in this exercise. SALES was created in an assignment at the end of Chapter 2. To retrieve the file SALES:

Press	/
Select	File
Select	Retrieve

When prompted for the file name:

Press	(F3)
Move	the cell pointer to SALES.WK1
Press	(↵)

To enter a formula that will compute the percentage of sales for each salesperson:

Move	the cell pointer to cell D8
Type	+
Move	the cell pointer to cell C8
Type	/

Move   the cell pointer to cell C15

Press   ⏎

Cell D8 should now display the following number: 0.140231

To copy the formula for the rest of the SALESPERSONS:

Press   /

Select   Copy

When prompted for the range to copy FROM:

Press   ⏎

Since the cell pointer was highlighting cell D8, it is now designated as the range to copy.

When prompted for the range to copy TO:

Move   the cell pointer to cell D9

Type   .

Move   the cell pointer to cell D13

Press   ⏎

ERR (Error) will appear in cells D9 through D13. The screen should look like Figure 3-1.

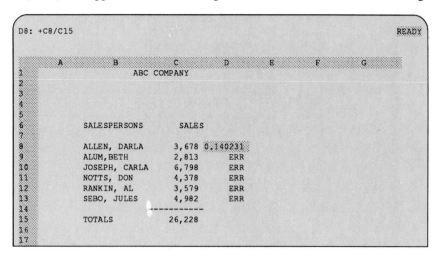

Figure 3-1

To see why the formula +C8/C15, when copied, did not compute the expected amount:

Move	the cell pointer to cell D9

Look in the control panel to see the formula in cell D9. The formula that was *intended* to be copied was +C9/C15. However, when the formula was copied, it became +C9/C<u>16</u>. The same results occurred for the formulas in cells D10 through D13 (+C10/C<u>17</u>, +C11/C<u>18</u>, and so on). Formulas are based upon **relative location** in Lotus 1-2-3. Lotus 1-2-3 interprets the formula that was copied not as **C8/C15** but as "divide the number one cell to the left by the number to the left and *seven rows down*". The problem occurs when the formula is copied; cell C15 is not ". . . to the left and seven rows down" for cells D9 through D13. Furthermore, since the cells C16, C17, and so forth are blank and a number cannot be divided by zero, the ERR message appears.

To solve the problem encountered above, keep cell C15 (the address for TOTAL SALES) *constant* in the formula, even when the formula is copied to other cells. Lotus 1-2-3 refers to constant cells as being **absolute**.

To enter a formula that will compute the percentage of SALES for each salesperson and keep the TOTAL SALES constant:

Move	the cell pointer to cell D8
Type	+
Move	the cell pointer to cell C8
Type	/
Move	the cell pointer to cell C15
Press	F4
Press	↵

Look at the formula for cell D8 in the control panel. It should appear as ÷C8/$C$15. The dollar signs in front of the C and the 15 indicate that the column (C) and the row (15) will remain constant, or absolute, when copied. Cell D8 should now display the following number: 0.140231.

Note that $C$15 can be typed directly into the cell without having to use the F4 ((Abs)) key.

The F4 (Abs) key actually has four **cycles** or ways of changing a cell. The following options provide ways to change rows and columns using the absolute feature.

Option	Example	Column	Row
1	$C$8	Absolute	Absolute
2	C$8	Relative	Absolute
3	$C8	Absolute	Relative
4	C8	Relative	Relative

You can continue pressing the F4 (Abs) key until the desired format has been selected.

To copy the formula to the rest of the SALESPERSONS:

> **Press**   /
>
> **Select**   Copy

When prompted for the range to copy FROM:

> **Press**   ⏎

Since the cell pointer was highlighting cell D8, it is now designated as the range to copy.

When prompted for the range to copy TO:

> **Move**   the cell pointer to cell D9
>
> **Type**   .
>
> **Move**   the cell pointer to cell D13
>
> **Press**   ⏎

The correct computation will occur. The screen should look like Figure 3-2.

```
D8: +C8/$C$15                                                    READY

        A          B          C          D        E        F        G
  1                        ABC COMPANY
  2
  3
  4
  5
  6             SALESPERSONS       SALES
  7
  8             ALLEN, DARLA       3,678 0.140231
  9             ALUM,BETH          2,813 0.107251
 10             JOSEPH, CARLA      6,798 0.259188
 11             NOTTS, DON         4,378 0.166920
 12             RANKIN, AL         3,579 0.136457
 13             SEBO, JULES        4,982 0.189949
 14                              ----------
 15             TOTALS            26,228
 16
 17
```

Figure 3-2

To see how the formula +C8/$C$15 was copied:

Move   the cell pointer to cell D9

The formula +C9/$C$15 should be visible in the control panel; $C$15 is held constant. If you so desire, move to cells D10 through D13 to see that $C$15 is held constant in the formulas for the cells.

■CELL PROTECTION

Cells can be locked to prevent changes from being made to them. This protection is accomplished through the **Worksheet Global Protect Enable** command sequence or through a range command.

The **Worksheet Global Protect Enable** command turns on the worksheet protection. Only when cells have been unprotected with the **Range Unprotect** command can they be changed. When you try to enter data or make changes in protected cells, an error message is displayed. 1-2-3 also uses screen colors or highlighting to distinguish between protected and unprotected cells.

Saving files with a password is an alternate method for limiting access to files.

Retrieve the BUDGET file to practice protecting cells. Your screen should look like Figure 3-3.

```
A1: [W18]                                                    READY

            A            B        C        D        E        F         G
1                                    ABC COMPANY
2                                      BUDGET
3
4
5                        QTR1     QTR2     QTR3     QTR4    YR TOTAL
6
7   SALES            $60,000  $61,200  $62,424  $63,672  $247,296
8
9   EXPENSES
10    SALARIES        35,000   35,500   36,200   37,000   143,700
11    RENT             9,000    9,000    9,000    9,000    36,000
12    TELEPHONE        1,000    1,050    1,103    1,158     4,311
13    OFFICE SUPPLIES    750      800      850      900     3,300
14    MISCELLANEOUS    1,000    1,030    1,061    1,093     4,184
15                    -------------------------------------------
16      TOTAL EXPENSES 46,750   47,380   48,214   49,151   191,495
17                    -------------------------------------------
18  GROSS PROFIT     $13,250  $13,820  $14,210  $14,521   $55,801
19                    ===========================================
20
                          UNDO
```

Figure 3-3

To protect all of the cells in the worksheet, use the following **Worksheet Global** commands:

Press	/
Select	Worksheet
Select	Global
Select	Protection
Select	Enable

Now all the cells are protected. To unprotect cells A1..B14, use the following range commands:

Press	/
Select	Range
Select	Unprot

When prompted to enter the range to unprotect, highlight cells A1..B14.

Press	⏎

The unprotected area will be a different color or highlighted depending upon the type of monitor being used.

Move	cell pointer to cell C10
Type	36000
Press	⏎

Your computer will sound a "beep" and a message will appear at the bottom of the screen reminding you that the cell is protected.

Press	Esc
Move	cell pointer to cell B10
Type	36000
Press	⏎

Notice that you are able to change the data in the unprotected cell, and the worksheet recalculates.

Using the range commands, return the unprotected cells to a protected status.

Press	/
Select	Range
Select	Prot

When prompted to enter the range to protect, highlight cells A1..B14.

Press	⏎

The entire worksheet is protected again and changes cannot be made to any of the cells.

■ERASING CELLS

Retrieve the file BUDGET2 for this exercise.

To erase the labels ABC COMPANY in cell F1 and BUDGET in F2:

Move	the cell pointer to cell F1
Press	/
Select	Range
Select	Erase

Press

The highlighted cells should appear as in Figure 3-4.

```
F2: '         BUDGET                                                    POINT
Enter range to erase: F1..F2

              A           B          C          D          E          F          G
1                                                                        ABC COMPANY
2                                                                          BUDGET
3
4
5                       YEAR 1     YEAR 2     YEAR 3     YEAR 4     YEAR 5     YEAR 6
6
7   SALES              $60,000    $61,200    $62,424    $63,672    $64,945    $66,244
8
9   EXPENSES
10      SALARIES        35,000     35,500     36,200     37,000     37,000     37,000
11      RENT             9,000      9,000      9,000      9,000      9,000      9,000
12      TELEPHONE        1,000      1,050      1,103      1,158      1,216      1,277
13      OFFICE SUPPLIES    750        800        850        900        950      1,000
14      MISCELLANEOUS    1,000      1,030      1,061      1,093      1,126      1,160
15                     -----------------------------------------------------------
16      TOTAL EXPENSES  46,750     47,380     48,214     49,151     49,292     49,437
17                     -----------------------------------------------------------
18  GROSS PROFIT       $13,250    $13,820    $14,210    $14,521    $15,653    $16,807
19                     ===========================================================
20
```

Figure 3-4

Press   ⏎

Cells F1 and F2 are now erased. Your screen should look like Figure 3-5.

```
F1:                                                          READY

         A          B        C        D        E        F        G
1
2
3
4
5                  YEAR 1   YEAR 2   YEAR 3   YEAR 4   YEAR 5   YEAR 6
6
7   SALES          $60,000  $61,200  $62,424  $63,672  $64,945  $66,244
8
9   EXPENSES
10    SALARIES      35,000   35,500   36,200   37,000   37,000   37,000
11    RENT           9,000    9,000    9,000    9,000    9,000    9,000
12    TELEPHONE      1,000    1,050    1,103    1,158    1,216    1,277
13    OFFICE SUPPLIES  750      800      850      900      950    1,000
14    MISCELLANEOUS  1,000    1,030    1,061    1,093    1,126    1,160
15                 -------------------------------------------------------
16    TOTAL EXPENSES 46,750   47,380   48,214   49,151   49,292   49,437
17                 -------------------------------------------------------
18  GROSS PROFIT   $13,250  $13,820  $14,210  $14,521  $15,653  $16,807
19                 =======================================================
20
                    UNDO
```

Figure 3-5

■ERROR CORRECTION AND CELL EDITING

There are various ways to correct errors on a worksheet. Two commonly used methods are illustrated below.

Replacing an Erroneous Entry

Clear your screen using the **Worksheet Erase Yes** command sequence.

In cell A1:

Type   100

Press   ⏎

Your screen should now look like Fig 3-6 Part 1.

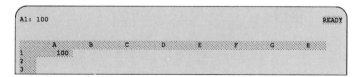

Figure 3-6
Part 1

To change the entry to 1000:

Type   1000

Press   ⏎

To replace an item that is incorrect, make sure the cell pointer is highlighting the incorrect cell entry and retype the entry. The screen should look like Figure 3-6 Part 2.

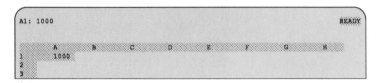

Figure 3-6
Part 2

Editing an Entry Using the F2 key

To change the cell entry in cell A1 from 1000 to 1000*1.03:

Move   the cell pointer to cell A1

Press   F2

The entry is displayed in the control panel and a cursor appears at the end of the entry. EDIT appears as the mode indicator to indicate that the EDIT mode has been activated. The screen should look like Figure 3-7 Part 1.

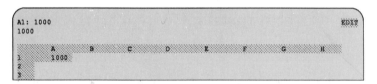

Figure 3-7
Part 1

To add to the end of the existing entry:

Type   *1.03

Press   ⏎

The entry in cell A1 has now been changed from 1000 to 1000*1.03. Your screen should look like Figure 3-7 Part 2.

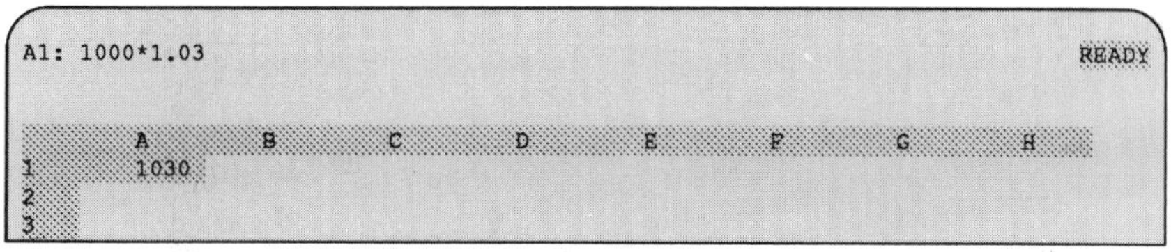

```
A1: 1000*1.03                                                    READY


       A         B         C         D         E         F         G         H
  1    1030
  2
  3
```

Figure 3-7
Part 2

When the EDIT mode is activated, the left and right pointer-movement keys as well as the [Home] and [End] keys can be used to move to various characters in an entry.

Clear your screen using the Worksheet Erase Yes command sequence.

| **Move** | the cell pointer to cell C3 |

| **Type** | ABC COMPANY |

| **Press** | [↵] |

To change the entry to THE ABC MANUFACTURING COMPANY, INC.:

| **Press** | [F2] |

| **Press** | [Home] |

The cursor is now under the apostrophe, which is the default label prefix. The [Home] key places the cursor at the first position of the cell entry.

| **Press** | [→] to move the cursor to the letter A in ABC |

| **Type** | THE |

| **Press** | the space bar |

When the additional text is typed, the remaining text **moves over** so that the new text is inserted. To insert MANUFACTURING:

| **Press** | [→] until the cursor appears under the space after ABC |

| **Press** | the space bar |

| **Type** | MANUFACTURING |

To move quickly to the end of the line, you can use the ⌈End⌉ key so that **, INC.** can be added.

Press   ⌈End⌉

Type   , INC.

Since the entry is completely edited:

Press   ⏎

The screen should look like Figure 3-8.

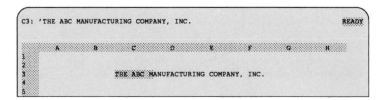

C3: 'THE ABC MANUFACTURING COMPANY, INC.   READY

    A   B   C   D   E   F   G   H
1
2
3   THE ABC MANUFACTURING COMPANY, INC.
4
5

Figure 3-8

When you are in EDIT mode, additional text can be typed and the remaining text is **moved over,** as illustrated in the example above.

The ⌈Ins⌉ or Insert key can be pressed to activate Overstrike (OVR will appear on the screen).

If the Overstrike function is activated, the new text will overstrike or type over the existing text. For example, to replace the letters ABC with XYZ:

Move   the cell pointer to cell C3

Press   ⌈F2⌉

Press   ⌈←⌉ to move the cursor to the letter A in ABC (or use the ⌈Home⌉ key and the ⌈→⌉ key to achieve the same result).

Press   ⌈Ins⌉

OVR appears at the bottom right corner of the screen.

Type   XYZ

Press   ⏎

The letters ABC have now been replaced with the letters XYZ. Your screen should look like Figure 3-9.

```
C3: 'THE XYZ MANUFACTURING COMPANY, INC.                              READY


        A        B        C        D        E        F        G        H
   1
   2
   3                   THE XYZ MANUFACTURING COMPANY, INC.
   4
   5
```

Figure 3-9

■ FILE COMMANDS

File Directory

The **File Directory** command changes the drive and path specifications from which files are retrieved and saved. To change from drive C to drive A, for example:

Press   /

Select   File

Select   Directory

Your screen should look similar to Figure 3-10.

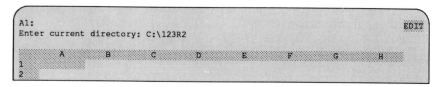

```
A1:                                                                  EDIT
Enter current directory: C:\123R2

        A        B        C        D        E        F        G        H
   1
   2
```

Figure 3-10

The current directory (where data files are being retrieved and saved) should be displayed. If you are currently saving the data in the root directory on drive C, your directory setting is C:\.

To change the directory to drive A, for example, the user could type A:\ and press ⏎ to save or retrieve files from drive A (do **not** do so at this time). To avoid changing the directory from its present setting:

Press   (Esc) until the menus disappear from the
              control panel

Note: to permanently change the directory, issue the Worksheet Global Default Directory sequence. Change the directory to the desired drive or path, press the ⏎ key and select **Update** to permanently save the directory as a default. Choose **Quit** to exit the menu.

File Erase

The **File Erase** command sequence erases a file. To erase a worksheet file:

Press   /

Select   File

Select   Erase

Four types of files are listed on the menu—Worksheet, Print, Graph and Other. When prompted for the type of file to erase:

Select   Worksheet

The screen should look similar to Figure 3-11.

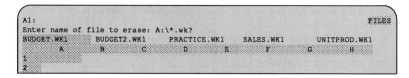

```
A1:                                                                      FILES
Enter name of file to erase: A:\*.wk?
BUDGET.WK1        BUDGET2.WK1        PRACTICE.WK1      SALES.WK1       UNITPROD.WK1
        A            B          C          D          E          F       G       H
 1
 2
```

Figure 3-11

To erase a file, you can press the $\boxed{\text{F3}}$ key and use the pointer movement keys to highlight the file to erase and press $\boxed{\leftarrow}$ (do **not** do so at this time). To escape from this process and not erase a file:

Press $\boxed{\text{Esc}}$ until the menus disappear

File List

The **File List** command sequence lists the files in the directory being used. To list the worksheet files:

Press   /

Select   File

Select   List

Note the five options—Worksheet, Print, Graph, Other, or Linked.

Worksheet: lists the worksheet files.

Print: lists print files (created using the **Print File** command sequence and printing a range to a file).

Graph: lists graph files (created using the Graph Save command sequence to print a graph from the graph settings in the current file).

Other: lists all files in the directory being used including those that were not created with Lotus 1-2-3.

Linked: lists the files that are linked to the current file.

Select   Worksheet

Your screen should look like Figure 3-12.

```
A1: [W18]                                                           FILES
Enter extension of files to list: A:\*.wk?
             BUDGET.WK1     09/20/89        09:16         3835
BUDGET.WK1        BUDGET2.WK1     PRACTICE.WK1     SALES.WK1      UNITPROD.WK1
```

Figure 3-12

To return to the worksheet:

Press

File Save Backup

When saving a file, 1-2-3 will automatically add a three-character extension to a file name.

The **File Save Backup** command is useful when you want to save the last version of a file without renaming the file. Before using this command, retrieve file BUDGET. To use this feature, follow these commands:

Press   /

Select   File

Select   Save

When prompted to enter the filename, a file name already appears above the control panel.

Press

Three choices appear on the screen as shown in Figure 3-13.

Cancel: cancels the Save command.

Replace: replaces the original file with the file being used.

Backup: creates a second file with a backup (BAK) extension.

```
A1: [W18]                                                           MENU
Cancel  Replace  Backup
Backup existing file (with a .BAK extension) and save the current file on disk
         A          B        C        D        E       F        G
1                              ABC COMPANY
2                               BUDGET
3
4
5                     QTR1     QTR2     QTR3     QTR4   YR TOTAL
6
7  SALES            $60,000  $61,200  $62,424  $63,672 $247,296
8
9  EXPENSES
10    SALARIES       35,000   35,500   36,200   37,000  143,700
11    RENT            9,000    9,000    9,000    9,000   36,000
12    TELEPHONE       1,000    1,050    1,103    1,158    4,311
13    OFFICE SUPPLIES   750      800      850      900    3,300
14    MISCELLANEOUS   1,000    1,030    1,061    1,093    4,184
15                   ------   ------   ------   ------  -------
16     TOTAL EXPENSES 46,750   47,380   48,214   49,151  191,495
17                   ------   ------   ------   ------  -------
18 GROSS PROFIT     $13,250  $13,820  $14,210  $14,521  $55,801
19                  =======  =======  =======  =======  =======
20
                                                            CAPS
```

Figure 3-13

Select   Backup

The file is now saved under its original extension (WK1) and also as a backup file with the backup extension (BAK).

File Admin Table

One of the features of the **File Admin Table** command sequence is its capability to create information in table form about files on the disk. From the following five selections, tables can be created.

Worksheet: worksheet files in a specific directory.

Print: files in a specific directory with PRN extension.

Graph: graph files in a specific directory.

Other: all files in a specific directory.

Linked: all files linked by formula references to current file.

Clear your screen using the **Worksheet Erase Yes** command sequence.

To create a table showing all the files on the disk in Drive C:

Press   /

Select	File
Select	Admin
Select	Table
Select	Other

When prompted to enter the directory:

Press	Esc
Type	C:*.* (or your directory)
Press	←

When prompted to enter a range, select an area which is blank since existing data will be written over by the table.

Press	←

A sample of a table appears in Figure 3-14.

```
A1:  'A.BAT                                                     READY

             A          B        C         D        E       F       G       H
1    A.BAT          32631 0.850092       69
2    A1.WK3         32631 0.900150      711
3    A2FILES.W      32663 0.929270     2350
4    A3CHART.       32631 0.900150      711
5    AHPT04FG.      32634 0.965590     1020
6    AL.EXE         32251 0.441921    61824
7    AR.DEF         32644 0.657939      122
8    AUTOEXEC.      32631 0.846053      100
9    AUTOEXEC.      32668 0.654305      174
10   AUTOEXEC.      32685 0.515393      174
11   AUTOEXEC.      32644 0.591805       18
12   B.BAT          32631 0.888368       46
13   BOATSALE.      32686 0.482210      785
14   BOOK.LIB       32588 0.643819      206
15   BUDGET.WK      32678 0.575023     4659
16   C.BAT          32645 0.467002       48
17   COMMAND.C      32114 0.781412    25276
18   CONFIG.BA      32644 0.636342       43
19   CONFIG.BA      32671 0.438923       76
20   CONFIG.OL      32644 0.591932       11
                                  UNDO
```

Figure 3-14

The first column indicates the filename; the second and third columns show the date and time before they are formatted. The last column indicates the file size.

Once the date and time are formatted and the columns have been widened to display the information, your table should look similar to Figure 3-15. The process of formatting the date and time is covered in Chapter 9.

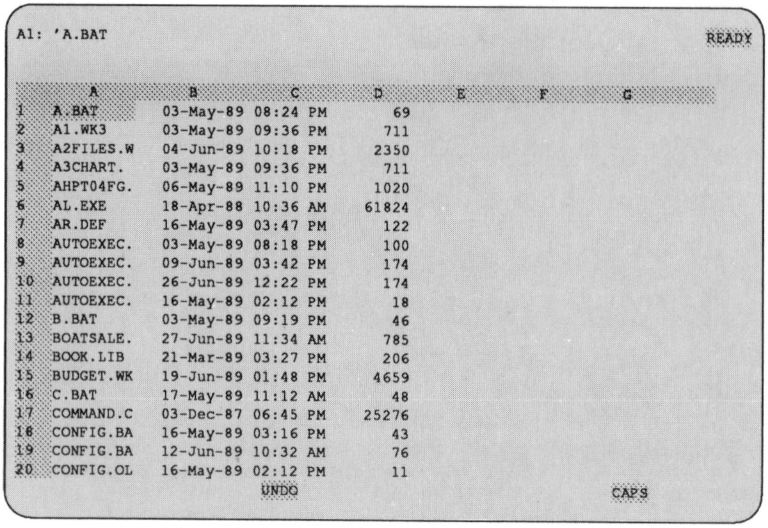
A1: 'A.BAT READY

	A	B	C	D	E	F	G
1	A.BAT	03-May-89	08:24 PM	69			
2	A1.WK3	03-May-89	09:36 PM	711			
3	A2FILES.W	04-Jun-89	10:18 PM	2350			
4	A3CHART.	03-May-89	09:36 PM	711			
5	AHPT04FG.	06-May-89	11:10 PM	1020			
6	AL.EXE	18-Apr-88	10:36 AM	61824			
7	AR.DEF	16-May-89	03:47 PM	122			
8	AUTOEXEC.	03-May-89	08:18 PM	100			
9	AUTOEXEC.	09-Jun-89	03:42 PM	174			
10	AUTOEXEC.	26-Jun-89	12:22 PM	174			
11	AUTOEXEC.	16-May-89	02:12 PM	18			
12	B.BAT	03-May-89	09:19 PM	46			
13	BOATSALE.	27-Jun-89	11:34 AM	785			
14	BOOK.LIB	21-Mar-89	03:27 PM	206			
15	BUDGET.WK	19-Jun-89	01:48 PM	4659			
16	C.BAT	17-May-89	11:12 AM	48			
17	COMMAND.C	03-Dec-87	06:45 PM	25276			
18	CONFIG.BA	16-May-89	03:16 PM	43			
19	CONFIG.BA	12-Jun-89	10:32 AM	76			
20	CONFIG.OL	16-May-89	02:12 PM	11			

UNDO CAPS

Figure 3-15

■ FORMATTING

Percent

Retrieve the file SALES so that the percent format can be illustrated.

Create an appropriate heading as follows:

Move the cell pointer to D6

Type "% SALES

The " right-justifies the label in cell D6. See the Label Prefixes section later in this chapter for additional information.

Press ↵

To format the data in column D so that percent signs and two decimal places are displayed:

Move the cell pointer to D8

Press /

Select Range

Select Format

Select   Percent

To accept the default of two decimal places:

Press   ↵

When prompted for the range to format:

Move   the cell pointer to cell D15

The range to format should be cells D8..D15. If it is not, press the Esc key to release the anchor and set the range to D8..D15. When the range is correct:

Press   ↵

To enter percentages in column D:

Move   the cell pointer to D8

Type   @ROUND(C8/$C$15,2)

Press   ↵

To copy the formula to the remaining cells in column D:

Press   /

Select   Copy

Press   ↵

Move   the cell pointer to cell D9

Press   .

Move   the cell pointer down to cell D15

Press   ↵

Move   the cell pointer to cell D14

Type   \-

Press   ↵

The percentages now use the Percent format which multiplies the data by 100, displays the desired number of decimal places, and attaches the % symbol to the end of the data. Note that percentages do not always add up to 100 percent, but may add up to 99 or 101 percent. Using the @ROUND function for percentages (e.g., @ROUND(+C8/$C$15,2)) may not solve the problem. It may be necessary to "plug" a number to obtain the desired results.

Your screen should look like Figure 3-16.

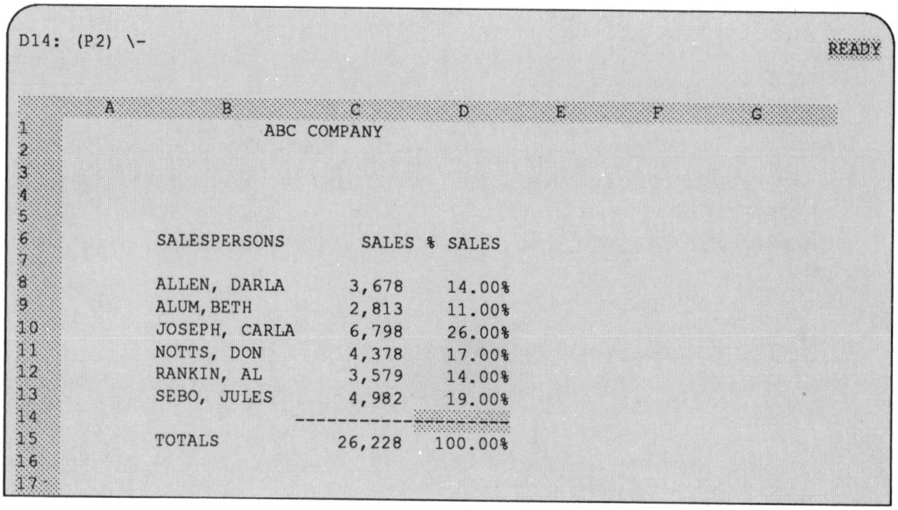

```
D14: (P2) \-                                                          READY

        A          B          C          D          E         F         G
 1                      ABC COMPANY
 2
 3
 4
 5
 6          SALESPERSONS          SALES  % SALES
 7
 8          ALLEN, DARLA          3,678    14.00%
 9          ALUM, BETH            2,813    11.00%
10          JOSEPH, CARLA         6,798    26.00%
11          NOTTS, DON            4,378    17.00%
12          RANKIN, AL            3,579    14.00%
13          SEBO, JULES           4,982    19.00%
14                             ----------
15          TOTALS               26,228   100.00%
16
17
```

Figure 3-16

■ HIDING AND REDISPLAYING DATA

Hiding a Column

One or more columns of a worksheet can be suppressed so that any data in them is not displayed or printed, but the data continues to be used in calculations.

Retrieve the BUDGET file. To hide column E:

Press	/
Select	Worksheet
Select	Column
Select	Hide

When prompted for the column(s) to hide:

Move	the cell pointer to a cell in column E
Press	↵

Column E is no longer visible on the screen. Your screen should look like Figure 3-17.

```
A1: [W18]                                                          READY

              A          B        C        D        F      G      H
  1                              ABC COMPANY
  2                                BUDGET
  3
  4
  5                      QTR1     QTR2     QTR3   YR TOTAL
  6
  7   SALES            $60,000  $61,200  $62,424 $247,296
  8
  9   EXPENSES
 10     SALARIES        35,000   35,500   36,200  143,700
 11     RENT             9,000    9,000    9,000   36,000
 12     TELEPHONE        1,000    1,050    1,103    4,311
 13     OFFICE SUPPLIES    750      800      850    3,300
 14     MISCELLANEOUS    1,000    1,030    1,061    4,184
 15                    -----------------------------------
 16      TOTAL EXPENSES 46,750   47,380   48,214  191,495
 17                    -----------------------------------
 18   GROSS PROFIT     $13,250  $13,820  $14,210  $55,801
 19                    ===================================
 20

                          UNDO                        CAPS
```

Figure 3-17

Redisplaying a Hidden Column

To make column E visible on the screen again:

Press	/
Select	Worksheet
Select	Column
Select	Display

Any column which had been hidden will now be visible and have an asterisk beside it.

When prompted for the column to redisplay:

| **Move** | the cell pointer to a cell in column E |
| **Press** | ↵ |

Column E should now appear on your screen.

Hiding a Range of Cells

To hide the GROSS PROFIT label and values and double underlines:

Move	the cell pointer to cell A18
Press	/
Select	Range
Select	Format
Select	Hidden
Move	the cell pointer to cell F19
Press	⏎

The GROSS PROFIT label and associated values as well as the double underlines have been hidden.

Redisplaying a Range of Cells

To restore the hidden information to your screen:

Move	the cell pointer to cell A18
Press	/
Select	Range
Select	Format
Select	Reset
Move	the cell pointer to cell F19
Press	⏎

The hidden data now appears on your screen. Note that the format of the cells is reset to the **Worksheet Global , 0** format setting.

■ LABEL PREFIXES

The use of the caret (the ^ symbol) to center labels was illustrated in Chapter 2. The caret is a **label prefix**. 1-2-3 has four label prefixes that affect the appearance of labels both on the screen and when they are printed. In this section, the label prefixes are discussed and demonstrated. Before starting the following exercise, erase your screen.

The apostrophe (the ' symbol located on the double-quote key) is the default label prefix in 1-2-3. When a nonnumeric character is the first character of an entry, 1-2-3 automatically places an apostrophe as the prefix to the label. The entry then appears at the left of the cell in which it is input. Enter the following label in cell A1:

Type   USA

Press   ⏎

Look at the control panel. Notice that an apostrophe appears in the control panel before USA. In the worksheet, notice that USA appears on the left side of cell A1. Because you did not specify a label prefix, the apostrophe was used. Your screen should look like Figure 3-18.

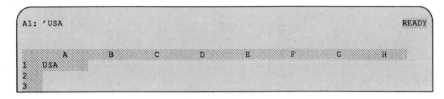

Figure 3-18

Erase the screen using the Worksheet Erase Yes command sequence. In cell A1, manually input the apostrophe before entering USA.

Type   'USA

Press   ⏎

Again, USA appears at the left side of the cell. The apostrophe appears before USA in the control panel when cell A1 is highlighted.

The caret symbol causes a label to appear in the center of a cell. The caret must be typed as the first character of the entry. To center a label:

Move   the cell pointer to cell A2

Type   ^USA

Press   ⏎

USA appears in the center of the cell. The caret appears before USA in the control panel when cell A2 is highlighted.

The double-quote symbol causes a label to appear at the right side of the cell. The double-quote must be typed as the first character of the entry. To right-justify a label:

Move   the cell pointer to cell A3

Type	"USA
Press	⏎

USA appears in the rightmost portion of the cell. The double-quote appears before USA in the control panel when cell A3 is highlighted.

The backward slash (the \ symbol) causes the characters entered after the backward slash to be repeated in the cell. To cause the label USA to be repeated in a cell:

Move	the cell pointer to cell A4
Type	\USA
Press	⏎

Cell A4 displays USAUSAUSA throughout the cell. If the width of column A is shortened or lengthened, the repeating label adjusts accordingly. This label prefix is useful for subtotal and total lines. For example, entering \- will cause repeating dashes to appear in a cell. Refer to Figure 3-19 to see how the label prefixes altered the appearance of the label USA.

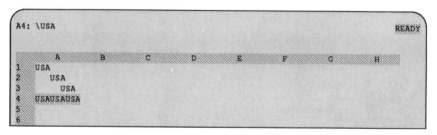

Figure 3-19

Note that label prefixes are to be used only for **labels**. If ^123 is entered in a cell, for example, 123 is centered and treated as a label in a cell and should not be used for computation.

■ MOVING CELL CONTENTS

To prepare to illustrate the process of moving the contents of cells from one location on a spreadsheet to another location, complete the following steps. First erase the spreadsheet on your screen. Make sure the cell pointer is in cell A1; then:

Type	100
Press	⏎
Move	the cell pointer to cell A4

Type	50
Press	➡
Type	25
Press	⬅

Make sure your screen looks like Figure 3-20.

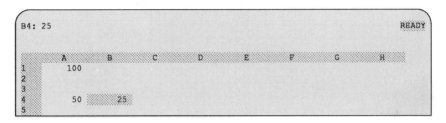

B4: 25   READY

	A	B	C	D	E	F	G	H
1	100							
2								
3								
4	50	25						
5								

Figure 3-20

Moving the Contents of One Cell to Another Cell

To move the contents of cell A1 to cell H1:

Move	the cell pointer to cell A1

When the cell pointer is already highlighting the cell to move, it is easier to use the Move command.

Press	/
Select	Move

When prompted for the range to move FROM:

Press	⬅

The cell to move (cell A1) was already highlighted, so only the ⬅ had to be pressed.

When prompted for the range to move TO:

Move	the cell pointer to cell H1
Press	⬅

Your screen should look like Figure 3-21.

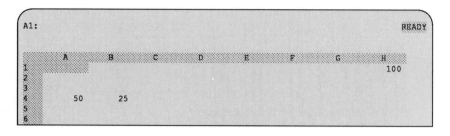

Figure 3-21

Moving the Contents of Several Cells to Another Location on the Worksheet

To move cells A4 through B4 to cells A14 through B14:

Move the cell pointer to cell A4

Press /

Select Move

When prompted for the range to move FROM:

Move the cell pointer to cell B4

Cells A4 through B4 are now highlighted and therefore specified as the cells to move.

Press ⏎

When prompted for the range to move TO:

Move the cell pointer to cell A14

Press ⏎

The contents of cells A4 through B4 have now been moved to cells A14 through B14. Note that it was only necessary to specify the upper left corner of the range to move to. Your screen should look like Figure 3-22.

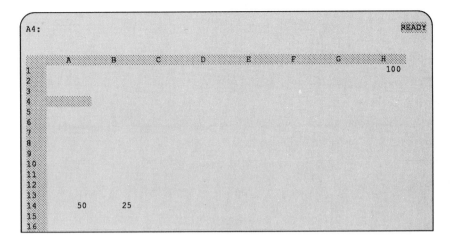

Figure 3-22

■PAGE BREAK

When printing a spreadsheet in Lotus 1-2-3, Lotus prints as much as it can on a single page based upon the default page length. The remaining rows are printed on the next page or set of pages. Sometimes, you may wish to specify where you want page breaks to occur. The Page Break command can be used in such situations.

Retrieve the BUDGET2 file for use in the following exercise. To set a print range:

Press	/
Select	Print
Select	Printer
Select	Range

If necessary, press the [Esc] key to delete the current print range. When prompted for the range to print:

Press	the [Home] key (if the cell pointer is not already in cell A1)
Type	.
Move	the cell pointer to cell G32

Cells A1. .G32 (the descriptions, data and assumptions for YEAR 1 through YEAR 6) are now highlighted.

Press   ↵

Select   Quit

To insert a page break at cell A12:

Move   the cell pointer to cell A12

Press   /

Select   Worksheet

Select   Page

Note that two colons (: :) now appear in cell A12. The data that was previously in rows 12 through 32 has been moved down one row. If the print range for BUDGET2 is printed, the data in row 13 (TELEPHONE expenses) will be printed at the top of the second page. Note that |: : (the pipe symbol and two colons) appear in the control panel as the contents of A12. The symbols |: : can be manually typed on the spreadsheet where a page break is desired. No data should be contained in the row with the designation for the page break if the symbol is typed. Note that the page break symbol can be erased just as though it were a typical data entry—one option is the **Range Erase** command sequence. The **Worksheet Delete Row** command sequence may be preferable because a row was added to accommodate the page break symbol. The screen should look like Figure 3-23 Part 1.

```
A12: [W18] |::                                                      READY


            A          B         C         D         E          F          G
1                                                                ABC COMPANY
2                                                                  BUDGET
3
4
5                      YEAR 1    YEAR 2    YEAR 3    YEAR 4     YEAR 5     YEAR 6
6
7    SALES            $60,000   $61,200   $62,424   $63,672    $64,945    $66,244
8
9    EXPENSES
10     SALARIES        35,000    35,500    36,200    37,000     37,000     37,000
11     RENT             9,000     9,000     9,000     9,000      9,000      9,000
12   ::
13     TELEPHONE        1,000     1,050     1,103     1,158      1,216      1,277
14     OFFICE SUPPLIES    750       800       850       900        950      1,000
15     MISCELLANEOUS    1,000     1,030     1,061     1,093      1,126      1,160
16                     -----------------------------------------------------------
17     TOTAL EXPENSES  46,750    47,380    48,214    49,151     49,292     49,437
18                     -----------------------------------------------------------
19   GROSS PROFIT     $13,250   $13,820   $14,210   $14,521    $15,653    $16,807
20                     ===========================================================
                            UNDO                               CAPS
```

Figure 3-23
Part 1

To print the spreadsheet:

Press	/
Select	Print
Select	Printer
Select	Align
Select	Go

After printing:

Select	Page
Select	Quit

Assuming that the printing was performed on 8 1/2 by 11 inch paper, your printout should look like Figure 3-23 Parts 2 and 3.

				ABC COMPANY		
				BUDGET		
	YEAR 1	YEAR 2	YEAR 3	YEAR 4	YEAR 5	YEAR 6
SALES	$60,000	$61,200	$62,424	$63,672	$64,945	$66,244
EXPENSES						
SALARIES	35,000	35,500	36,200	37,000	37,000	37,000
RENT	9,000	9,000	9,000	9,000	9,000	9,000

Figure 3-23
Part 2

TELEPHONE	1,000	1,050	1,103	1,158	1,216	1,277
OFFICE SUPPLIES	750	800	850	900	950	1,000
MISCELLANEOUS	1,000	1,030	1,061	1,093	1,126	1,160
	--------	--------	--------	--------	--------	--------
TOTAL EXPENSES	46,750	47,380	48,214	49,151	49,292	49,437
	--------	--------	--------	--------	--------	--------
GROSS PROFIT	$13,250	$13,820	$14,210	$14,521	$15,653	$16,807
	========	========	========	========	========	========
GROWTH RATE						
ASSUMPTIONS						
SALES		1.02	1.02	1.02	1.02	1.02
TELEPHONE		1.05	1.05	1.05	1.05	1.05
OFFICE SUPPLIES		50.00	50.00	50.00	50.00	50.00
MISCELLANEOUS		1.03	1.03	1.03	1.03	1.03

Figure 3-23
Part 3

To delete the page break symbol, you must delete the row containing it or erase the cell. In this case you will delete the row.

Move   the cell pointer to cell A12

Press   /

Select   Worksheet

Select   Delete

Select	Row
Press	⏎

The page break symbol no longer appears on your screen.

■PRINTING

Borders

The **Borders** option is useful when working with large spreadsheets or worksheets of more than one page. This command places headings or labels from the worksheet on every page either to the left of the data or at the top of the page, or both.

Row borders are useful when there are several pages to a report. They provide descriptive information at the top of each page. Column information can be printed on the left side of each page for ease in reading the worksheet.

When using the **Border** feature, there are two options to choose from:

Rows: horizontal headings above each print range and at the top of each page.

Columns: vertical headings to the left of each print range and at the left side of each page.

Before starting this exercise, retrieve the BUDGET2 file.

To print columns on every page of the worksheet:

Press	/
Select	Print
Select	Printer
Select	Options
Select	Borders
Select	Columns

To make the labels in column A appear on every page, highlight a cell in column A; then

Press	⏎
Select	Quit

When selecting the print range, do not include the borders. This would cause a double printing of the border. For this example:

Select   Range

To clear the current print range:

Press   Esc

To specify the new print range:

Move   the cell pointer to cell B1

Type   .

Move   the cell pointer to cell L32

Press   ↵

To undo a border selection, use **Print Printer Clear Borders**. Do **not** undo the border selection at this time.

Headers and Footers

The header is a line of text entered below the top margin of every page. The default reserves three lines for a header: one line for the text followed by two blank lines before the data. Headers may be placed at the left margin, right margin, or centered. Although headers are normally short, they may contain as many as 240 characters.

To place a header at the top of each page, use the following procedure:

Select   Options

Select   Header

When prompted to enter the header:

Type   ABC COMPANY

Notice the control panel in Figure 3-24.

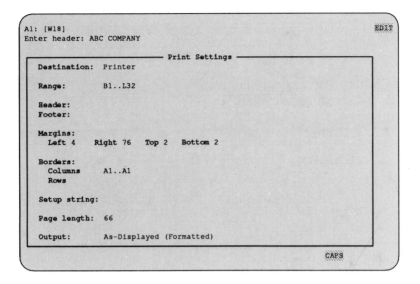

Figure 3-24

Press ⏎

Headers are entered only once, but they are reproduced on each printed page. Headers can be changed by repeating the procedure. They can be deleted by repeating the procedure and then pressing the Esc when you are prompted to enter the heading.

Headers and footers may also be entered by using special characters and symbols. The following symbols can be used to format them:

#	(pound sign) places the page number on every page.
##	(double pound sign) when followed by a page number specifies that page number as the first page of the printout.
@	(at sign) places current date (DD-MM-YY) on every page.
|	(vertical bar or pipe symbol) separates footers or headers (left, right, or centered).
\\	(backslash) followed by a cell address or range name whose contents become the header or footer text.

The vertical bar controls the position of the text on the page. Without the vertical bar, the text is left-justified. With one vertical bar preceding the text, it is centered. With two vertical bars preceding the text, it is right-justified.

To create a footer which will result in a right-justified page number:

Select   Footer

When prompted to enter the footer:

Type ||#

Your control panel should match the one shown in Figure 3-25.

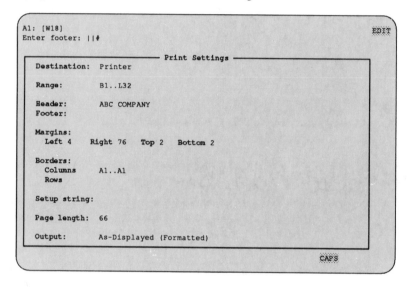

```
A1: [W18]                                                              EDIT
Enter footer: ||#

┌───────────────────────── Print Settings ─────────────────────────┐
│  Destination:  Printer                                            │
│                                                                   │
│  Range:        B1..L32                                            │
│                                                                   │
│  Header:       ABC COMPANY                                        │
│  Footer:                                                          │
│                                                                   │
│  Margins:                                                         │
│    Left 4     Right 76    Top 2    Bottom 2                       │
│                                                                   │
│  Borders:                                                         │
│    Columns    A1..A1                                              │
│    Rows                                                           │
│                                                                   │
│  Setup string:                                                    │
│                                                                   │
│  Page length:  66                                                 │
│                                                                   │
│  Output:       As-Displayed (Formatted)                          │
└───────────────────────────────────────────────────────────────────┘
                                                              CAPS
```

Figure 3-25

Press   ↵

Select   Quit

Note that the **Page** command must be issued for 1-2-3 to put a footer on the last page.

To print the worksheet with the borders, header and footer:

Select   Align

Select   Go

Select   Page (twice if necessary to advance paper to top of next page)

Select   Quit

■ RANGE NAMES

Creating a Range Name

Range names can be used rather than cell addresses to make it easier to remember the location of cells. A range name is associated with cell addresses.

Retrieve the BUDGET worksheet. To assign a range name to the cells containing the values of TOTAL EXPENSES for the four quarters:

Press	/
Select	Range
Select	Name
Select	Create

When prompted for the range name:

Type	TOTAL_EXP
Press	⏎

When prompted for the range to be assigned to the name TOTAL_EXP:

Press	Esc
Move	cell pointer to B16
Type	.
Move	cell pointer to E16

The screen should look like Figure 3-26.

```
E16: @SUM(E10..E14)                                          POINT
Enter name: TOTAL_EXP              Enter range: B16..E16

          A          B        C        D        E        F         G
 1                         ABC COMPANY
 2                            BUDGET
 3
 4
 5                        QTR1     QTR2     QTR3     QTR4    YR TOTAL
 6
 7   SALES            $60,000  $61,200  $62,424  $63,672  $247,296
 8
 9   EXPENSES
10     SALARIES        35,000   35,500   36,200   37,000   143,700
11     RENT             9,000    9,000    9,000    9,000    36,000
12     TELEPHONE        1,000    1,050    1,103    1,158     4,311
13     OFFICE SUPPLIES    750      800      850      900     3,300
14     MISCELLANEOUS    1,000    1,030    1,061    1,093     4,184
15                    -------- -------- -------- -------- ---------
16      TOTAL EXPENSES 46,750   47,380   48,214   49,151   191,495
17                    -------- -------- -------- -------- ---------
18   GROSS PROFIT     $13,250  $13,820  $14,210  $14,521   $55,801
19                    ======== ======== ======== ======== =========
20
                                                             CAPS
```

Figure 3-26

Press   ⏎

Range names are used in formulas in place of cell addresses. Cell addresses in formulas are changed to reflect that you have defined a range name.

Move   the cell pointer to cell F16

Note that TOTAL_EXP has replaced the B16..E16 in the @SUM function.

Range names may be up to 15 characters in length. Do not use special characters. The underline and dash symbols are exceptions and may be used.

Deleting a Range Name

When a range name is deleted, the range name is replaced in formulas with the cell address. It does not change the range. Remember to delete the name for a range of cells before assigning the name to a different set of cells.

To delete a range name for a range of cells:

Press   /

Select   Range

Select   Name

Select	Delete
Press	⟦F3⟧

Specify the range name TOTAL_EXP is to be deleted by highlighting it.

Press	⟦↵⟧

Notice that TOTAL_EXP in cell F16 has been replaced with B16..E16.

Table of Range Names

An alphabetical list of range names can be created by using the Range Name Table command. Decide upon a location for the table before beginning the command. This area should be blank so that the table does not overwrite existing data.

Retrieve the BUDGET file and create range names for SALES, SALARIES and TOTAL EXPENSES that include the values for QTR1 through QTR4 for each item. Then create an alphabetical list of the range names by using the following procedure:

Press	/
Select	Range
Select	Name
Select	Table

When prompted to enter the range for the table, place the cell pointer in the upper left corner of the output area.

Press	⟦Esc⟧
Move	the cell pointer to cell A35
Press	⟦↵⟧

The table should be placed below the worksheet assumptions and your screen should look like Figure 3-27.

```
A35: [W18] 'SALARIES                                                    READY

              A             B        C        D        E        F        G
21
22  GROWTH RATE
23  ASSUMPTIONS
24
25  SALES                           1.02     1.02     1.02
26  TELEPHONE                       1.05     1.05     1.05
27  OFFICE SUPPLIES                50.00    50.00    50.00
28  MISCELLANEOUS                   1.03     1.03     1.03
29
30
31  Prepared by H. Al Napier
32         11-Sep-89
33
34
35  SALARIES          B10..E10
36  SALES             B7..E7
37  TOTAL_EXPENSES    B16..E16
38
39
40
                            UNDO                            CAPS
```

Figure 3-27

■RECALCULATION OF A SPREADSHEET

Retrieve the file BUDGET2 for this exercise.

To change the value of a cell on the worksheet:

Move	the cell pointer to cell B7
Type	70000
Press	↵

The worksheet is recalculated with the new entry $70,000 for YEAR 1 of SALES. Your screen should look like Figure 3-28 Part 1. The initial settings for recalculation are Automatic and Natural; the worksheet recalculates automatically and in natural order every time any cell is changed. Sometimes when new data is input, it may take several seconds or even minutes for the worksheet to recalculate. If you have several changes to make, then time will be wasted while you wait for 1-2-3 to recalculate the worksheet as you make each change. A way to reduce the amount of time wasted is to set the Recalculation option to Manual.

To control the recalculation in a worksheet manually:

Press	/
Select	Worksheet
Select	Global

Select   Recalculation

Select   Manual

The recalculation options are described below.

Natural:	first recalculates other formulas upon which a particular formula depends.
Columnwise:	causes the worksheet to recalculate column by column.
Rowwise:	causes the worksheet to recalculate row by row.
Automatic:	causes the worksheet to recalculate every time the worksheet data is changed.
Manual:	causes the worksheet to recalculate only by pressing the [F9] function key.
Iteration:	causes the worksheet to recalculate a designated number of times, or iterations.

To change the sales amount in cell B7 again:

Type   80000

Press   [←]

Note that when the number 80000 was entered, the worksheet was not recalculated and the letters CALC appeared at the bottom of the screen. The screen should look like Figure 3-28 Part 2.

```
B7: (C0)  70000                                                    READY


          A          B          C          D          E          F          G
 1                                                                ABC COMPANY
 2                                                                  BUDGET
 3
 4
 5                   YEAR 1     YEAR 2     YEAR 3     YEAR 4     YEAR 5     YEAR 6
 6
 7  SALES            $70,000    $71,400    $72,828    $74,285    $75,771    $77,286
 8
 9  EXPENSES
10    SALARIES        35,000     35,500     36,200     37,000     37,000     37,000
11    RENT             9,000      9,000      9,000      9,000      9,000      9,000
12    TELEPHONE        1,000      1,050      1,103      1,158      1,216      1,277
13    OFFICE SUPPLIES    750        800        850        900        950      1,000
14    MISCELLANEOUS    1,000      1,030      1,061      1,093      1,126      1,160
15                   -----------------------------------------------------------
16      TOTAL EXPENSES 46,750     47,380     48,214     49,151     49,292     49,437
17                   -----------------------------------------------------------
18  GROSS PROFIT     $23,250    $24,020    $24,614    $25,134    $26,479    $27,849
19                   ===========================================================
20
                          UNDO                                  CAPS
```

Figure 3-28
Part 1

```
B7: (C0)  80000                                                    READY


          A          B          C          D          E          F          G
 1                                                                ABC COMPANY
 2                                                                  BUDGET
 3
 4
 5                   YEAR 1     YEAR 2     YEAR 3     YEAR 4     YEAR 5     YEAR 6
 6
 7  SALES            $80,000    $71,400    $72,828    $74,285    $75,771    $77,286
 8
 9  EXPENSES
10    SALARIES        35,000     35,500     36,200     37,000     37,000     37,000
11    RENT             9,000      9,000      9,000      9,000      9,000      9,000
12    TELEPHONE        1,000      1,050      1,103      1,158      1,216      1,277
13    OFFICE SUPPLIES    750        800        850        900        950      1,000
14    MISCELLANEOUS    1,000      1,030      1,061      1,093      1,126      1,160
15                   -----------------------------------------------------------
16      TOTAL EXPENSES 46,750     47,380     48,214     49,151     49,292     49,437
17                   -----------------------------------------------------------
18  GROSS PROFIT     $23,250    $24,020    $24,614    $25,134    $26,479    $27,849
19                   ===========================================================
20
                          UNDO                        CALC      CAPS
```

Figure 3-28
Part 2

To recalculate the worksheet:

Press   [F9]

The [F9] key is sometimes referred to as the CALC key.

Your worksheet is now recalculated. If another number is changed at this point, CALC will reappear on the screen. Multiple entries can be made without the worksheet recalculating after each new entry. The [F9] key must be pressed again before the worksheet will be recalculated. Your screen should look like Figure 3-28 Part 3.

```
B7: (C0)  80000                                                    READY

                A         B        C        D        E        F        G
 1                                                              ABC COMPANY
 2                                                                BUDGET
 3
 4
 5                      YEAR 1   YEAR 2   YEAR 3   YEAR 4   YEAR 5   YEAR 6
 6
 7   SALES            $80,000  $81,600  $83,232  $84,897  $86,595  $88,327
 8
 9   EXPENSES
10     SALARIES        35,000   35,500   36,200   37,000   37,000   37,000
11     RENT             9,000    9,000    9,000    9,000    9,000    9,000
12     TELEPHONE        1,000    1,050    1,103    1,158    1,216    1,277
13     OFFICE SUPPLIES    750      800      850      900      950    1,000
14     MISCELLANEOUS    1,000    1,030    1,061    1,093    1,126    1,160
15                    ------------------------------------------------------
16     TOTAL EXPENSES  46,750   47,380   48,214   49,151   49,292   49,437
17                    ------------------------------------------------------
18   GROSS PROFIT     $33,250  $34,220  $35,018  $35,746  $37,303  $38,890
19                    ======================================================
20
                         UNDO
```

Figure 3-28
Part 3

To cause the worksheet to recalculate automatically when the contents of a cell are changed or new data is entered:

Press   /

Select   Worksheet

Select   Global

Select   Recalculation

Select   Automatic

Your worksheet will now recalculate automatically whenever a change is made.

■SEARCH AND REPLACE

The **Range Search** command finds a string of characters in a label, formula, or both and highlights the string. Uppercase and lowercase letters are treated without sensitivity. If you specify the command to **Replace** the string, 1-2-3 finds the string and then replaces it with the exact string of characters that you enter. In the Find option, you are given the choice of continuing the search or quitting.

The **Replace** option highlights the matching cell. It provides the following four options:

Replace: inserts the replacement and moves to the next occurrence.

All: replaces each occurrence of the string.

Next: finds the next matching string without replacing the current one.

Quit: quits the search and replace procedure.

When there are no further matching strings, an error message is displayed. When this occurs, press ⏎ or Esc to return to the READY mode.

Retrieve the BUDGET file and search for the word SALES.

Press   /

Select   Range

Select   Search

When prompted to enter a range to be searched, highlight the entire worksheet.

Press   ⏎

When the prompt asks for the search string:

Type   SALES

Press   ⏎

Select   Both

Select   Find

Your screen should look like Figure 3-29.

```
A7: [W18] 'SALES                                                    MENU
Next  Quit
Find next matching string
          A              B        C        D        E        F      G
 1                              ABC COMPANY
 2                                BUDGET
 3
 4
 5                             QTR1     QTR2     QTR3     QTR4   YR TOTAL
 6
 7   SALES                   $60,000  $61,200  $62,424  $63,672 $247,296
 8
 9   EXPENSES
10      SALARIES              35,000   35,500   36,200   37,000  143,700
11      RENT                   9,000    9,000    9,000    9,000   36,000
12      TELEPHONE              1,000    1,050    1,103    1,158    4,311
13      OFFICE SUPPLIES          750      800      850      900    3,300
14      MISCELLANEOUS          1,000    1,030    1,061    1,093    4,184
15                           ---------------------------------------------
16      TOTAL EXPENSES        46,750   47,380   48,214   49,151  191,495
17                           ---------------------------------------------
18   GROSS PROFIT            $13,250  $13,820  $14,210  $14,521  $55,801
19                           =============================================
20
                                                                   CAPS
```

Figure 3-29

Select   Next

until you will hear a beep indicating there are no additional matches. When there are no other matching strings, press ⏎ or Esc to return to the READY mode.

To replace a string, choose **R**eplace and type in the replacement string at the prompt. You may then proceed in the same manner as the Find option.

■STATUS OF A WORKSHEET

Retrieve the BUDGET2 file.

To look at the Status (settings) of the worksheet:

Press   /

Select   Worksheet

Select   Status

Various settings are displayed. The displayed settings indicate available memory as well as the default or global settings for recalculation, format, label prefixes, column widths, and protected cells for the current file (in this example, the BUDGET2 file). Additional information is provided such as whether a math coprocessor is used, how many iterations are used to recalculate the worksheet, whether circular references exist and whether zero suppression is being used. Your screen should look similar to Figure 3-30. The available memory and math coprocessor settings depend upon the system being used.

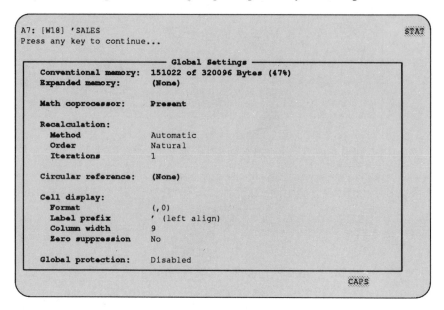

Figure 3-30

To exit from the status screen:

Press   [Esc]

The ↵ key can also be used to exit from the status screen.

■SYSTEM COMMAND

You may exit Lotus 1-2-3 temporarily to issue operating system level commands by using the System command.

To access the System command:

Press   /

Select   System

Lotus is still in memory, but the cursor is blinking at the operating system prompt. At this point, you can issue operating system commands.

To return to Lotus 1-2-3:

Type   EXIT

Your screen should look similar to Figure 3-31.

```
(Type EXIT and press ENTER to return to 1-2-3)


The IBM Personal Computer DOS
Version 3.00 (C)Copyright IBM Corp 1981, 1982, 1983, 1984

C:\123R22>EXIT
```

Figure 3-31

Press   ⏎

The cell pointer will appear in the same worksheet position as it was before you used the System command.

■TITLES

When working on a large spreadsheet and moving the cell pointer to a distant row or column, headings and row labels may "scroll" off the screen. When this happens, it is difficult to see exactly where data is to be input. The following example demonstrates how such a problem may occur, and how to solve the problem by "freezing" titles on the screen.

Retrieve the file BUDGET2 for use in the following exercise:

To move to a "distant" cell location:

Move   the cell pointer to cell H25

(In this example, use the pointer movement keys and **not** the F5 ((GOTO)) key to move to H25).

Note that it is difficult to tell what the numbers represent because neither the column titles nor the labels in column A are displayed on the screen as guides. Your screen should look like Figure 3-32.

```
H25:  (F2)  1.02                                                          READY

         B         C         D         E         F         G         H         I
  6
  7   $60,000   $61,200   $62,424   $63,672   $64,945   $66,244   $67,569   $68,920
  8
  9
 10    35,000    35,500    36,200    37,000    37,000    37,000    37,000    37,000
 11     9,000     9,000     9,000     9,000     9,000     9,000     9,000     9,000
 12     1,000     1,050     1,103     1,158     1,216     1,277     1,341     1,408
 13       750       800       850       900       950     1,000     1,050     1,100
 14     1,000     1,030     1,061     1,093     1,126     1,160     1,195     1,231
 15   -------------------------------------------------------------------------------
 16    46,750    47,380    48,214    49,151    49,292    49,437    49,586    49,739
 17   -------------------------------------------------------------------------------
 18   $13,250   $13,820   $14,210   $14,521   $15,653   $16,807   $17,983   $19,181
 19   ===============================================================================
 20
 21
 22
 23
 24
 25              1.02      1.02      1.02      1.02      1.02      1.02      1.02
                           UNDO                                         CAPS
```

Figure 3-32

To position the cell pointer so that the appropriate headings and descriptive labels are visible on the screen:

Press   Home

Move   the cell pointer to cell B6

Before using the menu to freeze the title, the cell pointer must already be in the correct position as described below:

> The column(s) you wish to keep displayed on the screen must be directly to the left of the cell pointer (in this example, column A will remain on the screen because the cell pointer is in column B).

> The row(s) you desire to keep displayed on the screen must be directly above the cell pointer (in this example, rows 1 through 5 will remain on the screen, because the cell pointer is in row 6).

To access the menu commands to freeze the titles and descriptive labels:

Press   /

Select   Worksheet

Select   Titles

Move   the cell pointer to the Vertical menu option

(Do **NOT** press **V** for Vertical)

The description "Freeze all columns to the left of the cell pointer" under the Vertical option explains how to freeze vertical titles. A similar description is displayed when the Horizontal option is highlighted. See Figure 3-33.

```
B6:                                                                     MENU
Both  Horizontal  Vertical  Clear
Freeze all columns to the left of the cell pointer
          A              B        C        D        E        F        G
1                                                                ABC COMPANY
2                                                                  BUDGET
3
4
5                       YEAR 1   YEAR 2   YEAR 3   YEAR 4   YEAR 5   YEAR 6
6
7   SALES               $60,000  $61,200  $62,424  $63,672  $64,945  $66,244
8
9   EXPENSES
10      SALARIES         35,000   35,500   36,200   37,000   37,000   37,000
11      RENT              9,000    9,000    9,000    9,000    9,000    9,000
12      TELEPHONE         1,000    1,050    1,103    1,158    1,216    1,277
13      OFFICE SUPPLIES     750      800      850      900      950    1,000
14      MISCELLANEOUS     1,000    1,030    1,061    1,093    1,126    1,160
15                      ------------------------------------------------------
16      TOTAL EXPENSES  46,750   47,380   48,214   49,151   49,292   49,437
17                      ------------------------------------------------------
18  GROSS PROFIT        $13,250  $13,820  $14,210  $14,521  $15,653  $16,807
19                      ======================================================
20
                                                                        CAPS
```

Figure 3-33

Select   Both   (for both columns and rows)

Note that you can choose to freeze only the columns or only the rows or both rows and columns as mentioned above.

To see the results of freezing the screen:

Move   the cell pointer to cell H25 (use the ⊕ and ⊕ arrow keys to move to cell H25)

Note that even though the cell pointer has been moved to a "distant" area of the spreadsheet, rows 1 through 5 and column A remain frozen on the screen. By using this option, it is possible to see the column and row descriptions and understand the content of the spreadsheet. For example, H18 contains the contents of GROSS PROFIT for YEAR 7. Your screen should look like Figure 3-34.

```
H25: (F2) 1.02                                                    READY

          A           C       D       E       F       G       H
 1                                                ABC COMPANY
 2                                                  BUDGET
 3
 4
 5                  YEAR 2  YEAR 3  YEAR 4  YEAR 5  YEAR 6  YEAR 7
11    RENT           9,000   9,000   9,000   9,000   9,000   9,000
12    TELEPHONE      1,050   1,103   1,158   1,216   1,277   1,341
13    OFFICE SUPPLIES  800     850     900     950   1,000   1,050
14    MISCELLANEOUS  1,030   1,061   1,093   1,126   1,160   1,195
15                  -------------------------------------------------
16      TOTAL EXPENSES 47,380 48,214 49,151 49,292 49,437 49,586
17                  -------------------------------------------------
18  GROSS PROFIT   $13,820 $14,210 $14,521 $15,653 $16,807 $17,983
19                  =================================================
20
21
22  GROWTH RATE
23  ASSUMPTIONS
24
25  SALES            1.02    1.02    1.02    1.02    1.02    1.02
                     UNDO                                    CAPS
```

Figure 3-34

Press   Home

Note that the cell pointer cannot move to cell A1 since the titles are frozen, but rather moves only to cell B6.

To cancel the title settings:

Press	/
Select	Worksheet
Select	Titles
Select	Clear
Press	Home

Notice the cell pointer is now in cell A1.

■ UNDO

The Undo feature creates a temporary copy of both the data and settings. 1-2-3 makes it possible to restore work to its original condition. The Alt-F4 key operates Undo. It works like a toggle switch and will restore canceled changes.

At times when only a small amount of memory is available, 1-2-3 will display a menu to turn Undo off with three possible choices. These choices are:

    Disable: turns off Undo; completes procedure.

    Proceed: turns off Undo; completes procedure; turns Undo on.

    Quit: quits procedure; saves changes made; Undo stays on.

Using `Ctrl-Break` or `Esc` produces the same results as **Quit**.

The primary purpose of Undo is to save time in having to redo procedures. However, it does not work with all commands. For a complete description of the operations which you cannot UNDO, see the Lotus 1-2-3 Reference Manual.

Note the Undo option is initially enabled when you install Lotus 1-2-3 Release 2.2.

If the Undo feature has been disabled, use these commands to turn it back on:

Press	/
Select	Worksheet
Select	Global
Select	Default
Select	Other
Select	Undo
Select	Enable
Select	Quit

Retrieve the BUDGET file.

Move	cell pointer to B10
Type	50000
Press	↵

The worksheet now appears like Figure 3-35.

```
B10: 50000                                                          READY

           A            B        C        D        E        F        G
  1
  2                              ABC COMPANY
  3                               BUDGET
  4
  5                      QTR1     QTR2     QTR3     QTR4   YR TOTAL
  6
  7   SALES            $60,000  $61,200  $62,424  $63,672 $247,296
  8
  9   EXPENSES
 10     SALARIES        50,000   35,500   36,200   37,000  158,700
 11     RENT             9,000    9,000    9,000    9,000   36,000
 12     TELEPHONE        1,000    1,050    1,103    1,158    4,311
 13     OFFICE SUPPLIES    750      800      850      900    3,300
 14     MISCELLANEOUS    1,000    1,030    1,061    1,093    4,184
 15                     -------------------------------------------
 16      TOTAL EXPENSES 61,750   47,380   48,214   49,151  206,495
 17                     -------------------------------------------
 18   GROSS PROFIT      ($1,750) $13,820  $14,210  $14,521  $40,801
 19                     ===========================================
 20
                          UNDO                              CAPS
```

Figure 3-35

To restore the figure in cell B10 to its original amount:

Press   [Alt-F4]

Your screen should look like Figure 3-36.

```
B10: 35000                                                          READY

           A            B        C        D        E        F        G
  1
  2                              ABC COMPANY
  3                               BUDGET
  4
  5                      QTR1     QTR2     QTR3     QTR4   YR TOTAL
  6
  7   SALES            $60,000  $61,200  $62,424  $63,672 $247,296
  8
  9   EXPENSES
 10     SALARIES        35,000   35,500   36,200   37,000  143,700
 11     RENT             9,000    9,000    9,000    9,000   36,000
 12     TELEPHONE        1,000    1,050    1,103    1,158    4,311
 13     OFFICE SUPPLIES    750      800      850      900    3,300
 14     MISCELLANEOUS    1,000    1,030    1,061    1,093    4,184
 15                     -------------------------------------------
 16      TOTAL EXPENSES 46,750   47,380   48,214   49,151  191,495
 17                     -------------------------------------------
 18   GROSS PROFIT      $13,250  $13,820  $14,210  $14,521  $55,801
 19                     ===========================================
 20
                          UNDO                              CAPS
```

Figure 3-36

Now the figure in cell B10 is restored to its original amount of 35,000.

To disable the Undo feature for the present example:

Press	/
Select	Worksheet
Select	Global
Select	Default
Select	Other
Select	Undo
Select	Disable
Select	Quit

Before proceeding, enable Undo again.

■WIDENING MULTIPLE COLUMNS ON THE WORKSHEET

When you plan on placing data in cells that require more space than allowed by the default, you need to widen the columns. Otherwise, the cells will display asterisks each time the data exceeds the column width. When a cell contains asterisks, the contents of the cell are no longer visible. This situation may occur in several contiguous columns. By using a Worksheet Global command, all of the columns can be widened at one time. However, this global command does not change any columns set with a Column-range command illustrated in this section.

Retrieve the BUDGET file. To widen columns B through E to 11 characters:

Move	the cell pointer to cell B1
Press	/
Select	Worksheet
Select	Column
Select	Column-Range
Select	Set-Width
Move	the cell pointer to cell E1

Press	⏎
Type	11
Press	⏎

Now the columns B through E have widths of 11. Your screen should look like Figure 3-37.

```
B1: [W11]                                                              READY


              A            B           C           D          E         F
1                                   ABC COMPANY
2                                     BUDGET
3
4
5                       QTR1        QTR2        QTR3       QTR4    YR TOTAL
6
7    SALES            $60,000     $61,200     $62,424    $63,672 $247,296
8
9    EXPENSES
10      SALARIES       35,000      35,500      36,200     37,000  143,700
11      RENT            9,000       9,000       9,000      9,000   36,000
12      TELEPHONE       1,000       1,050       1,103      1,158    4,311
13      OFFICE SUPPLIES   750         800         850        900    3,300
14      MISCELLANEOUS   1,000       1,030       1,061      1,093    4,184
15                    ------------------------------------------------------
16      TOTAL EXPENSES 46,750      47,380      48,214     49,151  191,495
17                    ------------------------------------------------------
18   GROSS PROFIT     $13,250     $13,820     $14,210    $14,521  $55,801
19                    ======================================================
20
                         UNDO                                  CAPS
```

Figure 3-37

■WINDOWS

Lotus 1-2-3 allows you to view two different areas of the spreadsheet on the screen at the same time by using the **Windows** command. Retrieve the BUDGET2 file for use in the following exercise.

When creating windows, the cell pointer must be in the desired position before the menus are accessed. To position the cell pointer so that the screen will be divided at column D.

Move	the cell pointer to cell D7

To access the menu commands to create the windows:

Press	/
Select	Worksheet

Select   Window

Select   Vertical

Two windows are visible on the screen. Note that Lotus 1-2-3 allows you to make either horizontal or vertical windows. Your screen should look like Figure 3-38.

```
C7: (C0) @ROUND(B7*C25,0)                                                  READY

                  A           B         C      │    D        E        F        G
                                                1                           ABC COMPANY
   1                                            2                             BUDGET
   2                                            3
   3                                            4
   4                                            5    YEAR 3   YEAR 4   YEAR 5   YEAR 6
   5            YEAR 1      YEAR 2               6
   6                                            7   $62,424  $63,672  $64,945  $66,244
   7   SALES    $60,000    $61,200              8
   8                                            9
   9   EXPENSES                                10   36,200   37,000   37,000   37,000
  10      SALARIES   35,000   35,500           11    9,000    9,000    9,000    9,000
  11      RENT        9,000    9,000           12    1,103    1,158    1,216    1,277
  12      TELEPHONE   1,000    1,050           13      850      900      950    1,000
  13      OFFICE SUPPLIES  750    800          14    1,061    1,093    1,126    1,160
  14      MISCELLANEOUS  1,000  1,030          15  ------------------------------------
  15                  -------------------      16   48,214   49,151   49,292   49,437
  16      TOTAL EXPENSES  46,750   47,380      17  ------------------------------------
  17                  -------------------      18  $14,210  $14,521  $15,653  $16,807
  18   GROSS PROFIT  $13,250   $13,820         19  ====================================
  19                  ===================      20
  20
                        UNDO                                         CAPS
```

Figure 3-38

To move around in the left window:

Move   the cell pointer to cell B7

Notice that the cell pointer can be moved anywhere in the spreadsheet.

To move to the right window:

Press   F6

Move   the cell pointer to cell L7 (YR TOTAL for SALES)

The F6 key is sometimes referred to as the **window** key.

To return to the left window:

Press   F6

Move   the cell pointer to cell B7

Type 65000

Press ⏎

By using windows, you are able to see the effect of changing SALES on another area of the worksheet. In this example, you can see the updated amount for the YR TOTAL of SALES when the value for SALES in YEAR 1 is changed.

Your worksheet should look like Figure 3-39.

```
B7: (C0) 65000                                                           READY


            A           B        C        I        J        K        L
   1                                    1
   2                                    2
   3                                    3
   4                                    4
   5                  YEAR 1   YEAR 2   5   YEAR 8   YEAR 9   YEAR 10 YR TOTAL
   6                                    6
   7   SALES          $65,000  $66,300  7   $74,665  $76,158  $77,681 $711,735
   8                                    8
   9   EXPENSES                         9
  10     SALARIES      35,000   35,500 10    37,000   37,000   37,000 $365,700
  11     RENT           9,000    9,000 11     9,000    9,000    9,000  $90,000
  12     TELEPHONE      1,000    1,050 12     1,408    1,478    1,552  $12,583
  13     OFFICE SUPPLIES  750      800 13     1,100    1,150    1,200   $9,750
  14     MISCELLANEOUS  1,000    1,030 14     1,231    1,268    1,306  $11,470
  15                   ------------------15  ----------------------------------
  16       TOTAL EXPENSES 46,750  47,380 16    49,739   49,896   50,058 $489,503
  17                   ------------------17  ----------------------------------
  18   GROSS PROFIT   $18,250  $18,920 18   $24,926  $26,262  $27,623 $222,232
  19                   ==================19  ==================================
  20                                   20

                        UNDO                              CAPS
```

Figure 3-39

To clear the window setting:

Press /

Select Worksheet

Select Windows

Select Clear

The windows are now deleted from your screen.

■WORKSHEET INSERTIONS AND DELETIONS

Columns and rows can be inserted into a worksheet after the worksheet has been created. They can also be deleted whenever that is necessary.

Inserting and Deleting Columns

To complete this exercise, create the worksheet in Figure 3-40 Part 1 and save the worksheet in a file named BOATSALE.

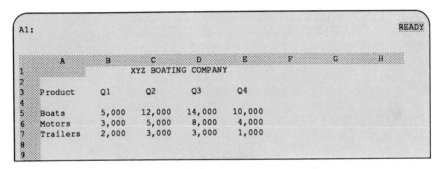

Figure 3-40
Part 1

To insert a column between the columns for Q3 and Q4:

Move	the cell pointer to cell E3
Press	/
Select	Worksheet
Select	Insert
Select	Column
Press	⏎

Your screen should now look like Figure 3-40 Part 2.

```
E3:                                                                    READY

         A         B         C         D         E         F         G         H
1                          XYZ BOATING COMPANY
2
3  Product     Q1        Q2        Q3                  Q4
4
5  Boats       5,000    12,000    14,000              10,000
6  Motors      3,000     5,000     8,000               4,000
7  Trailers    2,000     3,000     3,000               1,000
8
9
```

Figure 3-40
Part 2

To remove column E from the worksheet:

Move	the cell pointer to E3
Press	/
Select	Worksheet
Select	Delete
Select	Column
Press	⏎

Your screen should look like Figure 3-40 Part 3. If you want to delete more than one column, you can highlight the columns to be deleted with the cell pointer whenever they are adjacent to one another.

```
E3: ^Q4                                                                LABEL

         A         B         C         D         E         F         G         H
1                          XYZ BOATING COMPANY
2
3  Product     Q1        Q2        Q3        Q4
4
5  Boats       5,000    12,000    14,000    10,000
6  Motors      3,000     5,000     8,000     4,000
7  Trailers    2,000     3,000     3,000     1,000
8
9
```

Figure 3-40
Part 3

Inserting and Deleting Rows

Retrieve the BOATSALE file if necessary. To insert a blank row in a worksheet:

Move	the cell pointer to cell A3
Press	/
Select	Worksheet
Select	Insert
Select	Row
Press	⏎

Your screen should look like Figure 3-41. If more than one row is to be inserted, move the cell pointer down an additional time for each row. Rows can be deleted in a similar manner by using **delete** instead of **insert**.

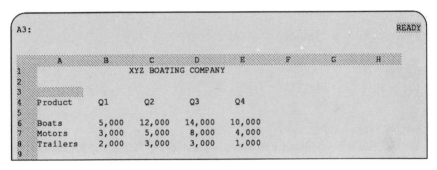

Figure 3-41

■ZERO VALUE SUPPRESSION

The Zero-value Suppression command in Lotus 1-2-3 allows you to eliminate the display of all zeros in a worksheet. This command places a blank in place of a cell entry of zero whether the cell entry consists of the number zero or a cell formula that currently evaluates to zero.

Retrieve the original file BUDGET2 for use in this exercise.

For the purposes of this example, a zero will be placed in YEAR1 of SALES. All of the projections for SALES in the following years are based upon this number and, therefore, will also display zeros.

Move	the cell pointer to cell B7
Type	0

Press ⏎

The row displaying the SALES data now contains zeros. Your screen should look like Figure 3-42.

```
B7: (C0)  0                                                          READY


               A            B        C        D        E        F        G
                                                                 ABC COMPANY
 1                                                                  BUDGET
 2
 3
 4
 5                         YEAR 1   YEAR 2   YEAR 3   YEAR 4   YEAR 5   YEAR 6
 6
 7   SALES                    $0       $0       $0       $0       $0       $0
 8
 9   EXPENSES
10     SALARIES            35,000   35,500   36,200   37,000   37,000   37,000
11     RENT                 9,000    9,000    9,000    9,000    9,000    9,000
12     TELEPHONE            1,000    1,050    1,103    1,158    1,216    1,277
13     OFFICE SUPPLIES        750      800      850      900      950    1,000
14     MISCELLANEOUS        1,000    1,030    1,061    1,093    1,126    1,160
15                        ----------------------------------------------------
16      TOTAL EXPENSES    46,750   47,380   48,214   49,151   49,292   49,437
17                        ----------------------------------------------------
18   GROSS PROFIT       ($46,750) ($47,380) ($48,214) ($49,151) ($49,292) ($49,437)
19                        ====================================================
20

                            UNDO                               CAPS
```

Figure 3-42

The **W**orksheet **G**lobal **Z**ero menu option allows you to suppress zeros from your screen. To suppress the zeros:

Press	/
Select	Worksheet
Select	Global
Select	Zero
Select	Y (for Yes)
Move	the cell pointer to cell C7

The zeros are now suppressed. Notice that even though the zero value is suppressed, the formula for cell C7 still appears in the control panel. Your screen should look like Figure 3-43.

```
C7: (C0) @ROUND(B7*C25,0)                                              READY

              A          B        C        D        E        F        G
                                                                 ABC COMPANY
 1                                                                 BUDGET
 2
 3
 4
 5                     YEAR 1   YEAR 2   YEAR 3   YEAR 4   YEAR 5   YEAR 6
 6
 7   SALES
 8
 9   EXPENSES
10      SALARIES       35,000   35,500   36,200   37,000   37,000   37,000
11      RENT            9,000    9,000    9,000    9,000    9,000    9,000
12      TELEPHONE       1,000    1,050    1,103    1,158    1,216    1,277
13      OFFICE SUPPLIES   750      800      850      900      950    1,000
14      MISCELLANEOUS   1,000    1,030    1,061    1,093    1,126    1,160
15                    ---------------------------------------------------------
16      TOTAL EXPENSES 46,750   47,380   48,214   49,151   49,292   49,437
17                    ---------------------------------------------------------
18   GROSS PROFIT     ($46,750) ($47,380) ($48,214) ($49,151) ($49,292) ($49,437)
19                    =========================================================
20
                          UNDO
```

Figure 3-43

To allow the zeros to be visible on the screen again:

Press	/
Select	Worksheet
Select	Global
Select	Zero
Select	No

The zeros should now be visible again. Your screen should look like Figure 3-44.

```
C7: (C0) @ROUND(B7*C25,0)                                           READY

           A            B         C         D         E         F         G
 1                                                               ABC COMPANY
 2                                                                 BUDGET
 3
 4
 5                    YEAR 1    YEAR 2    YEAR 3    YEAR 4    YEAR 5    YEAR 6
 6
 7  SALES               $0        $0        $0        $0        $0        $0
 8
 9  EXPENSES
10    SALARIES        35,000    35,500    36,200    37,000    37,000    37,000
11    RENT             9,000     9,000     9,000     9,000     9,000     9,000
12    TELEPHONE        1,000     1,050     1,103     1,158     1,216     1,277
13    OFFICE SUPPLIES    750       800       850       900       950     1,000
14    MISCELLANEOUS    1,000     1,030     1,061     1,093     1,126     1,160
15                   -------------------------------------------------------
16    TOTAL EXPENSES  46,750    47,380    48,214    49,151    49,292    49,437
17                   -------------------------------------------------------
18  GROSS PROFIT     ($46,750) ($47,380) ($48,214) ($49,151) ($49,292) ($49,437)
19                   =======================================================
20

                        UNDO
```

Figure 3-44

SUMMARY

Lotus 1-2-3 has various menu options and features that allow you to control how data is entered and viewed. These 1-2-3 commands allow you to work more effectively and efficiently when you are creating, editing or analyzing spreadsheets.

KEY CONCEPTS

Absolute cell reference
Borders
Cell protection
Error correction
File Directory
File Erase
File List
File Save Backup
File Admin Table
Footers
Headers
Hiding Columns
Label Prefix
Move
Page Break
Range Erase
Range Format Percent
Range Name
Range Name Table
Recalculation

Relative cell reference
Search and Replace
Status
System
Undo
Windows
Widening Multiple Columns
Worksheet Column Hide
Worksheet Delete Column
Worksheet Delete Row
Worksheet Global Recalculation Manual
Worksheet Global Zero
Worksheet Insert Column
Worksheet Insert Row
Worksheet Page
Worksheet Status
Worksheet Titles
Worksheet Window
Zero value suppression

CHAPTER THREE
EXERCISE 1

INSTRUCTIONS: Circle T if the statement is true and F if the statement is false.

T   F   1. An absolute cell reference means that the reference is kept constant, even when copied.

T   F   2. The F2 key allows you to correct a cell entry without having to retype the entire entry.

T   F   3. Worksheet **Titles** allows you to center titles on a spreadsheet.

T   F   4. Worksheet **Window** allows you to view two different areas of a spreadsheet at the same time.

T   F   5. Worksheet **Page** creates a page break in a spreadsheet.

T   F   6. If column D is hidden on a worksheet using Worksheet **Column Hide**, column D will not appear if the worksheet is printed.

T   F   7. Worksheet **Global Recalculation Manual** is activated so that data can be entered without the worksheet recalculating after each new entry.

T   F   8. Changing the **File Directory** changes the drive designation or path to which 1-2-3 saves and retrieves files.

T   F   9. File **Erase** erases a file from memory.

T   F   10. The **System** command permanently returns you to the operating system command.

T   F   11. Only one cell at a time can be erased.

T   F   12. The width for multiple contiguous columns can be changed to the same width at the same time.

CHAPTER THREE
EXERCISE 2

INSTRUCTIONS: Explain a typical situation when the following keystrokes or
Lotus 1-2-3 commands are used.

Problem   1:   F4

Problem   2:   / **Range Format Percent**

Problem   3:   / **Worksheet Titles**

Problem   4:   / **Worksheet Windows**

Problem   5:   F6

Problem   6:   / **Worksheet Insert Row**

Problem   7:   / **Worksheet Delete Column**

Problem   8:   / **Worksheet Column Hide**

Problem   9:   / **Worksheet Page**

Problem 10:   / **Worksheet Global Recalculation Manual**

Problem 11:   F9

Problem 12:   / **Worksheet Global Zero**

Problem 13:   / **Range Erase**

Problem 14:   / **File List**

Problem 15:   / **File Erase**

Problem 16:   / **File Directory**

Problem 17:   / **System**

Problem 18:   F2

Problem 19:   Ins in EDIT mode

Problem 20:   / **Worksheet Column Column-Range Set-Width**

Problem 21:   / **Worksheet Global Default Other Undo Enable**

CHAPTER THREE
EXERCISE 3
Making a Cell Entry Absolute

INSTRUCTIONS: The following example illustrates a common error. Follow the instructions below to create the error and solve the problem.

Clear the screen.

In cell A1, type REVENUE and press ⏎.
In cell A2, type ASSUMED REV RATE and press ⏎.
Widen column A to 16 characters.

In cell B1, type 10000 and press ⏎.
In cell B2, type .15 and press ⏎.
In cell C1, type +B1*(1+B2) and press ⏎.

Copy the formula in cell C1 to cells D1 and E1.

The screen should look like Figure 3-45.

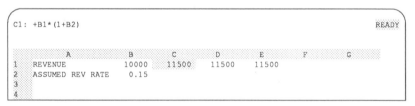

```
C1: +B1*(1+B2)                                                    READY

            A           B        C         D         E        F        G
1   REVENUE           10000    11500     11500     11500
2   ASSUMED REV RATE   0.15
3
4
```

Figure 3-45

Change the formula in cell C1 and recopy it so that the formulas in cells D1 and E1 also refer to cell B2 for the projected revenue rate.

Print the worksheet.

CHAPTER THREE
EXERCISE 4
Protecting Cells in a Worksheet

INSTRUCTIONS: Retrieve the file PRACTICE you created as an exercise in Chapter 2.

Protect all cells in the worksheet.

Try to change the value of any cell on the worksheet. What happens?

Unprotect the cells containing the revenue growth rates.

Change the revenue growth rates to 8%, 5%, 10% and 7% respectively for Year 2 through Year 5.

Print the worksheet after changing the growth rates.

CHAPTER THREE
EXERCISE 5
Erasing Cells

INSTRUCTIONS: Retrieve the file PRACTICE.

Erase the title line "PROJECTED PROFITS."

Print the worksheet after you erase the title line.

CHAPTER THREE
EXERCISE 6
Hiding and Displaying a Column

INSTRUCTIONS: Retrieve the file BUDGET that was created in Chapter 2.

Hide columns B and F.

Print the worksheet.

Display columns B and F on the screen.

Print the worksheet.

CHAPTER THREE
EXERCISE 7
Label Prefixes

INSTRUCTIONS: Clear your screen.

Enter the value 123 in cell B1.
Enter 123 as a label and left-justify the characters in cell B3.

Right-justify the characters ABC in cell B5.
Repeat the characters XYZ in cell B7.

Center the characters ABC in cell B9.

Print the worksheet.

CHAPTER THREE
EXERCISE 8
Entering Page Breaks in a Spreadsheet

INSTRUCTIONS: Retrieve the file BUDGET that was created in Chapter 2.

Create a page break after the subtotal line for TOTAL EXPENSES.

Print the spreadsheet.

CHAPTER THREE
EXERCISE 9
Printing Headers and Footers

INSTRUCTIONS: Retrieve the file SALES.

Create the following Header and Footer:

Header:

SALES RESULTS

Footer:

ANNUAL SALES—CURRENT YEAR

Center the Header and Footer. Include the current date to the right of the text information of the Footer.

Print the worksheet.

CHAPTER THREE
EXERCISE 10
Range Names

INSTRUCTIONS: Retrieve the file BUDGET2 that was created as an exercise in Chapter 2.

Create the range name SALES and include the cells containing the SALES amounts for the 10 years as its range.

Create the range name TOTAL_EXPENSES and include the cells containing the TOTAL EXPENSES values for the 10 years as its range.

Create the range name GROSS_PROFIT and include the cells containing the GROSS PROFIT amounts for the 10 years as its range.

Place a table of the range names beginning in cell A38 at the bottom of the worksheet and print the table containing the range names and cells contained in the named ranges.

Print the worksheet.

CHAPTER THREE
EXERCISE 11
Search and Replace

INSTRUCTIONS: Retrieve the file BUDGET.

Use the **S**earch and **R**eplace command to change the name ABC COMPANY to ABC, INC.

Change the word SALES to REVENUES using the **S**earch and **R**eplace command.

Print the worksheet.

CHAPTER THREE
EXERCISE 12
Widening Multiple Columns in One Worksheet

INSTRUCTIONS: Retrieve the file BUDGET.

Change the column width of columns B through E to 11 using the multiple column width option.

Print the worksheet.

CHAPTER THREE
EXERCISE 13
Inserting and Deleting Rows and Columns

INSTRUCTIONS: Retrieve the file SALES.

Insert a column at column C.

Insert two rows at row 12.

Print the worksheet.

Delete the column you inserted.

Delete the rows you inserted.

Print the worksheet.

CHAPTER THREE
EXERCISE 14
Suppressing Zero Values

INSTRUCTIONS: Retrieve the file PRACTICE.

Enter the value 0 for the revenue value in Year 1.

Suppress the zero values in the worksheet so that no zeros appear.

Print the worksheet.

CHAPTER FOUR

CREATING AND PRINTING GRAPHS

OBJECTIVES:

In this chapter, you will learn to:

- Create a Graph
- Create Various Types of Graphs
- Print a Graph
- Use Additional Graph Commands

■CHAPTER OVERVIEW

If a spreadsheet contains a large amount of data, it can be very difficult to detect trends and see relationships among various numbers. A graph depicting key elements of a spreadsheet can facilitate a more accurate analysis. Graphs can be easily created in Lotus 1-2-3 by using data that is entered on a spreadsheet. The graphic image can be viewed on the screen and may also be printed.

■CREATING A GRAPH

The first graph that will be created in this chapter is based upon data in the BUDGET worksheet that was created in Chapter 2. Retrieve the file BUDGET:

Press	/
Select	File
Select	Retrieve

When prompted for the file name:

Press	F3
Select	BUDGET
Press	←

The file BUDGET should now be visible on your screen (Figure 4-1).

```
A1: [W18]                                                              READY


         A              B        C        D        E        F        G
1                                 ABC COMPANY
2                                   BUDGET
3
4
5                      QTR1     QTR2     QTR3     QTR4    YR TOTAL
6
7  SALES              $60,000  $61,200  $62,424  $63,672 $247,296
8
9  EXPENSES
10    SALARIES         35,000   35,500   36,200   37,000  143,700
11    RENT              9,000    9,000    9,000    9,000   36,000
12    TELEPHONE         1,000    1,050    1,103    1,158    4,311
13    OFFICE SUPPLIES     750      800      850      900    3,300
14    MISCELLANEOUS     1,000    1,030    1,061    1,093    4,184
15                     -------------------------------------------
16      TOTAL EXPENSES 46,750   47,380   48,214   49,151  191,495
17                     -------------------------------------------
18 GROSS PROFIT       $13,250  $13,820  $14,210  $14,521  $55,801
19                     ===========================================
20
                         UNDO
```

Figure 4-1

You will first create a bar graph. The bars will represent the SALES, TOTAL EXPENSES and GROSS PROFIT variables for the four quarters in BUDGET. When the graph is completed, it will look like Figure 4-2.

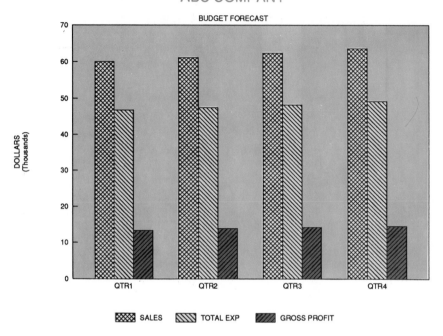

Figure 4-2

Specifying the Type of Graph

To specify the type of graph to create:

Press   /

Select   Graph

Select   Type

Select   Bar

The main graph menu appears again. The other types of graphs available are illustrated in exercises later in this chapter.

Specifying the X-axis and Data Ranges

To specify the labels that will be on the X-axis:

Select   X

When prompted for the X-axis range:

Move	the cell pointer to cell B5
Type	.
Move	the cell pointer to cell E5
Press	⏎

Do not include YR TOTAL label. If this label were accidentally highlighted, choose X again from the menu to reset the range. Press the [Esc] key to cancel the previous setting. Cells B5 through E5 contain the labels QTR1 through QTR4. QTR1 through QTR4 are the labels that will be used for the X-axis of the graph. See Figure 4-3, Part 1.

To indicate the data to display, use the menu options A through F. In this exercise, you use variables A through C to specify the data for SALES, TOTAL EXPENSES and GROSS PROFIT. To specify the first data range:

Select	A

When prompted to enter the first data range:

Move	the cell pointer to cell B7
Type	.
Move	the cell pointer to cell E7
Press	⏎

Cells B7 through E7 contain the data for SALES. The data for SALES for all four quarters will be the first data range displayed on the graph. See Figure 4-3 Part 2.

To specify the second data range:

Select	B

When prompted to enter the second data range:

Move	the cell pointer to cell B16
Type	.
Move	the cell pointer to cell E16

Press   ⏎

Cells B16 through E16 contain the data for TOTAL EXPENSES. The data for TOTAL EXPENSES will be the second data range displayed on the graph.

To specify the third data range:

Select   C

When prompted to enter the third data range:

Move   the cell pointer to cell B18

Type   .

Move   the cell pointer to cell E18

Press   ⏎

The data for GROSS PROFIT for all four quarters will be the third data range displayed on the graph.

Viewing the Graph

To view the graph:

Select   View

The graph should look similar to Figure 4-3 Part 3. If you are using a color monitor, you may see solid colors rather than hatching patterns. If the screen does not display a graph, it may be because the computer being used does not have a graphics card. If this is the case, a graph cannot be seen on the screen, but it can still be created and printed.

The X range highlights the data used for the X-axis labels in bar graphs.

```
E5: ^QTR4                                                    POINT
Enter x-axis range: B5..E5

         A            B       C       D       E       F       G
1                             ABC COMPANY
2                               BUDGET
3
4
5                     QTR1    QTR2    QTR3    QTR4   YR TOTAL
6
7    SALES            $60,000 $61,200 $62,424 $63,672 $247,296
8
9    EXPENSES
10     SALARIES       35,000  35,500  36,200  37,000  143,700
11     RENT            9,000   9,000   9,000   9,000   36,000
12     TELEPHONE       1,000   1,050   1,103   1,158    4,311
13     OFFICE SUPPLIES   750     800     850     900    3,300
14     MISCELLANEOUS   1,000   1,030   1,061   1,093    4,184
15                    -------------------------------------------
16     TOTAL EXPENSES 46,750  47,380  48,214  49,151  191,495
17
18   GROSS PROFIT     $13,250 $13,820 $14,210 $14,521  $55,801
19                    ===========================================
20
                                                        CAPS
```

Figure 4-3
Part 1

The A range highlights the data used for the first data range in the graph.

```
E7: (C0) @ROUND(D7*E25,0)                                    POINT
Enter first data range: B7..E7

         A            B       C       D       E       F       G
1                             ABC COMPANY
2                               BUDGET
3
4
5                     QTR1    QTR2    QTR3    QTR4   YR TOTAL
6
7    SALES            $60,000 $61,200 $62,424 $63,672 $247,296
8
9    EXPENSES
10     SALARIES       35,000  35,500  36,200  37,000  143,700
11     RENT            9,000   9,000   9,000   9,000   36,000
12     TELEPHONE       1,000   1,050   1,103   1,158    4,311
13     OFFICE SUPPLIES   750     800     850     900    3,300
14     MISCELLANEOUS   1,000   1,030   1,061   1,093    4,184
15                    -------------------------------------------
16     TOTAL EXPENSES 46,750  47,380  48,214  49,151  191,495
17
18   GROSS PROFIT     $13,250 $13,820 $14,210 $14,521  $55,801
19                    ===========================================
20
```

Figure 4-3
Part 2

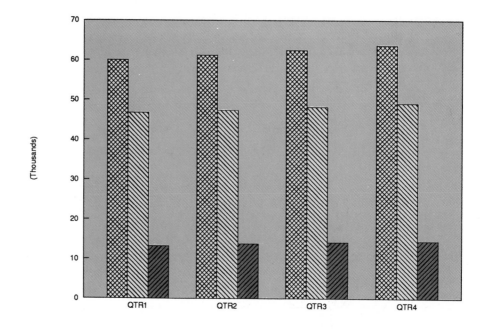

Figure 4-3
Part 3

To return to the graph menu after viewing the graph:

Press   the ⏎ key or the (Esc) key

Actually, any key on the keyboard can be used.

The basic settings for the graph have been specified. Now you will add the titles, legends and other features necessary to complete the graph.

If you are using a color monitor, you can display the graph in color. To display a color graph:

Select   Options

Select   Color

Select   Quit

To view the color graph:

Select   View

The graph is displayed in solid color bars. If the monitor is not a color monitor, the graph may be displayed as solid bars in varying shades of the monitor's primary color (e.g., green or amber). Note that the color graph is not an appropriate setting if the graph is to be printed on a one-color printer because all bars will appear in just one color. The colors on the screen are *not* indicative of the color the graph will be when it is printed with a color printer or plotter. The colors on the printed graph depend upon the *printer's* available ink or pen colors.

To return to the graph menu after viewing the color graph:

Press   ↵

To set the graph to print on a printer with only black ink (i.e., not a color plotter):

Select   Options

Select   B&W (Black and White)

Select   Quit

If the graph remained set as a color graph, a printer with only a black ribbon would have printed out a graph with solid black bars. The B&W setting sets cross-hatch patterns to distinguish the bars from each other. If you want to continue using the color option as you complete this chapter, repeat the Graph Options Color command sequence.

Entering the Titles for the Graph

Using the main graph menu, enter the first title:

Select   Options

Select   Titles

Select   First

When prompted to enter the top line of the graph title:

Type   ABC COMPANY

Press   ↵

To enter the second title:

Select   Titles

Select   Second

When prompted to enter the second line of the graph title:

Type   BUDGET FORECAST

Press   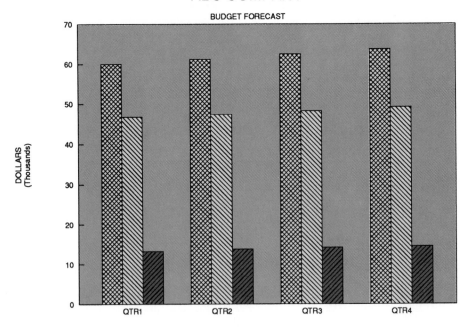⏎

To enter a title for the Y-axis:

Select   Titles

Select   Y-Axis

When prompted to enter the Y-axis title:

Type   DOLLARS

Press   ⏎

Select   Quit

To view the graph with titles on it:

Select   View

The graph should look like Figure 4-4.

ABC COMPANY

BUDGET FORECAST

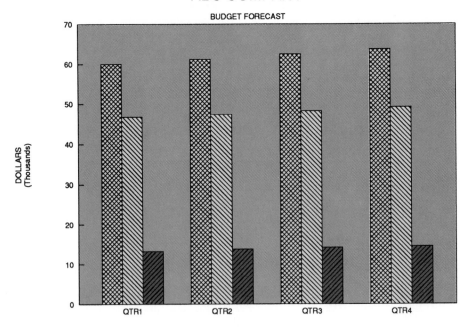

Figure 4-4

To return to the graph menu after viewing the graph:

Press   ⏎

Specifying the Legends

To enter the legend for the first data range (highlighted as data range A earlier in this exercise):

Select   Options

Select   Legend

Select   A

When prompted to enter the legend for data range A:

Type   SALES

Press   ⏎

To enter the legend for the second data range (placed in data range B earlier in this exercise):

Select   Legend

Select   B

When prompted for the legend for data range B:

Type   TOTAL EXP

Press   ⏎

To enter the legend for the third data range (placed in data range C earlier in this exercise):

Select   Legend

Type   C

When prompted for the legend for data range C:

Type   GROSS PROFIT

Press   ⏎

To view the graph with titles and legends:

Select   Quit

Select   View

The screen should look like Figure 4-5.

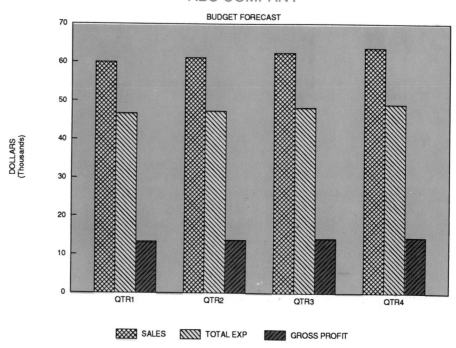

Figure 4-5

To return to the graph menu:

Press   ⏎

Naming and Saving the Graph

To name the graph:

Select   Name

Select   Create

When prompted for the graph name:

Type   BUDBAR

Press   ⏎

Naming a graph in a worksheet is especially important if more than one graph will be created from the data in a worksheet. When a particular graph setting is needed, **the** Graph Name Use command sequence displays all graph names so that the desired graph can be selected and viewed.

To save the graph as a file on the disk:

Select   Save

When prompted for the graph file name:

Type   BUDBAR

Press   ⏎

A file entitled BUDBAR is now saved. This file contains only a *picture* of the graph that can be used to print the graph. The file BUDBAR does not end with the extension .WK1 because it is not a worksheet file. BUDBAR is listed on the disk as BUDBAR.PIC (it is possible to see the file listing for graph files using the **File List Graph** command sequence).

The **Graph Name Create** command assigned the name BUDBAR to the graph settings *in the worksheet*. The file BUDBAR created with the Save command in the Graph menu is a separate file containing only the picture of the graph, *not* the graph settings. The graph settings are a part of the worksheet BUDGET. The settings sheet and the .PIC file do not have to have the same name. If BUDBAR.PIC does not print the desired graph, you must retrieve the worksheet file BUDGET and correct the settings sheet; if the settings sheet has the same name as the graph file, it will be easier to find and edit. The file BUDBAR.PIC would have to be saved again and replaced so that it would show the changes made the next time it was printed. Refer to Figure 4-6 Parts 1 and 2.

Graph Name Create assigns a name to the graph settings for a graph. (File Save will permanently save the graph settings as a part of the worksheet file.)

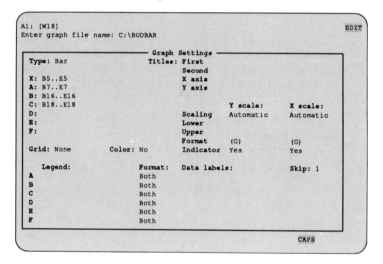

```
A1: [W18]                                                              EDIT
Enter graph name: BUDBAR

                          ─────── Graph Settings ───────
  Type: Bar                 Titles: First
                                    Second
  X: B5..E5                         X axis
  A: B7..E7                         Y axis
  B: B16..E16
  C: B18..E18                                 Y scale:      X scale:
  D:                                Scaling   Automatic     Automatic
  E:                                Lower
  F:                                Upper
                                    Format      (G)           (G)
  Grid: None      Color: No         Indicator   Yes           Yes

    Legend:               Format:   Data labels:            Skip: 1
  A                       Both
  B                       Both
  C                       Both
  D                       Both
  E                       Both
  F                       Both


                                                             CAPS
```

Figure 4-6
Part 1

Graph Save saves the graph in a .PIC file for later printing.

```
A1: [W18]                                                              EDIT
Enter graph file name: C:\BUDBAR

                          ─────── Graph Settings ───────
  Type: Bar                 Titles: First
                                    Second
  X: B5..E5                         X axis
  A: B7..E7                         Y axis
  B: B16..E16
  C: B18..E18                                 Y scale:      X scale:
  D:                                Scaling   Automatic     Automatic
  E:                                Lower
  F:                                Upper
                                    Format      (G)           (G)
  Grid: None      Color: No         Indicator   Yes           Yes

    Legend:               Format:   Data labels:            Skip: 1
  A                       Both
  B                       Both
  C                       Both
  D                       Both
  E                       Both
  F                       Both


                                                             CAPS
```

Figure 4-6
Part 2

The settings used to make the graph should be saved with the worksheet file BUDGET.WK1 in the event that changes will be made later. For this reason, the next step is to save and replace the BUDGET.WK1 file so that the file will include the graph settings.

To exit the graph menu:

Select   Quit

To save the graph settings with the worksheet BUDGET:

Press   /

Select   File

Select   Save

When prompted for the file name:

Press   ⏎

In response to the prompt to either Cancel the command, Replace the file or create a Backup file:

Select   Replace

The graph specifications and name are now saved on the BUDGET worksheet file.

■CREATING VARIOUS TYPES OF GRAPHS

In the previous exercise, a bar graph was created. Lotus 1-2-3 has four other types of graphs that can be created: Line, XY, Stacked-Bar and Pie graphs. The BUDGET worksheet is used to create some of the graphs.

To retrieve the BUDGET worksheet:

Press   /

Select   File

Select   Retrieve

When prompted for the file name:

Move   the cell pointer to the word BUDGET

Press

Creating a Bar Graph

The directions for creating the bar graph were covered in the previous section entitled "Creating a Graph" so they will not be duplicated here.

Creating a Line Graph

The graph settings saved on file BUDGET contain the graph data range specifications for SALES, TOTAL EXPENSES, and GROSS PROFIT. Because the graph settings are already designated, they can be used to redisplay the same data as a line graph. Only the graph type has to be changed. The newly designated graph can then be given a graph name.

To create a line graph:

Press   /

Select   Graph

Select   Type

Select   Line

To view the graph:

Select   View

The lines on the screen appear more jagged than they will when printed. Your screen should look similar to Figure 4-7.

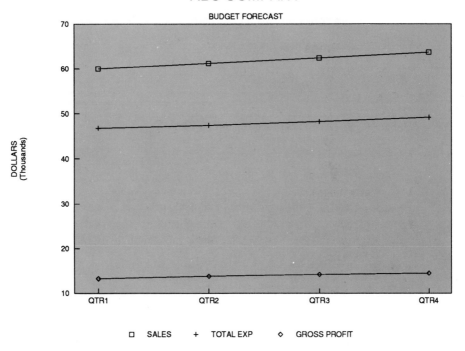

Figure 4-7

To return to the graph menu:

Press ⏎

Notice that since the graph settings were set in an earlier exercise, specifications such as data ranges, titles and legends do not have to be set again.

To name the graph:

Select Name

Select Create

When prompted for the graph name:

Type BUDLINE

Press ⏎

To save the graph image in a file:

Select   Save

When prompted for the graph file name:

Type   BUDLINE

Press   ⏎

The graph has now been saved to a graph file.

To leave the graph menu:

Select   Quit

To save the line graph specifications with the worksheet BUDGET:

Press   /

Select   File

Select   Save

The word BUDGET should appear. To replace the current version of BUDGET:

Press   ⏎

When prompted to either Cancel, Replace or Backup:

Select   Replace

The graph specifications and name for the line graph are now saved on the BUDGET worksheet file.

Creating a Stacked-Bar Graph

The BUDGET worksheet is again used in this exercise. The graph settings for the graph named BUDBAR saved on file BUDGET contain the graph range specifications for SALES, TOTAL EXPENSES and GROSS PROFIT. Because the graph settings are already set, they can be used to redisplay the same data as a stacked-bar graph. Only the graph type has to be changed. The newly designated graph will be given a graph name.

To use the BUDBAR graph, first retrieve file BUDGET and then:

Press   /

Select   Graph

Select   Name

Select	Use
Select	BUDBAR
Press	⏎

To create a stacked-bar graph:

Select	Type
Select	Stack-Bar

To view the graph:

Select	View

Your screen should look like Figure 4-8.

The data options and legends need to be altered so that the stacked-bar graph more accurately depicts the data on the worksheet.

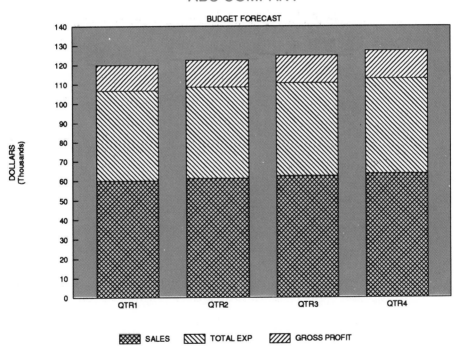

Figure 4-8

To return to the graph menu:

Press   ⏎

The graph settings were completed in an earlier exercise; therefore, specifications such as data ranges, titles and legends are already set. The settings are not appropriate, however, for a stacked-bar graph. The data options and legends need to be altered so the stacked-bar graph more accurately depicts the data on the BUDGET worksheet.

To reset data ranges:

Select   Reset

When prompted for the ranges to reset:

Select   A

Select   C

To leave the Reset menu:

Select   Quit

To reset range A:

Select   A

When prompted for the first data range:

Move   the cell pointer to cell B18

Type   .

Move   the cell pointer to cell E18

Press   ⏎

Variable A now contains the data for GROSS PROFIT.

Before the changes were made, data ranges A, B and C represented SALES, TOTAL EXPENSES and GROSS PROFIT respectively. The three data ranges added together were not appropriate on a stacked-bar graph. The data was rearranged as follows: data range A was changed to the data for GROSS PROFIT; data range B was left as TOTAL EXPENSES; data range C was cancelled. In this way the stacked-bar stacks ranges A and B (GROSS PROFIT and TOTAL EXPENSES) which add up to total SALES.

To change the legends:

Select	Options
Select	Legend
Select	A

The current legend is SALES. To replace the legend for range A:

Press	(Esc)
Type	GROSS PROFIT
Press	(←)

To reset the legend for range C:

Select	Legend
Select	C
Press	the (Esc) key
Press	(←)

The (Esc) key was pressed to cancel the legend for the C range.

To return to the main graph menu:

Select	Quit

To view the graph:

Select	View

Note that the data ranges are now appropriate. Data range A (GROSS PROFIT) and data range B (TOTAL EXPENSES) are stacked and result in a pictorial addition and representation of SALES. A third data range is not needed. Refer to Figure 4-9.

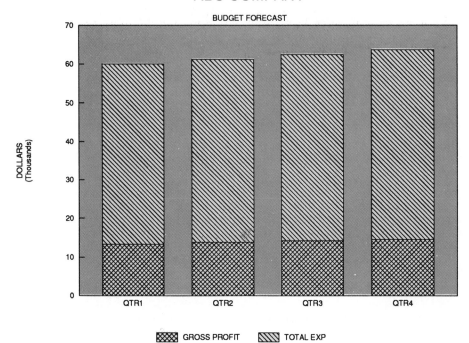

Figure 4-9

When you are through viewing the graph:

       Press   ⏎

To name the graph:

       Select   Name

       Select   Create

When prompted for the graph name:

       Type   BUDSTBAR

       Press   ⏎

To save the graph:

       Select   Save

When prompted for the graph file name:

Type   BUDSTBAR

Press

The graph has now been saved on a graph file.

To leave the graph menu:

Select   Quit

To save the stacked-bar graph specifications with the worksheet BUDGET:

Press   /

Select   File

Select   Save

The word BUDGET should appear. To replace the current version of BUDGET:

Press

When prompted to either Cancel, **R**eplace or **B**ackup:

Select   Replace

The graph specifications and name for the stacked-bar graph are now saved on the BUDGET worksheet file.

Creating a Pie Graph

The BUDGET worksheet is used in this exercise. You will create a pie graph, name the pie graph and save it for later use.

Before creating the pie graph, you need to reset all of the previously defined graph data and option ranges.

Press   /

Select   Graph

Select   Reset

To reset all previously defined graph settings:

| **Select** | Graph |

You will create a pie graph to show the breakdown of some of the expense items for QTR1.

To create the pie graph:

| **Select** | Type |
| **Select** | Pie |

To specify the labels for the pie segments:

Select	X
Move	the cell pointer to cell A10
Type	.
Move	the cell pointer to cell A12
Press	⏎

To indicate the QTR1 expense data to graph:

Select	A
Move	the cell pointer to cell B10
Type	.
Move	the cell pointer to cell B12
Press	⏎

To add titles to the graph:

Select	Options
Select	Titles
Select	First
Type	ABC COMPANY
Press	⏎
Select	Titles
Select	Second

Type	PARTIAL EXPENSE ANALYSIS
Press	⏎

To view the graph:

Select	Quit
Select	View

Your screen should look like Figure 4-10.

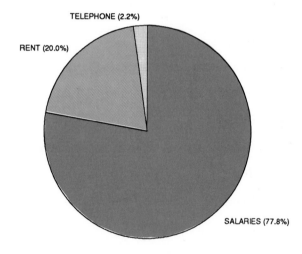

ABC COMPANY

PARTIAL EXPENSE ANALYSIS

Figure 4-10

When you are through viewing the graph:

Press	⏎

To name the graph:

> **Select**   Name
>
> **Select**   Create

When prompted for the graph name:

> **Type**   BUDPIE
>
> **Press**   ⏎

To save the graph:

> **Select**   Save

When prompted for the graph file name:

> **Type**   BUDPIE
>
> **Press**   ⏎

The graph has now been saved on a graph file.

To leave the graph menu:

> **Select**   Quit

To save the pie graph specifications with the worksheet BUDGET:

> **Press**   /
>
> **Select**   File
>
> **Select**   Save

The word BUDGET should now appear. To replace the current version of BUDGET:

> **Press**   ⏎

When prompted to either Cancel, Replace or Backup:

> **Select**   Replace

The graph specifications and name for the pie graph are now saved on the BUDGET worksheet file.

Creating an XY Graph

XY graphs are basically line graphs that use numeric values for both the X-axis and the Y-axis. Retrieve the file UNITPROD (Unit Production) for use in this exercise. The file UNITPROD was created in an exercise you completed in Chapter 2. Since the file has no graph settings, you will need to create all of the graph settings.

To designate the graph type:

Press	/
Select	Graph
Select	Type

When prompted for the graph type:

Select	XY

This graph will represent the number of UNITS PRODUCED on the X-axis and the number of UNITS SOLD on the Y-axis.

To designate the data for the X-axis:

Select	X

When prompted for the X-axis range:

Move	the cell pointer to cell C7
Type	.
Move	the cell pointer to cell C12
Press	⏎

To designate the data for the Y-axis:

Select	A

When prompted to enter the A range:

Move	the cell pointer to cell D7
Type	.
Move	the cell pointer to cell D12

Press   ⏎

A menu option that would clarify the data points is Data-Labels, which you can use to place data labels to the left of each data point:

Select	Options
Select	Data-Labels
Select	A
Move	the cell pointer to cell B7
Type	.
Move	the cell pointer to cell B12
Press	⏎
Select	Left

To exit the current menu:

Select	Quit

To enter the first title:

Select	Titles
Select	First

When prompted to enter the top line of the graph title:

Type	ABC COMPANY
Press	⏎

To enter an X-Axis title:

Select	Titles
Select	X-Axis

When prompted for the title:

Type	UNITS PRODUCED
Press	⏎

To enter a Y-Axis title:

Select	Titles

> **Select**   Y-Axis

When prompted for the title:

> **Type**   UNITS SOLD
>
> **Press**

To exit the current menu:

> **Select**   Quit

To view the graph:

> **Select**   View

The graph should look like Figure 4-11. Note that the graph on the screen and the printed graph may look slightly different since the scale on the printout may vary from the scale on the screen display. For example, the screen's Y-axis scale is in increments of 100 (300...400...800) while the printout's X-axis scale is in increments of 50 (350...400...800). The X-axis also has different increments in the screen display and the printed display.

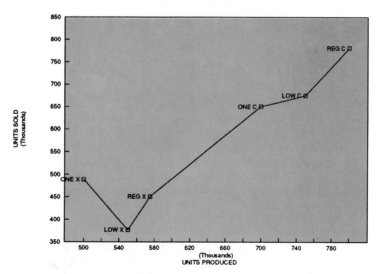

Figure 4-11

To return to the graph menu after viewing the graph:

Press ⏎

To exit the current menu:

Select Quit

You do not need to save the graph settings.

■ GROUP GRAPHING

In the previous section, you created graphs by specifying the type of graph and the individual data ranges to include on the graph.

Another way to quickly create a graph is through the Graph Group command sequence. If you use this option, the data ranges X and A through F are specified simultaneously. The X and A through F ranges must be in consecutive rows or columns in a range. When you finish this section, a graph like the one in Figure 4-13 will be displayed on your screen.

Before creating the graph, prepare the worksheet in Figure 4-12 and save it using the file name AUTOMATI.

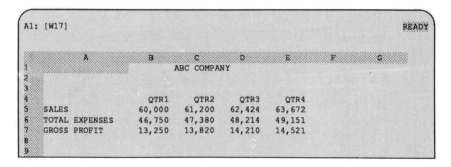

Figure 4-12

Selecting Graph Data Ranges

To create a graph using the group graphing option:

Press /

Select Graph

Select Group

To enter the group range of cells:

Move   the cell pointer to cell B4

Type   .

Move   the cell pointer to cell E7

Press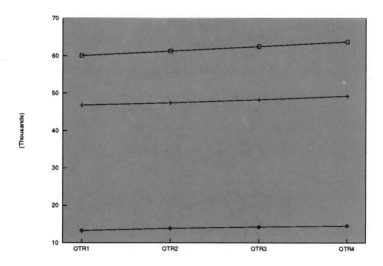

To specify that rows are to be used as the data ranges:

Select   Rowwise

You have indicated that the X data range consists of cells B4 through E4 (QTR1 through QTR4). You have also specified that the A, B and C data ranges include the data for SALES, TOTAL EXPENSES and GROSS PROFIT respectively.

To view the graph you have created:

Select   View

Your screen should look like Figure 4-13.

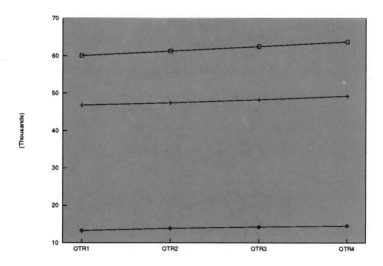

Figure 4-13

To return to the graph menu:

Press ⏎

Notice that since you did not indicate the type of graph to draw, 1-2-3 defaults to the line graph option.

Selecting a Group of Graph Legends

To indicate the legends in one step:

Select	Options
Select	Legend
Select	Range
Move	the cell pointer to cell A5
Type	.
Move	the cell pointer to cell A7
Press	⏎

To leave the graph options menu and view the graph:

Select	Quit
Select	View

Your screen should look like Figure 4-14.

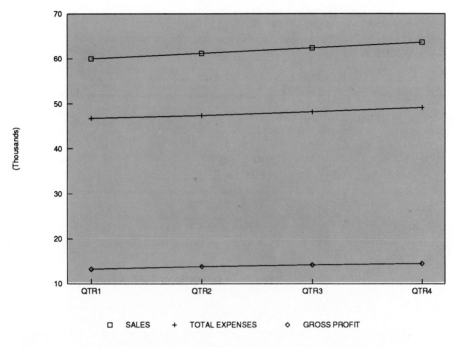

Figure 4-14

To return to the graph menu:

Press   ⏎

To exit the graph menu:

Select   Quit

■ PRINTING A GRAPH

After creating a graph, you will most likely want to print the graph. In many instances, you may want to print a graph that you created in an earlier 1-2-3 work session. In this section, you will learn how to print graphs.

Three steps are necessary to print a graph in Lotus. You must enter the Lotus PrintGraph menu, select the desired graph and send the graphic image to the printer.

Entering the Lotus PrintGraph Menu

To print the graph, the PrintGraph option must be accessed. To reach this option, you need to return to the 1-2-3 access menu.

To stop using 1-2-3:

Press   /

Select   Quit

Select   Yes

The Lotus Access System menu appears and your screen should look like Figure 4-15.

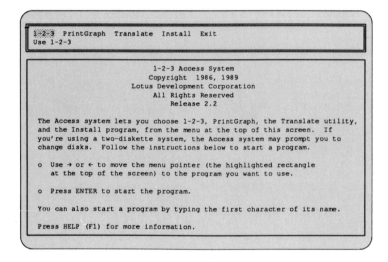

```
1-2-3   PrintGraph   Translate   Install   Exit
Use 1-2-3


                           1-2-3 Access System
                          Copyright  1986, 1989
                       Lotus Development Corporation
                           All Rights Reserved
                              Release 2.2

       The Access system lets you choose 1-2-3, PrintGraph, the Translate utility,
       and the Install program, from the menu at the top of this screen.  If
       you're using a two-diskette system, the Access system may prompt you to
       change disks.  Follow the instructions below to start a program.

       o  Use → or ← to move the menu pointer (the highlighted rectangle
          at the top of the screen) to the program you want to use.

       o  Press ENTER to start the program.

       You can also start a program by typing the first character of its name.

       Press HELP (F1) for more information.
```

Figure 4-15

With the Lotus Access System Menu on the screen:

Select   PrintGraph

If Lotus 1-2-3 is being used in drive A, a prompt will appear on the screen to remove the Lotus 1-2-3 System disk and insert the Lotus 1-2-3 PrintGraph disk in drive A. When ↵ is pressed, the PrintGraph program will be loaded. (Another way to load the PrintGraph program from the DOS prompt A> is to insert the Lotus PrintGraph disk in drive A and type PGRAPH ↵). If a hard disk contains the Lotus programs being used but the PrintGraph menu does not appear, it may be that the PrintGraph programs are not on the hard disk.

Your screen currently displays the primary PrintGraph menu. The screen also displays the default settings for graphs to be printed, such as the graph's size, the graph's directory (indicates what disk drive the graph file is located on), and the printer to use. All of the settings may be changed, if desired. Your screen should look like Figure 4-16.

```
Copyright 1986, 1989 Lotus Development Corp.  All Rights Reserved. V2.2    MENU

Select graphs to print or preview
Image-Select  Settings  Go  Align  Page  Exit

   GRAPHS    IMAGE SETTINGS                    HARDWARE SETTINGS
  TO PRINT   Size              Range colors   Graphs directory
             Top        .395   X Black           A:\22CH04
             Left       .750   A Black        Fonts directory
             Width     6.500   B Black           C:\123R22
             Height    4.691   C Black        Interface
             Rotation   .000   D Black           Parallel 1
                               E Black        Printer
             Font              F Black           PostScript
             1 BLOCK1                         Paper size
             2 BLOCK1                            Width     8.500
                                                Length   11.000

                                              ACTION SETTINGS
                                              Pause  No  Eject  No
```

Figure 4-16

Selecting the Graph to be Printed and Previewing the Graph

To select the graph to print:

Select   Image-Select

A screen displaying all of the defined graphs, like the one in Figure 4-17, should appear on your screen.

```
Copyright 1986, 1989 Lotus Development Corp.  All Rights Reserved. V2.2    POINT

Select graphs to print


  GRAPH FILE  DATE      TIME    SIZE
  --------------------------------------
  BUDBAR     09-14-89  13:51    8024    Space bar marks or unmarks selection
  BUDLINE    09-21-89   9:07     956    ENTER selects marked graphs
  BUDPIE     09-14-89  14:08    1831    ESC exits, ignoring changes
  BUDSTBAR   09-14-89  14:05    5056    HOME moves to beginning of list
                                        END moves to end of list
                                        ↑ and ↓ move highlight
                                           List will scroll if highlight
                                           moved beyond top or bottom
                                        GRAPH (F10) previews marked graph
```

Figure 4-17

To print the BUDBAR graph, make sure the graph name is highlighted.

Press   the space bar

A # sign should appear in front of the word BUDBAR. The # sign marks BUDBAR as a graph to be printed. If there are several graph files listed, you can select a particular graph to print by moving the cell pointer to the name using the arrow keys. Pressing the space bar causes a # sign to appear in front of the graph name and marks it to be printed. If desired, multiple graphs can be selected for printing by marking the graphs to print with the # sign. Your screen should look like Figure 4-18.

```
Copyright 1986, 1989 Lotus Development Corp.  All Rights Reserved. V2.2    POINT

Select graphs to print


    GRAPH FILE  DATE      TIME      SIZE
    ------------------------------------------
  # BUDBAR      09-14-89  13:51     8024      Space bar marks or unmarks selection
    BUDLINE     09-21-89   9:07      956      ENTER selects marked graphs
    BUDPIE      09-14-89  14:08     1831      ESC exits, ignoring changes
    BUDSTBAR    09-14-89  14:05     5056      HOME moves to beginning of list
                                              END moves to end of list
                                              ↑ and ↓ move highlight
                                                List will scroll if highlight
                                                moved beyond top or bottom
                                              GRAPH (F10) previews marked graph
```

Figure 4-18

To remove the # sign, press the space bar again. The # sign will disappear and the graph in question will not be printed. Note that the space bar is used to *place* and to *remove* the # sign from graph names. Make sure that the # sign is in front of BUDBAR before continuing with this exercise.

To preview the graph before printing it:

Press   [F10] (the Graph key)

The graph, as it will be printed, appears on the screen. If the bars are solid colors, the graph will only print correctly on a color plotter. There will be more detail on the printed graph than there is on your screen. Your screen should look similar to Figure 4-19. Note that a graph's appearance may differ slightly when viewed form within the PrintGraph menu, as compared to within the 1-2-3 menu when the graph was created using the spreadsheet settings. Even the scale may be different.

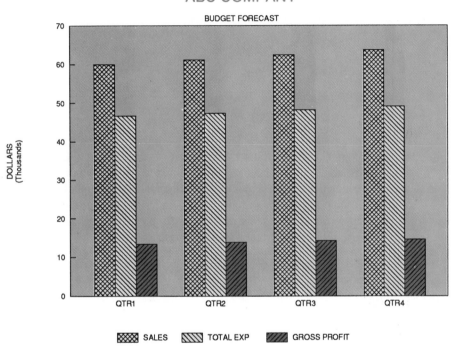

Figure 4-19

After viewing the graph:

Press ⏎ twice

Notice that BUDBAR is now listed under "Graph to Print."

Printing the Graph

To prepare the printer for operation:

Check	to see that the printer is connected to the computer
Align	the paper, if necessary
Turn	on the printer, if it is off

To print the graph:

Select	Align
Select	Go

1-2-3 loads the fonts and then starts generating the printed graph. This can be a slow process; do not disturb or interrupt the computer.

WAIT will appear in the top right corner of your screen. Even if the printer stops, do not assume the graph is finished until WAIT is replaced by MENU. Depending upon the type of printer you are using, expect the graph to take about 1 to 2 minutes to print. This may seem like a long time, but it is much faster than manually producing the graph. The amount of time a graph takes to print depends upon the quality of the printed version (a low or high density) and the type of printer used. Low density provides rough drafts; high density graphs are better-quality graphs and take longer to print.

If it is necessary to eject the printed graph when the graph has finished printing (and MENU appears in the top right corner of the screen):

Select	Page

To eject a second page so that the paper can be easily removed from the printer:

Select	Page

Your graph should look like Figure 4-20.

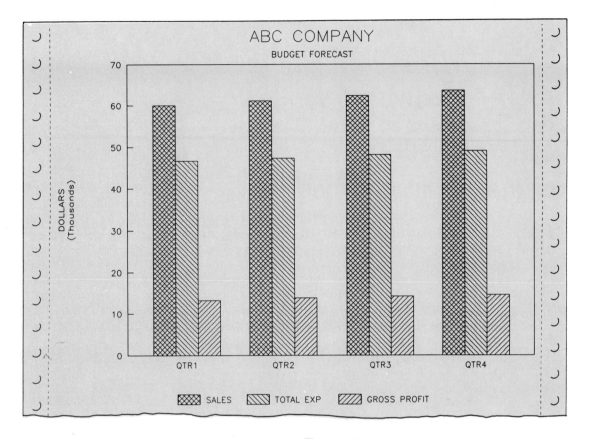

Figure 4-20

Exiting the PrintGraph Menu and Returning to Spreadsheet Mode

To exit the PrintGraph menu:

Select   Exit

Select   Yes

The Lotus Access System Menu will appear. If you are using Lotus 1-2-3 in drive A, you will need to replace the PrintGraph diskette with the Lotus System diskette.

To return to the Lotus spreadsheet area:

Type   1 (for 1-2-3)

A blank worksheet should appear on the screen.

■ OTHER GRAPH COMMANDS

A summary of commonly used graph commands is included for your reference. Tasks such as viewing a particular graph, deleting graph settings, erasing all graphs in a worksheet, erasing graph files and removing the scale indicator from a graph are discussed.

Viewing the Current Graph

Retrieve the file BUDGET for this exercise. It is assumed that the previous exercises on graphs have been completed. There are two ways to view the current graph in a worksheet.

Press   F10

or

Press   /

Select   Graph

Select   View

The current graph appears on your screen.

To return to the worksheet after viewing the graph:

Press   ↵

To exit the current menu if one appears on your screen:

Select   Quit

Selecting a Graph to View

In order to assign two or more graphs to a worksheet, each graph must be named and saved with the worksheet, just as BUDBAR and BUDLINE were two of the graphs named in the BUDGET file. As an example, you earlier named the bar graph BUDBAR and line graph BUDLINE. Then you saved the graph specifications and names on the BUDGET file.

To choose the graph to view:

Press	/
Select	Graph
Select	Name
Select	Use
Press	F3 (graphs names are listed)
Move	the pointer to the graph to view

In this example, highlight the name BUDBAR. When BUDBAR is highlighted:

Press	⏎

The graph will appear on the screen. Your screen should look like Figure 4-21.

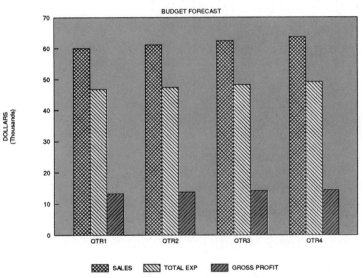

Figure 4-21

To return to the worksheet after viewing the graph:

> **Press** ⏎

To exit the graph menu:

> **Select** Quit

Note: The following steps give further information about graphs and are not a part of the exercise. If the exercises are completed, graphs that were created earlier will be erased. This will not cause a problem because the graphs are not used again in this book.

Deleting a Named Graph

To delete a named graph that was saved on a worksheet:

> **Press** /
>
> **Select** Graph
>
> **Select** Name
>
> **Select** Delete
>
> **Move** the cursor to the name of the graph to erase (in this case, BUDLINE)
>
> **Press** ⏎

To exit the menu:

> **Select** Quit

To delete the graph specifications for BUDLINE from the BUDGET file, you will need to complete the **File Save Replace** command sequence for the BUDGET file.

Erasing the Settings for a Graph

You can erase some or all of the settings associated with the current or named graph.

To erase the various settings for a specific graph, first specify a named graph to use. In this example you will use BUDBAR.

Press   /

Select   Graph

Select   Name

Select   Use

Press   F3

Move   the pointer to BUDBAR

Press   ⏎

To return to the main graph menu:

Press   ⏎

To illustrate the process of erasing some or all of the graph settings:

Select   Reset

The **R**eset menu now appears on your screen which should look like Figure 4-22.

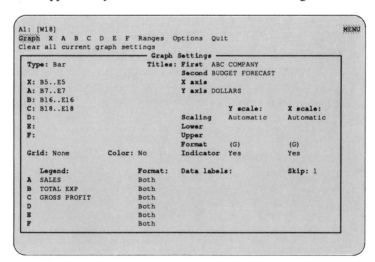

Figure 4-22

If you select **Graph**, all graph settings will be deleted. When you select **Ranger**, the **X** and **A-F** ranges will be eliminated. If the letter **X, A, B, C, D, E** or **F** is selected, then only the data associated with the item chosen will be deleted. When Options is selected, all settings related to the **Graph Options** menu are deleted. For example the titles and legend settings are deleted.

To exit from the graph menus:

Select	Quit twice

To permanently change the graph settings on the BUDGET file, you will need to complete the **File Save Replace** command sequence for the BUDGET file.

Erasing Graph Files from the Disk

Even if the BUDGET worksheet file is erased from the disk, any files saved as graph files will remain on the disk. To list the graph files on the disk for the current directory:

Press	/
Select	File
Select	List
Select	Graph

If there are any graph files in the directory, the graph file names will appear on your screen. If there are none saved, no name will appear on the screen and you will need to press the Esc key several times to exit the menu structure. Your screen should look like Figure 4-23.

To return to the worksheet screen:

Press	↵

```
A1: [W18]                                                               FILES
Enter extension of files to list: A:\*.pic
             BUDBAR.PIC    07/13/89      20:34        7814
BUDBAR.PIC      BUDLINE.PIC    BUDPIE.PIC    BUDSTBAR.PIC
```

Figure 4-23

To erase a graph file:

Press	/
Select	File
Select	Erase

| **Select** | Graph |
| **Press** | F3 |

A list of the graph files appears.

| **Move** | the cell pointer to the graph file to erase (BUDLINE in this case) |
| **Press** | ⏎ |

Menu choices of No and Yes appear. To erase the graph file:

| **Select** | Yes |

The graph file has been erased from the disk. In order for you to check if the file has been erased, complete the **File List Graph** command sequence again.

Removing the Scale Indicator from a Graph

In some situations, you may want to remove the scaling indicator.

If necessary, retrieve the file BUDGET for use in this exercise.

To pick a graph for use:

Press	/
Select	Graph
Select	Name
Select	Use

When prompted for the graph to use:

Press	F3
Move	the pointer to BUDBAR
Press	⏎

On the Y scale the word (**Thousands**) is displayed as the scale indicator as shown in Figure 4-24.

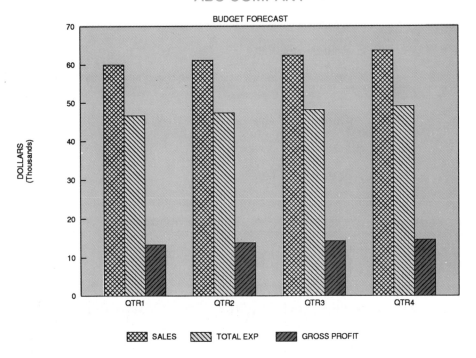

Figure 4-24

To return to the worksheet:

Press   ⏎

To remove the indicator from the Y Scale, select the following menu options:

Select   Options

Select   Scale

Select   Y-Scale

Select   Indicator

Select   No

To view the graph:

      Select   Quit twice

      Select   View

The Y-scale indicator no longer appears on the graph and your screen should look like Figure 4-25.

To return to the worksheet after viewing the graph, and exit the graph menus:

      Press   ⏎

      Select   Quit

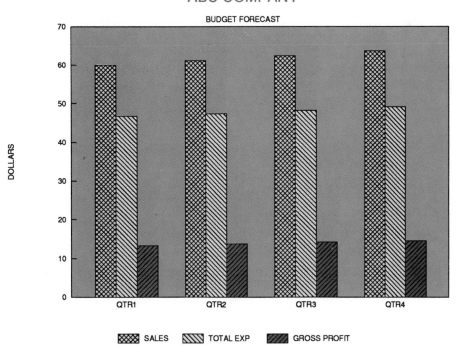

Figure 4-25

SUMMARY

1-2-3 allows you to integrate graphics with spreadsheets. Creating graphics using spreadsheet data is easy to do, because the data to be graphed does not have to be entered a second time. In fact, if the data on a spreadsheet is changed and the spreadsheet is recalculated, the graph reflects the changes in the data the next time the graph is viewed. Graphic representations of data on a spreadsheet allow you to use graphs as an aid not only in analyzing spreadsheet data, but in presenting the data to others.

KEY CONCEPTS

A-range
B-range
Bar graph
C-range
D-range
E-range
Erasing graphs
F-range
Graph
Group graph
Image-Select
Legend
Legend range
Line graph
Naming a graph

Pie graph
Printing a graph
Saving a graph
Scale Indicator
Stacked-Bar graph
Titles
Type of graph
Viewing a graph
X-Axis
X-Scale
X-range
XY graph
Y-Axis
Y-Scale

CHAPTER FOUR
EXERCISE 1

INSTRUCTIONS: Circle T if the statement is true and F if the statement is false.

T   F   1. A Lotus 1-2-3 graph can contain up to six different data ranges.

T   F   2. To change a bar graph into a line graph, change the **Graph Type** from **Bar** to **Line**.

T   F   3. If numbers are changed on the spreadsheet, the graph will reflect the changes when the graph is viewed again on the screen.

T   F   4. If numbers are changed on the spreadsheet, the changes will be automatically reflected on any graph file that was previously created from the worksheet.

T   F   5. It is possible to create three completely different graphs with data from one worksheet.

T   F   6. If **File Save** is not executed after a graph is made, the graph settings will not be saved.

T   F   7. If a computer is not configured to show graphics on the screen, it is not possible to create and print a Lotus 1-2-3 graph.

T   F   8. A color graph on the screen displays the colors in which the graph will be printed on a color printer or plotter.

T   F   9. A pie graph displays the data in data range A.

T   F   10. An XY graph is different from other Lotus graphs because it includes data for variable X.

T   F   11. The scale indicator can be deleted.

CHAPTER FOUR
EXERCISE 2

INSTRUCTIONS: Explain a typical situation when the following keystrokes or Lotus 1-2-3 commands are used.

Problem 1:	/ Graph A
Problem 2:	/ Graph Name Use
Problem 3:	/ Graph View
Problem 4:	/ Graph Name Create
Problem 5:	/ Graph Options Legends
Problem 6:	/ Graph Options Titles
Problem 7:	/ Graph Options Data-Labels
Problem 8:	/ Graph Type Pie

CHAPTER FOUR
EXERCISE 3
Creating a Bar Graph

INSTRUCTIONS: Retrieve file PRACTICE.

Create a bar graph that includes REVENUE, EXPENSES and PROFIT BEFORE TAX for 5 years as the graph ranges.

Include the YEAR 1 through YEAR 5 captions on the X-axis.
Place legend and title information on the graph.

Name and save the graph on a file using the name PROFIT.

Print the graph.

CHAPTER FOUR
EXERCISE 4
Creating a Stacked-Bar Graph

INSTRUCTIONS: Retrieve file PRACTICE.

Create a stacked bar graph for the REVENUE, PROFIT BEFORE TAX and PROFIT AFTER TAX data for the five-year period.

Include appropriate information for the X-axis range, legends and graph titles.

Name and save the graph using the name PROFSTBR.

Print the graph.

CHAPTER FOUR
EXERCISE 5
Creating a Pie Graph

INSTRUCTIONS: Retrieve file SALES.

Create a pie graph using the data for the individual salespersons.

Place appropriate titles on the graph.

Name and save the graph using the name SALESPCT.

Print the graph.

CHAPTER FOUR
EXERCISE 6
Creating an XY Graph

INSTRUCTIONS: Create the worksheet appearing in Figure 4-26.

```
A1: [W21]                                                        READY


                A          B        C           D          E
1                       ABC COMPANY
2
3
4                                NO. OF      NO. OF
5              UNITS      CODE  UNITS PRODUCED UNITS SOLD
6
7    FISHING BOAT        FISH         800        780
8    SKI BOAT            SKI          750        675
9    SAIL BOAT           SAIL         700        650
10   CANOE               CANOE        575        450
11   HOUSE BOAT          HOUSE        550        375
12   RAFT                RAFT         500        490
13
14
```

Figure 4-26

Create an XY graph using the number of units produced as the X item and the number of units sold as the Y item.

Include the code information on the graph to the right of each point to identify the points.

Place appropriate title, X-axis, and Y-axis information on the graph.

Print the graph.

CHAPTER FIVE

CREATING AND USING A TEMPLATE

OBJECTIVES

In this chapter, you will learn to:

■ Create and use a template

■ CHAPTER OVERVIEW

In Lotus 1-2-3, a **template** is a term used to describe a worksheet that can be used to create a series of other worksheets. A template usually consists of the general format (headings, labels, numeric format) and formulas that will be common to all of the worksheets. When data is entered in the template, the worksheet formulas calculate accordingly. The new data is then saved under a different file name. The use of a template can save you hours of time and effort in creating worksheets.

The template you will create computes the total salaries for employees in various divisions of the ABC Company example used earlier. Since the salaries for each division will be on a separate worksheet, you will build a template that can be used to create the worksheets for the various divisions of ABC Company. When you complete the template, your screen will look like Figure 5-1.

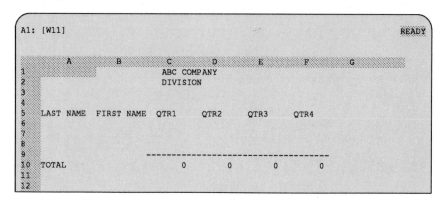

Figure 5-1

■CREATING A TEMPLATE

There are three steps for creating the template:

1. Create the worksheet title, column headings and labels.

2. Enter subtotal lines, total lines and formulas.

3. Set the numeric format for the worksheet.

It is also useful to name areas of the spreadsheet with range names where appropriate. The use of range names was introduced in Chapter 3.

Creating the Worksheet Title, Column Headings and Labels

If necessary, clear your screen.

To enter the titles for the template:

Press   the ⌈CapsLock⌋ key (if the CAPS indicator does not appear on the screen)

Move   the cell pointer to cell C1

Press   the space bar three times

Type   ABC COMPANY

Press   ⊡

Press   the space bar three times

Type   DIVISION

Press   ⊖

Move   the cell pointer to cell A5

Type   LAST NAME[1]

Press   ⊖

To widen column A:

Press   /

Select   Worksheet

Select   Column

Select   Set-Width

When prompted for the column width:

Enter   11

To enter the next heading:

Move   the cell pointer to cell B5

Enter   FIRST NAME

To widen column B:

Press   /

Select   Worksheet

Select   Column

Select   Set-Width

---

[1] By this point you should be thoroughly familiar with entering labels and data. Therefore, the remainder of the text uses the shortcut instruction Enter label or data. It is assumed that you will type the label or data and press the ⊖ key when asked to enter the information.

When prompted for the column width:

Enter   10

To enter the column headings in cells C5 through F5, respectively:

Enter   ^QTR1 in cell C5

Enter   ^QTR2 in cell D5

Enter   ^QTR3 in cell E5

Enter   ^QTR4 in cell F5

To enter the label TOTAL:

Move   the cell pointer to cell A10

Enter   TOTAL

Your screen should look like Figure 5-2.

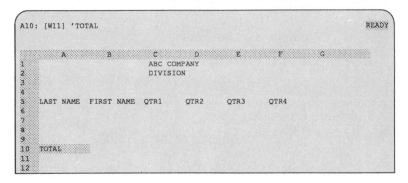

Figure 5-2

Entering Subtotal Lines, Total Lines and Formulas

To enter subtotal lines:

Move   the cell pointer to cell C9

Type   \ (for repeat)

Type   -

Press   ⏎

To copy the subtotal line to the rest of the row:

> **Press** /
>
> **Select** Copy

When prompted for the range to copy FROM:

> **Press** ⏎

C9 (the cell containing the subtotal line) is the selection for the range to copy. When prompted for the range to copy TO:

> **Move** the cell pointer to cell D9
>
> **Type** .
>
> **Move** the cell pointer to cell F9
>
> **Press** ⏎

To enter the formula to sum the salaries:

> **Move** the cell pointer to cell C10
>
> **Type** @SUM(
>
> **Move** the cell pointer to cell C5
>
> **Type** .
>
> **Move** the cell pointer to cell C9
>
> **Type**)
>
> **Press** ⏎

A zero (0) should appear in the cell, because the template does not contain any numbers to add. By including the rows above and below where data will be input, the @SUM formula allows the @SUM formula to adjust correctly in the event rows of data are inserted or deleted. Since the cells in the fifth and ninth rows contain labels, their **values** are assumed to be zero and therefore will not cause the results of using the @SUM formula to be incorrect.

To copy the formula to the rest of the row:

> **Press** /
>
> **Select** Copy

When prompted for the range to copy FROM:

Press   ↵

Cell C10 (the @SUM formula) is the selection for the cell to copy. When prompted for the range to copy TO:

Move   the cell pointer to cell D10

Type   :

Move   the cell pointer to cell F10

Press   ↵

Setting the Numeric Format for the Worksheet

To set the global format:

Press   /

Select   Worksheet

Select   Global

Select   Format

Select   , (for comma)

Type   0

Press   ↵

When numbers are entered, they will be formatted with commas and no decimal places. The template worksheet is now complete. Your screen should look like Figure 5-3.

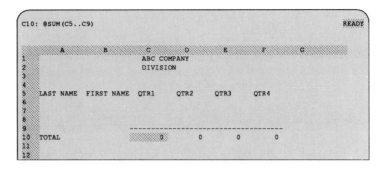

Figure 5-3

Saving the Template on a File

To save the file:

Press	Home
Press	/
Select	File
Select	Save

When prompted for the file name:

| **Type** | DIVTEMP |
| **Press** | ↵ |

Your worksheet has now been saved and can be used as a template for the various division worksheets.

An alternative way to create the template is to first create a spreadsheet for a division. After creating the file and making sure that all of the formulas and other elements of the worksheet are correct, save the file. Then erase the data for all lines that will be different for the other detail worksheets and save the **shell** as the template. In this example, the names, salary data and division number would be erased. This method may be preferable in some cases because it would be easier to check the appearance and accuracy of the worksheet, especially if it is large and complex.

Erase the template from your screen.

■USING A TEMPLATE

The purpose of having a template is to use it as a shell for other spreadsheets. In this section, the template DIVTEMP (Division Template) that was created in the previous section will be used to create the file DIV1 (Division 1).

Retrieve the Template

To use the template for inserting data, retrieve file DIVTEMP.

Enter Data into the Template

To enter the appropriate division number in the title:

Move	the cell pointer to cell C2
Press	F2
Press	the space bar
Type	1
Press	↵

To enter the data for Division 1:

Move	the cell pointer to cell A6

Using the data in Figure 5-4 as a reference, type the names and the quarterly salary information in rows 6 and 7 of columns A through F. The formulas in the TOTAL row will compute the totals as the data for each quarter is input. Notice that the appropriate numeric format is also used for the values.

```
A1: [W11]                                                              READY

           A         B          C         D        E        F       G
  1                             ABC COMPANY
  2                             DIVISION 1
  3
  4
  5    LAST NAME  FIRST NAME  QTR1      QTR2     QTR3     QTR4
  6    JOHNSON    ERNEST       8,000     8,000    8,800    8,800
  7    LYLIE      SUSAN        7,800     7,800    7,800    8,580
  8
  9                           --------------------------------------
 10    TOTAL                  15,800    15,800   16,600   17,380
 11
 12
```

Figure 5-4

Save the Worksheet Under Another Name

Use the **File Save** command sequence to save the salary data for DIVISION 1 as DIV1.

Press	/
Select	File
Select	Save
Type	DIV1
Press	⏎

Two files exist. DIVTEMP is the template, which can be used for creating worksheets of additional divisions. DIV1 contains the data for DIVISION 1. When DIVTEMP is in **memory**, it can be altered and saved under a different file name. The file DIVTEMP on the **disk** is not altered *unless* a File Save command is executed and the original file DIVTEMP is **Replaced**. Since it is very easy to accidentally save over a template, it is wise to keep a copy of the template file handy as a backup.

SUMMARY

A template is a shell document that can be used to create multiple spreadsheets that have the same basic format. The template contains the features that will be common to all other worksheets having a similar appearance. For example, titles, descriptions, formulas, range names and even print settings may be created in the template. When data is entered into the template, the results should be saved under a separate name so the template may be used to create additional worksheets.

KEY CONCEPTS

Template
Shell
Worksheet in memory
Worksheet on disk

CHAPTER FIVE
EXERCISE 1

INSTRUCTIONS: Circle T if the statement is true and F if the statement is false.

T   F   1. In Lotus 1-2-3, a template file must be combined with another file containing data to generate a new spreadsheet.

T   F   2. A template is a good way to keep spreadsheets standardized.

T   F   3. When data is added to a template in memory, it is automatically added to the template file on the disk.

T   F   4. A template can be used to create multiple worksheets.

T   F   5. After adding data to a template in order to create a new spreadsheet, the worksheet should be saved using a name other than the template file name.

CHAPTER FIVE
EXERCISE 2
Creating a Template from an Existing Worksheet

INSTRUCTIONS: Retrieve the file DIV1. Erase the number 1 from the title DIVISION 1. Erase the data for LAST NAME, FIRST NAME, and all four quarters for Ernest Johnson and Susan Lylie.

Save the file as DIVTEMP2. The file DIVTEMP2 should be identical to the file DIVTEMP that was created in this chapter. The screen should look like Figure 5-5.

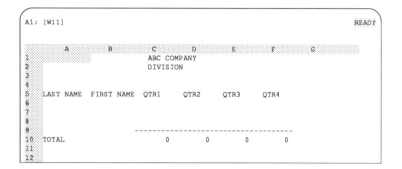

```
A1: [W11]                                                    READY

          A          B          C         D         E         F         G
    1                              ABC COMPANY
    2                              DIVISION
    3
    4
    5   LAST NAME  FIRST NAME  QTR1      QTR2      QTR3      QTR4
    6
    7
    8
    9                          ------------------------------------
   10   TOTAL                      0         0         0         0
   11
   12
```

Figure 5-5

CHAPTER FIVE
EXERCISE 3
Creating a Template

INSTRUCTIONS: Create the template in Figure 5-6.

```
A1: [W20]                                                    READY

          A                    B         C         D         E         F
    1                              XYZ, INC.
    2                              PROFIT FORECAST
    3
    4                          JAN       FEB       MAR       QTR1
    5
    6   SALES                  $0        $0        $0        $0
    7   EXPENSES               $0        $0        $0        $0
    8                          ----------------------------------
    9   PROFIT BEFORE TAX      $0        $0        $0        $0
   10                          ==================================
   11
   12   ASSUMPTIONS:
   13   INITIAL SALES AMOUNT
   14   SALES GROWTH RATE
   15   EXPENSE RATE
   16
   17
   18
   19
   20
                      UNDO                                CAPS
```

Figure 5-6

SALES for the month of January are determined from the amount entered in cell B13 by placing the formula +B13 in cell B6. The values for SALES in February and March are computed by multiplying the SALES amount for the previous month times the GROWTH RATE for the current month.

EXPENSES are calculated by multiplying the EXPENSE RATE for each month times the SALES amount for the month.

Save the template using the file name PROFTEMP.

Print the template worksheet.

After placing the values in the appropriate ASSUMPTION cells, the screen should look like Figure 5-7.

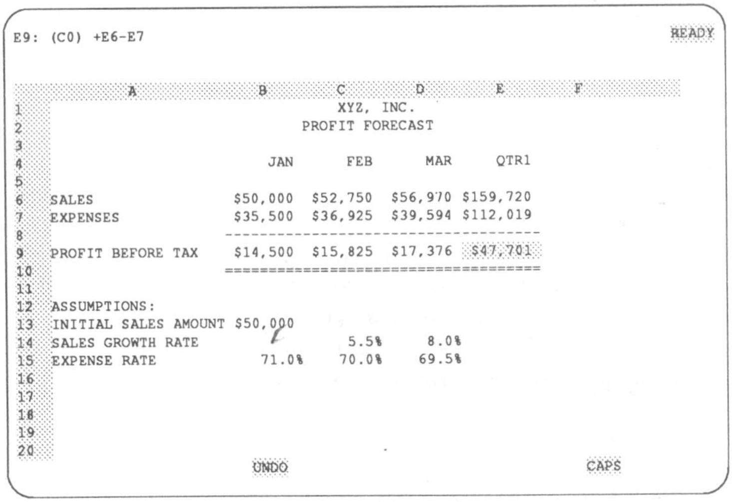

```
E9:  (C0)  +E6-E7                                                    READY

            A              B        C        D        E        F
 1                                XYZ, INC.
 2                               PROFIT FORECAST
 3
 4                         JAN      FEB      MAR      QTR1
 5
 6    SALES              $50,000  $52,750  $56,970 $159,720
 7    EXPENSES           $35,500  $36,925  $39,594 $112,019
 8                       ------------------------------------
 9    PROFIT BEFORE TAX  $14,500  $15,825  $17,376   $47,701
10                       ====================================
11
12    ASSUMPTIONS:
13    INITIAL SALES AMOUNT $50,000
14    SALES GROWTH RATE              5.5%     8.0%
15    EXPENSE RATE         71.0%    70.0%    69.5%
16
17
18
19
20
                           UNDO                              CAPS
```

Figure 5-7

Print the results after you use the template worksheet.

CHAPTER SIX

COMBINING INFORMATION BETWEEN WORKSHEETS AND LINKING FILES

OBJECTIVES

In this chapter, you will learn to:

- Consolidate information from a detail worksheet into a summary worksheet
- Consolidate information from several detail worksheets into a summary worksheet
- Use the Range Value command sequence for consolidating worksheets
- Link worksheets in separate files

■CHAPTER OVERVIEW

Sometimes it is necessary to move data from a detail worksheet to a summary worksheet. **Detail worksheets** may contain a considerable amount of information about a particular topic. For example, a company can have detail worksheets that contain information about the budgets for each department. A **summary worksheet** summarizes information contained in detail worksheets. When the totals or "bottom line" items for each department budget are brought into a summary worksheet, a manager can more effectively assess the overall picture.

In Chapter 5, you created the file DIV1 from a template and used it to record the salaries for DIVISION 1. In this chapter, DIVISION 1 will be used as a detail worksheet. In Chapter 2 the file BUDGET was created and contained a line for SALARIES data. In this chapter, BUDGET will be used as a summary worksheet. Using the **File Combine Add** command sequence, you will add the total salaries in DIV1 and additional worksheets into the BUDGET file. The summary worksheet BUDGET is displayed in Figure 6-1.

```
A1: [W18]                                                          READY

             A          B       C        D        E       F       G
 1                               ABC COMPANY
 2                                 BUDGET
 3
 4
 5                      QTR1     QTR2     QTR3     QTR4   YR TOTAL
 6
 7   SALES           $60,000  $61,200  $62,424  $63,672 $247,296
 8
 9   EXPENSES
10     SALARIES       35,000   35,500   36,200   37,000  143,700
11     RENT            9,000    9,000    9,000    9,000   36,000
12     TELEPHONE       1,000    1,050    1,103    1,158    4,311
13     OFFICE SUPPLIES   750      800      850      900    3,300
14     MISCELLANEOUS   1,000    1,030    1,061    1,093    4,184
15                    ------------------------------------------
16      TOTAL EXPENSES 46,750   47,380   48,214   49,151  191,495
17                    ------------------------------------------
18   GROSS PROFIT    $13,250  $13,820  $14,210  $14,521  $55,801
19                    ==========================================
20
                        UNDO                             CAPS
```

Figure 6-1

■ CONSOLIDATING INFORMATION FROM A DETAIL WORKSHEET INTO A SUMMARY WORKSHEET

In the following exercise, you will assign a range name to the cells on the worksheet containing the totals in the file DIV1. The data from those cells will then be consolidated into the summary worksheet BUDGET.

Define a Range Name in the Detail Worksheet

Retrieve the file DIV1. Your screen should look like Figure 6-2.

```
A1: [W11]                                                          READY

            A          B        C        D        E       F       G
 1                             ABC COMPANY
 2                             DIVISION 1
 3
 4
 5   LAST NAME  FIRST NAME    QTR1     QTR2     QTR3     QTR4
 6   JOHNSON    ERNEST        8,000    8,000    8,800    8,800
 7   LYLIE      SUSAN         7,800    7,800    7,800    8,580
 8
 9                          ------------------------------------
10   TOTAL                    15,800   15,800   16,600   17,380
11
12
```

Figure 6-2

To combine a specific area of one worksheet into another worksheet, you must indicate which area(s) is to be included. The most common procedure is to use a **range name**. The name TOTAL will be assigned to the range of cells on the TOTAL line in DIV1. To define the range name TOTAL:

Press	/
Select	Range
Select	Name
Select	Create

When prompted for the range name:

Type	TOTAL
Press	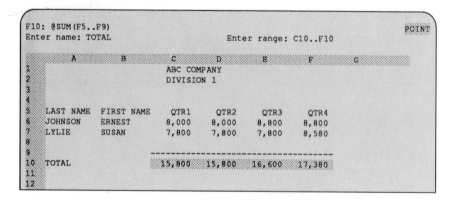

When you are prompted for the range to be assigned to the name TOTAL:

Press	(Esc)
Move	the cell pointer to cell C10
Type	.
Move	the cell pointer to F10

Cells C10 through F10 should be highlighted.

Your screen should look like Figure 6-3.

```
F10: @SUM(F5..F9)                                                    POINT
Enter name: TOTAL                        Enter range: C10..F10

           A          B          C        D        E        F        G
 1                             ABC COMPANY
 2                             DIVISION 1
 3
 4
 5    LAST NAME  FIRST NAME    QTR1     QTR2     QTR3     QTR4
 6    JOHNSON    ERNEST        8,000    8,000    8,800    8,800
 7    LYLIE      SUSAN         7,800    7,800    7,800    8,580
 8
 9                           ---------------------------------
10    TOTAL                    15,800   15,800   16,600   17,380
11
12
```

Figure 6-3

Press	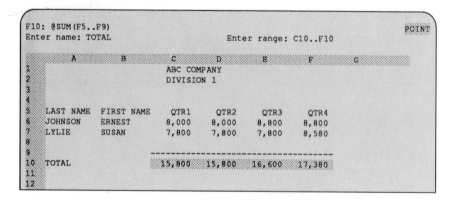

The range name TOTAL now has the cells C10 through F10 as its range.

Saving and Replacing the Worksheet to Keep the Range Name

Save the worksheet with the range name by using the File Save Replace command sequence.

The file DIV1 now contains the range name TOTAL.

Preparing the Summary Worksheet

The TOTAL range from DIV1 will be combined into the BUDGET file. For the purposes of this exercise, the BUDGET worksheet will be acting as a summary worksheet so you can combine DIV1 data into it. Retrieve the file BUDGET.

You must first erase the SALARIES data for the four quarters so the cells will be blank.

Move	the cell pointer to cell B10
Press	/
Select	Range
Select	Erase
Move	the cell pointer to cell E10
Press	⏎

Your screen should look like Figure 6-4.

```
B10:                                                                  READY

              A          B          C          D          E          F          G
1                                   ABC COMPANY
2                                     BUDGET
3
4
5                        QTR1       QTR2       QTR3       QTR4    YR TOTAL
6
7    SALES             $60,000    $61,200    $62,424    $63,672 $247,296
8
9    EXPENSES
10      SALARIES                                                        0
11      RENT             9,000      9,000      9,000      9,000   36,000
12      TELEPHONE        1,000      1,050      1,103      1,158    4,311
13      OFFICE SUPPLIES    750        800        850        900    3,300
14      MISCELLANEOUS    1,000      1,030      1,061      1,093    4,184
15                      --------------------------------------------------
16      TOTAL EXPENSES  11,750     11,880     12,014     12,151   47,795
17                      --------------------------------------------------
18   GROSS PROFIT      $48,250    $49,320    $50,410    $51,521 $199,501
19                      ==================================================
20
                                   UNDO                            CAPS
```

Figure 6-4

Moving the Detail Worksheet Data to the Summary Worksheet

The cell pointer must be placed on the summary worksheet in the proper cell so that the data from the detail worksheet will be placed in the proper cell. To position the cell pointer where the detail worksheet data is to be placed in the summary worksheet:

Move   the cell pointer to cell B10 (if necessary)

The cells in the range name TOTAL that contain the total quarterly salaries from the file DIV1 will be added in the BUDGET worksheet beginning at cell B10 (the first quarter for SALARIES).

To add the data in the range name TOTAL from the detail worksheet DIV1 to the summary worksheet BUDGET:

Press   /

Select   File

Select   Combine

Select   Add

Select   Named/Specified-Range

When prompted for the range name:

Select   TOTAL

Press   ⏎

The word TOTAL must be typed exactly as it was specified in the file DIV1. However, Lotus 1-2-3 is not "case sensitive" with range names; for example, "Total" or "total" is acceptable. Lotus 1-2-3 contains the menu option Named/Specified-Range. The Specified-Range portion of the Named/Specified-Range option means that you may specify either a range name or the exact range in the file that you wish to combine into the current worksheet. In this exercise, you can use the range name TOTAL or the specified range C10..F10. Cells C10..F10 are the set of cells in the range name TOTAL that exists in the DIV1 file.

When prompted for the file to combine:

Type   DIV1

Press   ⏎

The summary worksheet BUDGET now contains the data from the range name TOTAL in DIV1 on its SALARIES line, and the worksheet has recalculated accordingly. The SALARIES data from DIV1 now exists in both DIV1 and in the current worksheet. Your screen should look like Figure 6-5.

```
B10: 15800                                                          READY

              A            B        C        D        E        F        G
1                                   ABC COMPANY
2                                     BUDGET
3
4
5                         QTR1     QTR2     QTR3     QTR4    YR TOTAL
6
7     SALES             $60,000  $61,200  $62,424  $63,672 $247,296
8
9     EXPENSES
10       SALARIES        15,800   15,800   16,600   17.380   65,580
11       RENT             9,000    9,000    9,000    9,000   36,000
12       TELEPHONE        1,000    1,050    1,103    1,158    4,311
13       OFFICE SUPPLIES    750      800      850      900    3,300
14       MISCELLANEOUS    1,000    1,030    1,061    1,093    4,184
15                       -------------------------------------------
16       TOTAL EXPENSES  27,550   27,680   28,614   29,531  113,375
17                       -------------------------------------------
18    GROSS PROFIT      $32,450  $33,520  $33,810  $34,141 $133,921
19                       ===========================================
20
                              UNDO                              CAPS
```

Figure 6-5

Only numbers, not formulas or labels, are added when using the File Combine Add command sequence. (Use the File Combine Copy command to bring in labels and formulas; the data brought in *replaces* any existing data on a worksheet). The File Combine Add sequence cannot add values to cells where formulas exist on the current worksheet. A formula will override a number coming into the worksheet.

To see an example of how File Combine Add cannot add numbers to formulas, first erase cells B10 through E10. Do *not* save the result of the previous exercise. The original file BUDGET will be used in the next exercise.

Cell F10, which contains the formula @SUM(B10..F10), displays a zero because cells B10 through E10 have been erased.

For the purposes of this illustration, the range name TOTAL from DIV1 will be added beginning in cell C10.

Move	the cell pointer to cell C10
Press	/
Select	File
Select	Combine

Select   Add

Select   Named/Specified-Range

When prompted for the range name:

Type   TOTAL

Press   ⏎

When prompted for the file name:

Type   DIV1

Press   ⏎

The result is that the first number from the range name TOTAL will be added to cell C10, the second number from the range name TOTAL will be added to cell D10, and the third number will be added to cell E10. The fourth number, however, will not be added to cell F10 because F10 contains the formula @SUM(B10..E10).

Move   the cell pointer to cell F10

Instead of the number 17,380 from DIV1 being brought into the worksheet in cell F10, the number 48,200 will appear. The number 48,200 is a result of the formula @SUM(B10..E10) in cell F10, which "overrides" (prohibits) the number 17,380 from being brought into the cell. Your screen should look like Figure 6-6.

```
F10: @SUM(B10..E10)                                              READY

            A           B        C        D        E        F        G
 1                                   ABC COMPANY
 2                                     BUDGET
 3
 4
 5                       QTR1     QTR2     QTR3     QTR4    YR TOTAL
 6
 7   SALES            $60,000  $61,200  $62,424  $63,672  $247,296
 8
 9   EXPENSES
10     SALARIES                 15,800   15,800   16,600    48,200
11     RENT             9,000    9,000    9,000    9,000    36,000
12     TELEPHONE        1,000    1,050    1,103    1,158     4,311
13     OFFICE SUPPLIES    750      800      850      900     3,300
14     MISCELLANEOUS    1,000    1,030    1,061    1,093     4,184
15                     -------  -------  -------  -------  --------
16     TOTAL EXPENSES  11,750   27,680   27,814   28,751    95,995
17                     -------  -------  -------  -------  --------
18   GROSS PROFIT      $48,250  $33,520  $34,610  $34,921  $151,301
19                     =======  =======  =======  =======  ========
20

                        UNDO                               CAPS
```

Figure 6-6

■CONSOLIDATING INFORMATION FROM SEVERAL DETAIL WORKSHEETS INTO A SUMMARY WORKSHEET

In this exercise, you will alter the template DIVTEMP to include the range name TOTAL. If the template contains the range name, it is not necessary to add the range name to all future worksheets made from the template. A second file (DIV2) is then created using the template DIVTEMP so that the range TOTAL from both DIV1 and DIV2 can be consolidated into the summary BUDGET worksheet.

Modifying the Template

Retrieve the file DIVTEMP.

To set up the range name TOTAL on the template:

Press	/
Select	Range
Select	Name
Select	Create

When prompted for the range name:

Type	TOTAL
Press	⏎

When prompted for the range:

Press	Esc
Move	the cell pointer to cell C10
Type	.
Move	the cell pointer to F10
Press	⏎

The range name TOTAL is now part of the template and all future worksheets made from this template. It is a useful idea to include all range names when first creating the template.

To make the editing of the division number more efficient:

Move	the cell pointer to cell C2
Press	F2

Press   the space bar

Press   ⏎

The space after the word DIVISION on the worksheet keeps the user from having to add a space when entering the division number.

When a file is saved, the cell pointer is saved in the position where it is located when the File Save command sequence is executed. The next time the file is retrieved, the cell pointer will appear in the same position it was in when the file was last saved. In this exercise, the cell pointer is saved in cell C2 so that it is already highlighting the word DIVISION when retrieved. To save the cell pointer in cell C2, execute the File Save Replace command sequence.

The cell pointer is now saved in cell C2. When the template is retrieved, the cell pointer will already be highlighting C2, the cell that needs to be edited for every DIVISION worksheet created from the template.

Retrieving the Template and Entering Data

In this section, you use the revised template DIVTEMP to build a second detail worksheet named DIV2 for DIVISION 2.

Retrieve the template file DIVTEMP, if necessary.

To enter the division number:

Press   F2

Type   2

Press   ⏎

The cell pointer appears in cell C2, because the cell pointer was saved in this position. It is not necessary to press the space bar before typing the division number since a space was added in the template.

To enter the data for Division 2:

Move   the cell pointer to cell A6

Using the data in Figure 6-7 as a reference, type the names and the salary information for each quarter in rows 6 and 7 in columns A through F.

```
A1:  [W11]                                                          READY

            A         B         C        D        E        F        G
 1                             ABC COMPANY
 2                             DIVISION 2
 3
 4
 5    LAST NAME  FIRST NAME  QTR1     QTR2     QTR3     QTR4
 6    ARMOUR     CYNTHIA      5,200    5,200    5,400    5,400
 7    CHIN       TOMMY        5,000    5,000    5,200    5,200
 8
 9                           ------------------------------------
10    TOTAL                  10,200   10,200   10,600   10,600
11
12
```

Figure 6-7

Saving the Worksheet Under Another Name

Save the worksheet as DIV2 by using the File Save command sequence and using DIV2 as
the file name.

When prompted for the file name:

Type	DIV2
Press	⏎

Since the range name TOTAL was entered in the template in the section titled "Modifying
the Template," the range name already exists. To make sure that the range already exists,
use the **Range Name Create** command sequence. When prompted to enter the range name,
highlight TOTAL and press ⏎. The range for TOTAL (cells C10 through F10) should be
highlighted. Press the ⏎ key to return to READY mode.

Preparing the Summary Worksheet

In this section, the SALARIES data in the BUDGET worksheet is again erased. The BUDGET
worksheet will serve as a summary worksheet into which the TOTAL ranges for DIV1 and
DIV2 will be added.

First, retrieve the file BUDGET.

To erase the SALARIES line in BUDGET:

Move	the cell pointer to cell B10
Press	/
Select	Range
Select	Erase

Move   the cell pointer to cell E10

Press   ⏎

Your screen should look like Figure 6-8.

```
B10:                                                                    READY

            A           B        C        D        E        F       G
 1                              ABC COMPANY
 2                                BUDGET
 3
 4
 5                      QTR1     QTR2     QTR3     QTR4   YR TOTAL
 6
 7   SALES          $60,000  $61,200  $62,424  $63,672 $247,296
 8
 9   EXPENSES
10     SALARIES                                               0
11     RENT           9,000    9,000    9,000    9,000   36,000
12     TELEPHONE      1,000    1,050    1,103    1,158    4,311
13     OFFICE SUPPLIES  750      800      850      900    3,300
14     MISCELLANEOUS  1,000    1,030    1,061    1,093    4,184
15                    ------   ------   ------   ------  -------
16     TOTAL EXPENSES 11,750   11,880   12,014   12,151   47,795
17                    ------   ------   ------   ------  -------
18   GROSS PROFIT   $48,250  $49,320  $50,410  $51,521 $199,501
19                    ======   ======   ======   ======  =======
20
                          UNDO                          CAPS
```

Figure 6-8

Moving the Detail Worksheet Data to the Summary Worksheet

The cell pointer must be placed in the summary worksheet correctly so that the data will be added at the correct place in the worksheet. To position the cell pointer correctly:

Move   the cell pointer to cell B10 (if necessary)

The TOTAL range from the file DIV1 will be added beginning in cell B10 (the first quarter for SALARIES).

To move the salaries data in the range TOTAL from the detail worksheet DIV1 to the summary worksheet BUDGET:

Press   /

Select   File

Select   Combine

Select   Add

Select   Named/Specified-Range

When prompted for the range name:

Type   TOTAL

Press   ⏎

When prompted for the file to combine:

Type   DIV1

Press   ⏎

The summary worksheet BUDGET now contains the data from the TOTAL range name in DIV1 on its SALARIES line, and the worksheet has recalculated accordingly. Your screen should look like Figure 6-9.

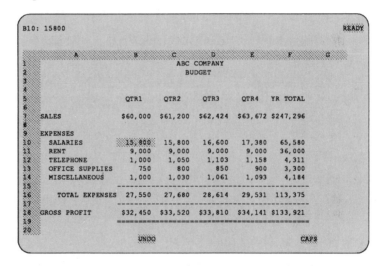

B10: 15800   READY

	A	B	C	D	E	F	G
1			ABC COMPANY				
2			BUDGET				
3							
4							
5		QTR1	QTR2	QTR3	QTR4	YR TOTAL	
6							
7	SALES	$60,000	$61,200	$62,424	$63,672	$247,296	
8							
9	EXPENSES						
10	SALARIES	15,800	15,800	16,600	17,380	65,580	
11	RENT	9,000	9,000	9,000	9,000	36,000	
12	TELEPHONE	1,000	1,050	1,103	1,158	4,311	
13	OFFICE SUPPLIES	750	800	850	900	3,300	
14	MISCELLANEOUS	1,000	1,030	1,061	1,093	4,184	
15							
16	TOTAL EXPENSES	27,550	27,680	28,614	29,531	113,375	
17							
18	GROSS PROFIT	$32,450	$33,520	$33,810	$34,141	$133,921	
19							
20							

UNDO   CAPS

Figure 6-9

To add the salary data from file DIV2 to the salary data from file DIV1:

Move   the cell pointer to cell B10 (if necessary)

The TOTAL range name from file DIV2 will now be added beginning at cell B10 (the first quarter for SALARIES) and then added to the data already moved (added) from file DIV1.

To add the salaries data in the range TOTAL from the detail worksheet DIV2 to the summary worksheet BUDGET:

Press   /

Select   File

Select	Combine
Select	Add
Select	Named/Specified-Range

When prompted for the range name:

| **Type** | TOTAL |
| **Press** | ⏎ |

When prompted for the file to combine:

| **Type** | DIV2 |
| **Press** | ⏎ |

The summary worksheet BUDGET now contains the data from range name TOTAL for both DIV1 and DIV2 files on its SALARIES line, and the other cells have been recalculated appropriately. Your screen should look like Figure 6-10.

```
B10: 26000                                                          READY

                A        B        C        D        E        F        G
 1                              ABC COMPANY
 2                                BUDGET
 3
 4
 5                        QTR1     QTR2     QTR3     QTR4   YR TOTAL
 6
 7    SALES            $60,000  $61,200  $62,424  $63,672 $247,296
 8
 9    EXPENSES
10      SALARIES        26,000   26,000   27,200   27,980  107,180
11      RENT             9,000    9,000    9,000    9,000   36,000
12      TELEPHONE        1,000    1,050    1,103    1,158    4,311
13      OFFICE SUPPLIES    750      800      850      900    3,300
14      MISCELLANEOUS    1,000    1,030    1,061    1,093    4,184
15                     -----------------------------------------------
16      TOTAL EXPENSES  37,750   37,880   39,214   40,131  154,975
17                     -----------------------------------------------
18    GROSS PROFIT     $22,250  $23,320  $23,210  $23,541  $92,321
19                     ===============================================
20
                                UNDO                          CAPS
```

Figure 6-10

Do *not* save the results of this exercise, as the original file BUDGET will be used for later exercises.

■ LINKING WORKSHEETS IN SEPARATE FILES

Another method of moving data between files is provided by the file linking capability available in 1-2-3. Files can be connected by using a linking formula. The general format of a linking formula is:

```
+<<file reference>>cell reference
```

The file reference identifies the name of the file and path to it, while cell reference is the address of the cell or a range name. Note: only one cell can be linked at a time. Before you use a link formula, you need to retrieve file BUDGET and erase the SALARIES data in cells B10 through E10. To link cell C10 in file DIV1 to cell B10 in the BUDGET worksheet:

Move	the cell pointer to cell B10
Type	+<<DIV1.WK1>>C10
Press	⏎

Then you need to copy the contents of cell B10 to cells C10 through E10. After completing the Copy command sequence, your screen should look like Figure 6-11.

```
B10: +<<C:DIV1.WK1>>C10                                              READY

              A            B         C         D         E         F        G
     1                              ABC COMPANY
     2                                BUDGET
     3
     4
     5                        QTR1      QTR2      QTR3      QTR4    YR TOTAL
     6
     7   SALES            $60,000   $61,200   $62,424   $63,672   $247,296
     8
     9   EXPENSES
    10     SALARIES        15,800    15,800    16,600    17,380     65,580
    11     RENT             9,000     9,000     9,000     9,000     36,000
    12     TELEPHONE        1,000     1,050     1,103     1,158      4,311
    13     OFFICE SUPPLIES    750       800       850       900      3,300
    14     MISCELLANEOUS    1,000     1,030     1,061     1,093      4,184
    15                     --------------------------------------------------
    16        TOTAL EXPENSES 27,550   27,680    28,614    29,531    113,375
    17                     --------------------------------------------------
    18   GROSS PROFIT     $32,450   $33,520   $33,810   $34,141   $133,921
    19                     ==================================================
    20
                                                                       CAPS
```

Figure 6-11

■USING THE RANGE VALUE COMMAND FOR CONSOLIDATING WORKSHEETS

Suppose you have two files named File A and File B. Sometimes it is necessary to add numbers from File A to a row or column of numbers in File B that have been created with formulas. When the **File Combine Add** command sequence is used, 1-2-3 will not add the File A numbers to File B if the cells in File B contain formulas. To solve this problem, change the cells in File B so that they only contain the numbers (the results of the calculated formulas) and not the formulas. This can be accomplished using the **Range Value** command sequence.

Retrieve the file BUDGET for the following exercise.

Move   the cell pointer to cell C14

Look at the control panel. Note that cell C14 contains the formula @ROUND(B14*C28,0). D14 and E14 contain similar formulas. In order to use the **File Combine Add** function to add data to the MISCELLANEOUS line, cells C14 through E14 need to be changed so that only numbers exist in the cell.

To change the formulas in cells C14 through E14 to values (rather than formulas):

Press   /

Select   Range

Select   Value

When prompted for the range to copy FROM:

Move   the cell pointer to cell E14

Cells C14 through E14 should be highlighted.

Press   ↵

When prompted for the range to copy TO:

Type   .

Move   the cell pointer to cell E14

Cells C14 through E14 should be highlighted. In this example, the values (the results of the calculated formulas) of cells C14 through E14 will be copied over the formulas themselves. In other instances, it may be appropriate to copy the values to another part of the worksheet (leaving the formulas intact in their original position).

Press   ↵

With the cursor in cell C14, look at the control panel. 1030 (the actual value of cell C14) is displayed in the control panel. The formula no longer exists in the cell. If you desire to keep the original file with the formulas intact, you must save the worksheet in memory (the worksheet with only values) using a different name.

To see the contents of cells D14 and E14:

> **Move**   the cell pointer to cell D14
>
> **Move**   the cell pointer to cell E14

Numbers exist in cells D14 and E14 rather than formulas.

If a File Combine Add is performed to the MISCELLANEOUS line in the BUDGET worksheet, there will be no problem adding the numbers from the incoming file to the BUDGET worksheet because the MISCELLANEOUS line now consists of numbers, not formulas.

SUMMARY

The File Combine Add command sequence allows you to bring data from one or more worksheets into a summary worksheet. Range names can be assigned so that only the specified ranges are pulled into the summary worksheet. There can be multiple range names in a worksheet. Only one range can be combined at a time, although the range can consist of multiple lines of data. Only one range and one file can be combined at a time.

An efficient way to standardize range names for all detail worksheets is to create them in a template. The template can then be used to create all of the detail worksheets.

Cells on separate worksheet files can be linked using a range name or a cell address.

The File Combine Add command sequence will not combine data into an area that consists of formulas or labels. The Range Value command sequence changes formulas into values so that the File Combine Add command sequence can be used.

KEY CONCEPTS

Detail worksheet
File Combine Add
File Combine Copy
Named/Specified-Range
Linking Files

Range name
Range Name Create
Range Value
Summary worksheet

CHAPTER SIX
EXERCISE 1

INSTRUCTIONS: Circle T if the statement is true and F if the statement is false.

T   F   1. The range name for a range of cells must be taken from a label already existing on the worksheet.

T   F   2. A template is a good way to keep range names standardized for several worksheets.

T   F   3. A detail worksheet is used for summarizing data from several worksheets.

T   F   4. The **File Combine Copy** command sequence is used to add numbers together from various worksheets.

T   F   5. If desired, the exact range location rather than a range name can be specified when using the **Named/Specified-Range** command to combine data between worksheets.

T   F   6. **File Combine Add** can add numbers to existing cells containing values or formulas.

T   F   7. The **Range Value** command can change values into formulas.

T   F   8. The **File Combine Copy** command sequence can be used to copy formulas from one worksheet to another worksheet.

T   F   9. When files are combined, the original detail worksheet and summary worksheet are automatically changed.

T   F   10. Cells on separate worksheet files cannot be linked.

CHAPTER SIX
EXERCISE 2
Creating a Detail Worksheet

INSTRUCTIONS: Follow the instructions below to create a worksheet from an existing template.

Using the template DIVTEMP, create a worksheet for DIVISION 3 as illustrated in Figure 6-12.

Save the file using the name DIV3. Print the worksheet.

```
A1: [W11]                                                          READY


            A          B           C        D        E        F        G
 1                                ABC COMPANY
 2                                DIVISION 3
 3
 4
 5     LAST NAME  FIRST NAME   QTR1     QTR2     QTR3     QTR4
 6     JONES      NINA          6,750    6,750    6,750    7,450
 7     SPROUT     AL            5,950    5,950    6,450    6,450
 8     VALETTI    GEORGE        5,900    5,900    6,300    6,300
 9                             -----------------------------------
10     TOTAL                   18,600   18,600   19,500   20,200
11
12
```

Figure 6-12

CHAPTER SIX
EXERCISE 3
Combining a Detail Worksheet with a Summary Worksheet

INSTRUCTIONS: Retrieve the file BUDGET.

Combine the TOTAL salary data for DIVISION 3 that was stored in file DIV3 into the BUDGET worksheet.

Print the BUDGET worksheet after combining the TOTAL salary data from file DIV3.

CHAPTER SIX
EXERCISE 4
Combining Multiple Detail Worksheets into a Summary Worksheet

INSTRUCTIONS: Retrieve the file BUDGET.

Combine the TOTAL salary data for DIVISIONS 1, 2 and 3 that are stored on files DIV1, DIV2 and DIV3 respectively into the BUDGET worksheet.

Print the BUDGET worksheet after combining the TOTAL salary data from files DIV1, DIV2 and DIV3.

CHAPTER SIX
EXERCISE 5
Correcting a Worksheet

INSTRUCTIONS: Follow the instructions below to combine multiple detail worksheets into a summary worksheet. Then answer the questions at the end of the exercise.

Erase the screen.

In cell A1, type 0.
In cell B1, type +A1*1.02.

Copy the formula in cell B1 to cells C1 and D1.

Your screen should look like Figure 6-13.

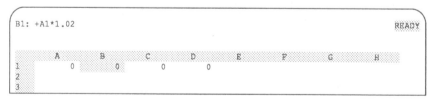

Figure 6-13

Place the cell pointer in cell A1.

Add the TOTAL data from DIV1 into the existing worksheet.

Your screen should look like Figure 6-14 Part 2.

The file DIV1.

```
A1: [W11]                                                          READY


              A          B          C          D        E        F        G
    1                               ABC COMPANY
    2                               DIVISION 1
    3
    4
    5   LAST NAME   FIRST NAME   QTR1       QTR2     QTR3     QTR4
    6   JOHNSON     ERNEST        8,000      8,000    8,800    8,800
    7   LYLIE       SUSAN         7,800      7,800    7,800    8,580
    8
    9                            -------------------------------------
   10   TOTAL                     15,800     15,800   16,600   17,380
   11
   12
```

Figure 6-14
Part 1

The results of using **File Combine Add** to consolidate the range TOTAL from the file DIV1 into the current worksheet.

```
A1: 15800                                                          READY


              A          B          C          D        E        F        G        H
    1       15800      16116 16438.32 16767.08
    2
    3
```

Figure 6-14
Part 2

Make sure that the numbers from DIV1 are not altered when the **File Combine Add** command is executed. Your screen should look like Figure 6-15 if the **File Combine Add** command sequence worked properly.

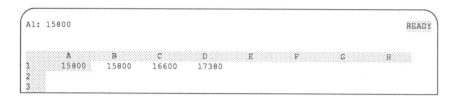

A1: 15800   READY

	A	B	C	D	E	F	G	H
1	15800	15800	16600	17380				
2								
3								

Figure 6-15

1. Why didn't the numbers from DIV1 appear correctly in the current worksheet?

2. How can the problem be solved?

CHAPTER SIX
EXERCISE 6
Using the Range Value Command

INSTRUCTIONS: Retrieve the file BUDGET.

Enter 40,000 for the SALARIES value in cell B10.

Place a formula in cells C10 through E10 that computes the SALARIES value by increasing the previous quarters' SALARIES by 4 percent. Use the **Range Value** command to change the SALARIES values in the BUDGET worksheet from formulas to values.

Add the cells in range TOTAL in file DIV1 to the SALARIES cells in the BUDGET worksheet.

Print the completed worksheet.

CHAPTER SEVEN

DATABASE CAPABILITIES OF 1-2-3

OBJECTIVES

In this chapter, you will learn to:

- Identify basic database terms
- Sort data on a spreadsheet
- Query for desired data on a spreadsheet
- Use additional Data Query options
- Fill cells with sequences of data
- Create data tables
- Use the Data Distribution command

■CHAPTER OVERVIEW

Lotus 1-2-3 can perform **database** capabilities such as sorting data and querying data in a worksheet. Suppose some of the personal information for all employees of an organization is entered into a single worksheet. To sort the names by division within the organization, you can use the **Data Sort** command sequence. To generate a report listing all employees who have been employed by the company for over 10 years, you can use the **Data Query** command sequence. However, 1-2-3 cannot perform database capabilities as extensively as a database management system such as dBASE III PLUS or IV[1], R:BASE System V,[2] or Paradox Release 3.0.[3] This chapter discusses the database capabilities of 1-2-3.

■ BASIC DEFINITIONS

Some of the basic terms used in database management are **field, record, file** and **key**.

A **field** is a collection of characters that are grouped together. In 1-2-3, each field is contained in a separate column within the database, or file. An example would be a person's last name. A **field name** is the term used to describe each field. For example, the title LAST NAME might be the field name for the field in which a person's last name is listed. In 1-2-3, each field name is listed in the column containing the field and is located in the cell *immediately* above the first field entry.

A **record** is a group of data fields that are combined in some logical pattern. For example, the personnel record for individuals in a company might include the individual's social security number, last name, first name, middle initial, department in which the individual works and so forth. In 1-2-3, each record is listed as a separate row.

A **file** is a group of records that are combined together. For example, the personnel file would include all of the personnel records. In 1-2-3, a group of records that is placed together on a worksheet in a logical manner is referred to as a **database table.**

A **key** is a specific field that can be used for distinguishing between records. For example, an identification number or the social security number for an employee can be used as a key for the personnel file.

■ SORTING

Sometimes you may need to sort data in order. For example, it may be necessary to sort transactions in order by type of transaction. The following exercises demonstrate how to sort information in 1-2-3.

---

[1] dBASE III PLUS and dBASE IV are registered trademarks of Ashton-Tate; Culver City, California.

[2] R:BASE System V is a registered trademark of Microrim, Inc.; Bellevue, Washington.

[3] Paradox Release 3.0 is a registered trademark of Ansa Software, a Borland Company; Belmont, California.

Sorting by a Primary Key

Create the worksheet appearing in Figure 7-1 and save it using the file name ABCSAL.

```
A1: [W7]                                                          READY

        A        B          C         D    E       F       G       H        I
1                                              ABC COMPANY
2                                             SALARY BUDGET
3
4
5   EMP NO LAST NAME FIRST NAME DIV   QTR1    QTR2    QTR3    QTR4    TOTAL
6      568 SPROUT    AL          3   5,950   5,950   6,450   6,450   24,800
7      123 LYLIE     SUSAN       1   7,800   7,800   7,800   8,580   31,980
8      390 CHIN      TOMMY       2   5,000   5,000   5,200   5,200   20,400
9      972 JOHNSON   SANDRA      1   8,200   8,200   9,000   9,000   34,400
10     898 VALETTI   GEORGE      3   5,900   5,900   6,300   6,300   24,400
11     239 ARMOUR    CYNTHIA     2   5,200   5,200   5,400   5,400   21,200
12     576 JOHNSON   ERNEST      1   8,000   8,000   8,800   8,800   33,600
13     833 JONES     NINA        3   6,750   6,750   6,750   7,450   27,700
14                                  ------- ------- ------- ------- --------
15            TOTAL                 52,800  52,800  55,700  57,180  218,480
16
17
18
19
20
                            UNDO
```

Figure 7-1

Suppose you need to sort the data in the ABCSAL worksheet in order by Division number.

Specifying the Data Range

Before sorting the spreadsheet, you need to specify the data range. The **data range** indicates where the database records you want to sort are located on the worksheet.

To specify the data range:

Press	/
Select	Data
Select	Sort
Select	Data-Range

When prompted for the data range:

Move	the cell pointer to cell A6
Type	.
Move	the cell pointer to cell I13

Press   ↵

All of the records in cells A6 through I13 comprise the data range. Note that only the records and *not* the field titles (EMP NO, LAST NAME, FIRST NAME, ...) are included in the data range. If the field titles are included, they will also be sorted. Another common error is to highlight only the column that needs to be sorted when indicating the data range. If this error occurs, only the column specified in the data range will be sorted; none of the data in the adjacent columns (e.g., EMP NO, LAST NAME, FIRST NAME) will be sorted with the appropriate division. Note that the underline and TOTAL rows should not be included in the data range.

Specifying the Primary Key

To specify the primary key:

Select   Primary-Key

Move   the cell pointer to cell D5 (or any other cell in column D)

Press   ↵

The **primary key** indicates the column containing the field by which the database should sort the records. Since column D contains the data to sort by (in this example, by division), any cell in the column containing the division numbers can be used to specify the primary key. When prompted for the desired sort order:

Type   A (for Ascending)

Press   ↵

The two options for sorting are Ascending and Descending. **Ascending** order refers to alphabetical order (from A to Z) or numerical order (from the smallest number to the largest number). **Descending** order refers to reverse alphabetical order (from Z to A) or numerical order (from the largest number to the smallest number).

Sorting the Data

To begin the sort procedure:

Select   Go

The records should be sorted in order by division number. Your screen should look like the final illustration in Figure 7-2. Figure 7-2, Parts 1 through 3 displays, the entire sort procedure.

Step 1 of the Sort Procedure: Specify the Data-Range

```
I13: @SUM(E13..H13)                                                POINT
Enter data range: A6..I13


       A       B          C       D    E       F       G       H      I
1                                    ABC COMPANY
2                                    SALARY BUDGET
3
4
5   EMP NO LAST NAME FIRST NAME DIV   QTR1    QTR2    QTR3    QTR4    TOTAL
6      568 SPROUT    AL          3   5,950   5,950   6,450   6,450   24,800
7      123 LYLIE     SUSAN       1   7,800   7,800   7,800   8,580   31,980
8      390 CHIN      TOMMY       2   5,000   5,000   5,200   5,200   20,400
9      972 JOHNSON   SANDRA      1   8,200   8,200   9,000   9,000   34,400
10     898 VALETTI   GEORGE      3   5,900   5,900   6,300   6,300   24,400
11     239 ARMOUR    CYNTHIA     2   5,200   5,200   5,400   5,400   21,200
12     576 JOHNSON   ERNEST      1   8,000   8,000   8,800   8,800   33,600
13     833 JONES     NINA        3   6,750   6,750   6,750   7,450   27,700
14                                 ------- ------- ------- ------- -------
15        TOTAL                   52,800  52,800  55,700  57,180 218,480
16
17
18
19
20
```

Figure 7-2
Part 1

Step 2 of the Sort Procedure: Specify the Sort Column and the Sort Order

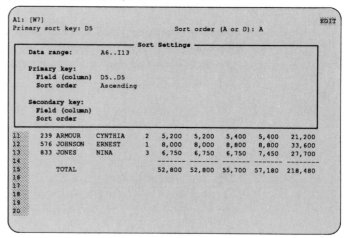

```
A1: [W7]                                                            EDIT
Primary sort key: D5                     Sort order (A or D): A

     ──────────────────── Sort Settings ────────────────────
    Data range:       A6..I13

    Primary key:
     Field (column)  D5..D5
     Sort order      Ascending

    Secondary key:
     Field (column)
     Sort order
     ──────────────────────────────────────────────────────

11     239 ARMOUR    CYNTHIA     2   5,200   5,200   5,400   5,400   21,200
12     576 JOHNSON   ERNEST      1   8,000   8,000   8,800   8,800   33,600
13     833 JONES     NINA        3   6,750   6,750   6,750   7,450   27,700
14                                 ------- ------- ------- ------- -------
15        TOTAL                   52,800  52,800  55,700  57,180 218,480
16
17
18
19
20
```

Figure 7-2
Part 2

Step 3 of the Sort Procedure: Select **Go** from the Sort Menu to Sort the Database

```
A1: [W7]                                                               READY

            A       B       C     D     E       F       G       H       I
 1                                      ABC COMPANY
 2                                      SALARY BUDGET
 3
 4
 5    EMP NO LAST NAME FIRST NAME DIV  QTR1    QTR2    QTR3    QTR4    TOTAL
 6       972 JOHNSON   SANDRA      1   8,200   8,200   9,000   9,000   34,400
 7       123 LYLIE     SUSAN       1   7,800   7,800   7,800   8,580   31,980
 8       576 JOHNSON   ERNEST      1   8,000   8,000   8,800   8,800   33,600
 9       239 ARMOUR    CYNTHIA     2   5,200   5,200   5,400   5,400   21,200
10       390 CHIN      TOMMY       2   5,000   5,000   5,200   5,200   20,400
11       898 VALETTI   GEORGE      3   5,900   5,900   6,300   6,300   24,400
12       568 SPROUT    AL          3   5,950   5,950   6,450   6,450   24,800
13       833 JONES     NINA        3   6,750   6,750   6,750   7,450   27,700
14                                     -------  -------  -------  -------  --------
15           TOTAL                     52,800  52,800  55,700  57,180  218,480
16
17
18
19
20
                          UNDO
```

Figure 7-2
Part 3

Sorting by Primary and Secondary Keys

In this exercise, the records in the file ABCSAL are sorted so that the names appear in alphabetical order within each division. It has been written with the assumption that the exercise in the previous section has just been completed and that the sorted records are currently displayed on your screen.

Specifying the Primary Key

A common error at this point is to indicate that the LAST NAME column is the **primary** key. This would not be correct. In this case, when the database is sorted, the last names would be sorted correctly, but the divisions would be out of order. The Division column will be the primary key so that the database is sorted *primarily* by division. The LAST NAME column will be specified as the **secondary** key so that the database is sorted *secondarily* by last name. This will cause the last names to appear in alphabetical order within each division.

To specify the primary key:

Press	/
Select	Data
Select	Sort
Select	Primary-Key

A cell in column D should be highlighted as a result of the previous exercise. If it is not, highlight a cell in column D by moving the cell pointer to cell D5 or any other cell in column D at this time.

With cell D5 highlighted:

Press ⏎

When prompted for the sort order, make sure that the letter A (for Ascending order) appears. The A should appear as a result of being selected in the previous exercise. If it does not, type A at this time.

With A specified as the sort order:

Press ⏎

Specifying the Secondary Key
To specify the secondary key:

Select Secondary-Key

Move the cell pointer to cell B5 (or any other cell in column B)

Press ⏎

Since column B contains the data to sort by (in this example, by LAST NAME), any cell in column B can be specified as the secondary key.

When prompted for the desired sort order:

Type A

Press ⏎

Sorting the Data
To begin the sort procedure:

Select Go

The database should now be sorted so that the last names are in alphabetical order within each division. Your screen should look like Figure 7-3.

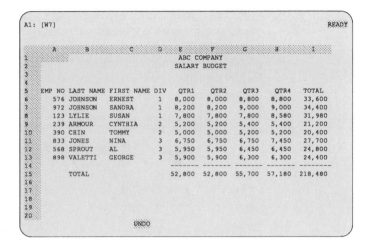

```
A1: [W7]                                                              READY

         A        B        C        D    E        F       G       H       I
 1                                        ABC COMPANY
 2                                        SALARY BUDGET
 3
 4
 5   EMP NO LAST NAME FIRST NAME DIV    QTR1     QTR2    QTR3    QTR4    TOTAL
 6      576 JOHNSON   ERNEST      1     8,000    8,000   8,800   8,800   33,600
 7      972 JOHNSON   SANDRA      1     8,200    8,200   9,000   9,000   34,400
 8      123 LYLIE     SUSAN       1     7,800    7,800   7,800   8,580   31,980
 9      239 ARMOUR    CYNTHIA     2     5,200    5,200   5,400   5,400   21,200
10      390 CHIN      TOMMY       2     5,000    5,000   5,200   5,200   20,400
11      833 JONES     NINA        3     6,750    6,750   6,750   7,450   27,700
12      568 SPROUT    AL          3     5,950    5,950   6,450   6,450   24,800
13      898 VALETTI   GEORGE      3     5,900    5,900   6,300   6,300   24,400
14                                     -------  ------- ------- ------- --------
15          TOTAL                      52,800   52,800  55,700  57,180  218,480
16
17
18
19
20
                              UNDO
```

Figure 7-3

■QUERYING

At times, you may need to perform a **query**, which is the process of searching through a file and selecting items which meet specific criteria. For example, you may wish to select all stores in a database file that have revenues in excess of $75,000 a year. The following exercises demonstrate how to perform queries in 1-2-3.

Querying with a Simple Criteria

In this exercise, the data in the database table ABCSAL will be queried to find each individual in the database table who has a total salary greater than $25,000.

Retrieve the original file ABCSAL for use in this exercise.

Placing the Criteria on the Worksheet

At this point, you need to place the criteria on the worksheet.

To place the descriptive information on the worksheet:

Move	the cell pointer to cell J3
Type	CRITERIA
Press	⊕
Type	RANGES
Press	⏎

The criteria must consist of at least two cells. The first cell specifies the field name that contains the data relevant to the query (in this case, the relevant field name is TOTAL). The second line of the criteria must consist of a formula or data that specifies the actual query. The name in the first cell of the criteria must match the field name in the database table exactly. Therefore, you will copy the field name TOTAL from the database to the criteria range.

To specify the criteria for the query:

Move	the cell pointer to cell J5
Press	/
Select	Copy

When prompted for the range to copy FROM:

Press	Esc
Move	the cell pointer to cell I5
Press	⏎

When prompted for the range to copy TO, the cell pointer will be in cell J5.

Press	⏎

As indicated earlier, the word TOTAL in the criteria must be listed exactly as it is specified in the database. It does not matter if the label is listed in lowercase or uppercase letters or which label prefix (^, " or ') is used. However, TOTAL must match the field name TOTAL character for character. For example, TOTALS would not render the correct results because the S in TOTALS is not present in the field name in the database table (cell I5).

To define the second line of the criteria:

Move	the cell pointer to cell J6
Type	+
Move	the cell pointer to I6
Type	>

Notice that the cell pointer returns to cell J6.

Type	25000
Press	⏎

The two cells required for the criteria—the field name TOTAL and the condition (+I6>25000) have been entered. In this example, the criteria indicates that the query will be for cells under the field name TOTAL that contain data greater than 25,000.

The number 0 appears in cell J6. This is not significant in terms of performing a query; 1-2-3 simply tested the condition +I6>25000 to see if cell I6 is greater than 25,000. Since I6 contains 24,800, the test was false and a 0 was placed in cell J6. If the condition had been true, the number 1 would have appeared in cell J6.

An optional step is to format cell J6 so that the formula for the criteria is displayed.

To format the cell to show the formula:

Press	/
Select	Range
Select	Format
Select	Text

When prompted for the range to format:

Press   ↵

Cell J6 now displays +I6>2500, which is not the complete formula. In order to show the complete criteria, widen column J so its width is set to 10. The formula +I6>25000 is now fully displayed in cell J6. Your screen should look like Figure 7-4.

```
J6: (T) [W10] +I6>25000                                              READY

        C     D     E       F       G       H       I         J
                          ABC COMPANY
1                         SALARY BUDGET
2
3                                                           CRITERIA
4                                                           RANGES
5    FIRST NAME DIV   QTR1    QTR2    QTR3    QTR4    TOTAL    TOTAL
6    AL         3    5,950   5,950   6,450   6,450   24,800  +I6>25000
7    SUSAN      1    7,800   7,800   7,800   8,580   31,980
8    TOMMY      2    5,000   5,000   5,200   5,200   20,400
9    SANDRA     1    8,200   8,200   9,000   9,000   34,400
10   GEORGE     3    5,900   5,900   6,300   6,300   24,400
11   CYNTHIA    2    5,200   5,200   5,400   5,400   21,200
12   ERNEST     1    8,000   8,000   8,800   8,800   33,600
13   NINA       3    6,750   6,750   6,750   7,450   27,700
14                 -------  ------- ------- ------- -------
15                 52,800   52,800  55,700  57,180  218,480
16
17
18
19
20
                              UNDO
```

Figure 7-4

Placing the Output Range on the Worksheet

Once the records matching the criteria have been located, it is possible to copy these records to another part of the worksheet called an output range. By specifying an output range, the desired records can be analyzed and manipulated without disturbing the database in which the records are contained.

In this exercise, the fields for LAST NAME, FIRST NAME and TOTAL for each record that satisfies the criteria will be copied to the specified output range. The field names define the **output range.** The records that match the criteria are be copied or **output** to the cells immediately beneath the field names in the output range. As illustrated by this example, the field names can be specified so that the entire record does not have to be output. In this case, only the LAST NAME, FIRST NAME and TOTAL will be output. The information for the employee number, division and the salaries in the four quarters will not be output.

To specify the output range, the appropriate field names must be copied. The field titles in the output range must match the names in the input range character for character. For this reason, you will use the copy command.

To copy the LAST NAME and FIRST NAME field names as two of the fields to output:

Move	the cell pointer to cell K5
Press	/
Select	Copy

When prompted for the range to copy FROM:

Press	[Esc]
Move	the cell pointer to cell B5
Type	.
Move	the cell pointer to cell C5
Press	[↵]

When prompted for the range to copy TO:

Press	[↵]

Widen columns K and L so that they are wide enough to display 12 characters.

To specify the TOTAL field as another field to output:

Move	the cell pointer to cell M5
Press	/
Select	Copy

When prompted for the range to copy FROM:

Press	[Esc]
Move	the cell pointer to cell I5
Press	[↵]

When prompted for the range to copy TO:

Press	[↵]

To document where the output ranges are located (an optional step):

Move	the cell pointer to cell K3
Type	OUTPUT
Press	[↓]
Type	RANGE
Press	[↵]

Your screen should look like Figure 7-5.

```
K4: [W12] 'RANGE                                                    READY

        G      H      I       J        K          L         M
 1
 2
 3                          CRITERIA  OUTPUT
 4                          RANGES    RANGE
 5     QTR3   QTR4   TOTAL   TOTAL    LAST NAME  FIRST NAME  TOTAL
 6     6,450  6,450  24,800  +I6>25000
 7     7,800  8,580  31,980
 8     5,200  5,200  20,400
 9     9,000  9,000  34,400
10     6,300  6,300  24,400
11     5,400  5,400  21,200
12     8,800  8,800  33,600
13     6,750  7,450  27,700
14     ------ ------ -------
15     55,700 57,180 218,480
16
17
18
19
20
                           UNDO
```

Figure 7-5

Specifying the Input Range

Now that the criteria and the headings for the output have been entered on the worksheet, you will indicate through the Lotus 1-2-3 menu where the records, criteria, and output range are located. After these steps are finished, you will complete the actual query operations.

First, indicate the input range. The **input range** is the term for the field names and data records located in the database table on the worksheet.

To specify the input range:

> **Press**   /
>
> **Select**   Data
>
> **Select**   Query
>
> **Select**   Input

When prompted to indicate the input range:

> **Move**   the cell pointer to cell A5
>
> **Type**   .
>
> **Move**   the cell pointer to cell I13

Your screen should look like Figure 7-6.

> **Press**   ⏎

Note that the input range includes the field names (EMP NO, LAST NAME, FIRST NAME, . . .TOTAL). If there are two lines of field titles, include only the bottom row in the input range and use only the words in the bottom row as the field names in your criteria and output ranges. Remember that the first database record must be in the row immediately under the field names without any rows separating the field name from the first record.

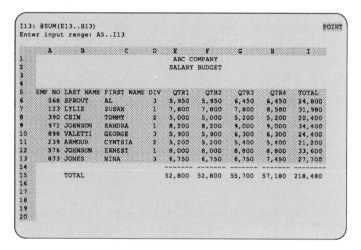

Figure 7-6

Specifying the Criteria Range

To specify where the criteria are located:

> **Select**   Criteria

When prompted for the criteria range:

> **Move**   the cell pointer to cell J5

> **Type**   .

> **Move**   the cell pointer to cell J6

Your screen should now look like Figure 7-7.

> **Press**   ⏎

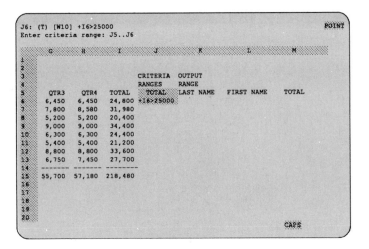

```
J6: (T) [W10] +I6>25000                                              POINT
Enter criteria range: J5..J6

          G        H        I        J        K        L        M
  1
  2
  3                                  CRITERIA  OUTPUT
  4                                  RANGES    RANGE
  5       QTR3     QTR4     TOTAL    TOTAL     LAST NAME  FIRST NAME  TOTAL
  6       6,450    6,450    24,800   +I6>25000
  7       7,800    8,580    31,980
  8       5,200    5,200    20,400
  9       9,000    9,000    34,400
 10       6,300    6,300    24,400
 11       5,400    5,400    21,200
 12       8,800    8,800    33,600
 13       6,750    7,450    27,700
 14       -------  -------  --------
 15       55,700   57,180   218,480
 16
 17
 18
 19
 20                                                               CAPS
```

Figure 7-7

Cells J5 and J6 define the criteria.

Performing a Find

The Find command highlights each record that satisfies the criteria. To determine whether the criteria has been specified correctly, you can use the following steps to perform a Find that will locate and highlight the records in the database that match the criteria.

To perform the Find procedure:

Select   Find

The first record that should be highlighted is that of SUSAN LYLIE on row 7. Since her salary total is $31,980, the criteria is satisfied.

To move to the next record that matches the criteria:

Press   ⊕

The record of SANDRA JOHNSON should be highlighted because the salary total is $34,400 and this amount matches the criteria.

To move to the next record that matches the criteria:

Press   ⊕

The record for ERNEST JOHNSON is highlighted.

Press   ⊕

The record for NINA JONES is highlighted.

Press   ⊕

Lotus 1-2-3 "beeps" when no more records that satisfy the criteria are in the database (not because NINA JONES is the last record in this database table).

To exit from Find mode:

Press   ⏎

The Data Query menu should be visible at the top of the screen.

Specifying the Output Range

To specify the output range:

Select   Output

Move   the cell pointer to cell K5

Type   .

Move   the cell pointer to cell M5

When the output range is highlighted, your screen should look like Figure 7-8.

Press   ⏎

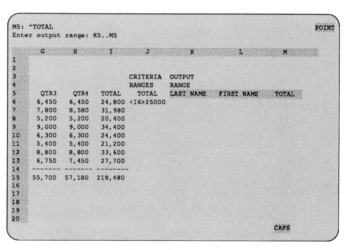

```
M5: ^TOTAL                                                          POINT
Enter output range: K5..M5

          G       H       I       J        K           L          M
  1
  2
  3                                 CRITERIA  OUTPUT
  4                                 RANGES    RANGE
  5      QTR3    QTR4    TOTAL    TOTAL     LAST NAME  FIRST NAME   TOTAL
  6     6,450   6,450   24,800  +I6>25000
  7     7,800   8,580   31,980
  8     5,200   5,200   20,400
  9     9,000   9,000   34,400
 10     6,300   6,300   24,400
 11     5,400   5,400   21,200
 12     8,800   8,800   33,600
 13     6,750   7,450   27,700
 14    -------  -------  -------
 15    55,700  57,180  218,480
 16
 17
 18
 19
 20
                                                                   CAPS
```

Figure 7-8

Extracting (Copying) the Desired Data Fields to the Output Range

After the Input range, the Criteria range and the Output range were specified in the Data Query menu, the Find option verified that the Criteria was set correctly. 1-2-3 located only the records in the database (Input range) that matched the Criteria. The records that match the Criteria can be copied to the area below the specified Output range using the Extract menu option. Only the fields specified in the Output range will be copied. Note that although the menu option you will use is Extract, the records are not really **extracted**—they are **copied**; in other words, the records are **not** omitted from the original database table.

To copy the records that satisfy the criteria to the output range:

Select   Extract

To view the extracted data:

Select   Quit

The LAST NAME, FIRST NAME and TOTAL are now listed for the specified records. Your worksheet should look like Figure 7-9.

K4: [W12] 'RANGE						READY
	C	H	I	J	K	L	M

```
K4: [W12] 'RANGE                                                    READY

        C       H       I         J         K          L            M
 1
 2
 3                              CRITERIA  OUTPUT
 4                              RANGES    RANGE
 5    QTR3    QTR4    TOTAL      TOTAL     LAST NAME  FIRST NAME   TOTAL
 6    6,450   6,450   24,800    +I6>25000  LYLIE      SUSAN        31,980
 7    7,800   8,580   31,980               JOHNSON    SANDRA       34,400
 8    5,200   5,200   20,400               JOHNSON    ERNEST       33,600
 9    9,000   9,000   34,400               JONES      NINA         27,700
10    6,300   6,300   24,400
11    5,400   5,400   21,200
12    8,800   8,800   33,600
13    6,750   7,450   27,700
14    ------- ------- -------
15   55,700  57,180  218,480
16
17
18
19
20
                                UNDO                              CAPS
```

Figure 7-9

Querying with Multiple Conditions Using #AND#

In this exercise, you will modify the criteria used in the previous exercise so that the criteria contains multiple conditions. The database table in the worksheet ABCSAL will be queried to find records for individuals who have a total salary between $20,000 and $22,000, including any salaries that are exactly $20,000 or $22,000. To perform this query, the logical operator #AND# will be used to combine two conditions.

Assuming you have just completed the previous exercise and the results are still visible on your screen, complete the following problem.

Changing the Current Criteria to the Desired Criteria

In this exercise you will change the current criteria from +I6>25000 to +I6>=20000#AND#I6<=22000.

To change the criteria:

Move	the cell pointer to cell J6
Type	+I6>=20000#AND#I6<=22000
Press	⏎

The **first** line of the criteria (in cell J5—TOTAL) should remain the same.

To see the entire formula, column J could be widened using the Worksheet Column Set-Width command sequence. This step is optional. The entire formula in the criteria does not have to be visible on the screen in order to perform a query. The entire formula can be viewed by placing the cell pointer in cell J6 and looking at the control panel, which shows the contents of a highlighted cell. Assuming that the cell pointer is in cell J6, your screen should look like Figure 7-10.

```
J6: (T) [W10] +I6>=20000#AND#I6<=22000                                    READY

        G         H         I         J         K         L         M
  1
  2
  3                                 CRITERIA  OUTPUT
  4                                 RANGES    RANGE
  5     QTR3      QTR4     TOTAL      TOTAL   LAST NAME  FIRST NAME  TOTAL
  6     6,450     6,450    24,800  +I6>=2000 LYLIE      SUSAN       31,980
  7     7,800     8,580    31,980            JOHNSON    SANDRA      34,400
  8     5,200     5,200    20,400            JOHNSON    ERNEST      33,600
  9     9,000     9,000    34,400            JONES      NINA        27,700
 10     6,300     6,300    24,400
 11     5,400     5,400    21,200
 12     8,800     8,800    33,600
 13     6,750     7,450    27,700
 14     -------   -------  --------
 15    55,700    57,180   218,480
 16
 17
 18
 19
 20
                              UNDO                                  CAPS
```

Figure 7-10

The output range, input range and criteria range were set and remain the same. Although the criteria now being used are different, the **range** where the criteria are located is the same.

To perform the query extract with the new criteria:

Press /

Select Data

Select Query

Select Extract

To view the data that has been extracted:

Select Quit

The desired data is now listed. Note that the data in the output range from the previous exercise using **Data Query Extract** was deleted completely and replaced with the data for the current **Data Query Extract**.

Your screen should look like Figure 7-11.

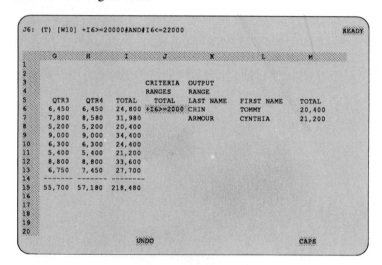

Figure 7-11

Querying with Multiple Conditions Using #OR# and Using the Query F7 Key

In this exercise, the database table in the ABCSAL worksheet will be queried to find individuals who have a salary less than $22,000 or greater than $30,000 using the logical operator #OR#. You will use the QUERY key (the F7 function key) rather than the **Data Query Extract** command sequence.

Changing the Current Criteria to the Desired Criteria

In this exercise, the current criteria will be changed from +I6>=20000#AND#I6<=22000 to +I6<22000#OR#I6>30000.

To change the criteria:

Move	the cell pointer to cell J6
Type	+I6<22000#OR#I6>30000
Press	⏎

(The **first** line of the criteria (in cell J5—TOTAL) will remain the same). Column J can be widened to see the entire formula using the **Worksheet Column Set-Width** command sequence. This step is optional. Because the same Output range, Input range and Criteria range that were set in a previous exercise will be used, they do not have to be reset. Although the criteria being used are different, the **range** where the criteria are located is the same. Instead of executing the **Data Query Extract** command sequence, the QUERY key (the F7 function key) can be used.

To perform a query extract using the new criteria:

Press	F7

The desired data are now listed. Note that the data from the previous **Data Query Extract** exercise was deleted completely and replaced with data for the current query. Assuming that the cell pointer is in cell J6, your screen should look like Figure 7-12.

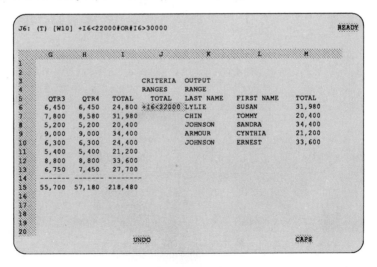

Figure 7-12

Querying with Multiple Criteria

In this exercise, you will query the ABCSAL database table to find the records for individuals who have a salary less than $25,000 and who are also in DIVISION 3. It is assumed that the results of the previous exercise are still displayed on your screen.

Changing the Current Criteria to the Desired Criteria

In this exercise, the current criteria +I6<22000#OR#I6>30000 will be changed to +I6<25000 and will serve as the **first** criteria. A **second** criteria (DIV equals 3) will appear in cells K5 and K6, respectively.

To change the criteria under TOTAL:

Move	the cell pointer to cell J6
Type	+I6<25000
Press	⏎

The **first** line of the criteria (in cell J5—TOTAL) will remain the same.

To insert a column for the new criteria:

Move	the cell pointer to cell K5
Press	/
Select	Worksheet
Select	Insert
Select	Column
Press	⏎

To place the new criteria on the worksheet:

Press	/
Select	Copy

When prompted for the range to copy FROM:

Press	Esc
Move	the cell pointer to cell D5
Press	⏎

When prompted for the range to copy TO:

Press   ⏎

The field name for division (DIV) now appears in cell K5.

To enter the specific value to be used:

Move   the cell pointer to cell K6

Type   3

Press   ⏎

To specify the proper criteria for the query:

Press   /

Select   Data

Select   Query

Select   Criteria

Notice that only the criteria in column J (cells J5 and J6) are highlighted from a previous exercise. Since you placed new criteria in cells K5 and K6, these cells need to be highlighted before performing the extract.

To include the new criteria in the Criteria Range setting:

Press   ➡

Cells J5 through K6 should be highlighted. These cells contain the criteria displayed in Figure 7-13. The results of the previous Data Query Extract are still visible on the screen.

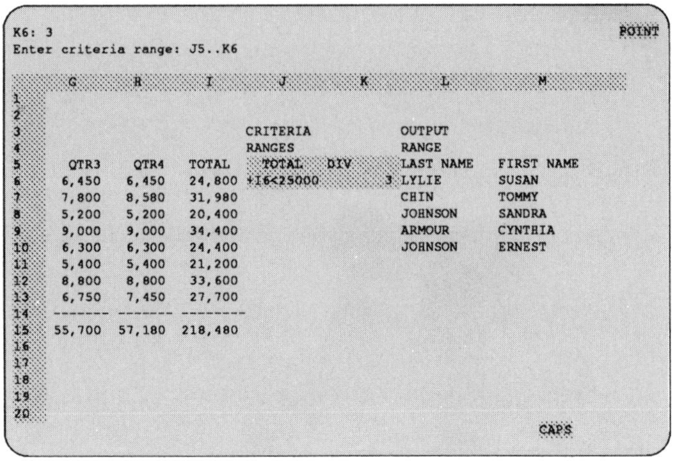

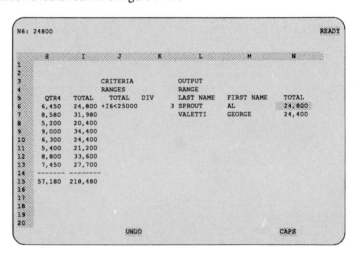

Figure 7-13

To accept cells J5..K6 as the criteria range:

Press   ⏎

To perform the query extract:

Select   Extract

Select   Quit

The data for the designated criteria now should be listed. Assuming you place the cell pointer in cell N6, your screen should look like Figure 7-14.

Figure 7-14

■USEFUL DATA QUERY OPTIONS

In this section, you will use the Data Query Unique and the Data Query Delete command sequences.

Using the Query Unique Command

You will continue to use the database table in the file ABCSAL with the results of the previous exercise. For the purposes of this exercise, use the instructions below to alter the file so that it has a duplicate record.

Move	the cell pointer to cell A9

To insert a row:

Press	/
Select	Worksheet
Select	Insert
Select	Row
Press	⏎

To copy Al Sprout's record from row 6 to row 9:

Move	the cell pointer to cell A6
Press	/
Select	Copy

When prompted for the range to copy FROM:

Move	the cell pointer to cell I6

Cells A6 through I6 should be highlighted.

Press	⏎

When prompted for the range to copy TO:

Move	the cell pointer to cell A9
Press	⏎

To execute a query:

Move	to cell N6

Press   ⑰ F7

Your screen should look like Figure 7-15.

```
N6: 24800                                                                    READY

        H        I        J        K        L            M            N
1
2
3                       CRITERIA              OUTPUT
4                       RANGES                RANGE
5     QTR4     TOTAL    TOTAL     DIV    LAST NAME    FIRST NAME   TOTAL
6     6,450    24,800  +I6<25000   3 SPROUT       AL           24,800
7     8,580    31,980                SPROUT       AL           24,800
8     5,200    20,400                VALETTI      GEORGE       24,400
9     6,450    24,800
10    9,000    34,400
11    6,300    24,400
12    5,400    21,200
13    8,800    33,600
14    7,450    27,700
15   -------  --------
16   63,630   243,280
17
18
19
20
                           UNDO                            CAPS
```

Figure 7-15

Because the record for Al Sprout was duplicated in the database, the name Al Sprout appears twice in the output range. By using the following command one of the duplicate records will be deleted from the output range.

Press   /

Select   Data

Select   Query

Select   Unique

To leave the Data menu:

Select   Quit

Al Sprout appears in the output range only once. Your screen should look like Figure 7-16.

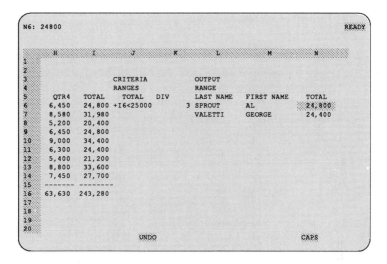

```
N6: 24800                                                              READY

         H        I        J        K        L         M          N
 1
 2
 3                        CRITERIA           OUTPUT
 4                        RANGES             RANGE
 5       QTR4    TOTAL    TOTAL    DIV       LAST NAME  FIRST NAME  TOTAL
 6       6,450   24,800  +I6<25000  3        SPROUT     AL          24,800
 7       8,580   31,980                      VALETTI    GEORGE      24,400
 8       5,200   20,400
 9       6,450   24,800
10       9,000   34,400
11       6,300   24,400
12       5,400   21,200
13       8,800   33,600
14       7,450   27,700
15       -------  -------
16      63,630  243,280
17
18
19
20
                          UNDO                              CAPS
```

Figure 7-16

Note that this option does **not** delete duplicate records in the database itself, only in the output range. Al Sprout's record still appears twice in the database.

Using the Query Delete Command

In this exercise you will use the Data Query Delete command. This command is **extremely powerful**, because it **deletes all records in the database that MATCH the criteria.** To make this change permanent on the ABCSAL file, you would perform a File Save. However, in this case, you will not save the file. In this example, all individuals in the file ABCSAL who earn less than $25,000 and are in DIVISION 3 will be deleted from the database. It is assumed that you have just completed the previous exercise.

To delete the records that satisfy the criteria:

Press	/
Select	Data
Select	Query
Select	Delete

The Cancel Delete menu appears so that you are given a chance to cancel this command or go ahead and delete the record.

To complete the process:

Select	Delete

To leave the current menu:

Select   Quit

To see the database table after the records have been deleted for individuals who are in DIVISION 3 with salaries less than $25,000:

Move   the cell pointer to cell A6

Your screen should look like Figure 7-17.

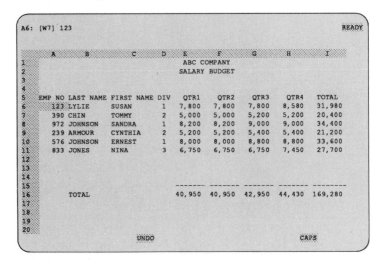

Figure 7-17

■ FILLING CELLS WITH DATA

In many situations, you may need to enter a sequence of numbers, dates or times on a worksheet. 1-2-3 facilitates the input of such data using the **Data Fill** command sequence to enter data into various cells on a worksheet.

Entering Sequences of Numbers on a Worksheet

Suppose that you want to enter the sequence of numbers 1 through 10 into cells B6 through B15. Make sure you have a blank worksheet on your screen.

To enter the sequence of numbers:

Press   /

Select   Data

Select   Fill

When you are prompted for the **fill** range:

Move	the cell pointer to cell B6
Type	.
Move	the cell pointer to cell B15
Press	↵

You have designated the set of cells B6 through B15 as the cells in which the sequence of numbers is to be placed.

When prompted for the **start** number:

Type	1
Press	↵

To indicate the **step** value between each number in the sequence is to be the default value of 1:

Press	↵

When you are prompted for the **stop** number:

Press	↵

You accept the stop number of 8191 because the capacity of the range to be filled will limit the maximum value to less than 8191.

Your screen should now have the sequence of numbers 1 through 10 in cells B6 through B15 and look like Figure 7-18.

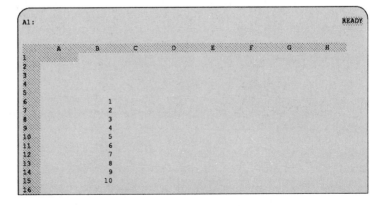

Figure 7-18

Now, suppose you are asked to enter a sequence of even numbers beginning in cell A3 and ending in cell H3.

To enter this sequence of numbers:

Press   /

Select   Data

Select   Fill

Note that the fill range from the previous exercise is highlighted. To escape from the previously defined range:

Press   [Esc]

To indicate the fill range for the present problem:

Move   the cell pointer to cell A3

Type   .

Move   the cell pointer to cell H3

Press   [←]

When prompted for the starting value:

Type   2

Press   [←]

To specify that the step value is 2:

Type   2

Press   [←]

When you are asked for the stopping point,

Press   [←]

because you have already indicated the fill range is A3 through H3.

Your screen should now look like Figure 7-19.

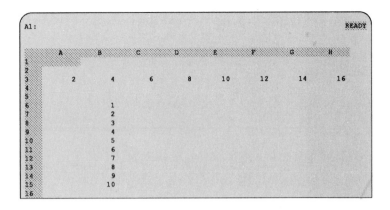

Figure 7-19

Entering a Sequence of Dates

At times, you may desire to place a series of dates on a worksheet. For example, it may be necessary to place the dates for 10 days in a column, or you may want to enter a series of dates that are a specified amount of time apart such as a week.

To illustrate the process of placing a sequence of 10 days on a worksheet, first make sure that you have a blank worksheet on your screen. Then,

Press	/
Select	Data
Select	Fill

To specify the fill range:

Move	the cell pointer to cell B3
Type	.
Move	the cell pointer to cell B12
Press	↵

When you are asked for the starting value, you can indicate that the initial date is July 1, 1989 as follows:

Type	@DATE (89,7,1)
Press	↵

To indicate that step value between dates is one:

Press   ⏎

To specify the ending date:

Type   @DATE (89,7,10)

Press   ⏎

You must enter a stop date and not use the default value of 8191.

Your screen should look like Figure 7-20.

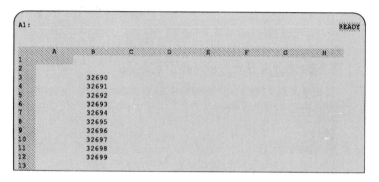

Figure 7-20

The numbers in cells B3 through B12 are called date serial numbers. Each number represents the number of days that have elapsed since December 31, 1899.

To properly format the dates:

Move	the cell pointer to cell B3
Press	/
Select	Range
Select	Format
Select	Date
Select	4 (to indicate the long international format to be used.)
Move	the cell pointer to cell B12
Press	⏎

The dates should now be properly formatted and your screen should look like Figure 7-21.

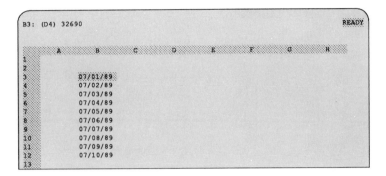

Figure 7-21

Suppose you are asked to create a worksheet in which the column headings are a series of six dates each a week apart with the initial date being August 2 and the last date being September 6 appearing in cells B2 through G2.

To place this series of dates on a worksheet, first make sure that you have a blank worksheet on your screen. Then,

Press	/
Select	Data
Select	Fill
Move	the cell pointer to cell B2
Type	.
Move	the cell pointer to cell G2
Press	⏎

To indicate that August 2, 1989 is the start date:

Type	@DATE (89,8,2)
Press	⏎

To specify that the step value is 1 week:

Type	7	(for 7 days)
Press	⏎	

When prompted for the stop date:

Type	@DATE (89,9,6)

Press ↵

You have indicated that the last date in the sequence is September 6. Your screen should look like Figure 7-22.

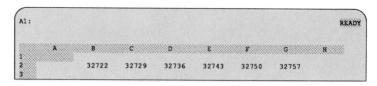

Figure 7-22

To format the data so only the month and day appear on your screen:

Move	the cell pointer to cell B2
Press	/
Select	Range
Select	Format
Select	Date
Select	5
Move	the cell pointer to cell G2
Press	↵

Your screen now should be properly formatted and look like Figure 7-23.

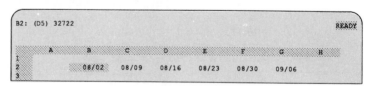

Figure 7-23

■USING DATA TABLES

Data tables are used to illustrate the impact of changing values of variables on the results obtained when formulas are used. A classic example of the need for using a data table occurs when a person tries to evaluate the monthly payment on a loan for various principal amounts, interest rates and time periods. Another example occurs when a sales manager desires to evaluate the impact on an employee's compensation of proposed changes in quotas and commission rates.

Suppose you are considering the purchase of a new luxury automobile by borrowing the money from a bank. The variables that can change include the principal amount, interest rate and number of time periods to repay the loan. In this section, you will use the **Data Table** command sequence available in 1-2-3 to evaluate the impact of changes in such loan variables.

Before using the data table options, you need to have a blank worksheet on your screen and then create a worksheet that looks like Figure 7-24.

The payment amount is computed by using the payment function, @PMT, that is available in 1-2-3. Cell A8 should contain the formula @PMT(A4,A7,A6). Cell A7 should have the formula +A5/12 and represents the monthly interest rate. Notice that since you want a monthly payment value, the annual interest rate must be converted to a monthly rate by dividing by 12. Each of the entries in the @PMT function is referred to as an argument. The three arguments, A4, A7 and A6, refer to the values used for the principal amount, interest rate and time period.

```
A1:                                                         READY

          A        B        C        D        E      F      G      H
1                 LUXURY CAR LOAN AMORTIZATION
2
3     ASSUMPTIONS
4      $40,000             PRINCIPAL
5       12.00%             ANNUAL INTEREST RATE
6          36              LOAN PERIOD IN MONTHS
7        1.00%             MONTHLY INTEREST RATE
8     1,328.57             CALCULATED PAYMENT AMOUNT
9
```

Figure 7-24

Changing the Values of One Variable

The **Data Table 1** sequence of commands can be used to change one of the variables used in computing the payment amount. Suppose you want to see the impact of changing the loan period while holding the principal amount and interest rate constant.

To construct a data table for varying the loan period:

Enter	LOAN in cell A11 and PERIOD in cell A12
Enter	the numbers 36, 48, 60, 72 and 84 in cells A15 through A19

You may use the **Data Fill** command sequence illustrated earlier in this chapter to expedite the process for entering the loan period values that represent 3 through 7 year loan periods.

Enter	PAYMENT in cell B11 and AMOUNT in cell B12

Data Table operations require the use of input cells. In this case the input cell will be A6 which is the loan period value.

To complete the data table:

Move   the cell pointer to cell B14

Type   +A8

Press   ⏎

The payment amount for a loan period of three years appears in cell B14. This indicates to 1-2-3 that you are using the @PMT function computation that appears in cell A8. Your screen should now look like Figure 7-25.

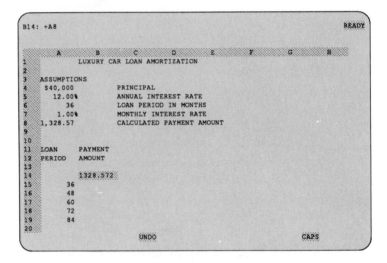

Figure 7-25

To initiate the **Data Table** command sequence for varying one input variable:

Press   /

Select   Data

Select   Table

Select   1

To specify the data table range:

Move	the cell pointer to cell A14
Type	.
Move	the cell pointer to cell B19
Press	⏎

When prompted for the input cell:

Move	the cell pointer to cell A6
Press	⏎

The values for the loan period in cells A15 through A19 will be substituted for the loan period parameter in the @PMT function one at a time and a value for the payment amount will be determined. In a few seconds, the payment amounts will be placed in column B next to the loan period numbers.

You can now format the values in cell B14 through B19 using the **Range Format ,** command sequence so your screen looks like Figure 7-26.

```
B14: (,2) +A8                                                    READY

        A         B         C         D         E       F       G       H
 1               LUXURY CAR LOAN AMORTIZATION
 2
 3   ASSUMPTIONS
 4    $40,000              PRINCIPAL
 5     12.00%              ANNUAL INTEREST RATE
 6        36              LOAN PERIOD IN MONTHS
 7      1.00%              MONTHLY INTEREST RATE
 8   1,328.57              CALCULATED PAYMENT AMOUNT
 9
10
11   LOAN      PAYMENT
12   PERIOD    AMOUNT
13
14              1,328.57
15        36  1,328.57
16        48  1,053.35
17        60    889.78
18        72    782.01
19        84    706.11
20
                          UNDO                            CAPS
```

Figure 7-26

As expected, the payment amount decreases as the loan period increases.

Using the Data Table 1 Command Sequence with Several Formulas

1-2-3 permits you to substitute the value of the input cell in more than one formula. For example, you may want to set up a table that lets you examine simultaneously a change in the principal amount and interest rate for the various loan periods.

Suppose you need to evaluate the following sensitivity cases for the car purchase decision discussed in the last section.

1. What is the payment amount for the various loan period options if the principal is $45,000 instead of $40,000?

2. What is the payment amount for the various loan period options if the interest rate is 10% instead of 12%?

Before starting this exercise, make sure that your screen looks like Figure 7-26. Prior to issuing the Data Table 1 sequence of commands, complete the following instructions:

To enter the additional @PMT function formulas:

Enter	the labels CASE1 in cell C10, LOAN in cell C11 and PAYMENT in cell C12
Enter	the labels CASE2 in cell D10, LOAN in cell D11 and PAYMENT in cell D12
Move	the cell pointer to cell C14
Type	@PMT (45000,A7,A6)
Press	⏎
Move	the cell pointer to cell D14
Type	@PMT (A4,0.1/12,A6)
Press	⏎

Notice that A6 (the loan period) is used in both formulas, because it is the input cell that will be used in the Data Table 1 command sequence. To see the text form of these formulas, first widen columns C and D so each can display 20 characters using the Worksheet Column Column-Range Set-Width command sequence. Then,

Move	the cell pointer to cell C14
Press	/
Select	Range

Select	Format
Select	Text
Move	the cell pointer to cell D14
Press	⏎

When you are finished, your screen should look like Figure 7-27.

```
C14:  (T)  [W20]  @PMT(45000,A7,A6)                                      READY

             A        B          C                  D            E
    1                     LUXURY CAR LOAN AMORTIZATION
    2
    3    ASSUMPTIONS
    4    $40,000           PRINCIPAL
    5      12.00%          ANNUAL INTEREST RATE
    6         36           LOAN PERIOD IN MONTHS
    7       1.00%          MONTHLY INTEREST RATE
    8    1,328.57          CALCULATED PAYMENT AMOUNT
    9
   10                      CASE 1             CASE 2
   11   LOAN      PAYMENT  LOAN               LOAN
   12   PERIOD    AMOUNT   PAYMENT            PAYMENT
   13
   14             1,328.57 @PMT(45000,A7,A6)  @PMT(A4,0.1/12,A6)
   15        36   1,328.57
   16        48   1,053.35
   17        60     889.78
   18        72     782.01
   19        84     706.11
   20
                            UNDO                       CAPS
```

Figure 7-27

To initiate the **Data Table** 1 command sequence:

Press	/
Select	Data
Select	Table
Select	1

To expand the data table range to include the additional formulas:

Move	the cell pointer to column D
Press	⏎

To accept A6 as the input cell:

Press	⏎

The values for the loan period will then be substituted into the original formula as well as the new formulas one at a time and values for the payment amounts will be determined. These payment amounts will appear in columns B through D next to the loan period values.

You can now format the payment amount data using the **Range Format** command sequence and right justify the labels in cells C10 through D12.

Move	the cell pointer to cell C10
Press	/
Select	Range
Select	Label
Select	Right

To highlight all cells that need to be right justified:

Move	the cell pointer to cell D12
Press	⏎

Your screen should look like Figure 7-28.

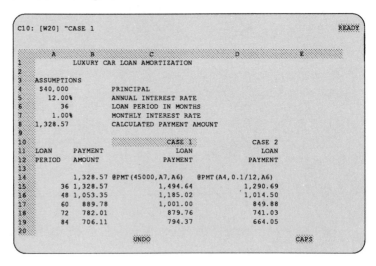

Figure 7-28

Changing the Values of Two Variables

In some situations, you may want to change two of the variables in a formula. 1-2-3 permits you to simultaneously modify two such input cells using the **Data Table 2** command sequence.

Suppose for the luxury car loan decision introduced in the previous section, you want to vary the loan period and interest rates in the loan payment calculation. You specifically want to determine the loan payment amount for 36, 48, 60, 72 and 84 months using 9%, 10%, 11%, 12%, 13% and 14% interest rates.

Before initiating the **Data Table** command sequence, create the worksheet in Figure 7-29. Cell A8 contains the function @PMT (A4,A7,A6).

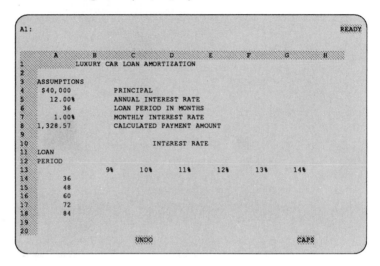

Figure 7-29

When you create a data table that allows you to modify the values of two input cells, the formula that uses the input cells must be placed in the top left corner cell of the data table. In this case you need to place the payment function formula in cell A13.

Move	the cell pointer to cell A13
Type	+A8
Press	↵

The payment amount using the initial assumptions now appears in cell A13. If you so desire, you can format the loan payment amount to two decimal places using the **Range Format** , (comma) command sequence.

To start the **Data Table** command sequence for varying two input cells:

Press	/
Select	Data
Select	Table

Select   2

When prompted for the data table range:

Press   (Esc) to delete the previous data table range, if needed

Move   the cell pointer to cell A13

Type   .

Move   the cell pointer to cell G18

Press   ⏎

To specify loan period as the first input cell:

Move   the cell pointer to cell A6

Press   ⏎

To indicate interest rate is the second input cell:

Move   the cell pointer to cell A5

Press   ⏎

The values for loan period and interest rate will then be substituted into the loan payment calculation formula and in a few seconds the values for the various combinations of loan period and interest rates will appear on the worksheet. The values in the left column of the data table (column A) were substituted into input cell 1 (loan period). The values in the top row of the data table (row 13) were substituted into input cell 2 (interest rate). Format the results using the Range Format , command sequence so your screen will look like Figure 7-30.

```
A1:                                                                    READY

          A        B          C          D        E          F        G        H
 1                 LUXURY CAR LOAN AMORTIZATION
 2
 3     ASSUMPTIONS
 4       $40,000            PRINCIPAL
 5        12.00%            ANNUAL INTEREST RATE
 6           36             LOAN PERIOD IN MONTHS
 7         1.00%            MONTHLY INTEREST RATE
 8      1,328.57            CALCULATED PAYMENT AMOUNT
 9
10                              INTEREST RATE
11     LOAN
12     PERIOD
13     1,328.57        9%        10%        11%      12%        13%       14%
14           36  1,271.99  1,290.69  1,309.55  1,328.57  1,347.76  1,367.11
15           48    995.40  1,014.50  1,033.82  1,053.35  1,073.10  1,093.06
16           60    830.33    849.88    869.70    889.78    910.12    930.73
17           72    721.02    741.03    761.36    782.01    802.96    824.23
18           84    643.56    664.05    684.90    706.11    727.68    749.60
19
20                              UNDO                            CAPS
```

Figure 7-30

■CREATING A FREQUENCY DISTRIBUTION

The **Data D**istribution menu option allows you to determine the frequency distribution of any column or row of numbers. A frequency distribution counts the number of values that fall within specified intervals. Retrieve the original file ABCSAL for use in this exercise.

In this example, you will determine the frequency distribution of salaries based on a bin range set up in cells B17 through B20. The **bin range** is a column containing numbers or formulas that specify the intervals for the frequency distribution. The intervals in the bin range are determined by the user and must always be in ascending order. A blank column should exist to the right of this column (with an additional blank row below the last value in the interval range) where the results will be placed after the **Data D**istribution procedure is invoked through the menu. First, set up the bin range. Use Figure 7-31 as a guide to enter this information in cells B17 through B20, C17 and D21.

```
D21: [W3] '(INDICATES NUMBERS ABOVE MAXIMUM RANGE)                          READY

       A       B            C         D     E        F        G        H        I
2                                        SALARY BUDGET
3
4
5    EMP NO LAST NAME FIRST NAME DIV     QTR1     QTR2     QTR3     QTR4     TOTAL
6       568 SPROUT     AL          3    5,950    5,950    6,450    6,450    24,800
7       123 LYLIE      SUSAN       1    7,800    7,800    7,800    8,580    31,980
8       390 CHIN       TOMMY       2    5,000    5,000    5,200    5,200    20,400
9       972 JOHNSON    SANDRA      1    8,200    8,200    9,000    9,000    34,400
10      898 VALETTI    GEORGE      3    5,900    5,900    6,300    6,300    24,400
11      239 ARMOUR     CYNTHIA     2    5,200    5,200    5,400    5,400    21,200
12      576 JOHNSON    ERNEST      1    8,000    8,000    8,800    8,800    33,600
13      833 JONES      NINA        3    6,750    6,750    6,750    7,450    27,700
14                                     -------  -------  -------  -------  --------
15          TOTAL                      52,800   52,800   55,700   57,180   218,480
16
17          BIN RANGE FREQUENCY
18            23,000
19            28,000
20            33,000
21                                  (INDICATES NUMBERS ABOVE MAXIMUM RANGE)
                                 UNDO                              CAPS
```

Figure 7-31

To find the data distribution for the salaries:

Press	/
Select	Data
Select	Distribution

The prompt "Enter values range:" appears. Since the distribution for this example is for salaries, highlight the total salary amounts:

Move	the cell cursor to cell I6
Type	.
Move	the cell cursor to cell I13
Press	⏎

The prompt "Enter bin range:" appears. The bin range chosen for this example is from 23,000 through 33,000, highlight the range:

Move	the cell cursor to cell B18
Type	.
Move	the cell cursor to cell B20

Press   ⏎

The frequency of the salary amounts appears in cells C18 through C21.

The 2 in cell C18 indicates the number of salaries that are less than or equal to $23,000.

The 3 in cell C19 indicates the number of salaries between $23,000 and $28,000, including $28,000.

The 1 in cell C20 indicates the number of salaries between $28,000 and $33,000, including 33,000.

The 2 in cell C21 indicates the number of salaries greater than $33,000.

Your screen should look like the final illustration in Figure 7-32. Figure 7-32, Parts 1 through 3, display the entire Data Distribution procedure.

Step One of the Data Distribution Procedure: Specify the Desired Values through the Menu.

```
I13: @SUM(E13..H13)                                              POINT
Enter values range: I6..I13

       A      B          C      D    E        F        G        H       I
2                                    SALARY BUDGET
3
4
5    EMP NO LAST NAME FIRST NAME DIV QTR1     QTR2     QTR3     QTR4    TOTAL
6      568 SPROUT    AL          3   5,950    5,950    6,450    6,450   24,800
7      123 LYLIE     SUSAN       1   7,800    7,800    7,800    8,580   31,980
8      390 CHIN      TOMMY       2   5,000    5,000    5,200    5,200   20,400
9      972 JOHNSON   SANDRA      1   8,200    8,200    9,000    9,000   34,400
10     898 VALETTI   GEORGE      3   5,900    5,900    6,300    6,300   24,400
11     239 ARMOUR    CYNTHIA     2   5,200    5,200    5,400    5,400   21,200
12     576 JOHNSON   ERNEST      1   8,000    8,000    8,800    8,800   33,600
13     833 JONES     NINA        3   6,750    6,750    6,750    7,450   27,700
14                                   -------  -------  -------  ------- --------
15          TOTAL                    52,800   52,800   55,700   57,180  218,480
16
17          BIN RANGE FREQUENCY
18             23,000
19             28,000
20             33,000
21                                   (INDICATES NUMBERS ABOVE MAXIMUM RANGE)
```

Figure 7-32
Part 1

Step Two of the Data Distribution Procedure: Specify the Desired Bin Range through the Menu.

```
B20: [W10] 33000                                                    POINT
Enter values range: I6..I13           Enter bin range: B18..B20

       A      B          C        D    E       F       G       H       I
 2                                     SALARY BUDGET
 3
 4
 5   EMP NO LAST NAME FIRST NAME DIV   QTR1    QTR2    QTR3    QTR4    TOTAL
 6     568 SPROUT    AL          3     5,950   5,950   6,450   6,450   24,800
 7     123 LYLIE     SUSAN       1     7,800   7,800   7,800   8,580   31,980
 8     390 CHIN      TOMMY       2     5,000   5,000   5,200   5,200   20,400
 9     972 JOHNSON   SANDRA      1     8,200   8,200   9,000   9,000   34,400
10     898 VALETTI   GEORGE      3     5,900   5,900   6,300   6,300   24,400
11     239 ARMOUR    CYNTHIA     2     5,200   5,200   5,400   5,400   21,200
12     576 JOHNSON   ERNEST      1     8,000   8,000   8,800   8,800   33,600
13     833 JONES     NINA        3     6,750   6,750   6,750   7,450   27,700
14                                     ------- ------- ------- ------- -------
15         TOTAL                       52,800  52,800  55,700  57,180  218,480
16
17         BIN RANGE FREQUENCY
18           23,000
19           28,000
20           33,000
21                                 (INDICATES NUMBERS ABOVE MAXIMUM RANGE)
```

Figure 7-32
Part 2

Step Three of the Data Distribution Procedure: After pressing ⊖ , the Frequency Distribution is displayed next to the Specified Bin Range.

```
D21: [W3] '(INDICATES NUMBERS ABOVE MAXIMUM RANGE)                  READY

       A      B          C        D    E       F       G       H       I
 2                                     SALARY BUDGET
 3
 4
 5   EMP NO LAST NAME FIRST NAME DIV   QTR1    QTR2    QTR3    QTR4    TOTAL
 6     568 SPROUT    AL          3     5,950   5,950   6,450   6,450   24,800
 7     123 LYLIE     SUSAN       1     7,800   7,800   7,800   8,580   31,980
 8     390 CHIN      TOMMY       2     5,000   5,000   5,200   5,200   20,400
 9     972 JOHNSON   SANDRA      1     8,200   8,200   9,000   9,000   34,400
10     898 VALETTI   GEORGE      3     5,900   5,900   6,300   6,300   24,400
11     239 ARMOUR    CYNTHIA     2     5,200   5,200   5,400   5,400   21,200
12     576 JOHNSON   ERNEST      1     8,000   8,000   8,800   8,800   33,600
13     833 JONES     NINA        3     6,750   6,750   6,750   7,450   27,700
14                                     ------- ------- ------- ------- -------
15         TOTAL                       52,800  52,800  55,700  57,180  218,480
16
17         BIN RANGE FREQUENCY
18           23,000        2
19           28,000        3
20           33,000        1
21                         2 (INDICATES NUMBERS ABOVE MAXIMUM RANGE)
                         UNDO
```

Figure 7-32
Part 3

■ GRAPHING A FREQUENCY DISTRIBUTION

Assuming that the previous exercise has just been completed and the data distribution worksheet is on your screen, you will now complete the exercise by graphing the distribution of salaries.

For the X-axis on the graph you will use the bin range. To document the cell indicating the numbers above the maximum range:

Move	the pointer to cell B21
Type	">33,000
Press	⏎

By performing this step, >33,000 will appear on the graph to indicate those numbers beyond the bin range. (The double quote right-justifies this label in cell B21.)

To create a graph depicting the results of the frequency distribution in the previous exercise:

Press	/
Select	Graph
Select	Type
Select	Pie

For the X-axis on the graph:

Select	X-Axis

For the X-axis, select the numbers in the bin range:

Type	B18.B21
Press	⏎

To choose the first data range for the frequency data:

Select	A
Type	C18.C21
Press	⏎

To enter a title for the graph:

Select	Options
Select	Titles

> **Select** First

For the graph title:

> **Type** FREQUENCY DISTRIBUTION OF SALARIES
>
> **Press** ⏎

To exit the current menu:

> **Select** Quit

To view the graph:

> **Select** View

The graph should look like Figure 7-33.

FREQUENCY DISTRIBUTION OF SALARIES

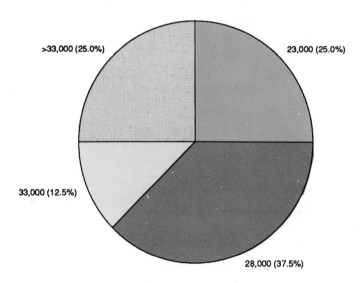

Figure 7-33

After viewing the graph:

Press   ↵

To leave the current menu:

Select   Quit

You do not need to save or print the graph.

SUMMARY

In Lotus 1-2-3, a spreadsheet may be set up as a database, or a collection of related records. The **Data Sort** command sequence can sort records in a database with up to two sort keys chosen by the user. The **Data Query** can perform a query upon a database according to criteria you specify. You must specify the database range, indicate the criteria, and may even specify an output range for the desired data. The **Data Fill** option provides an easy way to place sequences of numbers and dates on a worksheet. The **Data Table** capability allows you to create tables that illustrate the impact of changing values for a variable in a decision-making situation. Additional **Data Query** options allow you to delete duplicate records in an output range and also to delete specified records in a database (Unique and Delete). Lotus 1-2-3 also contains a **Data Distribution** command that you can use to determine the frequency distribution of data in a specified range.

KEY CONCEPTS

#AND#	Database
#OR#	Database table
Bin range	Field
Criteria	Field title
Data Distribution	Input range
Data Range	File
Data Sort	Key
Data Query Delete	Output range
Data Query Extract	Primary key
Data Fill	Query
Data Table	QUERY key [F7]
Data Query Find	Record
Data Query Unique	Secondary key

CHAPTER SEVEN
EXERCISE 1

INSTRUCTIONS: Circle T if the statement is true and F if the statement is false.

T   F   1. When sorting a database in Lotus 1-2-3, the data range must include the field titles.

T   F   2. The field titles must be located in the line directly above the first record of the database for the **Data Query** command sequence to work properly.

T   F   3. It is appropriate to have more than one line consisting of field titles designated in the input range.

T   F   4. Each criteria consists of at least two cells.

T   F   5. The input range, criteria and output range must be manually set up on the worksheet and then identified through the menu options.

T   F   6. The output range allows you to copy the desired fields that match the criteria to another area on the worksheet.

T   F   7. When designating the output range, you may highlight only the field names that are desired; the records will appear directly below the field names on the worksheet in the output range when the **Query Find** is executed.

T   F   8. The QUERY key allows the user to perform a query based upon previously set ranges.

T   F   9. The criteria for a worksheet can be chosen by setting the bin range.

T   F   10. The **Query Unique** command deletes multiple records in a database table on a file.

T   F   11. The **Data Table** option makes it possible to analyze changes in variables that impact decision-making situations.

CHAPTER SEVEN
EXERCISE 2
Sorting Records Using the Primary Key

INSTRUCTIONS: Create the file PERSON. Use Figure 7-34 as a guide.

Column A is 18 characters wide.

Column B is 11 characters wide.

Column C is 14 characters wide.

Column D is 5 characters wide.

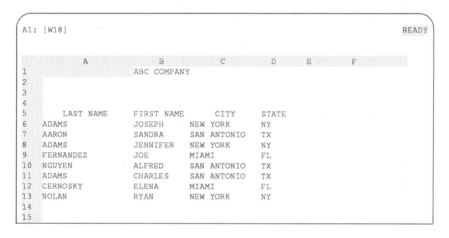

```
A1: [W18]                                                          READY

              A               B              C        D     E     F
 1                      ABC COMPANY
 2
 3
 4
 5       LAST NAME     FIRST NAME       CITY      STATE
 6    ADAMS           JOSEPH        NEW YORK      NY
 7    AARON           SANDRA        SAN ANTONIO   TX
 8    ADAMS           JENNIFER      NEW YORK      NY
 9    FERNANDEZ       JOE           MIAMI         FL
10    NGUYEN          ALFRED        SAN ANTONIO   TX
11    ADAMS           CHARLES       SAN ANTONIO   TX
12    CERNOSKY        ELENA         MIAMI         FL
13    NOLAN           RYAN          NEW YORK      NY
14
15
```

Figure 7-34

Sort the data in the file PERSON in alphabetical order by city.
Print the worksheet with the properly sorted data.

Sort
Person

CHAPTER SEVEN
EXERCISE 3
Sorting Records Using Primary and Secondary Keys

INSTRUCTIONS: Sort the last names in the file PERSON in alphabetical order within each city.

Print the worksheet with the properly sorted data.

CHAPTER SEVEN
EXERCISE 4
Querying Records Using One Criteria

INSTRUCTIONS: Retrieve the original file PERSON for use in this exercise.

Create the appropriate criteria to extract only individuals living in Miami, FL.

For the output range, extract the person's last name and first name.

Print the worksheet with the results.

CHAPTER SEVEN
EXERCISE 5
Querying Records Using Two Criteria

PERSON
SAVE UNER

INSTRUCTIONS: Retrieve the original file PERSON for use in this exercise.

Create the appropriate criteria to extract only those individuals living in New York, NY or San Antonio, TX.

For the output range, extract the person's last name, first name, city and state.

Print the worksheet with the results.

CHAPTER SEVEN
EXERCISE 6
Querying with Multiple Criteria

INSTRUCTIONS: Retrieve the original file PERSON for use in this exercise.

Create the appropriate criteria to extract only those individuals having a last name of Adams who live in New York, NY.

For the output range, extract the person's last name and first name.

Print the worksheet with the results.

CHAPTER SEVEN
EXERCISE 7
Filling Cells with Numbers

INSTRUCTIONS: Make sure you have a blank worksheet on your screen.

Using the Data Fill command sequence, place the sequence of numbers 1, 4, 7, 10, 13, 16, 19 in cells A2 through G2.

Using the Data Fill command sequence, place the sequence of numbers .1, .2, .3, .4, .5, .6 in cells A6 through A11.

Print the completed worksheet.

CHAPTER SEVEN
EXERCISE 8
Filling Cells with Dates

INSTRUCTIONS: Make sure you have a blank worksheet on your screen.

Using the Data Fill command sequence, place the sequence of dates May 3, May 7, May 11, May 15 for the year 1991 in cells B2 through E2.

As required, format the date serial numbers so that an appropriate form of the date appears. Print the worksheet after entering the indicated data.

CHAPTER SEVEN
EXERCISE 9
Changing the Values of One Variables in a Data Table

INSTRUCTIONS: Suppose you are considering the purchase of a house. The current interest rate is 11 percent for a 20-year fixed rate loan. Create a data table that contains the monthly payment for a house if the price is $75,000, $80,000, $85,000, $90,000 or $95,000 using the interest rate of 11 percent and assuming a 20-year loan period.

Print the data table after it is prepared.

CHAPTER SEVEN
EXERCISE 10
Changing the Values of Two Variables in a Data Table

INSTRUCTIONS: Suppose you are considering the purchase of some property that is priced in the $50,000 to $70,000 price range. Assume that you can obtain a 30-year fixed rate loan from several financial institutions with an interest rate varying between 9 percent and 11 percent.

Create a data table that contains the monthly payment amount after varying the purchase price from $50,000 to $70,000 in increments of $5,000. You also need to use an initial interest rate of 9 percent and increase it to a maximum of 11 percent using one-half percent increments.

Use a 30-year loan period for all calculations.

Print the data table after the monthly payment values have been determined.

CHAPTER SEVEN
EXERCISE 11
Creating a Frequency Distribution

INSTRUCTIONS: Retrieve the original file ABCSAL for use in this exercise.

Use the **D**ata **D**istribution menu option to determine the number of people in each division in the ABCSAL data table.

The bin range should encompass the division numbers in the database Print the worksheet after calculating the number of people there are in each division.

CHAPTER SEVEN
EXERCISE 12
Graphing a Frequency Distribution

INSTRUCTIONS: Use the results of Exercise 11 in this exercise.

Create a pie graph using the data for the distribution of people for the three divisions in ABC Company.

Print the pie graph depicting the frequency distribution.

CHAPTER EIGHT

SPECIAL FUNCTIONS IN LOTUS 1-2-3

String Functions

Special Characters and Creating Characters
Extracting Portions of a String from a Label
Changing the Case of a String
Converting Values to Strings and Strings to Values
Determining the Characteristics of a String

Summary
Key Concepts

OBJECTIVES

In this chapter, you will learn to use and apply the following types of special functions available in Lotus 1-2-3:

- ■ Statistical Analysis
- ■ Financial Analysis
- ■ Date and Time
- ■ Logical
- ■ Database
- ■ Mathematical
- ■ Special
- ■ String

■ CHAPTER OVERVIEW

Lotus 1-2-3 has 93 special functions. Suppose you want to compute the monthly payment for a 30-year, $100,000 bank loan with an 11 percent interest rate. 1-2-3 has the @PMT function that allows you to compute the payment amount. In earlier exercises, you have used some of the other special functions such as @SUM and @ROUND. In this chapter, you will learn to use many of the special functions in the following categories: statistical analysis, financial analysis, date and time, logical, database, mathematical, special, and string. Each of the special functions has a specific structure that you must use. The general format of a special function is:

```
@function name(argument1,argument2,...argumentn)
```

You must enter the function on your worksheet using the correct syntax or errors will occur. In some cases, an argument may be optional. If an argument is optional, brackets will appear in the text, but are not required when the function is used. Press the ⏎ key after entering the function.

Since each function requires various types of data to utilize it, you will need to erase your screen each time you work through the example for a new function. You do not need to save the results of any of the example problems covered in this chapter.

■STATISTICAL ANALYSIS FUNCTIONS

Lotus 1-2-3 has 7 statistical analysis functions. They include:

@SUM	Compute the sum of a list of cell values
@COUNT	Compute the number of items in a list of cell values
@AVG	Compute the arithmetic mean for a list of cell values
@MIN	Identify the minimum value for a list of cell values
@MAX	Identify the maximum value for a list of cell values
@VAR	Compute the population variance for a list of cells
@STD	Compute the population standard deviation for a list of cells

The general format for the statistical analysis functions is as follows:

```
@function name(first cell..last cell)
```

For example, to compute the sum of the numbers in cells A1 through G1 in a worksheet, the formula @SUM(A1..G1) is used. The function name should be used exactly as it is listed above (e.g. the function name for averaging numbers is written as AVG).

Using the Statistical Analysis Functions

In this section you will learn to use each of the statistical functions. First, create a worksheet like Figure 8-1.

```
A1: [W30] 'STATISTICAL ANALYSIS FUNCTIONS                                READY


                         A                    B        C        D        E
 1   STATISTICAL ANALYSIS FUNCTIONS
 2
 3
 4                                            58
 5                                            50
 6                                            67
 7                                            89
 8
 9   SUM
10   COUNT
11   AVERAGE
12   MINIMUM
13   MAXIMUM
14   POPULATION VARIANCE
15   POPULATION STANDARD DEVIATION
16
17
```

Figure 8-1

@SUM

To compute the sum of the four numbers in cells B4 through B7 using the @SUM function:

Move   the cell pointer to cell B9

Type   @SUM(

Move   the cell pointer to cell B4

Type   .

Move   the cell pointer to cell B7

Type   )

The formula @SUM(B4..B7) should now appear in the control panel.

Press   ⏎

The formula was entered into cell B9; the result is 264.

When using the @SUM formula in worksheets, you may wish to include the cell immediately above and below the range of numbers actually being added. For example, the formula @SUM(B3..B8) could be used instead of @SUM(B4..B7) to total the numbers in this exercise. If a row is inserted (or deleted) at the top or bottom of the range to add (or delete) a number, the @SUM command will adjust correctly to the change. If a label such as a subtotal line is included in the range, it will not be a problem because Lotus 1-2-3 considers labels to have a value of 0. For the purposes of this example, this technique was not used.

Rather than moving the cell pointer to the cells to be used in computation, you can type the formula @SUM(B4.B7) directly in cell B9 and press ⏎ to obtain the same result. The advantage of highlighting the numbers to be used in the formula is that you will be less likely to make errors and enter the wrong cells. When entering the remaining statistical analysis functions, the formula will be typed directly into the cell to save you some time.

@COUNT

To count the items in cells B4 through B7 using the @COUNT function:

      Move   the cell pointer to cell B10

      Enter   @COUNT(B4.B7)

Note that only one period needs to be typed within the formula. Typing @COUNT(B4.B7) produces the same result as typing @COUNT(B4..B7). The formula @COUNT(B4..B7) appears in the control panel. The number 4 appears in cell B10.

@AVG

To compute the average of the numbers in cells B4 through B7 using the @AVG function:

      Move   the cell pointer to cell B11

      Enter   @AVG(B4.B7)

The formula @AVG(B4..B7) appears in the control panel. The number 66 appears in cell B11.

@MIN

To determine the smallest value of the items in cells B4 through B7 using the @MIN function:

      Move   the cell pointer to cell B12

      Enter   @MIN(B4.B7)

The formula @MIN(B4..B7) appears in the control panel. The number 50 appears in cell B12.

@MAX

To determine the largest value of the items in cells B4 through B7 using the @MAX function:

      Move   the cell pointer to cell B13

Enter   @MAX(B4.B7)

The formula @MAX(B4..B7) appears in the control panel. The number 89 appears in cell B13.

@VAR for a Population

To determine the population variance of the numbers in cells B4 through B7 using the @VAR function:

Move   the cell pointer to cell B14

Enter   @VAR(B4.B7)

The formula @VAR(B4..B7) appears in the control panel. The number 212.5 appears in cell B14. It is assumed you have all the values that need to be considered and the data is not a sample of values from a larger set of data.

@STD for a Population

To determine the standard deviation of the numbers in cells B4 through B7 using the @STD function:

Move   the cell pointer to cell B15

Enter   @STD(B4.B7)

The formula @STD(B4..B7) appears in the control panel. The number 14.57737 appears in cell B15. It is assumed you have all the values that need to be considered and the data is not a sample of values from a larger set of data. Your screen should look like Figure 8-2.

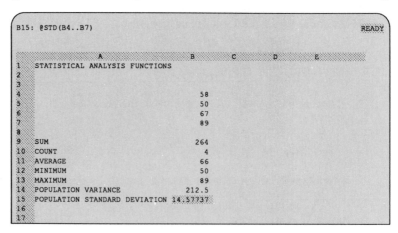

Figure 8-2

When using the statistical analysis functions, it is important to note that labels have a value of zero and can distort the desired computations. In the following exercise, you will erase one of the numbers in the range B4..B7 by pressing the space bar. The results are then discussed.

Move   the cell pointer to cell B6

Press   the space bar

Press   ⏎

Although cell B6 appears to be blank, it actually contains a label. In the control panel, an apostrophe appears. Whenever a label is typed, the default label prefix is the apostrophe. The cell is not really blank; it contains a space. A space is treated as a label and therefore is given a value of 0 when used in a computation. For example, the minimum value computed by the @MIN function is now zero. The count computed by the @COUNT function still shows four items since the @COUNT function counts both numeric and non-numeric items. Refer to Figure 8-3 to see how the label distorts the results of the computations.

A label counts as the value 0 in computations.

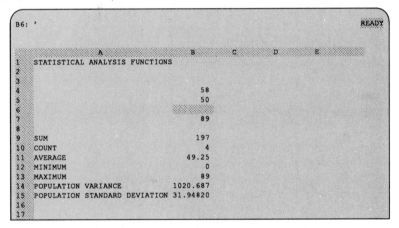

```
B6: '                                                              READY

              A                    B      C      D      E
 1  STATISTICAL ANALYSIS FUNCTIONS
 2
 3
 4                                   58
 5                                   50
 6
 7                                   89
 8
 9  SUM                             197
10  COUNT                             4
11  AVERAGE                       49.25
12  MINIMUM                           0
13  MAXIMUM                          89
14  POPULATION VARIANCE         1020.687
15  POPULATION STANDARD DEVIATION 31.94820
16
17
```

Figure 8-3

You can correct this problem by erasing the contents of cell B6. To truly erase cell B6, use the **Range Erase** command sequence. Notice that the formulas have accurately calculated the desired results. Your screen should look like Figure 8-4.

A blank cell will not count as any value in computations.

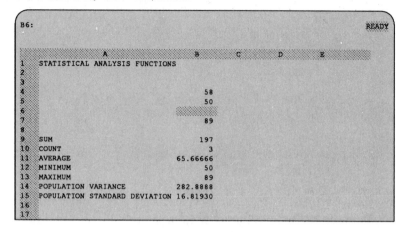

Figure 8-4

■FINANCIAL ANALYSIS FUNCTIONS

The 11 financial analysis functions available in Lotus 1-2-3 include:

CAPITAL BUDGETING:

@IRR   Internal rate of return

@NPV   Net present value

ANNUITIES:

@FV   Future value

@PV   Present value

@TERM   Number of time periods needed in the term of
                 an ordinary annuity earning a specific periodic
                 interest rate to accumulate a future value

@PMT   Payment amount

DEPRECIATION:

@SLN   Straight-line depreciation

@DDB   Double-declining balance depreciation

@SYD   Sum-of-the-Years' digits depreciation

SINGLE-SUM COMPOUNDING:

@CTERM   Number of time periods necessary for the
                        value of an investment to increase to a specific
                        value in the future

@RATE   Periodic interest rate necessary for the value
                        of an investment to grow to a specific
                        future value

Capital Budgeting

The two financial functions that can be used in capital budgeting and project evaluation activities are @IRR and @NPV.

@IRR

The @IRR function computes the internal rate of return for a series of cash flows that occur at regular periodic intervals. You must supply the cash flows and a guess rate for the internal rate of return. The format of the @IRR function is as follows:

```
@IRR(rate,range of cash flows)
```

Two sets of information are needed in the formula—the guess rate and the cash flows. Sets of information needed for a function to compute accurately are referred to as **arguments**. Arguments must be entered in the correct order and must be separated by a comma. Note that no space should be entered after the comma that separates the two arguments in the @IRR function.

In this exercise, suppose that an investment is being considered that requires a cash investment of $2,100 the first year and the anticipated cash flows in years 2 through 5 are respectively $1,300, $700, $500 and $300.

If necessary, erase your screen. Create a worksheet like Figure 8-5.

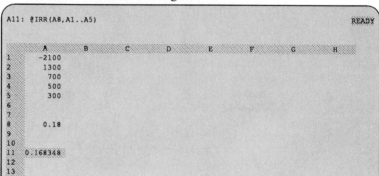

```
A8:  0.18                                                        READY

          A         B         C         D         E         F         G         H
1       -2100
2        1300
3         700
4         500
5         300
6
7
8        0.18
9
10
```

Figure 8-5

The initial investment, actually a cash outflow, is in cell A1. The negative number indicates the initial cash investment made by the investor. The range of anticipated cash flows from the investment appear in cells A2 through A5. The guess at the internal rate of return of 18 percent appears in cell A8.

To find the internal rate of return for the investment on which you entered data:

Move   the cell pointer to cell A11

Type   @IRR(A8,A1.A5)

The first argument in the @IRR formula identifies A8 as the cell with the guess rate of 18 percent. The second argument identifies A1..A5 as the cash flows beginning with the initial investment of $2,100 and ending with the cash flow in YEAR 5 of $300.

To enter the function in cell A11:

Press   ⏎

The function appears in the control panel. The result .168348 or about 16.83 percent is displayed. The screen should look like Figure 8-6.

```
A11:  @IRR(A8,A1..A5)                                           READY

          A         B         C         D         E         F         G         H
1       -2100
2        1300
3         700
4         500
5         300
6
7
8        0.18
9
10
11   0.168348
12
13
```

Figure 8-6

Note that the guess rate could have been entered directly into the function as @IRR(.18,A1..A5). The advantage of the guess rate being entered outside of the function is that it can be changed more readily. The cash flows must be entered as a range that is located elsewhere on the worksheet. A single-cell item, however, either can be either entered directly into the formula or referenced with a cell address (e.g., .18 or A8 is acceptable in the @IRR function in the previous exercise).

ERR may appear as a result of using the @IRR function if convergence to within .0000001 does not occur within 30 iterations. Change the guess rate to a higher or lower value until a value appears for the internal rate of return.

@NPV

The net present value computes the present value for a set of cash flows using a specified discount rate. All cash flows are assumed to occur at the end of each year. The format of the NPV function is:

```
@NPV(rate,range of cells)
```

In this exercise, consider an investment project that requires you to invest $2,000 initially and you receive payments of $900, $850, $600, $350, $200, and $50 at the end of the first through the sixth years. Assume that 10 percent is an appropriate discount rate.

To solve this problem, create the worksheet in Figure 8-7.

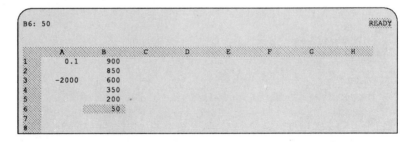

Figure 8-7

The discount rate is 10 percent and appears in cell A1. The initial investment is in cell A3. The cash flow payments are in cells B1 through B6.

To compute the net present value of the cash flows and add it to the initial investment of $2,000 (in cell A3):

Move	the cell pointer to cell C1
Type	@NPV(A1,B1.B6)+A3

The first argument identifies A1 as the discount rate of 10 percent. The second argument identifies B1..B6 as the cash flows beginning with the first year of $900 and ending with the last year at $50. Note that A3 (the initial investment) must be added to the net present value of the cash flows because, if it were included in the formula, it would be discounted.

To enter the function in cell C1:

Press ⏎

The formula appears in the control panel. The result 362.9127 or $362.91 is displayed. Your screen should look like Figure 8-8.

```
C1: @NPV(A1,B1..B6)+A3                                              READY

         A         B          C        D      E      F      G      H
1       0.1       900  362.9127
2                 850
3     -2000       600
4                 350
5                 200
6                  50
7
8
```

Figure 8-8

If desired, you can format the results with a dollar sign and two decimal places by using the **Range Format Currency** command sequence.

Annuities

The four functions that are available in 1-2-3 that are related to ordinary annuities include: @FV, @PV, @TERM and @PMT.

@FV

The future value function computes the future value of an annuity given the payment per period, an interest rate per period and the number of periods. The general format of the @FV function is as follows:

            @FV(payment, interest rate, term)

Assume you want to compute the future value of an annuity when the payment amount is $1,500, the interest rate is 13 percent and the term is 10 years.

In the previous exercises in this chapter, single-cell items used in the financial analysis functions were not placed directly into the function, but were referenced by cell address. In this example, all three arguments are single-cell items. Instead of entering a formula in a format such as the following —@FV(C1,C2,C3) —all of the arguments in this formula can be placed directly into the formula—@FV(1500,.13,10).

To find the future value of the given data:

Press   [Home] (if necessary)

Type   @FV(1500,.13,10)

The first argument specifies the payment per year as $1,500. The second argument specifies the interest rate as 13 percent. The third argument specifies the term as 10 years. To enter the function:

Press   [←]

The function appears in the control panel. The result 27629.62 or $27,629.62 is displayed on the worksheet. Your screen should look like Figure 8-9.

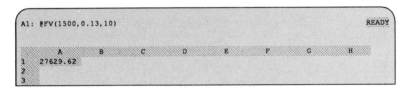

A1: @FV(1500,0.13,10)   READY

	A	B	C	D	E	F	G	H
1	27629.62							
2								
3								

Figure 8-9

@PV

The present value function computes the present value of an annuity given a payment per period, interest rate per period, and the number of time periods. The general format of the @PV function is as follows:

        @PV(payment, rate, number of periods)

In this exercise, you will determine the present value of an annuity where payments are $1,500 per year, the interest rate is 13 percent and the term is 10 years.

To find the present value of the given data:

Press   [Home] (if necessary)

Type   @PV(1500,.13,10)

The first argument identifies the payment amount of $1,500. The second argument identifies the interest rate of 13 percent. The third argument identifies the term as 10 years.

To enter the function:

Press   ⏎

The function appears in the control panel. The result is 8139.365 or $8,139.37. The screen should look like Figure 8-10.

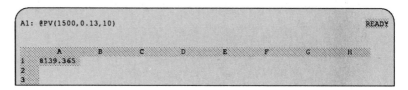

Figure 8-10

@TERM

@TERM calculates the number of payment periods in a term of an ordinary annuity earning a periodic interest rate necessary to accumulate a future value. Each payment is equal to the given payment amount in the formula. The general format for the @TERM function is as follows:

@TERM(payment,periodic interest rate,future value)

In this exercise, assume that $4,500 has been deposited each year on the same date into an account that pays an interest rate of 6 percent, compounded annually. The @TERM function will be used to determine how long it will take for you to have $20,000 in the account.

Using the given data:

Press   (Home) (if necessary)

Type   @TERM(4500,.06,20000)

The first argument identifies $4,500 as the payment amount. The second argument identifies .06 as the periodic interest rate. The third argument represents $20,000 as the future value.

To enter the function:

Press   ⏎

The answer is 4.056859, or about 4 years. Your screen should look like Figure 8-11.

```
A1: @TERM(4500,0.06,20000)                                    READY

        A        B        C        D        E        F        G        H
1   4.056859
2
3
```

Figure 8-11

@PMT

You can compute the payment per period if you are given the principal amount, the interest rate per period and the number of periods. The general format for the @PMT function is as follows:

```
@PMT(principal, interest rate, term)
```

Suppose the principal of a loan is $1,200, the interest rate is 15 percent and the number of time periods is 10 years.

To determine the payment per year of the given data:

Press   ⎡Home⎤   (if necessary)

Type   @PMT(1200,.15,10)

The first argument identifies the principal of $1,200. The second argument identifies the interest rate of 15 percent. The third argument identifies the term as 10 years.

To enter the function:

Press   ⏎

The function appears in the control panel. The result is 239.1024 or $239.10 payment per year. Your screen should look like Figure 8-12.

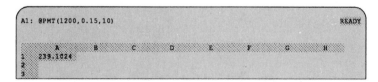

```
A1: @PMT(1200,0.15,10)                                        READY

        A        B        C        D        E        F        G        H
1   239.1024
2
3
```

Figure 8-12

Depreciation

The three depreciation functions included in Lotus 1-2-3 are: @SLN, @DDB, and @SYD.

@SLN

The straight-line depreciation of an asset can be computed for one period given the cost, salvage value, and estimated useful life of the asset. The general format for the @SLN function is as follows:

@SLN(cost,salvage value,estimated useful life)

In this exercise, you will determine the straight-line depreciation for equipment that is purchased for $13,000. The estimated useful life of the equipment is 6 years and the salvage value is estimated at $1,000.

To complete the next three exercises, create the worksheet in Figure 8-13, but do not include the function for computing the straight line depreciation.

To determine the straight-line depreciation for the equipment data:

Move   the cell pointer to cell B5

Type   @SLN(B1,B2,B3)

The first argument identifies B1 as the cell containing the cost of $13,000. The second argument identifies B2 as the cell containing the salvage value of $1,000. The third argument identifies B3 as the cell containing the useful life of 6 years. The formula @SLN(13000,1000,6) could have been entered as an alternative to using cell addresses for the various arguments.

To enter the function:

Press   ↵

The function appears in the control panel. The result 2000 or $2,000 is displayed on the worksheet. Your screen should look like Figure 8-13.

```
B5:  @SLN(B1,B2,B3)                                                  READY

                   A                B       C      D      E      F
1   COST                          13000
2   SALVAGE VALUE                  1000
3   USEFUL LIFE                       6
4
5   STRAIGHT LINE                  2000
6   DOUBLE DECLINING BALANCE
7   SUM-OF-THE-YEARS DIGITS
8
9
```

Figure 8-13

If you desire, you can format the results with a dollar sign and two decimal places.

@DDB

This exercise assumes you have just finished the previous exercise and the results are still displayed on the screen.

The depreciation of an asset using the double-declining balance method can be computed for a specified period given the cost, salvage value, estimated useful life and the desired time period. The general format for the @DDB function is as follows:

@DDB(cost,salvage value,estimated useful life,period)

In this exercise, you will use the data given in the previous exercise to compute the depreciation for the equipment for the first year using the double-declining balance method.

To document that the depreciation will be computed only for YEAR 1 in this example (an optional step):

Move   the cell pointer to cell C6

Enter   YEAR 1

To compute the depreciation using the double-declining balance method:

Move   the cell pointer to cell B6

Type   @DDB(B1,B2,B3,1)

The first argument identifies B1 as the cell containing the cost at $13,000. The second argument identifies B2 as the cell containing the salvage value at $1,000. The third argument identifies B3 as the cell containing the useful life of the equipment at 6 years. The fourth argument indicates that this computation represents the depreciation for YEAR 1.

To enter the function:

Press   ⏎

The function appears in the control panel. The result 4333.333 or $4,333.33 is displayed.
Your screen should look like Figure 8-14.

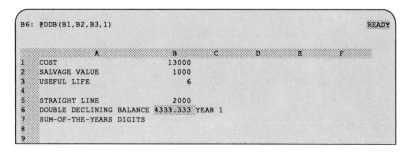

Figure 8-14

To compute the depreciation for the other time periods, you would have to enter the function
again for each of the desired time periods.

@SYD

This exercise assumes you have just finished the previous exercise and the results are still
displayed on the screen.

The depreciation of an asset using the sum-of-the-years' digits method can be computed for
a specified period given the cost, salvage value, estimated useful life and the desired time
period. The general format for the @SYD function is as follows:

        @SYD(cost,salvage value,estimated useful life,period)

In this exercise, you will use the data given in the previous exercise to calculate the
depreciation for the equipment for the third year using the sum-of-the-years' digits method.

To indicate that the depreciation will be computed only for YEAR 3 in this example (an
optional step):

        Move   the cell pointer to cell C7

        Type   YEAR 3

To compute the depreciation using the sum-of-the-years' digits method:

        Move   the cell pointer to cell B7

        Type   @SYD(B1,B2,B3,3)

The first argument identifies B1 as the cell containing the cost at $13,000. The second argument identifies B2 as the cell containing the salvage value at $1,000. The third argument identifies B3 as the cell containing the useful life of 6 years. The fourth argument indicates that this computation is for YEAR 3.

To enter the function:

Press   ⏎

The function appears in the control panel. The result 2285.714 or $2,285.71 is displayed on the worksheet. Your screen should look like Figure 8-15.

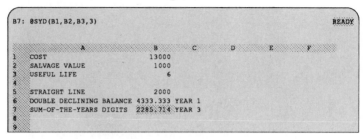

```
B7: @SYD(B1,B2,B3,3)                                               READY

                    A                B       C        D       E       F
1   COST                          13000
2   SALVAGE VALUE                  1000
3   USEFUL LIFE                       6
4
5   STRAIGHT LINE                  2000
6   DOUBLE DECLINING BALANCE 4333.333 YEAR 1
7   SUM-OF-THE-YEARS DIGITS  2285.714 YEAR 3
8
9
```

Figure 8-15

If you desire, the results could be formatted with a dollar sign and two decimal places. To compute the depreciation values for the other time periods, you would have to enter the function again for each of the desired time periods.

Single-Sum Compounding

The two single-sum compounding functions available in 1-2-3 are @CTERM and @RATE.

@CTERM

The @CTERM function calculates the number of compounding periods it will take for an investment with a specified initial value to increase to a future value. A fixed interest rate per compounding period is used. The general format for the @CTERM function is as follows:

```
@CTERM(periodic interest rate,future value, present
value)
```

In this exercise, assume that $4,500 was deposited in an account that pays an annual interest rate of 6 percent, compounded monthly. The @CTERM function can be used to determine how long it will be before you have $20,000 in the account.

Using the given data:

Press   (Home)

Type   @CTERM(.06/12,20000,4500)

The first argument identifies the periodic interest rate compounded monthly as .06/12. The second argument specifies the future value at $20,000. The third argument indicates the present value of $4,500.

To enter the function:

Press   ⏎

The answer is 299.0761 (represented in months) or about 25 years. Your screen should look like Figure 8-16.

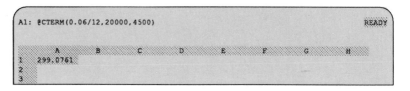

A1: @CTERM(0.06/12,20000,4500)   READY

	A	B	C	D	E	F	G	H
1	299.0761							
2								
3								

Figure 8-16

If you desire, you can format the number 299.0761 to 2 decimal places and place MONTHS in cell B1.

@RATE

@RATE calculates the periodic interest rate necessary for a specific initial value to increase to a particular future value over the number of compounding periods in the term. If the investment is compounded monthly, you must multiply the @RATE by 12 to determine the annual rate. The general format for the @RATE function is as follows:

    @RATE(future value,present value,term)

Suppose $4,500 has been invested in a bond which matures in 14 years to $20,000. Interest is compounded monthly. You must use the @RATE function to determine the periodic interest rate.

Using the given data:

Press   ⟨Home⟩

Type   @RATE(20000,4500,14*12)

The first argument identifies $20,000 is the future value. The second argument identifies $4,500 as the present value. The third argument specifies the terms in 168 months (14 years times 12 months).

To enter the function:

Press   ⏎

The answer is 0.008918 per month. You must multiply the value in cell A1 by 12 and place the results in A2 to calculate an annual rate. Your screen should look like Figure 8-17.

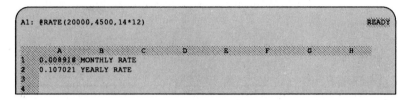

A1: @RATE(20000,4500,14*12)   READY

	A	B	C	D	E	F	G	H
1	0.008918	MONTHLY RATE						
2	0.107021	YEARLY RATE						
3								
4								

Figure 8-17

If you desire, you can format the rates as you deem appropriate. You may also place the MONTHLY RATE and YEARLY RATE labels on your worksheet.

■ DATE AND TIME FUNCTIONS

There are 12 date and time functions available in 1-2-3. They can be grouped as follows:

DATE:

@DATE	Determines date number for a specified date
@DATEVALUE	Changes a string of characters that looks like a date into a date number
@DAY	Calculates the day of the month from a date number
@MONTH	Computes the month from a date number
@YEAR	Determines the year from a date number

TIME:

@TIME	Computes a time number for a specific time consisting of an hour, minute and second
@TIMEVALUE	Changes a string of characters that looks like a time into a time number
@HOUR	Calculates the hour from a time number
@MINUTE	Computes the minute from a time number
@SECOND	Determines the second from a time number

CURRENT DATE AND TIME:

@TODAY	Computes the date number for the current date
@NOW	Calculates a value that corresponds to the current date and time

Date

The five date functions available in 1-2-3 include @DATE, @DATEVALUE, @DAY, @MONTH and @YEAR.

@DATE

The format of the @DATE function is:

@DATE(year,month,day)

where year is any two-digit number between 00 and 99; month is any integer between 1 and 12; and day is any integer between 1 and 31. If the year number used is 100, 101 and so forth, a date for the year 2000, 2001 and so forth will be returned.

To enter the date June 24, 1992 with the @DATE function in cell A1:

Move	the cell pointer to cell A1
Type	@DATE(92,6,24)
Press	⏎

The number 33779 appears in cell A1. This number indicates that 33,779 days have passed since December 31, 1899. If the number used is 100, 101, and so forth, a date for the year 2000, 2001, and so forth will be returned. To format the date appropriately:

Press	/
Select	Range
Select	Format
Select	Date

Five different options for ways to display the date appear on the menu. The sixth option for displaying the time is discussed later in this chapter. Your screen should look like Figure 8-18.

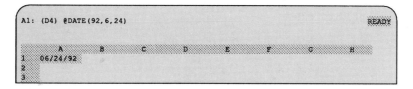

```
A1: @DATE(92,6,24)                                              MENU
1 (DD-MMM-YY)  2 (DD-MMM)  3 (MMM-YY)  4 (Long Intn'l)  5 (Short Intn'l)  Time
Lotus standard long form
         A         B         C         D         E         F         G         H
1     33779
2
3
```

Figure 8-18

Depending upon which option is chosen, the date in cell A1 can be displayed in one of the following five formats:

24-Jun-92

24-Jun

Jun-92

06/24/92

06/24

There are other formats for options 4 and 5 that can be accessed through the **Worksheet Global Default Other International Date** command sequence.

To choose option 4 from the Data Format menu:

Type   4

When prompted for the range to format:

Press   ⏎

The date format 06/24/92 is now displayed. Your screen should look like Figure 8-19.

```
A1: (D4) @DATE(92,6,24)                                        READY

         A         B         C         D         E         F         G         H
1    06/24/92
2
3
```

Figure 8-19

@DATEVALUE

This function returns the number of days that have elapsed since December 31, 1899 just as the @DATE function does. However, a single string of characters can be entered for the argument in the parentheses. The date string used in the @DATEVALUE function must be one of the acceptable Lotus 1-2-3 date formats.

The format of the @DATEVALUE function is:

@DATEVALUE(string of characters)

Suppose you want to use the @DATEVALUE function to place June 24, 1992 on your worksheet.

Move   the cell pointer to cell A1 (if necessary)

Type   @DATEVALUE("24-Jun-92")

Press   ⏎

Then you decide to determine the number of days between December 31, 1992 and June 24, 1992. To calculate the number of days between the two dates:

Move   the cell pointer to cell A2

Type   @DATEVALUE("31-Dec-92")
             -@DATEVALUE("24-Jun-92")

Press   ⏎

An alternative way to determine the number of days between June 24, 1992 and December 31, 1992 is:

Move   the cell pointer to cell A3

Type   @DATEVALUE("31-Dec-92")-A1

Press   ⏎

Your screen should look like Figure 8-20.

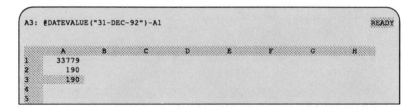

A3: @DATEVALUE("31-DEC-92")-A1   READY

         A   B   C   D   E   F   G   H
1   33779
2   190
3   190
4
5

Figure 8-20

Note the values in cells A2 and A3 are the same, because you used two different approaches for entering the formulas.

@MONTH

At times, you may be given a date number and you need to determine the month, day or year corresponding to the date number. For example, suppose that you need to determine the month, day and year represented by the date number 33779.

The @MONTH function determines the month in which a particular date number occurs. The value computed using the @MONTH function will be an integer between 1 and 12 for the months January through December respectively.

The format of the @MONTH function is:

    @MONTH(date number)

To determine the month in which the date number 33779 occurs:

Move	the cell pointer to cell A1
Enter	Month
Move	the cell pointer cell B1
Type	@MONTH(33779)
Press	↵

Your screen should look like Figure 8-21. The value of 6 appearing in cell B1 indicates the date number occurs in the month of June.

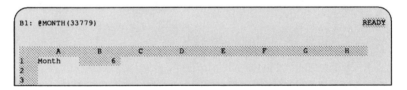

Figure 8-21

@DAY

The @DAY function determines on what day of the month a date occurs for a date number. An integer between 1 and 31 is entered into the cell in which the @DAY function is used.

The format of the @DAY function is:

    @DAY(date number)

For example, suppose you want to know the day of the month on which the date number 33779 occurred. To calculate the day of the month while leaving the results of the previous example in your worksheet:

Move	the cell pointer to cell A2
Enter	Day
Move	the cell pointer to cell B2
Type	@DAY(33779)
Press	⏎

Your screen should look like Figure 8-22.

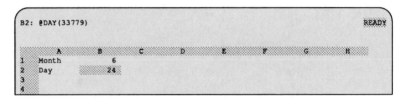

Figure 8-22

@YEAR

The @YEAR function determines the year in which a date number occurs. The value that appears in a cell in which the function is used will be a number between 0 and 99 representing the last two digits in the year. The number sequence 100, 101 and so on indicates years 2000, 2001 and so on.

The format of the @YEAR function is:

```
@YEAR(date number)
```

Keep the results of the previous example in your worksheet. To determine the year in which the date number 33779 occurs:

Move	the cell pointer to cell A3
Enter	Year
Move	the cell pointer to cell B3
Type	@YEAR(33779)
Press	⏎

Your screen should look like Figure 8-23.

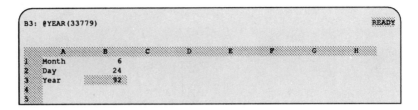

	A	B	C	D	E	F	G	H
1	Month	6						
2	Day	24						
3	Year	92						
4								
5								

Figure 8-23

The value of 92 in cell B3 indicates the date number 33779 occurs in the year 1992. Combining the information appearing in Figure 8-23, the date number represents June 24, 1992. This result is consistent with the date number you computed using the @DATE function for June 24, 1992 earlier in this chapter.

Time

The five time functions available in 1-2-3 include @TIME, @HOUR, @TIMEVALUE, @MINUTE and @SECOND.

@TIME

This function is used to calculate a time serial number that represents the percentage of the day for the time specified by you. The function returns a value between 0 and .99999. For example, the number 0 represents 12:00 midnight.

The format of the @TIME function is:

    @TIME(hour,minute,second)

Suppose you want to know the time serial number for the time 7:10:59 PM. To obtain the time serial number:

Move   the cell pointer to cell A1

Type   @TIME(19,10,59)

Press   ⏎

The number .799293 now appears in cell A1. This time serial number indicates that 7:10:59 is about 80 percent through the day.

Your screen should look like Figure 8-24.

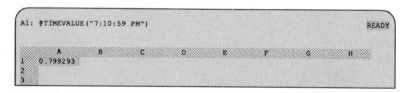

```
A1:  @TIME(19,10,59)                                                          READY

           A          B          C          D          E          F          G          H
  1    0.799293
  2
  3
```

Figure 8-24

@TIMEVALUE

This function returns the time serial number just as the @TIME function does. However, a single string of characters can be entered for the arguments instead of the hour, minute and second. The time string used in the @TIMEVALUE function must be one of the acceptable time formats available in Lotus 1-2-3.

The format of the @TIMEVALUE function is:

@TIMEVALUE(string of characters)

Suppose you want to determine the time serial number for the time 7:10:59 PM.

Move	the cell pointer to cell A1
Type	@TIMEVALUE("7:10:59 PM")
Press	↵

Your screen should look like Figure 8-25.

```
A1:  @TIMEVALUE("7:10:59 PM")                                                 READY

           A          B          C          D          E          F          G          H
  1    0.799293
  2
  3
```

Figure 8-25

Notice that the time serial number 0.799923 is the same value that you obtained when you used the @TIME function.

To format your screen so you can see the time:

Press	/
Select	Range
Select	Format
Select	Date

Select	Time
Select	1
Press	⏎

You will need to widen column A to 12 characters using the Worksheet Column Set-Width command sequence to see the time.

@HOUR

In some situations, you may be given a time serial number for which you need to determine the hour, minute and second corresponding to the time serial number.

The format for the @HOUR function is:

```
@HOUR(time serial number)
```

Suppose you are given the time serial number 0.799293. To determine the hour of the day represented by this time serial number:

Move	the cell pointer to cell A1
Enter	Hour
Move	the cell pointer to cell B1
Type	@HOUR(0.799293)
Press	⏎

Your screen should look like Figure 8-26.

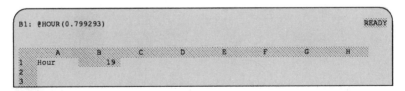

Figure 8-26

The value 19 appearing in cell B1 indicates that the time serial number represents a time between 7:00 PM and 8:00 PM.

@MINUTE

The @MINUTE function calculates the minute of the hour represented by a time serial number. The format of the @MINUTE function is:

    @MINUTE(time serial number)

Using the example time serial number 0.799293 again, you can compute the minute indicated by the time serial number using this function.

To compute the minute number while leaving the results of the previous example in your worksheet:

Move	the cell pointer to cell A2
Enter	Minute
Move	the cell pointer to cell B2
Type	@MINUTE(0.799293)
Press	⏎

Your screen should look like Figure 8-27.

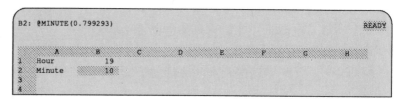

Figure 8-27

The value of 10 appearing in cell B2 specifies that the tenth minute is represented by the time serial number.

@SECOND

This function computes the second associated with a specific time serial number. The format for the @SECOND function is:

    @SECOND(time serial number)

To determine the second associated with the time serial number 0.799293 that was used in the last two examples:

| **Move** | the cell pointer to cell A3 |
| **Enter** | Second |

Move	the cell pointer to cell B3
Type	@SECOND(0.799293)
Press	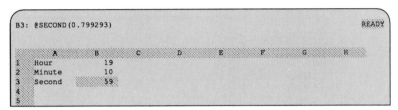

Your screen should look like Figure 8-28.

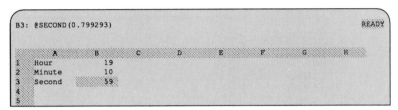

```
B3: @SECOND(0.799293)                                              READY


        A        B        C        D        E        F        G        H
1   Hour            19
2   Minute          10
3   Second          59
4
5
```

Figure 8-28

The value of 59 in cell B3 indicates the second represented by the time serial number is 59. Combining the information appearing in Figure 8-28, the time serial number 0.799293 represents the time 7:10:59 PM. This result is consistent with the time serial number you calculated using the @TIME function for 7:10:59 PM.

Current Date and Time

The two functions available in 1-2-3 to specify the current date and time are @TODAY and @NOW. These functions are very useful in documenting when a worksheet was last calculated. It is a good idea to use one of these functions on all of your worksheets.

@TODAY

The @TODAY function determines the date based on the current system date used by your computer.

The format for the @TODAY function is:

@TODAY

To illustrate the use of the @TODAY function:

Move	the cell pointer to cell A1
Enter	Today
Move	the cell pointer to cell B1
Type	@TODAY
Press	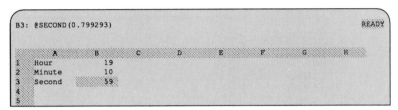

The date number for the current date now appears in cell B1. To format the date so you can determine the date, use the **Range Format Date** command sequence and select the first format option. You will need to set the column width to at least 10 using the **Worksheet Column Set-Width** command sequence.

Your screen should look similar to Figure 8-29.

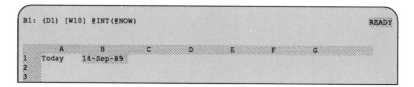

Figure 8-29

You should use this function when you only need to place the current date on your worksheet.

@NOW

The @NOW function returns the current date and time. You can format the resulting value using any of the date or time formats available in 1-2-3. The format of the @NOW function is:

    @NOW

Suppose you want to place the current time on your worksheet with today's date from the last example.

Move	the cell pointer to cell A2
Enter	Now
Move	the cell pointer to cell B2
Type	@NOW
Press	↵

The value on your screen includes the current date number and the time serial number. The integer portion of the value is the date number and the decimal portion is the time serial number.

Use the **Range Format Date Time** command sequence and select the second format option to format cell B2 so you can see a time.

Your screen should look similar to Figure 8-30.

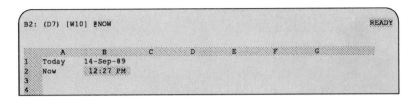

Figure 8-30

The current time should now appear on your screen. Note that if you enter anything in the worksheet, the time will also be updated on the screen. The @NOW function is particularly useful if you make changes to a worksheet several times in one day for "what-if" analysis purposes.

■ LOGICAL FUNCTIONS

There are nine logical special functions available in 1-2-3. The logical functions are:

@IF	Used to test a condition to determine if it is true or false
@FALSE	Returns a value of 0 (false)
@TRUE	Returns a value of 1 (true)
@ISAAF	Tests a name and returns a 1 (true) if it is a defined add-in function; otherwise a 0 (false) is returned
@ISAPP	Tests a name and returns a 1 (true) if it is an attached add-in; otherwise a 0 (false) is returned
@ISERR	Returns a value of 1 (true) if the cell contains an error (ERR); otherwise the value returned is 0
@ISNA	Returns a value of 1 if not available (NA) appears in a cell; otherwise the value is 0
@ISNUMBER	Returns a value of 1 if a value or blank cell is present; otherwise the value is 0
@ISSTRING	Returns a value of 1 if a string of characters is present; otherwise the value is 0

@IF

The @IF function allows you to test a condition and select one of two options depending upon the results of the test. The general format of the @IF function is:

```
@IF(condition,result  if  condition  is  true,result  if
condition is false)
```

To illustrate the use of the @IF function, suppose the income before taxes for a company is $250,000 and the tax rate is 40 percent. Assume you enter 250000 in cell A1 of a worksheet and .40 in A2. To compute the taxes due, you could create the formula +A1*A2 and place it in cell A3.

However, in some situations, an organization may lose money. Therefore, the formula will not work properly, because the company cannot pay a negative amount of taxes. In fact, the tax amount should be zero.

The @IF function can be used so that the formula can work properly. To illustrate the use of the @IF function:

Move	the cell pointer to cell A1
Enter	250000
Move	the cell pointer to cell A2
Enter	.40
Move	the cell pointer to cell A3
Type	@IF(A1>0,A1*A2,0)

The first argument, A1>0, is the condition. This condition is used to determine whether the value in A1 is greater than 0. The second argument, A1*A2, is the formula that will be used to place a value in cell A3 if the condition is true. The third argument, 0, indicates that a 0 will be entered in cell A3 if the condition is false.

To enter the @IF function in cell A3:

Press	⏎

The formula appears in the control panel, and the number 100000 is in cell A3. Since the condition, A1>0, is true, the formula A1*A2 is calculated and the value of 100000 is placed in the cell. Your screen should look like Figure 8-31.

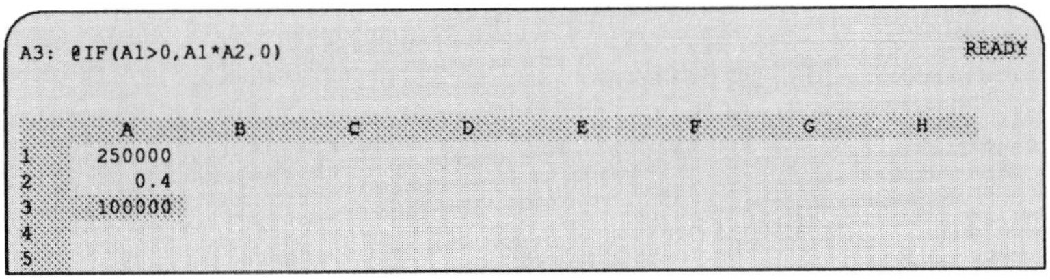

```
A3:  @IF(A1>0,A1*A2,0)                                              READY

          A         B         C         D         E         F         G         H
1      250000
2        0.4
3      100000
4
5
```

Figure 8-31

To test the **false** argument in the @IF function:

> **Move** the cell pointer to cell A1
>
> **Enter** -250000

Notice that the value in cell A3 changes to 0. The remaining portion of the @IF function section includes illustrations of logical operators that can be used in an @IF function and nested @IF functions.

Logical Operators

Logical operators combine the conditional statements or formulas. The logical operators for simple logical statements are as follows:

Operator	Definition
=	equal
<	less than
<=	less than or equal to
>	greater than
>=	greater than or equal to
<>	not equal

Logical Operators for Compound Statements

Logical operators can be used to combine multiple conditions. The #AND#, #OR# and #NOT# logical operators for Lotus 1-2-3 are now discussed.

#AND#

#AND# can be used to combine multiple statements. For example, @IF(A5=0#AND#B5=0,Z5,C5) tests two conditions. More than one #AND# may be used in a formula. When the #AND# statement is used to link multiple conditions, *all* conditions must be true before the true result (Z5) can be executed.

#OR#

#OR# can be used to test if one argument *or* the other is true. For example, @IF(A5=0#OR#B5=0,Z5,C5) would result in the *true* result (Z5) if *either* A5=0 or B5=0. When the #OR# statement is used to link multiple conditions, *all* conditions must be false for the false result (C5) to be executed.

#NOT#

#NOT# can be used to indicate that a condition is not true. For example, @IF(#NOT#A5=0#OR#B5=0,Z5,C5) tests whether A5 is *not* equal to zero or if B5=0. Unlike the logical operators #OR# and #AND#, the #NOT# logical operator is used *before* a condition.

Nested IF

One @IF function may be nested inside another, as illustrated by the following example:

@IF(B1=25,B2*B1,@IF(B1=35,B3*B1,@IF(B1=45,B4*B1,0)))

The @IF function is read from left to right. The first two @IF functions have @IF functions for the false response. The parentheses used to end the @IF functions are at the end of the formula.

@FALSE

When the @FALSE function is used, it returns a value of 0. The format of the @FALSE function is:

@FALSE

Suppose you want to pay someone a commission of 10 percent of the sales amount if their sales are at least $1,000 and nothing if their sales are less than $1,000.

To illustrate the use of the @FALSE function to solve this problem:

Move	the cell pointer to cell A1
Enter	Sales
Move	the cell pointer to cell A2

Enter	Commission	
Move	the cell pointer to cell C1	
Enter	900	
Move	the cell pointer to cell C2	
Type	@IF(C1>=1000,C1*.10,@FALSE)	

In this @IF function, the @FALSE function will place a value of 0 in cell C2 whenever the sales amount is less than $1,000. To enter the @IF function in cell C2:

Press ⏎

Your screen should look like Figure 8-32.

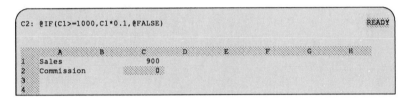

Figure 8-32

Notice that since the sales amount is less than $1,000, a value of 0 appears in cell C2. Change the value of sales to $1,000 and then $1,500 to make sure the @FALSE functions work properly.

@TRUE

The @TRUE function returns a value of 1 when it is used. The format of the @TRUE function is:

@TRUE

Assume that you need to determine whether the value in a cell is less than 500. You can use the @TRUE and @FALSE functions together with an @IF function to indicate whether the value is less than 500.

To illustrate the use of the @TRUE function:

Move	the cell pointer to cell A1
Enter	450
Move	the cell pointer to cell A2
Type	@IF(A1<500,@TRUE,@FALSE)

Press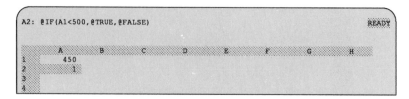

Your screen should look like Figure 8-33.

```
A2: @IF(A1<500,@TRUE,@FALSE)                                    READY

            A        B        C        D        E        F        G        H
     1          450
     2            1
     3
     4
```

Figure 8-33

The value of 1 in cell A2 indicates that the @TRUE function was used. Change the value in A1 to 500 and then 750 to make sure the functions work properly.

@ISAAF

The @ISAAF function determines whether a name is a defined add-in @ function. The format of the @ISAAF is:

@ISAAF(name)

where **name** is any literal string, a string formula or a reference to a cell containing a label. Do not include the @ symbol in **name**. For example, if you place @ISAAF("AVG") in cell A1, the value 0 will appear in cell A1 because AVG is a 1-2-3 @ function and not an add-in @ function.

@ISAPP

The @ISAPP function determines whether a specific add-in has been attached. The format of the @ISAPP function is:

@ISAPP(name)

where **name** is any literal string, a string formula or reference for a cell containing a label. Do not include the extension .ADN in the **name**. For example, if you place @ISAPP("ALLWAYS") in cell B1 and ALLWAYS.ADN is attached, then a value of 1 will appear in cell B1.

@ISERR

The @ISERR function determines whether the contents of a cell contain ERR. For example, the characters are placed in a cell by 1-2-3 whenever you try to divide by zero. If ERR is present when the @ISERR function is used, the value of 1 (true) is returned; otherwise a value of 0 (false) is returned.

The format of the @ISERR function is:

@ISERR(x)

where *x* can be a cell location, string of characters, condition or value.

Suppose that you need to divide the value in one cell by the value in another cell. In some cases the denominator may be zero, but you do not want ERR to appear in the cell where the division occurs. The @ISERR function can be used in such a situation.

To illustrate the use of the @ISERR:

Move   the cell pointer to cell B1

Enter   50

Move   the cell pointer to cell B2

Enter   0

Move   the cell pointer to cell B3

Enter   +B1/B2

You now have the characters ERR in cell B3. Suppose you want the number 0 to appear in cell B3 if an attempt to divide by 0 occurs.

Type   @IF(@ISERR(B1/B2),0,B1/B2)

If division by 0 is attempted, then a 0 is placed in cell B3, otherwise the cell B1 is divided by B2.

To enter the function in cell B3:

Press   ↵

Your screen should look like Figure 8-34.

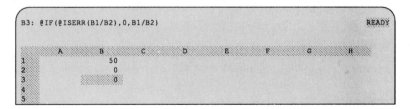

Figure 8-34

The value of 0 appearing in cell B3 indicates division by 0 was attempted. Change the value in B2 to 10 to verify the @ISERR function works properly.

@ISNA

The @ISNA function is used to verify whether NA appears in a cell. The format of the @ISNA function is :

@ISNA(x)

where *x* can be a cell location, string of characters, condition or value.

To illustrate the use of the @ISNA function:

> **Move**   the cell pointer to cell A1
>
> **Enter**   @NA

Note the characters NA, meaning not available, appear in cell A1. Assume that you would like to place a 1 in cell B1 if NA is present and a 0 if NA does not appear.

> **Move**   the cell pointer to cell B1
>
> **Type**   @IF(@ISNA(A1),1,0)
>
> **Press**   ⏎

Your screen should now look like Figure 8-35.

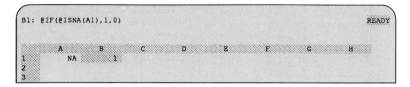

Figure 8-35

The value 1 in cell indicates NA appears in cell A1. To illustrate another approach to the problem enter @IF(@ISNA(A1), @TRUE, @FALSE) in cell B1. The value of 1 should also appear in cell B1. Change the contents of cell A1 to 100 and verify the @ISNA function works properly when A1 does not contain NA.

@ISNUMBER

The @ISNUMBER function determines if a value or a blank is present. The format of the @ISNUMBER function is:

@ISNUMBER(x)

where *x* can be any cell location, string of characters, condition or value. If a value or a blank cell is present, a 1 is returned, otherwise a 0 is returned.

Suppose you need to check a cell to determine what type of data is included in the cell. To ascertain whether a value or blank cell is present:

Move   the cell pointer to cell B1

Enter   100

Move   the cell pointer to cell A3

Type   @ISNUMBER(B1)

Press   ⏎

Your screen should look like Figure 8-36.

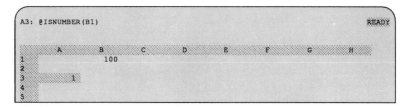

Figure 8-36

The number 1 appears in cell A3 indicating that a value appears in cell B1. Use the **R**ange **E**rase command sequence to erase cell B1. The value 1 remains in cell A3, because the B1 is now a blank cell. If you press the space bar and press the ⏎ key, a 0 will appear in cell A3 specifying that B1 does not contain a value or it is not a blank cell.

@ISSTRING

The @ISSTRING function is used to determine whether a string of characters is present. The format for the @ISSTRING function is:

@ISSTRING(x)

where *x* can be a cell location, string of characters, condition or value. If a string of characters is present, a 1 is returned. When a value or a blank cell is present, a value of 0 is returned.

Suppose you have a set of characters in a cell and you need to determine whether the cell contains a set of alphanumeric characters.

To illustrate how you can use the ISSTRING function to determine what type of characters are present in the cell:

Move   the cell pointer to cell C1

Enter   Lotus 1-2-3

Move   the cell pointer to cell C3

Type   @ISSTRING(C1)

Press   ⏎

Your screen should look like Figure 8-37.

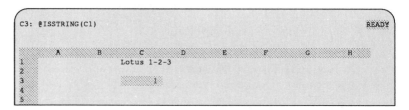

Figure 8-37

The value 1 appears in cell C3 indicating that the contents of C1 are a string of alphanumeric characters or a space. Use the **Range Erase** command sequence to erase cell C1. A zero then appears in cell C3 indicating C1 is a blank cell. Enter the value 200 in cell C1. The zero value remains in cell C3, because a value is present in cell C1.

■ DATABASE STATISTICAL FUNCTIONS

There are seven database functions available in 1-2-3.

DATABASE STATISTICAL FUNCTIONS:

@DSUM	Calculates the sum of values for a field in a database table satisfying a criteria range
@DCOUNT	Determines the number of nonblank cells for a field in a database table satisfying a criteria range
@DAVG	Computes the arithmetic mean of values for a field in a database table satisfying a criteria range
@DMIN	Determines the minimum value for a field in a database table satisfying a criteria range
@DMAX	Determines the maximum value for a field in a database table satisfying a criteria range

@DVAR   Calculates the population variance for a field
                         in a database table satisfying a criteria range

@DSTD   Computes the population standard deviation
                         for a field in a database table satisfying a
                         criteria range

The seven database statistical functions available in 1-2-3 are: @DSUM, @DCOUNT, @DAVG, @DMIN, @DMAX, @DVAR, and @DSTD. These functions are very similar to the statistical analysis functions discussed earlier in this chapter. As mentioned in Chapter 7, a **database** is a collection of related data or records. With the database statistical functions, you can complete statistical analysis on a set of cells that satisfy a particular criteria.

For example, you may have a database of all employees located in California, but you only want to know how many of the people live in Los Angeles. @COUNT can determine how many employees are in the database. @DCOUNT can be used to obtain a count for only those individuals living in Los Angeles. The database statistical functions are designed for use on databases and database tables. The D in front of each function indicates that it is a database statistical function.

The format for all of the database statistical functions is:

@function name(input range,field location,criteria)

The **input range** is the database area that includes the field names and records in the database. The **field location** is used to indicate which column should be used for the calculations. When specifying the column in the database, start counting with the number zero. Therefore, if the third column in a database is the desired field location, it is referred to as field number two in the function. The **criteria** range specifies the criteria that must be satisfied.

Before you use the database statistical functions, you need to create the database table in Figure 8-38.

```
A1: 'NAME                                                              READY

         A          B         C       D        E        F        G        H
1    NAME      SALARY    ST
2    BROWN       32000   TX
3    CHIN        28000   CA
4    JONES       45000   TX
5    MARTINEZ    31000   TX
6    SMITH       27000   CA
7    WHITE       35000   NY
8
9
```

Figure 8-38

The database table includes the last name, salary and state location of employees working for an organization. Save the worksheet on a file using the name SALS.

Assume that you want to apply the database statistical functions to those individuals earning more than $30,000. The individuals satisfying this criteria are Brown, Jones, Martinez and White.

To place the criteria on your worksheet:

Move	the cell pointer to cell D2
Enter	SALARY
Move	the cell pointer to cell D3
Enter	+B2>30000

The number 1 should appear in cell D2. Use the **Range Format Text** command sequence to place the text version of the criteria on your screen. You will need to set the column width to 10 characters so you can see the entire formula. Create the range name CRITERIA and include the cells D2 through D3 as the range. Place the word CRITERIA in cell D1 and names of the database statistical functions in cells D6 through D14. Your screen should look like Figure 8-39.

```
E6:                                                          READY

        A         B        C        D         E      F      G
1   NAME      SALARY    ST       CRITERIA
2   BROWN      32000   TX        SALARY
3   CHIN       28000   CA        +B2>30000
4   JONES      45000   TX
5   MARTINEZ   31000   TX
6   SMITH      27000   CA        DSUM
7   WHITE      35000   NY        DCOUNT
8                                DAVG
9                                DMIN
10                               DMAX
11                               DVAR
12                               DSTD
13
14
```

Figure 8-39

Create the range name DATABASE and include cells A1 through C7 as the range.

@DSUM

The @DSUM function computes the sum of values for a field that satisfies a criteria. To compute the sum for the cells satisfying the criteria in the SALS worksheet:

Move	the cell pointer to cell E6
Type	@DSUM(DATABASE,1,CRITERIA)
Press	⏎

DATABASE identifies cells A1 through C7 as the input range, the 1 indicates SALARY is the field location, and CRITERIA specifies D2 through D3 as the criteria range. The value 143000 appears in cell E6. This is the sum of the salaries for Brown, Chin, Martinez and White who each earn more than $30,000.

@DCOUNT

This function counts the number of nonblank cells for a field in a database table that satisfy a specified criteria.

To illustrate the use of the @DCOUNT function for the SALS worksheet:

Move	the cell pointer to cell E7
Type	@DCOUNT(DATABASE,1,CRITERIA)
Press	⏎

The value 4 appears in cell E7 indicating there are four individuals in the database who have a salary greater than $30,000.

@DAVG

The @DAVG function calculates the arithmetic mean of the values for a field in a database table that satisfy a criteria.

To demonstrate the use of the @DAVG function for the SALS worksheet:

Move	the cell pointer to cell E8
Type	@DAVG(DATABASE,1,CRITERIA)
Press	⏎

The value 35,750 appearing is the average salary for the four individuals who have a salary greater than $30,000.

@DMIN

The @DMIN function determines the minimum value for a field in a database table that satisfies a criteria.

To illustrate the use of the @DMIN function for the SALS worksheet:

Move	the cell pointer to cell E9
Type	@DMIN(DATABASE,1,CRITERIA)
Press	⏎

The value 31,000 that appears in cell E9 indicates that the lowest salary among the individuals having a salary greater than $30,000 is $31,000.

@DMAX

The @DMAX function determines the maximum value for a field in a database table that satisfies a criteria.

To demonstrate the use of the @DMAX function for the SALS worksheet:

Move	the cell pointer to cell E10
Type	@DMAX(DATABASE,1,CRITERIA)
Press	⏎

The value 45,000 that appears in cell E9 specifies that the highest salary among the employees having a salary greater than $30,000 is $45,000.

@DVAR

This function computes the population variance for the values in a field in a database table that satisfy a criteria. It is assumed that the database table represents all of the data that can be considered.

To illustrate the use of the @DVAR function for the SALS worksheet:

Move	the cell pointer to cell E11
Type	@DVAR(DATABASE,1,CRITERIA)
Press	⏎

The value 30,687,500 that appears in cell E10 is the population variance for the salaries for the persons having a salary greater than $30,000.

@DSTD

The @DSTD function computes the population standard deviation for the values in a field of a database table that satisfy a criteria.

To demonstrate the use of the @DSTD function for the SALS worksheet:

Move	the cell pointer to cell E12
Type	@DSTD(DATABASE,1,CRITERIA)
Press	⏎

The value 5,539.629 is the population standard deviation for the salaries of the employees who have a salary greater than $30,000. After entering all of the database statistical functions, your screen should look like Figure 8-40.

```
E12: @DSTD(DATABASE,1,CRITERIA)                                    READY

          A         B        C         D          E        F        G
 1  NAME       SALARY   ST        CRITERIA
 2  BROWN       32000 TX         SALARY
 3  CHIN        28000 CA         +B2>30000
 4  JONES       45000 TX
 5  MARTINEZ    31000 TX
 6  SMITH       27000 CA         DSUM       143000
 7  WHITE       35000 NY         DCOUNT          4
 8                               DAVG        35750
 9                               DMIN        31000
10                               DMAX        45000
11                               DVAR     30687500
12                               DSTD      5539.629
13
14
```

Figure 8-40

■ MATHEMATICAL FUNCTIONS

The 17 mathematical functions available in Lotus 1-2-3 include:

GENERAL:

@ABS	Computes the absolute value of a number in a cell
@EXP	Computes the number *e* raised to a specific power
@INT	Determines the integer portion of a value
@LN	Computes the natural logarithm (base *e*) of a value
@LOG	Computes the common logarithm (base 10) of a value
@MOD	Computes the remainder (modulus) of two values
@RAND	Generates a random number value between 0 and 1
@ROUND	Rounds a value to a specific number of decimal places

@SQRT	Computes the positive square root of a number

TRIGONOMETRIC:

@COS	Computes the cosine of an angle
@ACOS	Computes the arc cosine of a value
@SIN	Computes the sine of an angle
@ASIN	Computes the arc sine of a value
@TAN	Computes the tangent of an angle
@ATAN	Computes the arc tangent of a value
@ATAN2	Computes the four-quadrant arc tangent of two values
@PI	Returns the value for π (calculated at 3.14159265358979324)

General Functions

There are nine general mathematical functions. The general mathematical functions are @ABS, @EXP, @INT, @LN, @LOG, @MOD, @RAND, @ROUND, and @SQRT.

@ABS

The @ABS function determines the absolute value. The number returned will always be positive.

The format of the @ABS function is:

@ABS(x)

where *x* is any value.

To illustrate the use of the @ABS function:

Move	the cell pointer to cell A1
Enter	25
Move	the cell pointer to cell A2
Enter	-50
Move	the cell pointer to cell B1

Type	@ABS (A1)
Press	⏎
Move	the cell pointer to cell B2
Type	@ABS (A2)
Press	⏎

Your screen should look like Figure 8-41.

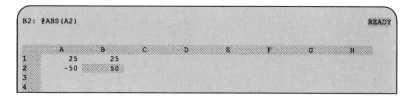

Figure 8-41

Notice that the absolute value of a positive number is the same positive number while the absolute value of a negative number is a positive number.

@EXP

The @EXP function computes the value of the number *e* raised to a specific power. The number *e* used in 1-2-3 has the approximate value of 2.718282.

The format of the @EXP function is:

@EXP (x)

where *x* is any value within the limits specified by the Lotus 1-2-3 reference manual. These limits are approximately from -11356 to 11356.

To demonstrate the use of the @EXP function:

Move	the cell pointer to cell A1
Type	@EXP (3)
Press	⏎

Your screen should look like Figure 8-42.

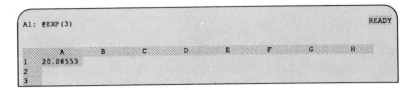

Figure 8-42

The value 20.08553 appearing in cell A1 is *e* (2.718282) raised to the power of 3.

@INT

The @INT function determines the integer portion of a value in a cell. The format for the @INT function is:

@INT(x)

where *x* is any value.

To demonstrate the use of the @INT function:

Move	the cell pointer to cell B1
Enter	33.1
Move	the cell pointer to cell B2
Type	@INT(B1)
Press	⏎

Your screen should look like Figure 8-43.

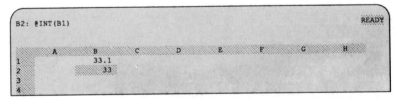

Figure 8-43

Notice that the value in cell B2 is 33 and the decimal portion of the number appearing in B1 has been omitted.

@LN

This function calculates the natural logarithm (base *e*) of a value. The format of the @LN function is:

    @LN(x)

where *x* is any value greater than 0.

To illustrate the use of the @LN function:

Move	the cell pointer to cell A1
Enter	2
Move	the cell pointer to cell A2
Type	@LN(A1)
Press	⏎

Your screen should look like Figure 8-44.

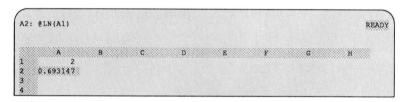

A2: @LN(A1)   READY

	A	B	C	D	E	F	G	H
1	2							
2	0.693147							
3								
4								

Figure 8-44

The value 0.693147 in A2 is the natural logarithm of the number 2.

@LOG

The @LOG function computes the common logarithm (base 10) for a value. The format for the @LOG function is:

    @LOG(x)

where *x* is any value greater than 0.

To demonstrate the use of the @LOG function:

Move	the cell pointer to cell B1
Enter	20
Move	the cell pointer to cell B2

Type   @LOG(B1)

Press   ⏎

Your screen should look like Figure 8-45.

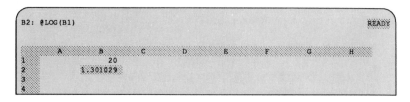

```
B2: @LOG(B1)                                                    READY

          A         B         C         D         E         F         G         H
1                        20
2               1.301029
3
4
```

Figure 8-45

The value 1.301029 in cell B2 is the common logarithm for the number 20.

@MOD

The @MOD function computes the remainder (modulus) when you divide one number by another. The format for the @MOD function is:

@MOD(x,y)

where *x* is any value and *y* is any value other than 0. The sign (+ or -) of the value *x* specifies the sign of the result.

To illustrate the use of the @MOD function:

Move   the cell pointer to cell A1

Enter   X

Move   the cell pointer to cell B1

Enter   15

Move   the cell pointer to cell A2

Enter   Y

Move   the cell pointer to cell B2

Enter   6

Move   the cell pointer to cell C1

Type   @MOD(B1,B2)

Your screen should look like Figure 8-46.

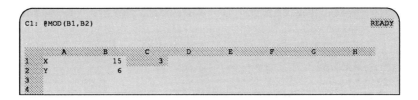

Figure 8-46

The value 3 is computed by dividing 15 by 6 and determining that the answer is 2 plus a remainder (modulus) of 3.

@RAND

The @RAND function calculates a random number between 0 and 1. The format of the @RAND function is:

@RAND

If you need to have a random number within a particular interval you must multiply the @RAND function by an appropriate value.

To illustrate the use of the @RAND function:

Move	the cell pointer to cell A1
Type	@RAND
Press	⏎
Move	the cell pointer to cell A2
Type	100*@RAND
Press	⏎

Your screen should look similar to Figure 8-47.

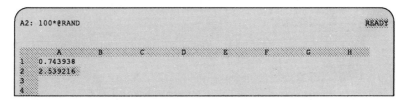

Figure 8-47

The value appearing in cell A1 is a random number between 0 and 1. The value in cell A2 is a random number between the interval 0 and 100. It was computed by multiplying a value determined using the @RAND function by 100.

@ROUND

The @ROUND function is use to round a value to a specific number of decimal places. The format for the @ROUND function is:

@ROUND(x,y)

where x is any value or formula and y is the number of decimal places you desire to the right of the decimal point. Chapter 2 includes an extensive discussion of the @ROUND function and several illustrations of its use.

@SQRT

The @SQRT function determines the positive square root for a value. The format of the @SQRT function is:

@SQRT(x)

where x is any positive value or formula that results in a positive number.

To demonstrate the use of the @SQRT function:

Move	the cell pointer to cell A1
Enter	25
Move	the cell pointer to cell A2
Type	@SQRT(A1)
Press	⏎

Your screen should look like Figure 8-48.

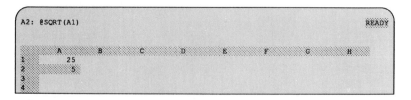

Figure 8-48

The value 5 appearing in cell A2 is the square root of 25. If you attempt to compute the square root of a negative value, the characters ERR will appear on your screen.

Trigonometric Functions

The trigonometric related functions available in 1-2-3 are @COS, @ACOS, @SIN, @ASIN, @TAN, @ATAN, @ATAN2 and @PI. These functions are used primarily by engineers and scientists. If you need to use these functions, please see the Lotus 1-2-3 reference manual.

■ SPECIAL FUNCTIONS

There are 11 special functions available in 1-2-3. They can be categorized as follows:

CELL AND RANGE INFORMATION:

@@	Returns the contents of the cell whose name or address another cell contains
@CELL	Returns information about a cell or its contents
@CELLPOINTER	Returns information about the current cell or its contents
@COLS	Determines the number of columns in a range
@ROWS	Determines the number of rows in a range

ERROR TRAPPING:

@ERR	Returns the characters ERR for error
@NA	Returns the characters NA for not available

LOOKUP CALCULATIONS:

@CHOOSE	Finds a specific value or string in a list
@HLOOKUP	Finds the contents of a cell in a specified row in a horizontal lookup table
@VLOOKUP	Finds the contents of a cell in a specified column of a vertical lookup table
@INDEX	Finds the contents of the cell in a specified row and column in a range

Cell and Range Information

The five cell and range information functions available in 1-2-3 are @@, @CELL, @CELLPOINTER, @COLS, and @ROWS.

@@

The @@ function returns the contents of the cell whose name or address another cell contains. The format of the @@ function is:

@@(location)

where location is the name or address of a single-cell range.

To illustrate the use of the @@ function:

Move	the cell pointer to cell A1
Enter	15
Move	the cell pointer to cell C1
Enter	A1
Move	the cell pointer to cell C3
Type	@@(C1)
Press	⏎

C1 has as it contents the label A1. The @@ function directs 1-2-3 to go to the cell referenced in cell C1, and place the contents of cell A1 in C3.

Your screen should look like Figure 8-49.

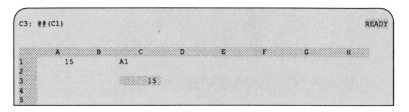

Figure 8-49

If the location you use refers to more than one cell, ERR will be returned.

@CELL

The @CELL function returns information about a cell or its contents. The format of the @CELL function is:

    @CELL(attribute,location)

The attribute can be any of 10 strings allowed by 1-2-3. The location can be any cell address or range name. The 1-2-3 reference manual contains a list of the 10 strings that can be used for the attribute argument and the value returned for each of the possible attributes.

@CELLPOINTER

The @CELLPOINTER function returns information about the current cell. The format of the @CELLPOINTER function is:

    @CELLPOINTER(attribute)

The attribute can be any of 10 strings allowed by 1-2-3 for the @CELL function. Refer to the 1-2-3 reference manual for the possible attributes and the value returned for each of the possible attributes.

@COLS

The @COLS function counts the number of columns in a specified range. The format of the @COLS function is:

    @COLS(range)

where the range can be specified or a range name can be used.

To demonstrate the use of the @COLS function:

Move	the cell pointer to cell A1
Type	@COLS(B1.M1)
Press	⏎

Your screen should look like Figure 8-50.

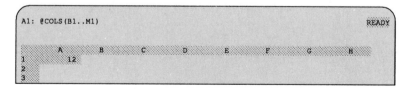

Figure 8-50

The value 12 appearing in cell A1 indicates there are 12 columns in the specified range B1 through M1.

@ROWS

The @ROWS function counts the number of rows in a range. The format of the @ROWS function is:

@ROWS(range)

where range can be a specified range or a range name.

To illustrate the use of the @ROWS function:

Move   the cell pointer to cell A1

Type   @ROWS(B32.B297)

Press   ⏎

Your screen should look like Figure 8-51.

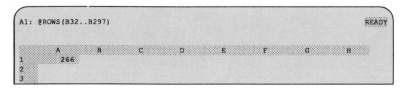

A1: @ROWS(B32..B297)   READY

```
       A          B          C          D          E          F          G          H
1      266
2
3
```

Figure 8-51

The value 266 appearing in cell A1 indicates that there are 266 rows in the range B32 through B297.

Error Trapping

The two error trapping functions available in 1-2-3 are @ERR and @NA.

@ERR

The @ERR function returns the characters ERR (Error). The format of the @ERR function is:

@ERR

To illustrate the use of the @ERR function:

Move   the cell pointer to cell A1

Enter   25

Move	the cell pointer to cell A2
Enter	5

Suppose you want to place a formula in cell A3 that will divide the value in cell A1 by the value in cell A2 only if the value in A2 is greater than 10. If the value is less than or equal to 10, you want to place the ERR characters in cell A3. To accomplish this task:

Move	the cell pointer to cell A3
Type	@IF(A2>10,A1/A2,@ERR)
Press	↵

Your screen should look like Figure 8-52.

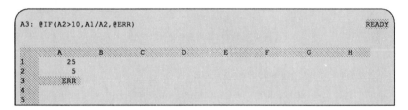

A3: @IF(A2>10,A1/A2,@ERR)   READY

```
         A        B        C        D        E        F        G        H
1       25
2        5
3      ERR
4
5
```

Figure 8-52

The characters ERR appear in cell A3, because the value in cell A2 is not greater than 10. Change the value in A2 to a value greater than 10 to verify that the function works properly.

@NA

The @NA function returns the characters NA (not available). The format for the @NA function is:

@NA

To demonstrate the use of the @NA function:

Move	the cell pointer to cell B1
Enter	0

Suppose you want to place the characters NA in cell A4 if the value in cell B1 is 0 meaning the data is not available yet. Otherwise you want to place the value appearing in cell B1 in cell A4.

Move	the cell pointer to cell A4
Type	@IF(B1=0,@NA,B1)

Press   ⏎

Your screen should look like Figure 8-53.

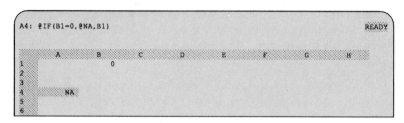

Figure 8-53

The NA appearing in cell A4 indicates that the value in cell B1 is a 0 and NA should therefore appear in cell A4. Change the value in cell B1 to some other number and the value will appear in cells B1 and A4.

Lookup Calculations

The four lookup calculation functions available in 1-2-3 include: @CHOOSE, @HLOOKUP, @VLOOKUP and @INDEX.

@CHOOSE

The @CHOOSE function finds a value or a string in a specified list. The format of the @CHOOSE function is:

```
@CHOOSE(offset number,list)
```

The offset number is the position of an item in a list. The initial item in the list has an offset number of 0. The second item has an offset number of 1 and so on. The final offset number is the total number of items minus 1. The offset number must be a positive integer and have a value less than or equal to 49. The list can contain any set of values, strings and range references or any combination of them. Before using the @CHOOSE function, you need to create the worksheet appearing in Figure 8-54.

```
D17: (P0) 0.15                                                    READY

          A         B         C         D         E       F       G       H
  1                          ABC COMPANY
  2
  3                           YEARS
  4                ORIGINAL     IN    DEPRECIATION
  5     EQUIPMENT   VALUE    SERVICE   AMOUNT
  6     TRACTOR     16,000      1
  7     CAR         10,000      4
  8     TRUCK       15,000      3
  9     WAGON        8,000      2
 10
 11
 12               DEPRECIATION        DEPRECIATION
 13               YEAR                RATE
 14                     1                25%
 15                     2                40%
 16                     3                20%
 17                     4                15%
 18
 19
 20                          UNDO
```

Figure 8-54

You need to compute the annual depreciation for the four pieces of equipment in cells A6 through A9. Suppose that each of the properties has an economic useful life of four years. The depreciation rate used for the properties depends on how long the property has been in service. For example, the depreciation rate for the tractor is 25 percent, because it has been in service for only one year. The depreciation amount for the tractor is 4,000 (.25 times 16,000).

To demonstrate the use of the @CHOOSE function to compute the depreciation amount for the tractor:

Move	the cell pointer to cell D6
Type	+B6*@CHOOSE(C6,@ERR,$D$14,$D$15, $D$16,$D$17,@ERR)
Press	⏎

The value 4,000 appearing in cell D6 is the depreciation amount based on the depreciation rate of 25 percent. Cell C6 is the cell having the offset number and has the value 1 in it. Since the YEARS IN SERVICE value in cell C6 is 1, the second item in the list is used. Note that @ERR is used for the items in the list if the offset number is 0 and greater than 4. In this manner, if YEARS IN SERVICE is entered incorrectly, the ERR will appear for the depreciation amount.

Verify that the @CHOOSE function works for the other equipment by copying the formula in cell D6 to cells D7 through D9.

Your screen should look like Figure 8-55.

```
D6: +B6*@CHOOSE(C6,@ERR,$D$14,$D$15,$D$16,$D$17,@ERR)                    READY


        A         B         C         D         E       F       G       H
 1                         ABC COMPANY
 2
 3                        YEARS
 4             ORIGINAL     IN    DEPRECIATION
 5  EQUIPMENT   VALUE    SERVICE    AMOUNT
 6  TRACTOR     16,000      1        4000
 7  CAR         10,000      4        1500
 8  TRUCK       15,000      3        3000
 9  WAGON        8,000      2        3200
10
11
12            DEPRECIATION         DEPRECIATION
13            YEAR                 RATE
14                1                   25%
15                2                   40%
16                3                   20%
17                4                   15%
18
19
20
                         UNDO
```

Figure 8-55

Change the value for the YEARS OF SERVICE to 0 and 5 for one of the equipment types. ERR will appear in the cell in both cases.

@HLOOKUP

The @HLOOKUP function determines the contents of a cell for a specified row in a horizontal lookup table. A horizontal lookup table is a range of cells that has value or label information in ascending order in the first row. The format of the @HLOOKUP function is:

    @HLOOKUP(x,range,row-offset)

where x is a value or label and range is the set of cells contained in the horizontal lookup table. Row-offset is the number of rows down a column to the cell whose contents are to be returned.

The column that is searched is determined by comparing x with the cells in the first row beginning with the leftmost cell in the row. 1-2-3 locates the cell in the first row having a label that matches x or a value that is greater than or equal to x and less than the value in the cell to the immediate right of the cell being compared. It then moves down the column based on the row-offset number and returns the contents of the cell. If labels appear in the first row instead of values, 1-2-3 checks for exact matches.

The row offset number is the position a row occupies in the range. The first row has an offset number of zero, the second row has an offset number of 1 and so on. The row offset number can be 0 or any positive integer between 1 and 19. The maximum value that row-offset can have is 19.

Before illustrating the use of the @HLOOKUP function, you need to create the worksheet in Figure 8-56.

```
C18: (,0) [W12] 1                                                    READY

             A            B           C            D            E         F
1    HORIZONTAL LOOKUP TABLE FOR TAX WITHHOLDING
2
3        ALLOWANCES                          SALARY
4                        1,760       1,800       1,840       1,880
5                 0        248         257         266         275
6                 1        229         238         247         256
7                 2        211         220         228         238
8                 3        196         203         210         220
9                 4        182         189         196         202
10
11
12                               WITHHOLDING     AMOUNT
13           EMPLOYEE     SALARY   ALLOWANCES   WITHHELD
14   AVERY               1,850          2
15   CHEN                1,875          0
16   GONZALEZ            1,825          3
17   SMITH               1,800          4
18   WOODS               1,775          1
19
20
                           UNDO
```

Figure 8-56

The horizontal lookup table contains the cells B4 through E9. The information in cells A5 through A9 is for documentation purposes only. The table is used to determine the amount of withholding tax an employee must pay depending on the salary and number of exemptions declared. For example, an individual earning more than $1,840 and less than or equal to $1,880 who has 2 exemptions must have $228 withheld from his paycheck.

To demonstrate the use of the @HLOOKUP function for this situation:

Move   the cell pointer to cell D14

Type   @HLOOKUP(B14,$B$4.$E$9,C14+1)

Press   ⏎

Make sure you include the $ signs to specify the absolute references. The value 228 appearing in cell D14 is the amount of withholding for an individual who has 2 withholding allowances, earning more than $1,840 and less than $1,880. Note that the value 1,850 is greater than or equal to 1,840 and less than 1,880. Therefore, the third column in the horizontal lookup table is used. The offset number is the value of cell C14 plus one because the row offset is one more than the corresponding number of allowances.

To verify the @HLOOKUP function works properly for the remaining employees, copy the formula in cell D14 to cells D15 through D18. When you are finished, your screen should look like Figure 8-57.

```
D14: (,0) [W12] @HLOOKUP(B14,WITHHOLD,C14+1)                              READY

              A           B            C            D           E           F
 1  HORIZONTAL LOOKUP TABLE FOR TAX WITHHOLDING
 2
 3      ALLOWANCES                              SALARY
 4                      1,760        1,800        1,840       1,880
 5              0         248          257          266         275
 6              1         229          238          247         256
 7              2         211          220          228         238
 8              3         196          203          210         220
 9              4         182          189          196         202
10
11
12                                WITHHOLDING     AMOUNT
13          EMPLOYEE      SALARY   ALLOWANCES    WITHHELD
14  AVERY                 1,850         2            228
15  CHEN                  1,875         0            266
16  GONZALEZ              1,825         3            203
17  SMITH                 1,800         4            189
18  WOODS                 1,775         1            229
19
20
                          UNDO
```

Figure 8-57

@VLOOKUP

The @VLOOKUP function determines the contents of a cell for a specified column in a vertical lookup table. A vertical lookup table is a range of cells that has label or value information in ascending order in the first column. The format of the @VLOOKUP function is:

@VLOOKUP(x,range,column-offset)

where x is a label or value and range is the set of cells contained in the vertical lookup table. Column-offset is the number of columns across a row to the cell whose contents are to be returned.

The column that is searched is determined by comparing x with the values in the first column of the range beginning with the top cell in the column. 1-2-3 locates the cell in the first column having a label that matches x or a value that is greater than or equal to x and less than the value in the cell immediately below the cell being compared. It then moves across the row based on the column-offset number and returns the contents of the cell. If labels are used in the first column instead of values, 1-2-3 checks for exact matches.

The column-offset number is the position a column occupies in the range. The first column has a value of 0; the second column has an offset number of 1 and so on. The column-offset number can be 0 or any positive integer between 1 and 19. The maximum value that the column-offset can have is 19.

Before illustrating the use of the @VLOOKUP function, you need to create the worksheet in Figure 8-58. The AMOUNT cells are calculated by multiplying QUANTITY times PRICE, and the total AMOUNT is determined by summing the individual item sales amounts.

```
E20:  (C2)  @SUM(E14..E19)                                           READY

          A          B           C          D         E        F
1                  VERTICAL LOOKUP TABLE
2
3        ITEM      QUANTITY
4       NUMBER     ON HAND       PRICE
5
6          2         150        $2.25
7          7         200        $3.75
8          8          95        $1.75
9         10          75        $4.25
10
11
12   SALES INVOICE
13       ITEM       ITEM       QUANTITY
14      NUMBER   DESCRIPTION   PURCHASED    PRICE    AMOUNT
15         8    JUICE            3                   $0.00
16         2    BEEF STEW        9                   $0.00
17        10    CANDY           10                   $0.00
18         7    COFFEE           5                   $0.00
19                                                 ---------
20              TOTAL                               $0.00
                         UNDO
```

Figure 8-58

The vertical lookup table is in cells A6 through C9. This table includes information on the prices for four items sold by a distributor. The table is used to specify the proper sales price for items on a sales invoice.

To demonstrate the use of the @VLOOKUP function for this situation:

Move	the cell pointer to cell D15
Type	@VLOOKUP(A15,$A$6.$C$9,2)
Press	↵

Make sure you include the $ signs to specify the absolute references. The value of $1.75 in cell D15 is the price for juice (item number 8). Note that the column offset number is 2, because the prices for the items are in the third column of the vertical lookup table.

To verify that the @VLOOKUP function works properly for the other sales items, copy the contents of cell D15 to cells D16 through D18.

– When you are finished, your screen should look like Figure 8-59.

```
D15:  (C2) [W14] @VLOOKUP(A15,PRICE,2)                              READY

          A          B           C          D        E        F
 1              VERTICAL LOOKUP TABLE
 2
 3       ITEM      QUANTITY
 4      NUMBER     ON HAND       PRICE
 5
 6         2         150        $2.25
 7         7         200        $3.75
 8         8          95        $1.75
 9        10          75        $4.25
10
11
12   SALES INVOICE
13       ITEM       ITEM      QUANTITY
14      NUMBER   DESCRIPTION  PURCHASED       PRICE   AMOUNT
15         8  JUICE              3           $1.75    $5.25
16         2  BEEF STEW          9           $2.25   $20.25
17        10  CANDY             10           $4.25   $42.50
18         7  COFFEE             5           $3.75   $18.75
19                                                  ---------
20            TOTAL                                   $86.75
                              UNDO
```

Figure 8-59

@INDEX

The @INDEX function determines the contents of a cell in a range of cells for a specific set of column-offset and row-offset numbers. The format of the @INDEX function is:

@INDEX(range,column-offset,row-offset)

The range can be any specified range of cells or range name.

Column-offset and row-offset are offset numbers. These numbers correspond to the column or row position of the desired cell in the range. The first column and row in the range has an offset of 0. Subsequent columns and rows are numbered as positive integers to a maximum value of 19.

Before illustrating the use of the @INDEX function, you need to create the worksheet in Figure 8-60.

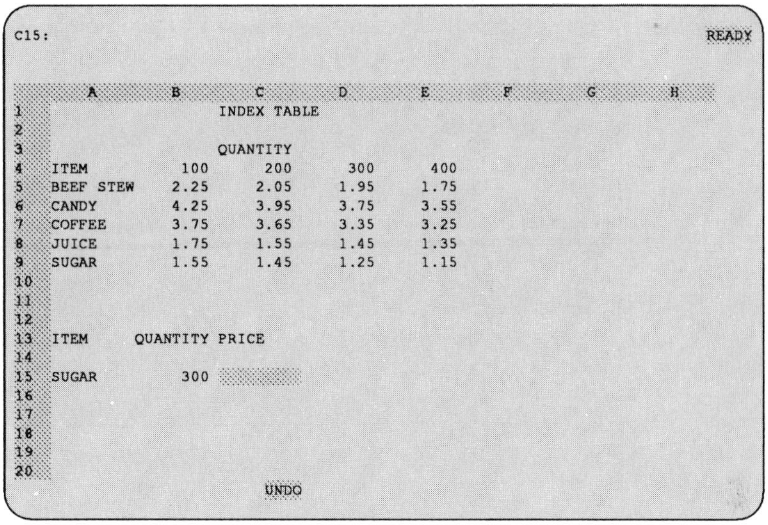

```
C15:                                                                    READY

          A         B         C         D         E        F       G       H
1                             INDEX TABLE
2
3                             QUANTITY
4       ITEM        100       200       300       400
5       BEEF STEW   2.25      2.05      1.95      1.75
6       CANDY       4.25      3.95      3.75      3.55
7       COFFEE      3.75      3.65      3.35      3.25
8       JUICE       1.75      1.55      1.45      1.35
9       SUGAR       1.55      1.45      1.25      1.15
10
11
12
13      ITEM     QUANTITY PRICE
14
15      SUGAR       300
16
17
18
19
20
                            UNDO
```

Figure 8-60

This worksheet includes an index table containing the price for some items based on the quantity purchased. You also need to create the range name PRICE_TABLE and include cells B5 through E9 as its range.

To demonstrate the use of the @INDEX function:

Move   the cell pointer to cell C15

Type   @INDEX(PRICE_TABLE,2,4)

Press   ⏎

Your screen should look like Figure 8-61.

```
C15: @INDEX(PRICE_TABLE,2,4)                                          READY
```

	A	B	C	D	E	F	G	H
1			INDEX TABLE					
2								
3			QUANTITY					
4	ITEM	100	200	300	400			
5	BEEF STEW	2.25	2.05	1.95	1.75			
6	CANDY	4.25	3.95	3.75	3.55			
7	COFFEE	3.75	3.65	3.35	3.25			
8	JUICE	1.75	1.55	1.45	1.35			
9	SUGAR	1.55	1.45	1.25	1.15			
10								
11								
12								
13	ITEM	QUANTITY	PRICE					
14								
15	SUGAR	300	1.25					
16								
17								

Figure 8-61

The value 1.25 appears in cell C15 indicating price for SUGAR when the purchase QUANTITY is 300 units.

■ STRING FUNCTIONS

There are 19 string functions available in 1-2-3. The term string refers to any set of characters. The string functions can be categorized as follows:

SPECIAL CHARACTERS AND CREATING CHARACTERS:

@CHAR	Returns the character which the Lotus Multibyte Character Set (LMBCS) code produces
@CLEAN	Removes control characters from a string
@CODE	Returns the LMBCS code corresponding to the first character in a string
@REPEAT	Duplicates a string of characters a specified number of times

EXTRACTING PORTIONS OF A STRING FROM A LABEL:

@FIND	Determines the position of the first character of a string within another string
@LEFT	Returns a specified number of characters beginning with the first character in the string

@LENGTH	Determines the number of characters in a string
@MID	Returns an indicated number of characters beginning with a specific character
@REPLACE	Replaces the characters in one string with another specified string of characters
@RIGHT	Returns a specified number of characters at the end of a string

CHANGING THE CASE OF A STRING:

@LOWER	Changes all letters in a string to lowercase
@PROPER	Changes the first letter of each word in a string to uppercase; all other letters in the string are lowercase
@UPPER	Changes all letters in a string to uppercase

CONVERTING VALUES TO STRINGS AND STRINGS TO VALUES:

@STRING	Changes a value into a label with a specified number of decimal places
@TRIM	Deletes all leading, trailing, and consecutive spaces from a string
@VALUE	Changes a string of characters from a label to a number

DETERMINING THE CHARACTERISTICS OF A STRING:

@EXACT	Determines whether two strings of characters are the same
@N	Returns the value (number) in the first cell in a range if it contains a number; otherwise a zero is returned
@S	Returns the label in the first cell in a range if it contains a label; otherwise a blank cell is returned

Special Characters and Creating Characters

The three functions for manipulating special characters in 1-2-3 are @CHAR, @CODE and @REPEAT.

@CHAR

The @CHAR returns the character that the Lotus Multibyte Character Set (LMBCS) code provides. The format of the @CHAR function is:

> @CHAR(x)

where *x* is an integer. See the Lotus 1-2-3 reference manual for further information.

@CLEAN

The @CLEAN function removes control characters from a string. The format of the @CLEAN function is:

> @CLEAN(x)

where *x* is a string. See the 1-2-3 reference manual for additional information.

@CODE

The @CODE function returns the Lotus Multibyte Character set (LMBCS) code for the first character in a string. The format of the @CODE function is:

> @CODE(x)

where *x* is a string. See the Lotus 1-2-3 reference manual for further information.

@REPEAT

The @REPEAT function is used to duplicate a string of characters a specific number of times. The format of the @REPEAT function is:

> @REPEAT(string,n)

where string is a set of characters and *n* is the number of times the string is to be repeated. The value of *n* can be any positive integer.

To illustrate the use of the @REPEAT function:

Move	the cell pointer to cell A1
Enter	@REPEAT("Worksheet ",3)
Press	⏎

Your screen should look like Figure 8-62.

```
A1: @REPEAT("Worksheet ",3)                                          READY


        A       B       C       D       E       F       G       H
1    Worksheet Worksheet Worksheet
2
3
```

Figure 8-62

The set of characters "Worksheet " is repeated three times in cell A1. Note that a space occurs between the words because you placed a space before the second " in the string definition.

Extracting Portions of a String from a Label

The six string functions in 1-2-3 used to extract portions of a string from a label are @FIND, @LEFT, @LENGTH, @MID, @REPLACE and @RIGHT.

@FIND

The @FIND function determines the position within a string where another string starts. The format of the @FIND function is:

@FIND(search-string,string,start-number)

where search-string is the set of characters being sought in the string. The search-string and string can be any string of characters, a reference to a cell or a formula that evaluates to a label. Start-number is an offset number of a character in a string. It can have a value of 0 or any positive integer. The first character in the string is the number zero, the second is number one and so on.

To illustrate the use of the @FIND function:

Move	the cell pointer to cell A1
Enter	Spreadsheet Analysis
Move	the cell pointer to cell A3
Type	@FIND("sheet",A1,0)
Press	↵

Your screen should look like Figure 8-63.

```
A3: @FIND("sheet",A1,0)                                            READY


        A        B        C        D        E        F        G        H
1   Spreadsheet Analysis
2
3           6
4
5
```

Figure 8-63

The number 6 is the position of the first character of search-string within the string being searched. If the @FIND function cannot locate the search string in the string, ERR is returned and will appear in cell A3. @FIND is case sensitive. For example, if "Sheet" had been specified in the example, ERR would have appeared in cell A3, because sheet is not capitalized in the string.

@LEFT

The @LEFT function returns a specified number of characters from a string beginning with the first character in the string. The format of the @LEFT function is:

@LEFT(string,n)

String can be any string of characters, a reference to a cell or a formula that evaluates to a label. The *n* is the number of characters to be returned from the string.

To demonstrate the use of the @LEFT function:

Move	the cell pointer to cell B1
Enter	Mastering and Using Lotus 1-2-3

Suppose you want to return the characters *Mastering* and place them in cell B3.

Move	the cell pointer to cell B3
Type	@LEFT(B1,9)
Press	⏎

Your screen should look like Figure 8-64.

```
B3: @LEFT(B1,9)                                                    READY

       A          B         C         D        E        F        G        H
1                Mastering Lotus 1-2-3
2
3                Mastering
4
5
```

Figure 8-64

The string of characters *Mastering* now appears in cell B3.

@LENGTH

The @LENGTH function counts the number of characters in a string. The format of the @LENGTH function is:

> @LENGTH(string)

where a string is any string of characters, a reference to a cell or a formula that evaluates to a string.

To illustrate the use of the @LENGTH function:

Move	the cell pointer to cell A1
Enter	Boyd & Fraser Publishing Company
Move	the cell pointer to cell A4
Type	@LENGTH(A1)
Press	⏎

Your screen should look like Figure 8-65.

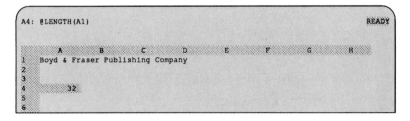

```
A4: @LENGTH(A1)                                                    READY

       A          B         C         D        E        F        G        H
1  Boyd & Fraser Publishing Company
2
3
4       32
5
6
```

Figure 8-65

The number 32 appears in cell A4 indicating there are 32 characters in the string that is contained in cell A1.

@MID

The `@MID` function is used to return a specific number of characters beginning at a particular point in a string. The format of the `@MID` function is:

        `@MID(string,start-number,n)`

where string is any string of characters, reference to a cell or formula that evaluates to a string, and *n* is the number of characters to return. Start-number can be zero or any positive integer.

To demonstrate the use of the `@MID` function:

Move	the cell pointer to cell B1
Enter	Mastering and Using Lotus 1-2-3 Release 2.2
Move	the cell pointer to cell B3
Type	`@MID(B1,20,11)`
Press	⏎

Your screen should look like Figure 8-66.

```
B3: @MID(B1,20,11)                                                  READY

        A        B        C        D        E        F        G        H
1                Mastering and Using Lotus 1-2-3 Release 2.2
2
3                Lotus 1-2-3
4
```

Figure 8-66

The set of characters Lotus 1-2-3 appears in cell B3 as a result of using the `@MID` function.

@REPLACE

The `@REPLACE` function finds a set of characters in a string and replaces the characters with another set of characters. The format of the `@REPLACE` function is:

        `@REPLACE(original-string,start-number,n,new-string)`

where original-string and new-string can be any string of characters, a reference to a cell or a formula that evaluates to a string. The *n* is the number of characters to be replaced and start-number is an offset number identifying where to start replacing characters in the original-string. Start-number and *n* can have a value of zero or any positive integer.

To illustrate the use of the @REPLACE function:

Move	the cell pointer to cell A1
Enter	Softball and Feetball are popular sports

To replace the *ee* in Feetball with *oo*:

Move	the cell pointer to cell A3
Type	@REPLACE(A1,14,2,"oo")
Press	⏎

Your screen should look like Figure 8-67.

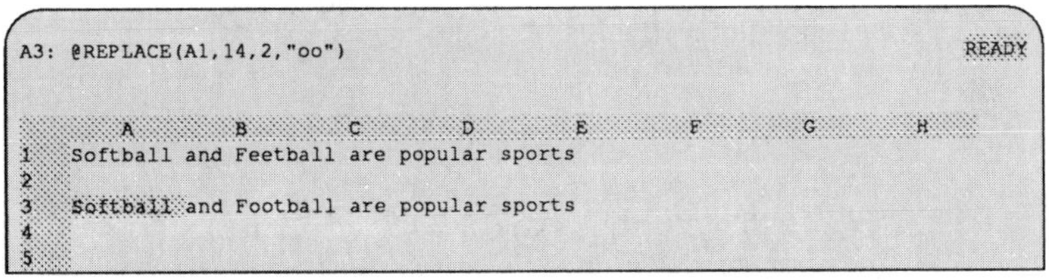

```
A3:  @REPLACE(A1,14,2,"oo")                                    READY

         A        B        C        D        E        F        G        H
  1  Softball and Feetball are popular sports
  2
  3  Softball and Football are popular sports
  4
  5
```

Figure 8-67

The spelling error appearing in cell A1 is now corrected in cell A3.

@RIGHT

The @RIGHT function returns characters from the end of a string. The format of the @RIGHT function is:

@RIGHT(string,n)

where string is any string of characters, a reference to a cell or a formula that evaluates to a string. The *n* is the number of characters to return and can be any positive integer.

To demonstrate the use of the @RIGHT function:

Move	the cell pointer to cell B1
Enter	Software Package
Move	the cell pointer to cell B3
Type	@RIGHT(B1,7)
Press	⏎

Your screen should look like Figure 8-68.

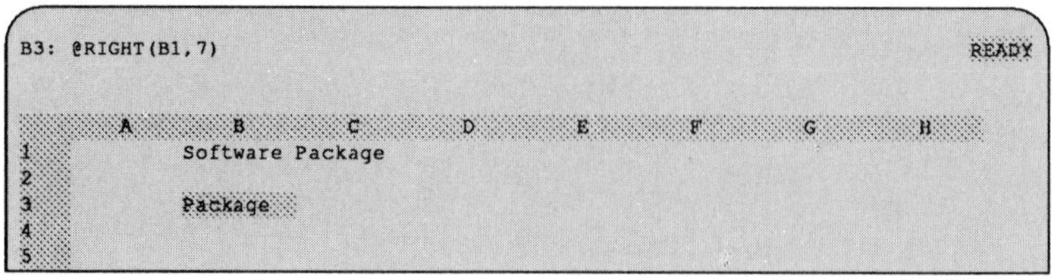

Figure 8-68

The word Package now appears in cell B3, because it represents the last seven characters of the string in B1.

Changing the Case of a String

The three functions available in 1-2-3 to change the case of a string are @LOWER, @PROPER and @UPPER.

@LOWER

The @LOWER function changes all letters in a string to lowercase. The format of the @LOWER function is:

@LOWER(string)

where string is any string of characters, a reference to a cell or a formula that evaluates to a string.

To illustrate the use of the @LOWER function:

Move	the cell pointer to cell A1
Enter	SOUTHWEST
Move	the cell pointer to cell A3
Type	@LOWER(A1)
Press	⏎

Your screen should look like Figure 8-69.

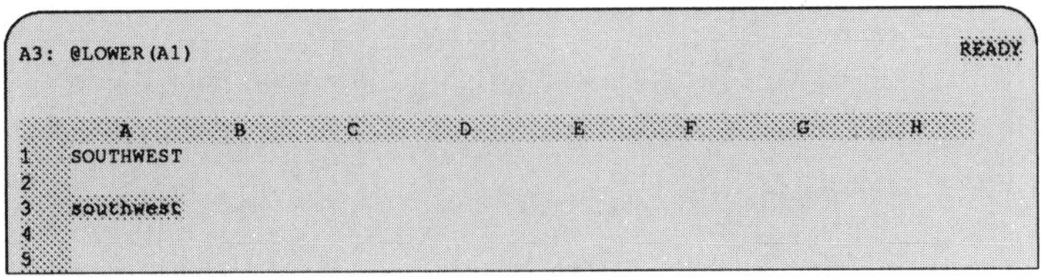

```
A3: @LOWER(A1)                                                    READY

          A         B         C         D         E         F         G         H
1    SOUTHWEST
2
3    southwest
4
5
```

Figure 8-69

The letters appearing in cell A3 are all lowercase.

@PROPER

The @PROPER function makes the first letter of each word in a string uppercase. The remaining letters are lowercase. The format of the @PROPER function is:

@PROPER(string)

where string is any string of characters, a reference to a cell or a formula that evaluates to a string.

To demonstrate the use of the @PROPER function:

Move	the cell pointer to cell B1
Enter	mastering and using lotus 1-2-3 release 2.2
Move	the cell pointer to cell B3
Type	@PROPER(B1)
Press	⏎

Your screen should look like Figure 8-70.

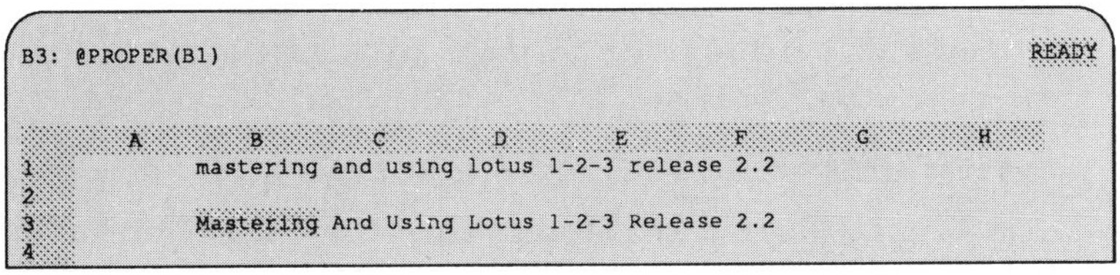

```
B3: @PROPER(B1)                                                   READY

          A         B         C         D         E         F         G         H
1              mastering and using lotus 1-2-3 release 2.2
2
3              Mastering And Using Lotus 1-2-3 Release 2.2
4
```

Figure 8-70

The first letter of each word in row 3 is uppercase and the other letters are lowercase.

@UPPER

The @UPPER function converts all lowercase letters in a string to uppercase letters. The format of the @UPPER function is:

@UPPER(string)

where string is any string of characters, a reference to a cell or a formula that evaluates to a string.

To illustrate the use of the @UPPER function:

Move	the cell pointer to cell A1
Enter	California
Move	the cell pointer to cell A3
Type	@UPPER(A1)
Press	↵

Your screen should look like Figure 8-71.

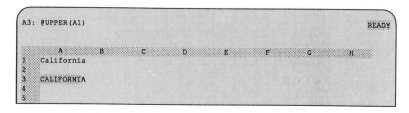

Figure 8-71

All letters in California are now uppercase in cell A3.

Converting Values to Strings and Strings to Values

The three functions available in 1-2-3 related to converting values to strings and strings to values are: @STRING, @TRIM and @VALUE.

@STRING

The @STRING function changes a value into a label with a specified number of decimal places. The format of the @STRING function is:

@STRING(x,n)

where x can be a value, a reference to a cell or a formula that evaluates to a value. The n can be 0 or any positive integer between 1 and 15.

To demonstrate the use of the @STRING function:

Move	the cell pointer to cell B1
Enter	123.45
Move	the cell pointer to cell B3
Type	@STRING(B1,0)
Press	↵

Your screen should look like Figure 8-72.

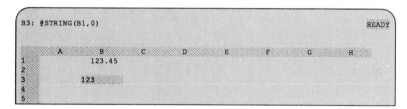

Figure 8-72

The value in cell B1 has been converted to the string 123 that appears in cell B3. Note the characters in cell B3 are left-justified indicating the data is considered as a label and not a value.

@TRIM

The @TRIM function deletes all leading, trailing and consecutive spaces from a string. Single spaces in the string are preserved. The format of the function is:

    @TRIM(string)

where string is any string of characters, a reference to a cell or a formula that evaluates to a string.

To illustrate the use of the @TRIM function:

Move	the cell pointer to cell A1
Enter	Worksheets are fun to create

Note that there are two spaces before Worksheets and between the words Worksheets, are, fun and to.

Move	the cell pointer to cell A3
Type	@TRIM(A1)

Press   ⏎

Your screen should look like Figure 8-73.

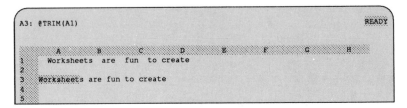

Figure 8-73

The leading spaces and extra spaces in the string have been deleted. Note that the space between to and create remains because there was only one space originally.

@VALUE

The @VALUE function changes a string of characters that looks like a number into a value. The format of the @VALUE function is:

        @VALUE(string)

where string can only include numbers or numeric symbols.

To demonstrate the use of the @VALUE function:

Move	the cell pointer to cell B1
Enter	'97.5%
Move	the cell pointer to cell B3
Type	@VALUE(B1)
Press	⏎

Your screen should look like Figure 8-74.

Figure 8-74

The string in cell B1 has been converted into the numeric value appearing in cell B3.

Determining the Characteristics of a String

The three functions available in 1-2-3 for determining the characteristics of a string are: @EXACT, @N and @S.

@EXACT

The @EXACT function determines whether two strings of characters are the same. The format of the @EXACT function is:

@EXACT(string1,string2)

where string1 and string2 can be any string of characters, a reference to a cell or a formula that evaluates to a string.

If string1 and string2 are exactly the same, a value of one is returned; otherwise a zero is returned.

To illustrate the use of the @EXACT function:

Move	the cell pointer to cell A1
Enter	Southwestern states
Copy	cell A1 to cell A3
Move	the cell pointer to A5
Type	@EXACT(A1,A3)
Press	⏎

Your screen should look like Figure 8-75.

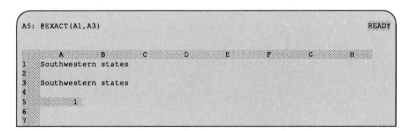

```
A5: @EXACT(A1,A3)                                                    READY

         A           B         C        D        E        F        G        H
1    Southwestern states
2
3    Southwestern states
4
5            1
6
7
```

Figure 8-75

The number 1 appears in cell A5 indicating the strings in cells A1 and A3 are the same. Edit cell A3 so that the string ends with a space.

Move	the cell pointer to cell A3
Press	F2
Press	the spacebar
Press	←

The number 0 appears in cell A5 because the strings in cells A1 and A3 are not exactly alike. Any differences in case between the two strings would also result in a 0 in cell A5.

@N

The @N function returns the value appearing in the first cell of a range if the content of the cell is a numeric value, otherwise a zero is returned. The format of the @N function is:

    @N(range)

where range is any specified set of cells, or a range name.

To demonstrate the use of the @N function:

Move	the cell pointer to cell B1
Enter	125
Move	the cell pointer to cell C1
Enter	150

Create the range name NUM_TEST that has cells B1 and C1 as its range.

Move	the cell pointer to cell B3
Type	@N(NUM_TEST)
Press	←

Your screen should look like Figure 8-76.

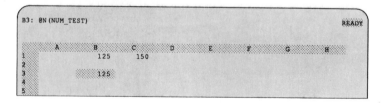

Figure 8-76

The number 125 appearing in cell B3 indicates that the first cell in the range NUM_TEST is a value. Change the contents of B1 to a label and a value of zero will appear in cell B3, indicating that the content of the first cell of the range NUM_TEST is not a number.

@S

The format of the @S function is:

    @S(range)

where range is any specified set of cells or a range name.

To illustrate the use of the @S function:

Move	the cell pointer to cell A1
Enter	June
Move	the cell pointer to cell B1
Enter	July

Create the range name LABEL_TEST that has cells A1 and B1 as its range.

Move	the cell pointer to cell A3
Type	@S(LABEL_TEST)
Press	⏎

Your screen should look like Figure 8-77.

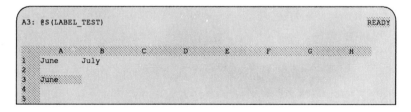

A3: @S(LABEL_TEST)   READY

	A	B	C	D	E	F	G	H
1	June	July						
2								
3	June							
4								
5								

Figure 8-77

The month June appears in cell A3 indicating that the first cell in the range LABEL_TEST has a label as its contents. Enter a number in cell A1, and A3 will appear as a blank cell. If you erase cell A1, cell A3 will also appear as a blank cell.

SUMMARY

Lotus 1-2-3 has many functions that can perform standard calculations. There are eight different categories of functions: statistical analysis, financial analysis, date and time, logical, database statistical, mathematical, special and string.

KEY CONCEPTS

Database Statistical Functions
Date and Time Functions
Financial Analysis Functions
Logical Functions
Mathematical Functions
Special Functions
Statistical Analysis Functions
String Functions

CHAPTER EIGHT
EXERCISE 1

INSTRUCTIONS: Circle T if the statement is true and F if the statement is false.

T F 1. @MIN determines the minute for a given serial number.

T F 2. Multiple items in a range may be listed individually (e.g.the syntax in the formula @COUNT(B1,B3,B4) is correct).

T F 3. Arguments within an @ function may be placed in any order desired by the user.

T F 4. Extra spaces are not acceptable within @ functions.

T F 5. A label has a value of 0 and will be counted as such if included in a range for an @ function.

T F 6. It is possible to alter an @ function with arithmetic operations to get the desired result (e.g., the formula @PMT(B1,B2/12,B3*12) is syntactically correct).

T F 7. If a worksheet file containing the @NOW function (formatted to show the date) is retrieved from a file and actively recalculates, the @NOW function will display the *current* system date.

T F 8. A single-cell item in an argument may not be entered directly into the formula (e.g., the formula @NPV(A1,B1..B6) cannot be entered as @NPV(.1,B1..B6).

T F 9. More than one @ function may be used in a formula.

T F 10. The @IF statement allows you to test one or more conditions in a worksheet and provide appropriate responses either a true result or a false result.

T F 11. Date and time special functions are available in 1-2-3.

T F 12. XLOOKUP allows you to look up values in a row or a table.

T   F   13. You can modify the appearance of a series of characters using the string functions.

T   F   14. Data queries cannot be accomplished using special functions.

CHAPTER EIGHT
EXERCISE 2
Using the Statistical Analysis Functions

INSTRUCTIONS: Using the data 111, 125, 116, 130, and 127, apply the statistical analysis functions available in Lotus 1-2-3 to:

1. Determine the sum of the numbers

2. Count the number of values

3. Compute the arithmetic mean of the values

4. Determine the minimum value

5. Calculate the maximum value

6. Compute the population variance

7. Determine the population standard deviation

Print the worksheet after completing the calculations.

CHAPTER EIGHT
EXERCISE 3
Using the Financial Analysis Functions

INSTRUCTIONS: Use the Financial Analysis Functions available in Lotus 1-2-3 to solve the following exercises.

1. Compute the internal rate of return for the following cash flow stream using .15 as the guess rate:

    -1000, -500, 900, 800, 700, 600, 400, 200, 100

2. Compute the net present value for the following cash flow stream using .10 as the discount rate:

    -1500, 900, 800, 700, 600, 400, 200, 100

3. Compute the future value if the payment per period is 500, the interest rate is 10%, and the term is 15 years.

4. Compute the present value using the arguments previously given in problem number 3.

5. Compute the payment amount for a 100,000 loan that has an interest rate of 10% and is to be paid on an annual basis for a period of 12 years.

6. Compute the *monthly* payment amount assuming all arguments in problem 5 stay the same except the time period is 30 years.

7. Compute the straight-line depreciation for an office machine having an initial cost of $13,000, an estimated useful life of 8 years, and a salvage value of $200.

8. Using the data given in problem 7, compute the depreciation of the office machine for the sixth year using the double-declining balance method.

9. Using the data given in problem 7, compute the depreciation of the office machine for the sixth year using the sum-of-the-years'digits method.

10. Suppose $10,000 has been invested in an account that pays an annual interest rate of 10 percent, compounded monthly. Determine how long it will take to get $30,000 in the account.

11. Suppose that $5,000 is deposited at the end of each year into a bank account. If 8% interest is earned per year, compute how long it will take to earn $20,000.

12. Suppose $15,000 has been invested in a bond which matures in 9 years to $25,000. Interest is compounded monthly. Determine the monthly interest rate.

Print the worksheet(s) showing your answers.

CHAPTER EIGHT
EXERCISE 4
Using the Date and Time Functions

INSTRUCTIONS:

1. Using the @DATE function, enter the date January 19, 1989 into cell A1. Format the date using option 1 from the Date format menu. Notice that the cell fills with asterisks; widen column A appropriately.

2. Using the @TIME function, enter the time 9:49 PM in cell A2.

3. Calculate the number of days between January 3, 1991, and June 27, 1989.

4. Use the @NOW function to place the current date on your screen.

5. For the time 8:14:10 AM, place the hour in cell B1, the minute in cell B2 and the second in cell B3.

6. Determine the time of day represented by the time serial number .481234.

Print your worksheet after completing all parts of the exercise.

CHAPTER EIGHT
EXERCISE 5
Using the Logical Functions

INSTRUCTIONS: Make sure you have a blank worksheet on your screen. Then enter the following data on the worksheet.

Cell	Data
A1	20
A2	30
A3	50
A10	@NA
A11	10
A12	Worksheet

1. In cell B1, determine whether the value in A1 is within the range from 30 to 40. If the value is in the range, place the word **True** in cell B1; otherwise, place the word **False** in cell B1.

2. In cell B2, determine whether the value in A2 is greater than 25. If the value in cell A2 is greater than 25, use the @TRUE function to enter a value of 1 in cell B2. If the value is less than or equal to 25, use the @FALSE function to place the value 0 in cell B2.

3. In cell B3, determine whether the value in A3 is greater than 60. If the value in cell A3 is greater than 60, use the @TRUE function to enter a value of 1 in cell B3. If the value is less than or equal to 60, use the @FALSE function to place the value 0 in cell B3.

Print the worksheet with the results of the first three questions.

4. Change the values entered in cells A1, A2, A3 to:

Cell	Data
A1	35
A2	10
A3	75

Print the worksheet with the results after entering the new values. Print a list of the cell formulas for cells A1 through B3.

Define the range name ABC and include cells A10 through A12 as its range.

5. In cell B10, determine if the content of cell A10 contains @NA; if so, place a 1 in cell B10; otherwise place a 0 in cell B10.

6. In cell B11, determine if the content of cell A11 is a value. If cell A11 contains a value, place a 1 in cell B11; otherwise enter a 0 in cell B11.

7. In cell B12, determine if cell A12 contains a string of characters. If a string of characters appears in cell A12, place a 1 in cell B12; otherwise, place a 0 in cell B12.

Print the results for questions 5 through 8. Include a list of cell formulas for cells A10 through B14.

CHAPTER EIGHT
EXERCISE 6
Using the Data Statistical Functions

INSTRUCTIONS: Create the database table in Figure 8-78.

```
A1: 'PRODUCT                                                          READY


        A          B          C        D        E        F        G        H
 1  PRODUCT    SALES
 2  NUTS       $38,000
 3  BOLTS      $27,000
 4  HAMMERS    $42,000
 5  NAILS      $34,500
 6  SAWS       $28,900
 7  LIGHTS     $41,000
 8
 9
10  SUM
11  COUNT
12  AVERAGE
13  MINIMUM
14  MAXIMUM
15  POPULATION VARIANCE
16  POPULATION STANDARD DEVIATION
17
18
19
20
                            UNDO
```

Figure 8-78

1. Construct a criteria that will determine if a product included in the database table has sales of more than $35,000.

2. Place the appropriate database statistical functions in cells E10 through E16 to compute the indicated items.

Print the worksheet after answering questions 1 and 2.

CHAPTER EIGHT
EXERCISE 7
Using the Mathematical Functions

INSTRUCTIONS: Make sure you have a blank worksheet on your screen. Then enter the following data on the worksheet.

Cell	Data
B1	-45
B2	45
B3	2
B4	52.9876
B5	1.5
B6	10
B7	20
B8	12
B9	67.3468
B10	225

1.   In cell C1, compute the absolute value of the contents of cell B1. Calculate the absolute value of the contents of cell B2 and place the results in cell C2.

2.   In cell C3, determine the value for *e* raised to the power of the number included in cell B3.

3.   In cell C4, calculate the integer portion of the value appearing in cell B4.

4.   In cell C5, compute the natural logarithm for the value in cell B5.

5.   In cell B6, specify the common logarithm for the value in cell B6.

6.   In cell C7, determine the remainder (modulus) for the values in cells B7 and B8. In computing the remainder, divide the value in cell B7 by the value in B8.

7.   In cell C8, enter a random number between 0 and 1.

8. In cell C9, round the value appearing in cell B9 to three decimal places.

9. In cell C10, compute the square root of the value in cell B10.

Print the worksheet with the answers to questions 1 through 9. Also print the cell formulas.

CHAPTER EIGHT
EXERCISE 8
Using the Cell, Range and Error Trapping Functions

INSTRUCTIONS: Make sure you have a blank worksheet on your screen.

1. Enter the number 25 in cell A2. Place A2 in cell D1. Use the @@ function to place 25 in cell B3.

2. Define the range name COLUMNS that includes cells A1 through K1. In cell A5, specify the number of columns in the range named COLUMNS.

3. Define the range named ROWS that includes cells B2 through B233. In cell A9, specify the number of rows in the range named ROWS.

4. Enter a 10 in cell B14 and a 0 in cell C14. In cell A14, place a formula that enters ERR in cell A14 when the value in cell C14 is zero; otherwise, compute the product of the values in cells B14 and C14.

5. Enter the number 100 in cell B16. Place the characters @NA (meaning not available) in cell A16 if the value in cell B16 is less than 500; otherwise, place the contents of cell B16 in cell A16.

Print the worksheet after solving questions one through five. Also print the cell formulas.

CHAPTER EIGHT
EXERCISE 9
Using the Lookup Functions

INSTRUCTIONS: 1. Create the worksheet appearing in Figure 8-79.

```
A1:                                                                    READY

           A          B         C          D       E       F       G
1                               Sales Tax    Sales
2       Product      Price   Rate Code      Tax
3    Beans           0.79           1
4    Hammer          2.59           2
5    Nail            0.25           2
6    Cake            1.25           1
7
8
9                            Sales Tax
10                           Rate Code  Tax Rate
11                                   1       0%
12                                   2       8%
13
14
```

Figure 8-79

You need to compute the Sales Tax amount for the four products based on the Sales Tax Rate Code. Use the @CHOOSE function to assist you in computing the proper sales tax amount for the four items.

Print the worksheet after completing the calculation of the sales tax amounts. Also print the cell formulas.

2. Create the worksheet appearing in Figure 8-80.

```
D9: [W12] ^AMOUNT                                                    READY

          A            B         C         D         E       F
1
2    COMMISSION                SALES AMOUNT
3       CODE        $2,000     $3,000     $4,000   $5,000
4            1         200        300        400      500
5            2         100        150        200      250
6            3          40         60         80      100
7
8                     SALES   COMMISSION COMMISSION
9    EMPLOYEE        AMOUNT      CODE      AMOUNT
10   ABRAMS         $2,500         3
11   CHEN           $3,500         1
12   MARTINEZ       $3,100         1
13   SMITH          $4,900         2
14   ZACHARY        $3,000         3
15
16
```

Figure 8-80

You need to calculate the commission owed each of the salespersons. The amount of commission is based on a commission code assigned to each individual and the sales amount for the individuals. For example, a person that has a sales amount of $2,800 and a commission code of 2 is owed a commission of $100. Use the @HLOOKUP function to help calculate the proper commission amounts.

Print the worksheet after computing the commission amounts. Also print the cell formulas.

3. Create the worksheet appearing in Figure 8-81.

```
D9: "TAXES                                                              READY


          A         B         C        D        E        F        G        H
1
2                  TAX
3       SALARY     RATE
4      $25,000       2%
5      $50,000       7%
6      $75,000      15%
7
8
9    EMPLOYEE    SALARY TAX RATE      TAXES
10   ABBOTT     $78,000
11   GARCIA     $52,000
12   MONTEGUET  $60,000
13   SMITH      $48,000
14
15
```

Figure 8-81

You must compute the state income taxes owed by the individuals. The tax amount owed by each employee is computed by multiplying the salary amount times the appropriate tax rate. For example, if a person has a salary equal to $50,000, then the amount of state income tax due is $3,500. Use the @VLOOKUP function to determine the proper tax rate for each employee.

Print the worksheet after calculating the tax amount due for each of the employees. Also print the cell formulas.

CHAPTER EIGHT
EXERCISE 10
Using the String Functions

INSTRUCTIONS: Make sure you have a blank worksheet on your screen.

1. Repeat the string of characters "Graph" 6 times in cell A1. Do not include the quotes.

2. Enter the label: "Lotus 1-2-3 is a great software package" in cell A3. Do not include the quotes. Find the position of the word *great* in the label and place the answer in cell B4.

3. Using the label in cell A3, place the characters *Lotus 1-2-3* in cell D4.

4. Using the label in cell A3, determine the number of characters in the label and place the answer in cell F4.

5. Using the label in cell A3, place the word *software* in cell B6.

6. Copy the label in cell A3 to cell A8. Using the label in cell A8, replace the word *great* with *wonderful*.

7. Using the label in cell A8, place the words *software package* in cell B9.

8. Enter the words "Fall is a beautiful time of year" in cell A11. Do not include the quotes.

9. Using the label in cell A11, change all of the letters to lowercase and place the results in cell A12.

10. Using the label in cell A11, change all of the letters to uppercase and place the results in cell A13.

11. Using the label in cell A11, capitalize the first letter in each word and make all other letters lowercase and place the results in cell A14.

Print the worksheet with the answers to questions 1 through 11. Also print the cell formulas.

CHAPTER EIGHT
EXERCISE 11
Using the String Functions

INSTRUCTIONS: Make sure you have a blank worksheet on your screen.

1. Enter the number 592.783 in cell A1. Using the value in cell A1, change the value to a label with three decimal places and place the results in cell B1.

2. Enter the label " Lotus 1-2-3   is   fun   to   use" in cell A3. Do not include the quotes. Remove the leading spaces and extra spaces between the words. Place the results in cell A4.

3. Enter 123.456 as a label in cell A6. Change the label in cell A6 to a number and place the results in cell B6.

4. Enter the string of characters "Northeast" in cell A8. Do not include the quotes. Place the same characters in cell A9 except omit the letter s. In cell A10, determine whether the contents of cells A8 and A9 are exactly the same. If they are not exactly the same, place a 0 in cell A10; otherwise, a 1 should appear in cell A10.

5. Place the values 1, 2, 3 in cells A12, B12 and C12 respectively, and create the range name NUM that includes these cells as the range. In cell A13, place the contents of the first cell in the range if the first cell in the range is a value.

Print the worksheet with the answers to questions 1 through 5. Also print the cell formulas.

CHAPTER NINE

INTRODUCTION TO MACROS

OBJECTIVES

In this chapter you will learn to:

- Use a standard procedure for creating a macro
- Define range names for use in a macro
- Place a macro in a suitable location on a worksheet
- Create and execute a macro
- Create a print macro
- Create a macro using the learn feature

■CHAPTER OVERVIEW

A **macro** is a set of written instructions representing keystrokes in Lotus 1-2-3. The macro keystrokes represent the keystrokes exactly as they are typed when you select them from various worksheet menus, enter data or move the cell pointer.

Macros are especially useful when performing detailed, repetitive routines. You can write macros that consolidate worksheets, perform special edit routines or print reports. Advanced uses of macros can involve using macro commands that allow you to perform loops, subroutines, *IF* statements, and many other features common to programming languages. A macro enables you to do intricate spreadsheet analysis. In this chapter, you will learn the basics of macros. The next chapter contains more advanced topics related to macros.

■DEFINING RANGE NAMES

A range name is a name that is assigned to a specific cell or group of cells. Range names are used to specify the location of macros. They are also used to identify ranges of cells within macros. By using range names, you can create macro programs that are more self-sufficient and require less editing and maintenance.

To illustrate the use of a range name, retrieve the BUDGET file you created in Chapter 2. Your screen should now look like Figure 9-1.

```
A1: [W18]                                                    READY

              A           B       C       D       E       F        G
1                                  ABC COMPANY
2                                    BUDGET
3
4
5                        QTR1    QTR2    QTR3    QTR4   YR TOTAL
6
7   SALES             $60,000 $61,200 $62,424 $63,672 $247,296
8
9   EXPENSES
10    SALARIES         35,000  35,500  36,200  37,000  143,700
11    RENT              9,000   9,000   9,000   9,000   36,000
12    TELEPHONE         1,000   1,050   1,103   1,158    4,311
13    OFFICE SUPPLIES     750     800     850     900    3,300
14    MISCELLANEOUS     1,000   1,030   1,061   1,093    4,184
15                    ---------------------------------------------
16      TOTAL EXPENSES 46,750  47,380  48,214  49,151  191,495
17                    ---------------------------------------------
18  GROSS PROFIT      $13,250 $13,820 $14,210 $14,521  $55,801
19                    =============================================
20
                         UNDO                            CAPS
```

Figure 9-1

Suppose you want to use a range name to represent the SALES values in cells B7 through E7.

To specify the range name SALES for these cells:

Move	the cell pointer to cell B7
Press	/
Select	Range
Select	Name
Select	Create

When prompted for a range name:

Type	SALES
Press	⏎

To define the range of cells to include:

Move	the cell pointer to cell E7

After highlighting the cells B7 through E7:

Press	⏎

The range of cells associated with the named range SALES was substituted in the @SUM formula for the word SALES and the proper total was computed. Your screen should look like Figure 9-1. Move the cell pointer to cell F7 and note that the @SUM formula now has SALES in it rather than B7..E7.

You can use the F5 key to go to the first cell in a range on a worksheet. For example:

Press   F5

When prompted for the address to go to:

Type   SALES

Press   ⏎

The cell pointer should now be in cell B7.

■ PROCESS FOR CREATING A MACRO

The steps you use to create a macro are:

1. Create a macro by first *practicing the procedure* that the macro is to perform; manually press the keystrokes necessary to execute the macro.

2. While going through the macro steps, *record every keystroke* exactly as it is typed.

3. After practicing the macro manually, *record the keystrokes on the worksheet.*

   The macro instructions must be in the proper order and must appear as labels contained in one column. Begin each of the macro instructions with an apostrophe (the ' symbol is located on the double quote key). This procedure will prevent the macro from executing some commands as they are being entered (for example, typing / to bring up the command menu). Using the apostrophe will also allow 1-2-3 to accept all macro instructions when they contain a combination of numeric and alphabetic characters.

4. After entering the complete macro, *name the macro as a named range.* There are two ways to name a macro. You can use the \ key and a single letter, or a range name that consists of any combination of 15 allowable characters, such as PRINT_MACRO. Only the first cell in the macro is needed for the range name; however, the entire macro can be specified in the range. The macro will stop executing when it attempts to process a blank cell in the column containing the macro.

5. Before running and testing the macro, *save the worksheet containing the macro.* Then, if the macro does not work properly, you can retrieve the worksheet and the macro as they were before any changes were made by the macro.

6. *Execute the macro.* If you named your macro using the \ key and a single letter, you can run the macro by holding down the [Alt] key and then pressing the letter. If the macro name consists of any other combination of characters, you need to hold down the [Alt] key and press the [F3] key. Then you must move the pointer to the proper macro name and press the [↵] key, or else type the name of the macro and press the [↵] key.

7. The macro should perform automatically. If it does not, the macro instructions are incorrect and you will have to *edit and revise the macro.* You may need to press the [Esc] key to exit a macro that has stopped because it encountered an error. Another way to stop a macro once it has begun execution is to hold down the [Ctrl] key and to press the [Break] key. The [Break] key is located on the [Pause] key on most keyboards.

   After determining the error, **retrieve** the worksheet containing the macro. Edit the macro on the retrieved worksheet, then **save** and **replace** it before testing the macro again. If the original worksheet and macro are not retrieved from the disk after it has incorrectly run, the worksheet may contain unwanted changes that were made to the worksheet during execution.

8. After a macro has executed correctly, you should *document* (*write an explanation of what the macro instructions do*) the macro in a column to the right of the macro steps and then write the macro's name either above or to the left of the macro steps. The documentation process is optional. However, a written explanation of a macro's purpose will prove valuable to a user who did not create the macro but needs to know what the macro does without having to spend extra time analyzing the macro. Documentation is also useful for the macro's author, saving time from having to decipher the macro at a later date when the macro may need to be altered or used in another application.

■ LOCATION OF A MACRO

It is recommended that you place the macro to the right and below the data on the worksheet. For example, suppose you are using cells A1 through F35 on your worksheet; your macros should be below row 35 and to the right of column F. By using this approach, you are less likely to accidentally delete or modify one of the macro instructions. For ease of presentation purposes we vary from this approach in this text.

■ CREATING AND EXECUTING A MACRO

In Chapter 6, you combined salary information for three divisions of ABC Company into the SALARIES row in the BUDGET file. In this section, you will build a macro to combine the total salary data from the file DIV1 that contains SALARIES data for DIVISION 1 into the BUDGET file. You will create a macro to combine the SALARIES data for all three divisions into the BUDGET file as an exercise at the end of this chapter.

In this example, you will place the macro immediately below the worksheet. By placing the macro in this position, you are less likely to accidentally modify the keystrokes.

Make sure the BUDGET worksheet is on your screen.

Manually Practicing the Macro Keystrokes and Recording Every Keystroke on Paper

For the purposes of this exercise, it is assumed that you have gone through the process for combining files and written the required keystrokes on a sheet of paper.

Entering the Keystrokes on the Worksheet

Begin this process of entering the keystrokes by placing the name of the macro as a title on the worksheet.

Move	the cell pointer to cell A35
Type	Macro \C
Press	⏎
Move	the cell pointer to cell B35
Type	Macro for combining data from the DIV1 file
Press	⏎
Move	the cell pointer to B36
Type	into the BUDGET file
Press	⏎

When you name the macro later using the Range Name command sequence, you will give it the name \C.

You will place the macro instructions as labels beginning in cell B38. To enter the first macro instruction:

Move	the cell pointer to cell B38
Type	'/reSALARIES~
Press	⏎

SALARIES is a range name for the cells B10 through E10. You will create the range name prior to executing the macro.

The first macro instruction records the keystrokes for pressing the / key, selecting the **Range Erase** command from the menu structure, using the SALARIES range name to specify the range of cells to erase, and pressing the ⏎ key to complete the procedure. The entry must begin with an apostrophe to enter the keystrokes as a label. The ~ character represents the ⏎ key in a macro instruction. Notice that the command letters for **Range Erase** are lowercase letters and that the range name SALARIES is in uppercase letters. This procedure is optional. Many macro authors use this convention so that the macro can be read more easily; the uppercase characters represent what you input, such as range names, cell addresses or file names.

To enter the second macro instruction:

Move	the cell pointer to cell B39
Type	'{goto}SALARIES~
Press	⏎

This second instruction records pressing the ⦅F5⦆ key, typing the named range SALARIES and pressing the ⏎ key. As a result of executing this macro instruction, the cell pointer is moved to the initial cell in the range name SALARIES which is cell B10 in this example.

To enter the third macro instruction:

Move	the cell pointer to cell B40
Type	'/fcanTOTAL~
Press	⏎

In this third macro instruction, you have indicated that you want to execute the **File Combine Add Named/Specified-Range** command sequence. TOTAL is the range name for the total salary cells in the DIV1 file that will be added to the SALARIES cells in the BUDGET file.

To specify the fourth macro instruction:

Move	the cell pointer to cell B41
Type	'DIV1~
Press	⏎

This fourth instruction indicates that the range name TOTAL is in file DIV1. When this macro instruction is executed, the values from the range name TOTAL in the DIV1 file are added to the respective cells of the range name SALARIES in the BUDGET file.

To enter the final macro instruction:

Move	the cell pointer to cell B42

Type   '{goto}A1~

Press   ⏎

This last instruction is optional. It was included so that the cell pointer will be moved to cell A1 after the macro is executed. If the cell pointer is not in cell A1 after the macro is executed, you will know that the macro has not executed correctly. When all of the macro instructions are entered, your screen should look like Figure 9-2.

```
B42: '{goto}A1~                                                          READY


              A              B        C        D        E        F        G
23  ASSUMPTIONS
24
25  SALES                            1.02     1.02     1.02
26  TELEPHONE                        1.05     1.05     1.05
27  OFFICE SUPPLIES                 50.00    50.00    50.00
28  MISCELLANEOUS                    1.03     1.03     1.03
29
30
31  Prepared by Al Napier
32          27-Sep-89
33
34
35  MACRO \C            Macro for combining data from the DIV1 file
36                      into the BUDGET file
37
38                      /reSALARIES~
39                      {goto}SALARIES~
40                      /fcanTOTAL~
41                      DIV1~
42                      {goto}A1~
                             UNDO
```

Figure 9-2

To create the range name SALARIES:

Move   the cell pointer to cell B10

Press   /

Select Range

Select Name

Select Create

To specify the range name to create:

Type   SALARIES

Press   ⏎

When you are prompted to enter the range of cells:

Move the cell pointer to cell E10

Press

To save the range name permanently and the macro commands, save the file with the name BUDGET3 using the **File Save** command sequence.

Naming the Macro

To define \ C as the name for the macro:

Move the cell pointer to cell B38

Note that B38 is the first cell that contains a macro instruction.

Press /

Select Range

Select Name

Select Create

When prompted enter the name:

Type \C

Press

To indicate the first cell of the macro as the range:

Press

The macro is now named \ C. The macro will execute the instructions in cell B38 and continue executing macro instructions in column B below cell B38 until it encounters a blank cell. When a blank cell is found, the macro will stop executing. If you so desire, you can include all macro instructions in the range name \ C.

Saving the File Containing the Macro Keystrokes

Before executing or testing the macro, you should save the file containing the macro and any worksheets that will be modified as a result of using the macro. In this case, you need to save the BUDGET3 file using the **File Save Replace** command sequence.

Executing the Macro

To execute the macro:

Press   Alt

While holding down the Alt key,

Type   C

Release both keys. The macro will now execute.

If the macro has executed properly, your screen should look like Figure 9-3.

```
A1: [W18]                                                        READY

              A         B        C        D        E        F        G
 1                               ABC COMPANY
 2                                 BUDGET
 3
 4
 5                            QTR1     QTR2     QTR3     QTR4   YR TOTAL
 6
 7    SALES                $60,000  $61,200  $62,424  $63,672 $247,296
 8
 9    EXPENSES
10       SALARIES          15,800   15,800   16,600   17,380   65,580
11       RENT               9,000    9,000    9,000    9,000   36,000
12       TELEPHONE          1,000    1,050    1,103    1,158    4,311
13       OFFICE SUPPLIES      750      800      850      900    3,300
14       MISCELLANEOUS      1,000    1,030    1,061    1,093    4,184
15                         ------------------------------------------
16       TOTAL EXPENSES    27,550   27,680   28,614   29,531  113,375
17                         ------------------------------------------
18    GROSS PROFIT        $32,450  $33,520  $33,810  $34,141 $133,921
19                         ==========================================
20
                               UNDO                         CAPS
```

Figure 9-3

Notice that the cells in range name TOTAL (cells C10 through E10 in the DIV1 file) have been added to the cells in the range name SALARIES of the BUDGET3 file.

Editing and Correcting the Macro

If the macro stops and *beeps*, look carefully at the screen to determine at what point the macro seemed to have trouble executing. To exit the macro, press the Ctrl and Break keys simultaneously. Depending upon the macro, the Esc key may need to be pressed after pressing Ctrl-Break. (The Break key is located on the Pause key). Move to the area where the macro instructions are written to see if the error can be determined. Compare keystrokes with the macro keystrokes in Figure 9-2.

Typical errors include:

■ Macro steps were preceded with the incorrect apostrophe (use the apostrophe on the double quote key).

■ Another character was entered instead of the tilde or a tilde was omitted in an instruction.

■ Parentheses (the ( ) symbols) or brackets (the [ ] symbols) were entered instead of braces (the { } symbols).

■ The backward slash (the \ symbol) was used instead of the slash (the / symbol) (Recall that the backward slash is a repeating prefix that repeats any characters following it).

■ A space was inserted in an inappropriate place.

■ The letter O was typed instead of a zero; the lowercase letter *l* was typed instead of the number one.

If the macro doesn't execute at all or attempts to enter a label and stops, consider these two typical errors:

■ The forward slash was used for the range name instead of the backward slash (use **Range Name Create** to see if the range was named / C instead of \ C) or no range name was given to the macro.

■ The range name was correct, but the first line of the macro is not a macro step (for example, if the top cell of the macro is a blank cell, the macro will never start executing).

Once the error is determined, **retrieve** the file BUDGET3 and correct the appropriate macro steps(s). Then **save** the file before trying to execute the macro again. If the original file is not retrieved, the results of the incorrect macro will remain on the spreadsheet. Save the file after the macro executes properly using the **File Save Replace** command sequence.

Documenting the Macro

Documenting a macro is optional, but you can save valuable time later when you are trying to edit or execute the macro. The documentation in this example explains every cell of the macro. Sometimes it is more appropriate to document a macro by writing a paragraph to explain a macro's overall purpose and then write additional paragraphs to explain sections.

To enter the corresponding explanations of the macro commands in column D to document what the macro does, retrieve the file BUDGET3 using the **File Retrieve** command sequence.

To create a title for the macro (an optional step):

Move the cell pointer to cell A38

Type   ' \C

Press   ⏎

Recall that you placed Macro \C in cell A35.

Creating a title is optional because it is not necessary to make the macro execute; however, the macro title is useful as documentation. A common convention is to put the macro name in the column to the left of the macro keystrokes. In this way, if several macros are on a single worksheet, the names will be clearly visible in the column to the left of the multiple macros.

To document the macro steps:

Move   the cell pointer to cell D38

Refer to Figure 9-4 to enter the documentation for the macro in cells D38 through D42.

```
D42: ' MOVE TO CELL A1                                            READY


            A              B        C        D        E        F        G
24
25  SALES                          1.02     1.02     1.02
26  TELEPHONE                      1.05     1.05     1.05
27  OFFICE SUPPLIES                50.00    50.00    50.00
28  MISCELLANEOUS                  1.03     1.03     1.03
29
30
31  Prepared by Al Napier
32          27-Sep-89
33
34
35  MACRO \C           Macro for combining data from the DIV1 file
36                     into the BUDGET file
37
38  \C                 /reSALARIES~        ERASE THE RANGE B10..E10
39                     {goto}SALARIES~     MOVE THE CELL POINTER TO CELL B10
40                     /fcanTOTAL~         COMBINE THE RANGE NAME TOTAL
41                     DIV1~               FROM THE DIVISION FILE
42                     {goto}A1~           MOVE TO CELL A1
43
                             UNDO
```

Figure 9-4

After entering the documentation:

Press   (Home)

Save the BUDGET3 file using the **F**ile **S**ave **R**eplace command sequence.

■ PROCESS FOR DEBUGGING A MACRO

Whenever a macro contains many instructions, it may be difficult to determine which macro entry may be causing an error. Fortunately, Lotus 1-2-3 has a feature that allows you to execute the macro one macro keystroke at a time. This process can be used to help eliminate errors, sometimes referred to as "bugs" and is, therefore, called "debugging".

To use the single-step mode of execution:

Press   Alt-F2

The word STEP now appears at the bottom of your screen. When you execute the macro you are examining, it will be executed one keystroke at a time by pressing the ↵ key each time you want to move to the next keystroke in the macro. As you start executing the macro, the macro commands replace the date and time indicator. If you execute the \C macro created in the last section, the cell address and characters for the macro keystrokes in cell B38 should now appear in the bottom left corner of your screen. As you press the ↵ key, the next character that will be used is highlighted.

When an error is determined, press the Ctrl-Break combination of keys to end the process. You can then edit the appropriate cell contents in the macro so the macro will execute properly.

To leave the STEP mode:

Press   Alt-F2

If execution of the macro has not been completed and you did not use the Ctrl Break key combination, then the remaining macro steps will be executed as soon as you leave STEP mode and press the ↵ key.

■ CREATING A PRINT MACRO

Macros can be used to print worksheets. In the last section you wrote a macro to combine data from one file to another file. In this section, you will write a macro to print the BUDGET3 worksheet.

You developed the macro \C to combine some information from the DIV1 file into the BUDGET3 file.

Before creating the print macro, erase whatever you presently have on your screen and retrieve the BUDGET3 file.

You will place the macro for printing the BUDGET worksheet below the macro you previously developed.

To give the macro a title:

Move	the cell pointer to cell A45
Type	'PRINT_MACRO
Press	⏎

The macro will be named later.

To enter the first instruction of the macro:

Move	the cell pointer to cell B45
Type	'{goto}A1~
Press	⏎

This instruction makes sure that the cell pointer is in the cell at the top left corner of the worksheet before you attempt to print.

Move	the cell pointer to cell B46
Type	'/pprPRINT_RANGE~
Press	⏎

This instruction specifies that the range of cells defined by the range name PRINT_RANGE is to be printed on the printer.

To place the third instruction of the macro on the worksheet:

Move	the cell pointer to cell B47
Type	'agppq
Press	⏎

This instruction specifies that 1-2-3 is to accept the present alignment of the paper in the printer, print the worksheet range, eject to the top of the next page, eject another page to make it easy to remove the paper from the printer and quit the print menu.

Your screen should now look like Figure 9-5.

```
B47: 'agppq                                                          READY


              A           B        C        D        E        F        G
28  MISCELLANEOUS                  1.03     1.03     1.03
29
30
31  Prepared by Al Napier
32          27-Sep-89
33
34
35  MACRO \C              Macro for combining data from the DIV1 file
36                        into the BUDGET file
37
38  \C                    /reSALARIES~      ERASE THE RANGE B10..E10
39                        {goto}SALARIES~   MOVE THE CELL POINTER TO CELL B10
40                        /fcanTOTAL~       COMBINE THE RANGE NAME TOTAL
41                        DIV1~             FROM THE DIVISION FILE
42                        {goto}A1~         MOVE TO CELL A1
43
44
45  PRINT_MACRO           {goto}A1~
46                        /pprPRINT_RANGE~
47                        agppq
                          UNDO
```

Figure 9-5

To name the macro:

Move	the cell pointer to cell B45
Press	/
Select	Range
Select	Name
Select	Create

When you are prompted to enter the name to create:

Type	PRINT_MACRO
Press	⏎

Notice that you used a different naming mechanism. This approach was taken so you can learn to execute a macro using a method other than the one used in the last section.

You can specify the initial cell of the macro as the range as follows:

Press	⏎

Before executing the macro, you need to specify the range of cells to be printed by creating the named range of cells, PRINT_RANGE, and save the modified file.

Move	the cell pointer to cell A1
Press	/
Select	Range
Select	Name
Select	Create

When prompted for the name of the range to create:

Type	PRINT_RANGE
Press	⏎

To specify that the entire worksheet is to be included in the print range:

Move	the cell pointer to cell F32
Press	⏎

To save the modified file:

Press	/
Select	File
Select	Save
Press	⏎
Select	Replace

You have saved the file prior to executing the macro.

To execute PRINT_MACRO:

Press	Alt-F3 keys simultaneously
Press	F3
Select	PRINT_MACRO

The BUDGET3 worksheet will then be printed.

Document your print macro using the information in Figure 9-6.

```
D47: 'PRINT; QUIT THE PRINT MENU                                    READY

              A           B         C        D        E        F       G
28  MISCELLANEOUS                   1.03     1.03     1.03
29
30
31  Prepared by Al Napier
32        27-Sep-89
33
34
35  MACRO \C              Macro for combining data from the DIV1 file
36                        into the BUDGET file
37
38  \C                    /reSALARIES~      ERASE THE RANGE B10..E10
39                        {goto}SALARIES~   MOVE THE CELL POINTER TO CELL B10
40                        /fcanTOTAL~       COMBINE THE RANGE NAME TOTAL
41                        DIV1~             FROM THE DIVISION FILE
42                        {goto}A1~         MOVE TO CELL A1
43
44
45  PRINT_MACRO           {goto}A1~         MOVE THE CELL POINTER TO CELL A1
46                        /pprPRINT_RANGE~  SPECIFY THE PRINT RANGE
47                        agppq             PRINT; QUIT THE PRINT MENU
                          UNDO
```

Figure 9-6

Save the worksheet on the BUDGET3 file so the documentation will be permanently attached to the macro instructions.

■CREATING A MACRO USING THE LEARN FEATURE

In the first part of this chapter you created a macro by entering the macro keystrokes that comprise the macro instructions one keystroke at a time. As you work through the remaining portion of this chapter, you will use an easier way to create a macro.

You will create the macro that appeared in the last section using the "learn" capability of 1-2-3. Prior to recording the macro, make sure the worksheet from the original file BUDGET is on your screen and that the range name SALARIES has been created and contains cells B10 through E10.

In this exercise, you will place the macro below the worksheet.

To place a title for the macro on the worksheet:

Move	the cell pointer to cell A38
Type	\C
Press	↵

Rather than recording the macro keystrokes on paper as you go through the process of combining the data from the DIV1 file into the worksheet in the BUDGET file, you can have 1-2-3 record the keystrokes for you.

1. Move the cell pointer to the first cell to be included in the macro.

2. Specify the range of cells in which the macro will be placed.

3. Enter Learn mode by pressing the ⎡Alt-F5⎤ keys.

4. Perform the tasks that you want to record.

5. After completing the tasks, stop the recording of your keystrokes by pressing the ⎡Alt-F5⎤ keys.

6. Examine the keystrokes that you recorded. Correct any mistakes.

7. Name the macro and save the file you are using.

8. Execute the macro.

Recording the Macro Keystrokes

To specify the Learn range:

Move	the cell pointer to cell B38
Press	/
Select	Worksheet
Select	Learn
Select	Range
Type	.
Move	the cell pointer to cell B45
Press	⎡←⎤

It is important that you have at least enough cells in the Learn range to include your macro keystrokes. You may include more than the required number of cells if you so desire.

To initiate the recording of keystrokes:

Press	⎡Alt-F5⎤

Note the word LEARN now appears at the bottom of the screen.

To complete the recording of the keystrokes for the macro:

Press	/
Select	Range
Select	Erase
Type	SALARIES
Press	⏎
Press	F5
Type	SALARIES
Press	⏎
Press	/
Select	File
Select	Combine
Select	Add
Select	Named/Specified-Range
Type	TOTAL
Press	⏎
Type	DIV1
Press	⏎
Press	F5
Type	A1
Press	⏎

To stop recording keystrokes:

Press	Alt-F5

The CALC indicator appears at the bottom of the screen. To remove it:

Press	F9

To see the recorded keystrokes:

Move   the cell pointer to cell A41

Your screen should look like Figure 9-7.

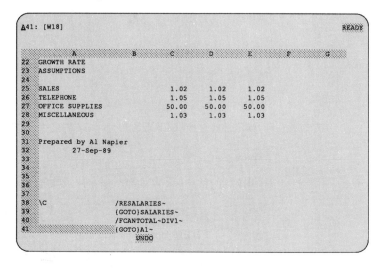

```
A41: [W18]                                                    READY

              A           B        C         D         E        F        G
22  GROWTH RATE
23  ASSUMPTIONS
24
25  SALES                        1.02      1.02      1.02
26  TELEPHONE                    1.05      1.05      1.05
27  OFFICE SUPPLIES             50.00     50.00     50.00
28  MISCELLANEOUS                1.03      1.03      1.03
29
30
31  Prepared by Al Napier
32          27-Sep-89
33
34
35
36
37
38  \C                  /RESALARIES~
39                      {GOTO}SALARIES~
40                      /FCANTOTAL~DIV1~
41                      {GOTO}A1~
                             UNDO
```

Figure 9-7

To name the macro:

Move   the cell pointer to cell B38

Press   /

Select   Range

Select   Name

Select   Create

When prompted for a range name:

Type   \C

Press   ⏎

To specify the first cell in the macro as the range:

Press   ⏎

Executing the Macro

Before executing the macro, save the file on BUDGET4.

To execute the macro:

Press   (Alt)

While holding down the (Alt) key:

Type   C

The macro will then execute. Your screen should now look like Figure 9-8.

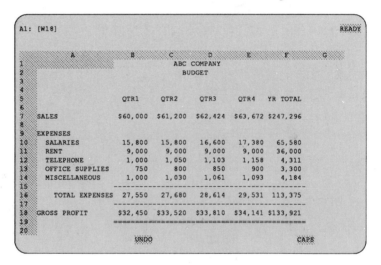

```
A1: [W18]                                                          READY

              A            B        C        D        E        F        G
 1                                ABC COMPANY
 2                                  BUDGET
 3
 4
 5                          QTR1     QTR2     QTR3     QTR4   YR TOTAL
 6
 7   SALES                $60,000  $61,200  $62,424  $63,672 $247,296
 8
 9   EXPENSES
10      SALARIES           15,800   15,800   16,600   17,380   65,580
11      RENT                9,000    9,000    9,000    9,000   36,000
12      TELEPHONE           1,000    1,050    1,103    1,158    4,311
13      OFFICE SUPPLIES       750      800      850      900    3,300
14      MISCELLANEOUS       1,000    1,030    1,061    1,093    4,184
15                        -------  -------  -------  -------  -------
16      TOTAL EXPENSES     27,550   27,680   28,614   29,531  113,375
17                        -------  -------  -------  -------  -------
18   GROSS PROFIT         $32,450  $33,520  $33,810  $34,141 $133,921
19                        ===================================================
20
                            UNDO                               CAPS
```

Figure 9-8

Document your macro using the comments in Figure 9-9 to specify the macro title and what the individual instructions do.

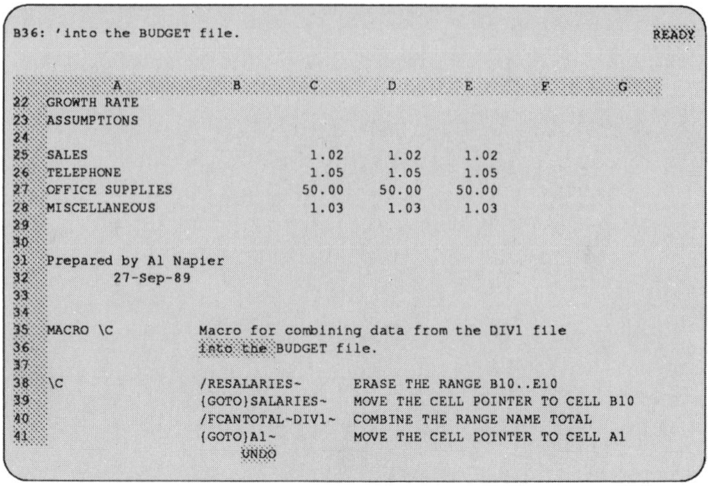

```
B36: 'into the BUDGET file.                                              READY

              A              B          C          D          E        F        G
22  GROWTH RATE
23  ASSUMPTIONS
24
25  SALES                               1.02       1.02       1.02
26  TELEPHONE                           1.05       1.05       1.05
27  OFFICE SUPPLIES                    50.00      50.00      50.00
28  MISCELLANEOUS                       1.03       1.03       1.03
29
30
31  Prepared by Al Napier
32           27-Sep-89
33
34
35  MACRO \C           Macro for combining data from the DIV1 file
36                     into the BUDGET file.
37
38  \C                 /RESALARIES~      ERASE THE RANGE B10..E10
39                     {GOTO}SALARIES~   MOVE THE CELL POINTER TO CELL B10
40                     /FCANTOTAL~DIV1~  COMBINE THE RANGE NAME TOTAL
41                     {GOTO}A1~         MOVE THE CELL POINTER TO CELL A1
                       UNDO
```

Figure 9-9

Save the completed worksheet on file BUDGET4 using the **F**ile **S**ave **R**eplace command sequence.

SUMMARY

A macro is a way to automate Lotus 1-2-3 keystrokes. Macros are an efficient way to automate repetitive procedures. Macros allow people who do not know 1-2-3 to use it to process spreadsheet operations such as printing a worksheet. It is important to define range names for specific cells and use the range names in macro instructions. Macros can be as simple or as complex as you desire to make them.

KEY CONCEPTS

[Alt]
[Alt-F2]
[Alt-F3]
[Alt-F5]
[Ctrl-Break]
Documentation
Learn
Location of a macro
Macro
Macro name
Step
Tilde

CHAPTER NINE
EXERCISE 1

INSTRUCTIONS: Circle T if the statement is true and F if the statement is false.

T   F   1. The range name for a macro must be taken from a label already existing on the worksheet.

T   F   2. The range name for a macro must begin with a forward slash and a letter of the alphabet.

T   F   3. A macro is a way to automate a repetitive procedure.

T   F   4. Certain keystrokes in a macro must be enclosed in braces (the { and } characters).

T   F   5. In a macro, the tilde (the ~ symbol) represents pressing the forward slash (the command key /).

T   F   6. To execute the macro named \ Z, the user must hold down the [Ctrl] key and tap the letter Z.

T   F   7. A range name for a macro must contain the first macro step as the first line in the range.

T   F   8. When entering data on a worksheet manually, the tilde can be used instead of pressing ⏎

T   F   9. Either apostrophe (the ' or the ') can be used to preface a macro step.

T   F   10. Documentation must be included in a macro.

T   F   11. You can automatically record macro keystrokes.

T   F   12. Macro instructions can be executed one step at a time by using [Alt-F1].

T   F   13. It does not matter where you place macros on a worksheet.

CHAPTER NINE
EXERCISE 2
Creating a Macro

INSTRUCTIONS: Retrieve the file BUDGET3.

Edit the existing macro to combine DIV1, DIV2 and DIV3 into the BUDGET worksheet . (The files DIV1, DIV2 and DIV3 were created in Chapter 6.

Document the new instructions. Delete the macro name \ C and name the macro \ A.

Save the file as BUDMAC.

Execute the macro.

Print the BUDGET worksheet and the macro.

CHAPTER NINE
EXERCISE 3
Creating a Print Macro

INSTRUCTIONS: Retrieve the file BUDMAC.

Create a separate macro for printing the worksheet and place both of the macros on the worksheet.

Save the macros on file BUDMAC.

Execute the macro.

Print the worksheet including the macros.

CHAPTER NINE
EXERCISE 4
Using a Macro to Sort Data

INSTRUCTIONS: Retrieve the file PERSON you created as an exercise in Chapter 7.

Write a macro that sorts the database in order by state and last name.

Create a macro that prints the sorted database table. Document both macros properly.

Print the sorted database table including the macros for sorting and printing the database table.

CHAPTER NINE
EXERCISE 5
Using Macros to Create a Graph

INSTRUCTIONS: Retrieve the file PRACTICE you created as an exercise in Chapter 2.

Reset all graph settings associated with the file and delete any graph files present.

Write a macro to create a bar graph that includes the data of the variables REVENUE, PROFIT BEFORE TAX and PROFIT AFTER TAX for the four quarters. Include appropriate graph title and legend information.

Document the macro properly.

Print the macro.

CHAPTER TEN

ADVANCED MACRO COMMANDS AND EXAMPLES

OBJECTIVES

In this chapter, you will learn to:

■ Create macros for various types of worksheet operations such as sorting data, restricting input to specific cells, and automatically executing a macro.

■ Use advanced macro commands to:
Create interactive macros
Change program flow and loop through a series of instructions
Develop subroutines
Create user-designed menus

■ Create and use a macro library

■ CHAPTER OVERVIEW

In Chapter 9 the use of macros in Lotus 1-2-3 was introduced. The process for creating a macro was defined. In the first part of this chapter, some additional macro examples are illustrated. The command language available in Lotus 1-2-3 is then presented. Finally, you will learn to use the command language by creating several macros.

■ MACRO SYMBOLS

In the process of creating a macro, many symbols are used to represent operations that are available in Lotus 1-2-3. For example, the **down** pointer movement key is designated by the symbol {down} or {D}. A list follows of symbols used to designate keystrokes including symbols for function keys and directional keys.

The symbols have been placed in alphabetical order. Symbols that include special characters appear at the end of the list.

Keys	Macro Instruction
Abs F4	{abs}
App1 Alt-F7	{app1}
App2 Alt-F8	{app2}
App3 Alt-F9	{app3}
App4 Alt-F10	{app4}
Backspace	{backspace} or {bs}
Ctrl-Left	{bigleft}
Ctrl-Right	{bigright}
Calc F9	{calc}
Delete Del	{delete} or {del}
Down ↓	{down} or {d}
Edit F2	{edit}
End	{end}
Escape Esc	{esc}
GoTo F5	{goto}
Graph F10	{graph}
Help F1	{help}
Home	{home}
Insert Ins	{ins}
Left ←	{left} or {l}
Name F3	{name}
PgDn PgDn	{pgdn}
PgUp PgUp	{pgup}
Query F7	{query}
Right →	{right} or {r}
Table F8	{table}
Up ↑	{up} or {u}
Window F6	{window}
/ (slash) or < (less than)	/, < or {menu}
Enter ←	~
{~} to have tilde appear as ~	{~}
{{} and {}} to have braces appear as { and }	{{} and {}}

Sometimes it is desirable to specify two or more repetitions of the same key. This repeating can be accomplished by including a repetition factor within the braces. For example, to move the cell pointer down four cells you can use either of the following macro instructions:

{down 4} or {d 4}

■ SOME ADDITIONAL MACRO EXAMPLES

To help you learn more about using macros, you will create and execute macros in this section for sorting data, restricting the entry of data to specific cells in a worksheet, and automatically executing a macro.

Sorting Data

In Chapter 7 you created a worksheet that had salary information for the employees of ABC Company and saved it on a file named ABCSAL. To complete this example problem, you need to retrieve file ABCSAL. Your screen should look like Figure 10-1.

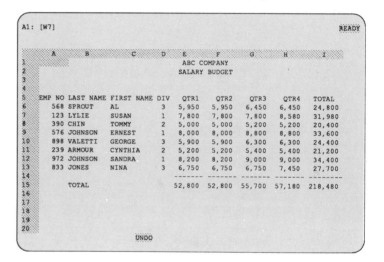

Figure 10-1

Suppose that you want to sort the data in ascending order by division and alphabetically within each division.

To accomplish the sort, you must:

1. Erase any previously set sort ranges

2. Specify the data range to sort

3. Define sort keys for the division number and last name

4. Indicate that the data is to be sorted

To enter the macro title:

Move	the cell pointer to cell A21
Type	Macro Sort
Press	↵
Move	the cell pointer to cell C21
Type	Macro for Sorting Data
Press	↵

To enter the macro name:

Move	the cell pointer to A23
Type	SORT
Press	↵

To make sure no sort settings are on the file:

Move	the cell pointer to cell B23
Type	'/dsrq
Press	↵

To specify the data range to sort:

Move	the cell pointer to cell B24
Type	'/dsdSORT_DATA~
Press	↵

To indicate that DIV is the primary sort key and that it is to be sorted in ascending order:

Move	the cell pointer to cell B25
Type	'pD5~a~
Press	↵

To define LAST NAME as the secondary key and that the names are to be sorted in alphabetical order:

Move	the cell pointer to cell B26
Type	'sB5~a~

Press   ⏎

To indicate it is appropriate to execute the sort and then exit the sort menu:

Move   the cell pointer to cell B27

Type   'g

Press   ⏎

Except for the documentation that appears on the macro worksheet, your screen should now look like Figure 10-2.

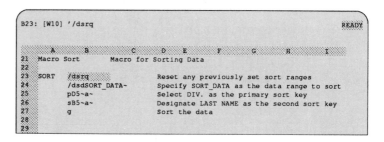

Figure 10-2

Before you can execute the macro, you need to define the named range SORT_DATA and name the macro.

Move   the cell pointer to cell A6

Create   the range name SORT_DATA including in it
the range of cells A6..I13

Move   the cell pointer to cell B23

Create   the macro name SORT and indicate the macro instructions
begin in cell B23

After checking your macro with the one in Figure 10-2 and making any necessary corrections, save the file on ABCSAL2.

Move the cell pointer to cell A1 and execute the macro SORT.

Move   the cell pointer to cell A1

Press   Alt-F3

Press   F3

Select   SORT

After the macro is executed, your screen should look like Figure 10-3. Notice that the data has been sorted in proper order.

```
A1: [W7]                                                          READY

         A       B          C        D     E        F       G       H        I
                                          ABC COMPANY
                                          SALARY BUDGET


   EMP NO LAST NAME FIRST NAME DIV   QTR1     QTR2    QTR3    QTR4    TOTAL
      576 JOHNSON   ERNEST      1    8,000    8,000   8,800   8,800   33,600
      972 JOHNSON   SANDRA      1    8,200    8,200   9,000   9,000   34,400
      123 LYLIE     SUSAN       1    7,800    7,800   7,800   8,580   31,980
      239 ARMOUR    CYNTHIA     2    5,200    5,200   5,400   5,400   21,200
      390 CHIN      TOMMY       2    5,000    5,000   5,200   5,200   20,400
      833 JONES     NINA        3    6,750    6,750   6,750   7,450   27,700
      568 SPROUT    AL          3    5,950    5,950   6,450   6,450   24,800
      898 VALETTI   GEORGE      3    5,900    5,900   6,300   6,300   24,400
                                     -------  ------- ------- ------- --------
          TOTAL                      52,800   52,800  55,700  57,180  218,480




                        UNDO                                    CAPS
```

Figure 10-3

Retrieve ABCSAL2 and document your macro using the comments in Figure 10-2. After completing the documentation, save the worksheet on file ABCSAL2.

Restricting Data Entry to Specific Cells in a Worksheet

To complete this exercise, you will need to create a loan amortization worksheet. This loan amortization worksheet will also be used in later sections of this chapter. Enter the labels and values for the worksheet by referring to Figure 10-4 Part 1.

```
A1: [W5]                                                              READY

     A       B         C         D          E          F          G
 1                         LOAN AMORTIZATION
 2
 3         ASSUMPTIONS
 4         ================================================================
 5         $50,000.00              PRINCIPAL
 6             12.00%              INTEREST RATE PER YEAR
 7                 60              TIME PERIOD IN MONTHS
 8              1.00%              MONTHLY INTEREST RATE
 9          1,112.22              CALCULATED PAYMENT AMOUNT
10         ================================================================
11
12    ********************************************************************
13                                                      PRINCIPAL   INTEREST
14  PMT    PAYMENT   PRINCIPAL  INTEREST   PRINCIPAL       PAID       PAID
15  NUM    AMOUNT    AMOUNT     AMOUNT     BALANCE        TO DATE    TO DATE
16    ********************************************************************
17
18
19
20

                           UNDO                              CAPS
```

Figure 10-4
Part 1

To assist you in the preparation of the worksheet, the column widths are:

Column	Width
A	5
B	11
C	10
D	11
E	12
F	12
G	11

Use the **Data Fill** command sequence to enter the numbers 1 through 60 in cells A18 through A77.

Enter formulas into cells as described below.

Cell	Formula
B8	+B6/12
B9	@PMT(B5,B8,B7)
E17	+B5
B18	+B9
C18	+B18-D18
D18	+B5*B8
E18	+E17-C18
F18	+C18

G18	+D18
B19	@IF($B$9>E18,$B$8*E18+E18,$B$9)
C19	+B19-D19
D19	+$B$8*E18
E19	+E18-C19
F19	+F18+C19
G19	+G18+D19

After you have entered the formulas for cells B19..G19, copy these cell formulas to cells B20..G77. You have created an amortization schedule worksheet that can be used for loan repayment periods from one to 60 months. Use the **Range Format , 2** command sequence to properly format cells B17 through G77. Your screen should now look like Figure 10-4 Part 2.

```
A1: [W5]                                                            READY


         A       B        C        D        E        F        G
1                       LOAN AMORTIZATION
2
3              ASSUMPTIONS
4              ================================================
5              $50,000.00       PRINCIPAL
6                  12.00%        INTEREST RATE PER YEAR
7                     60         TIME PERIOD IN MONTHS
8                   1.00%        MONTHLY INTEREST RATE
9               1,112.22  ·      CALCULATED PAYMENT AMOUNT
10             ================================================
11
12     ************************************************************
13                                             PRINCIPAL   INTEREST
14     PMT     PAYMENT  PRINCIPAL INTEREST  PRINCIPAL    PAID      PAID
15     NUM     AMOUNT    AMOUNT   AMOUNT     BALANCE    TO DATE   TO DATE
16     ************************************************************
17                                          50,000.00
18      1     1,112.22   612.22   500.00   49,387.78    612.22    500.00
19      2     1,112.22   618.34   493.88   48,769.43  1,230.57    993.88
20      3     1,112.22   624.53   487.69   48,144.90  1,855.10  1,481.57
                                   UNDO
```

Figure 10-4
Part 2

Save the worksheet using the file name AMORT.

Sometimes it may be useful to limit an individual's ability to enter data in only a certain set of cells. For example, in the loan amortization schedule worksheet, suppose you want an individual to only be allowed to change the principal, interest rate and time period. Such an approach prohibits users of the amortization worksheet from accidentally changing any of the formulas on the worksheet.

The steps that you need to have in a macro for restricting the data entry to the principal, interest rate and time period cells are as follows:

1. Change the calculation mode to manual so you do not have to wait for the worksheet to be recalculated before you enter the next data item.

2. Protect all of the cells in the worksheet.

3. Unprotect those cells that can be modified.

4. Calculate the worksheet after all data entry is completed.

To place a title for the macro on the worksheet:

Move	the cell pointer to cell A101
Enter	Macro Data Entry
Move	the cell pointer to cell C101
Enter	Macro for Restricting Data Entry to the Cells
Move	the cell pointer to cell C102
Enter	for Principal, Interest Rate and Time Period

To place the name of the macro on the worksheet:

Move	the cell pointer to cell A104
Enter	\D
Move	the cell pointer to cell B104
Enter	'{goto}A1~

To specify that manual calculation mode is to be used:

Move	the cell pointer to cell B105
Enter	'/wgrm

You can protect all cells in the worksheet as follows:

Move	the cell pointer to cell B106
Enter	'/wgpe

To allow data entry for the principal, interest rate and time period, you must unprotect the range of cells B5 through B7:

Move	the cell pointer to cell B107

Enter	'/ruB5.B7~

The **Range Input** command in 1-2-3 is used to restrict the cells in which you can enter data on the worksheet. Since you have protected all cells on the worksheet and unprotected the cells in which data entry is allowed, you can specify the entire worksheet (cells A1 .. G77) in the **Range Input** command.

Move	the cell pointer to cell B108
Enter	'/riA1.G77~

To specify that the worksheet is to be recalculated after the data entry is completed and move the cell pointer to cell A1:

Move	the cell pointer to cell B109
Enter	'{calc}
Move	the cell pointer to cell B110
Enter	'{goto}A1~

Except for the documentation on the macro worksheet, your screen should look like Figure 10-5.

```
B110: [W11] '{goto}A1~                                              READY

        A        B         C         D         E         F         G
101 Macro Data EntryMacro for Restricting Data Entry to the Cells
102                     for Principal, Interest Rate and Time Period
103
104 \D    {goto}A1~              Move to cell A1
105       /wgrm                  Change to manual recalculation
106       /wgpe                  Protect all cells in the worksheet
107       /ruB5.B7~              Unprotect the cells for prin., int. and time
108       /riA1.G77~             Specify range input cells
109       {calc}                 Recalculate the worksheet
110       {goto}A1~              Move the cell pointer to cell A1
111
112
```

Figure 10-5

Before you execute the macro, name it \ D.

Move	the cell pointer to cell B104
Press	/
Select	Range
Select	Name
Select	Create

Type \D

Press ⏎ twice

After checking your macro with the one in Figure 10-5 and making any necessary changes, save the file on AMORTRI.

Suppose that you want to use the loan amortization schedule worksheet to determine the monthly payment if you borrow $15,000 at an interest rate of 10 percent and have 48 months to repay the loan. To determine the payment amount, execute the macro:

Press (Alt-D)

The macro pauses at cell B5 to wait for you to enter the data for the new principal, interest rate and time period. Notice that the cells for these items are a different color if you are using a color monitor. If you are using a monochrome monitor, the cells will appear to be brighter. Press the ⏵, ⏷, ⏴ and ⏶ keys several times and note that you can only enter data in cells B5 through B7. The characters CMD appear at the bottom of the screen indicating that the macro is being executed and is waiting for you to enter the new data.

To enter the appropriate values:

Move the cell pointer to cell B5

Type 15000

Press ⏷

Type .10

Press ⏷

Type 48

Press ⏎

To finish execution of the macro:

Press ⏎

Your screen should look like Figure 10-6.

```
A1: PR [W5]                                                              READY

      A       B         C          D          E          F          G
 1                        LOAN AMORTIZATION
 2
 3         ASSUMPTIONS
 4         ====================================================================
 5         $15,000.00           PRINCIPAL
 6              10.00%           INTEREST RATE PER YEAR
 7                 48            TIME PERIOD IN MONTHS
 8              0.83%            MONTHLY INTEREST RATE
 9             380.44            CALCULATED PAYMENT AMOUNT
10         ====================================================================
11
12    ***********************************************************************
13                                                        PRINCIPAL   INTEREST
14    PMT    PAYMENT   PRINCIPAL  INTEREST   PRINCIPAL      PAID        PAID
15    NUM    AMOUNT     AMOUNT     AMOUNT     BALANCE      TO DATE     TO DATE
16    ***********************************************************************
17                                          15,000.00
18     1     380.44     255.44    125.00    14,744.56     255.44      125.00
19     2     380.44     257.57    122.87    14,486.99     513.01      247.87
20     3     380.44     259.71    120.72    14,227.28     772.72      368.60
                                      UNDO
```

Figure 10-6

Retrieve the file AMORTRI and disable worksheet protection by using the **W**orksheet **G**lobal **P**rotection **D**isable command. Document your macro using the information in Figure 10-5. After placing the documentation on the macro worksheet, save the worksheet file on AMORTRI.

Executing a Macro Automatically

In some situations, you may want to execute a macro automatically when the file on which it is saved is retrieved. For example, you may want the macro on the file that contains the loan amortization schedule to execute immediately so the individual using the loan amortization schedule only has to enter the new values for the principal, interest rate and time period.

When a macro is named \0 (zero), it will be executed when the file on which it resides is retrieved. Before you can execute the loan amortization schedule macro automatically, you must retrieve the file containing the macro, change the name of the macro to \0, and save the file.

To accomplish these steps:

Retrieve	the file AMORTRI
Move	the cell pointer to cell A104
Enter	\0
Delete	the range name \D

Move   the cell pointer to cell B104

Create   the range name \0 that includes cell B104 as the range

Save the worksheet using the file name AUTOMAC. Your screen should look like Figure 10-7.

```
B104: PR [W11] '{goto}A1~                                              READY

       A        B          C          D          E          F          G
101 Macro Data EntryMacro for Restricting Data Entry to the Cells
102                      for Principal, Interest Rate and Time Period
103
104 \0   {goto}A1~                    Move to cell A1
105      /wgrm                        Change to manual recalculation
106      /wgpe                        Protect all cells in the worksheet
107      /ruB5.B7~                    Unprotect the cells for prin., int. and time
108      /riA1.G77~                   Specify range input cells
109      {calc}                       Recalculate the worksheet
110      {goto}A1~                    Move the cell pointer to cell A1
111
112
113
114
115
116
117
118
119
120
                             UNDO
```

Figure 10-7

Suppose that you want to determine the monthly payment amount for a loan of $10,000 at an interest rate of 11 percent and time period of 36 months to pay the loan.

To illustrate the use of the automatic execution of a macro for this situation:

Erase   the worksheet from your screen

Retrieve   the file AUTOMAC

Notice that the macro has been initiated and the cell pointer is in cell B5. You now need to enter the data for the principal, interest rate and time period.

Enter   10000 in cell B5

Enter   .11 in cell B6

Enter   36 in cell B7

Press   ⏎

The macro has finished executing. Your screen should look like Figure 10-8.

```
B5: (C2) U [W11] 10000                                              READY

     A         B         C          D          E            F          G
 1                       LOAN AMORTIZATION
 2
 3            ASSUMPTIONS
 4            ============================================================
 5            $10,000.00             PRINCIPAL
 6                 11.00%            INTEREST RATE PER YEAR
 7                     36            TIME PERIOD IN MONTHS
 8                  0.92%            MONTHLY INTEREST RATE
 9                 327.39            CALCULATED PAYMENT AMOUNT
10            ============================================================
11
12  ***********************************************************************
13                                                        PRINCIPAL   INTEREST
14  PMT      PAYMENT   PRINCIPAL   INTEREST   PRINCIPAL      PAID       PAID
15  NUM      AMOUNT     AMOUNT      AMOUNT      BALANCE     TO DATE    TO DATE
16  ***********************************************************************
17                                            10,000.00
18    1      327.39     235.72      91.67      9,764.28      235.72     91.67
19    2      327.39     237.88      89.51      9,526.40      473.60    181.17
20    3      327.39     240.06      87.33      9,286.34      713.66    268.50
                                    UNDO
```

Figure 10-8

You do not need to save the new loan amortization schedule.

■ADVANCED MACRO COMMANDS

Lotus 1-2-3 Release 2.2 has 50 advanced macro commands. In this section, a list of the commands is introduced, groupings of the commands by typical use are presented, and a brief explanation of each command is given.

Listing of Advanced Macro Commands

The advanced macro commands available in Release 2.2 are:

{beep}	{let}
{blank}	{look}
{bordersoff}/{borderson}	{menubranch}
{branch}	{menucall}
{break}	{onerror}
{breakoff}/{breakon}	{open}
{close}	{paneloff}/{panelon}
{contents}	{put}
{define}	{quit}
{dispatch}	{read}
{filesize}	{readln}
{for}	{recalc}
{forbreak}	{recalccol}
{frameoff}	{restart}

{frameon}	{return}
{get}	{setpos}
{getlabel}	{subroutine}
{getnumber}	{system}
{getpos}	{wait}
{graphon}	{windowsoff}/{windowson}
{graphoff}	{write}
{if}	{writeln}
{indicate}	{?}

Summary by Type of Use of the Advanced Macro Commands

In this section, the advanced macro commands are grouped together by typical use. For ease of reference they are placed in alphabetical order within each grouping.

Controlling the Appearance of the Screen

In some situations, you may want to change the appearance of the screen. The following macro commands can be used to alter the appearance of the screen:

{beep}	{graphon}
{bordersoff}	{indicate}
{borderson}	{paneloff}
{frameoff}	{panelon}
{frameon}	{windowsoff}
{graphoff}	{windowson}

Interaction between User and Keyboard

The following commands can be employed to create macros that provide interactive use:

{?}	{getnumber}
{break}	{look}
{breakoff}	{menubranch}
{breakon}	{menucall}
{get}	{wait}
{getlabel}	

Changing the Flow of Instructions in a Macro

In some cases, it may be desirable to modify the exact sequence of commands in a macro. The following commands permit you to control the sequence of command execution.

{branch}	{onerror}
{define}	{quit}
{dispatch}	{restart}
{for}	{return}
{forbreak}	{system}
{if}	{subroutine}

Manipulating the Format and Location of Data

The listed commands can be used to manipulate the format and location of data in a worksheet:

{blank}	{put}
{contents}	{recalc}
{let}	{recalccol}

File Operations

In some cases, it may be useful to execute tasks related to files. The following commands permit you to manipulate files during the execution of a macro.

{close}	{readln}
{filesize}	{setpos}
{getpos}	{write}
{open}	{writeln}
{read}	

Specific Advanced Macro Commands

Explanations of the various advanced macro commands are contained in this section. For additional details on the many commands, see the Lotus 1-2-3 reference manual that comes with the software package.

The following format is used in the descriptions of the commands:

```
{Keyword arg1,arg2,...,argn}
```

Arguments which are shown within angle brackets (<>) are optional.

{beep}

The {beep} command causes the computer bell to sound. The number is optional. There are four tones to the *beep*. Therefore, the numbers 1, 2, 3 or 4 can appear within the {beep} command. If no number is specified, the default is the first tone.

The {beep} command has the following format:

```
{beep <number>}
```

The {beep} command does not produce a tone if you turn off the bell by using the **Worksheet Global Default Other Beep No** command sequence.

{blank}

The {blank} command erases the contents of the designated cell. The cell pointer does not move to the designated cell location.

The {blank} command has the following format:

```
{blank cell-location}
```

{bordersoff}

The {bordersoff} command suppresses the display of the worksheet frame that includes the column letters and row numbers. It works the same as {frameoff}.

The bordersoff command has the following format:

```
{bordersoff}
```

{borderson}

The {borderson} command restores the display of the worksheet frame that includes the column letters and row numbers.

The {borderson} command has the following format:

```
{borderson}
```

{branch}

The {branch} command directs control to the designated cell and continues the execution of the macro using the instructions in the designated cell.

The {branch} command has the following format:

```
{branch cell-location}
```

{break}

The {break} command stops the execution of a macro. It has the effect of pressing the `Ctrl-Break` keys.

The {break} command has the following format:

```
{break}
```

{breakoff} and {breakon}

The {breakoff} command disables the `Ctrl-Break` functionality that interrupts a macro. The {breakon} command reverses the {breakoff} command.

The {breakoff} and {breakon} commands have the following format:

```
{breakoff}
{breakon}
```

{close}

The {close} command closes a file that was previously opened using the {open} command.

The {close} command has the following format:

```
{close}
```

{contents}

The {contents} command stores the data from one cell in another cell as a label. The width of the label as well as the type of format desired can be specified for the target location. Refer to the 1-2-3 reference manual for the codes for the format numbers.

The {contents} command has the following format:

```
{contents target-location,source-location,
<width-number>,<format-number>}
```

{define}

The {define} command allocates where variables that are passed to a subroutine are stored. If used, it is the first command in the subroutine.

The {define} command has the following format:

```
{define cell-location1:type1,cell-location2:type 2...}
```

{dispatch}

The {dispatch} command directs control to another cell for instructions on where the macro should branch.

The {dispatch} command has the following format:

```
{dispatch cell-location}
```

{filesize}

The {filesize} command records the number of bytes in the currently open file. The number is recorded in the specified cell-location.

The {filesize} command has the following format:

```
{filesize cell-location}
```

{for}

The {for} command allows a set of commands to be repeated a specified number of times. The process of repeating a set of commands is often referred to as looping.

The {for} command has the following format:

```
{for counter-location,begin-number,end-number,step,
starting-location}
```

The counter-location is used to keep track of the number of times the loop of instructions is to be executed. The begin-number specifies the initial number with which the loop should begin its count, and the end-number specifies the number at which the loop should stop executing. The step tells what increment the loop count should use. The starting-location indicates the first cell or range name of the subroutine to be executed.

{forbreak}

The {forbreak} command breaks or interrupts the current {for} loop.

The {forbreak} command has the following format:

```
{forbreak}
```

{frameoff}

The {frameoff} command suppresses the display of the worksheet frame that includes the column letters and row numbers.

The {frameoff} command has the following format:

```
{frameoff}
```

{frameon}

The {frameon} command restores the display of the worksheet frame that includes the column letters and row numbers.

The {frameon} command has the following format:

```
{frameon}
```

{get}

The {get} command stops the macro and allows an individual to enter a single character in the designated cell-location.

The {get command} has the following format:

```
{get cell-location}
```

{getlabel}

The {getlabel} command stops the macro and prompts a person to enter a label that will be placed in the specified cell-location.

The {getlabel} command has the following format:

```
{getlabel prompt-string,cell-location}
```

{getnumber}

The {getnumber} command stops the macro and prompts an individual to enter a value that will be placed in the specified cell-location.

The {getnumber} command has the following format:

```
{getnumber prompt-string,cell-location}
```

{getpos}

The {getpos} command determines where the file pointer is in the open file and stores the position in the designated cell-location.

The {getpos} command has the following format:

```
{getpos cell-location}
```

{graphoff}

The {graphoff} command erases a graph displayed by the {graphon} command and displays the current worksheet on the screen.

The {graphoff command has the following format:

```
{graphoff}
```

{graphon}

The {graphon} command has the following format:

```
{graphon <named-graph>,<nodisplay>}
```

The named-graph and nodisplay arguments are optional.

Depending on the options selected, three things can happen when the {graphon} command is used. If {graphon} is used with no arguments, then a full-screen view of the current graph will be displayed on your screen as the macro continues to execute. If {graphon named-graph} is used, then the named-graph will appear on your screen while the macro continues to execute. If {graphon named-graph, nodisplay} is executed, the named-graph will become the current graph and there will be no graph displayed on your screen.

{if}

The {if} command tests the condition following the word *if.* When the *if* condition is true, the commands that immediately follow the {if} command in the same cell are then executed. If the condition is false, the command in the cell immediately below the {if} command is executed.

The {if} command has the following format:

```
{if condition}
```

{indicate}

The {indicate} command allows you to change the mode indicator, located at the top right corner of the screen.

The {indicate} command has the following format:

```
{indicate <string>}
```

If this command is used, Lotus 1-2-3 replaces the mode indicator with the specified string of characters.

{let}

The {let} command stores the specified entry in the designated cell-location. The entry may be a number, string of text, formula or cell reference.

The {let} command has the following format:

```
{let cell-location,entry}
```

{look}

The {look} command keeps track of whether or not you typed a keystroke while a macro was running. The keystroke (if any) is stored in the designated cell-location.

The {look} command has the following format:

```
{look cell-location}
```

{menubranch}

The {menubranch} command allows you to select a menu item and then execute the corresponding macro commands for the menu item. Menu items begin in the designated cell-location.

The {menubranch} command has the following format:

```
{menubranch cell-location}
```

{menucall}

The {menucall} command allows you to select a menu item and then execute the corresponding subroutine for the menu item. Menu items begin in the designated cell-location.

The {menucall} command has the following format:

```
{menucall cell-location}
```

{onerror}

The {onerror} command continues a macro at a designated branch-location if a command error occurs during macro execution. The {onerror} command does not affect macro failure caused by syntax errors.

If desired, an error message can be included in the cell designated for the message-location.

The {onerror} command has the following format:

```
{onerror branch-location,<message-location>}
```

{open}

The {open} command allows you to open a text file for the purposes of reading or writing.

The {open} command has the following format:

```
{open filename,access-mode}
```

The access-mode indicates R(Read), W(Write) or M(Modify) the file.

{paneloff} and {panelon} commands

The {paneloff} command prevents the appearance of information in the control panel during macro execution. The {panelon} command reverses the {paneloff} command.

The {paneloff} and {panelon} commands have the following format:

```
{paneloff}
{panelon}
```

{put}

The {put} command places an entry (number or string of characters) at the designated column and row within the designated two-dimensional range.

The {put} command has the following format:

```
{put range,column-number,row-number,entry}
```

For example, if the range was A1..B3, the column number was 0 and the row number was 1, the number or string would be placed in cell A2.

{quit}

The {quit} command stops the execution of the macro.

The {quit} command has the following format:

```
{quit}
```

{read}

The {read} command reads a specified number of characters or bytes (0 to 511 characters can be used) from a file and places the characters at the designated cell-location.

The {read} command has the following format:

```
{read byte-number,cell-location}
```

{readln}

The {readln} command reads and copies one line of information from the open file to the designated cell location.

The {readln} command has the following format:

```
{readln cell-location}
```

{recalc}

The {recalc} command recalculates the cells in the designated cell-location row by row.

The {recalc} command has the following format:

```
{recalc cell-location,<condition>,<iterations>}
```

{recalccol}

The {recalccol} command recalculates the cells in designated cell-location column by column.

The {recalccol} command has the following format:

```
{recalccol cell-location,<condition>,<iterations>}
```

{restart}

The {restart} command clears the subroutine stack. When {restart} is encountered, 1-2-3 continues to the end of the current subroutine. Instead of returning to the original macro location, the macro then stops executing.

The {restart} command has the following format:

```
{restart}
```

{return}

The {return} command transfers control from a subroutine to the next instruction in the macro from which the subroutine was called.

The {return} command has the following format:

```
{return}
```

{setpos}

The {setpos} command sets the new position for the byte pointer in the currently open file to the indicated position.

The {setpos} command has the following format:

```
{setpos byte-position}
```

{subroutine}

The {subroutine} command calls a subroutine. The optional arguments can be utilized to pass information to a subroutine.

The {subroutine} command has the following format:

```
{subroutine <argument>,<argument>...}
```

{system}

The {system} command temporarily halts execution of 1-2-3 and the specified operating system command is processed.

The {system} command has the following format:

```
{system command}
```

The command is any legal operating system command that needs to be executed.

{wait}

The {wait} command suspends macro execution until the designated time.

The {wait} command has the following format:

```
{wait time-number}
```

{windowsoff} and {windowson}

The {windowsoff} command prevents redrawing the screen (except for the control panel) during macro execution. The {windowson} command reverses the {windowsoff} command.

The {windowsoff} and {windowson} commands have the following format:

```
{windowsoff}
{windowson}
```

{write}

The {write} command writes characters into the currently open file.

The {write} command has the following format:

```
{write string}
```

{writeln}

The {writeln} command writes the specified string of characters to the currently open file and adds a carriage-return line-feed sequence to the end of the string.

The {writeln} command has the following format:

```
{writeln string}
```

{?}

The {?} command halts the execution of a macro to allow you to either move the cell pointer or menu pointer to enter data in a cell or to complete part of a command. When you press the ↵ key, the macro continues execution.

The {?} has the following format:

    {?}

■ Some Examples of Using Advanced Macro Commands

In this section, you will create several macros that illustrate some typical applications of advanced macro commands.

Interactive Macros

In many situations, you may want to allow users of a macro to enter data while a macro is executing. For example, you may want to prompt an individual to enter values or labels into some specific cells.

Entering a Sequence of Numbers

Sometimes you may need to enter rows or columns of numbers on a worksheet. Suppose you wanted to enter the set of numbers 10, 25, 15 and 32 in cells B10 through B14 on a worksheet. You will create a macro that moves the cell pointer down one cell after entering each of the numbers to expedite the process of entering the data.

Before creating the macro, make sure you have a blank worksheet on your screen.

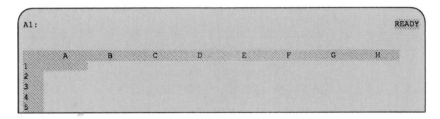

Figure 10-9

To place a title for the macro that will be used for entering the set of numbers.

Move	the cell pointer to cell A1
Enter	Macro Input

> **Move**   the cell pointer to cell C1
>
> **Enter**   Macro for entering numbers in a column

To place the name of the macro on the macro worksheet:

> **Move**   the cell pointer to cell A3
>
> **Enter**   COL_INPUT

Widen column A so it will display 12 characters.

To enter the first macro instruction:

> **Move**   the cell pointer to cell B3
>
> **Enter**   {?}

This instruction halts the execution of the macro until you input a value and press the ↵ key.

To indicate that you want to move the cell pointer down one cell after the value is entered.

> **Move**   the cell pointer to cell B4
>
> **Enter**   {down}

You could also have used {d}.

To specify that another number may need to be input:

> **Move**   the cell pointer to cell B5
>
> **Enter**   {branch COL_INPUT}

This instruction directs 1-2-3 to move to the first instruction in the macro so that you may enter another number if you so desire.

Before you execute the macro:

> **Name**   the macro COL_INPUT and include cell
>   B3 as the cell in the range

After moving the cell pointer to cell B3 and except for the documentation, your screen should look like Figure 10-10.

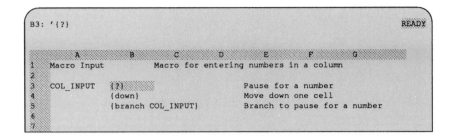

Figure 10-10

After comparing your macro with Figure 10-10 and making any necessary modifications, save the macro on file ENTRYMAC.

Before executing the macro, move the cell pointer to the cell in which you want to enter the first number.

Move   the cell pointer to cell B10

Execute the macro. Note that as soon as you start executing the macro, CMD appears at the bottom of the screen indicating that the macro is executing and in this case is waiting for you to enter a number.

Enter   10

After you press the ⏎ key, the cell pointer will be moved down one cell and the macro will pause again for you to enter another number in cell B11. Continue to enter the numbers until 25, 15 and 32 appear in cells B10 through B13.

To terminate the execution of the macro:

Press   [Ctrl-Break]

Press   [Esc]

A beep will be sounded to indicate the macro has been terminated. Your screen should now look like Figure 10-11. Do not save the results that appear on your screen.

```
B14:                                                                   READY

        A         B         C         D         E         F         G
1   Macro Input              Macro for entering numbers in a column
2
3   COL_INPUT    {?}                         Pause for a number
4                {down}                      Move down one cell
5                {branch COL_INPUT}          Branch to pause for a number
6
7
8
9
10                10
11                25
12                15
13                32
14
```

Figure 10-11

Prompting Users to Enter Labels and Numeric Data

At times it is helpful to place a message at the top of the screen to prompt a user to enter a specific label or a value. In this section, you will use the {getlabel} and {getnumber} commands to display prompts requesting the entry of labels and numbers.

Suppose you want to create a macro that prompts a person using the loan amortization schedule worksheet to enter the purpose for obtaining the loan, the principal amount, interest rate and time period.

You will need to retrieve the file AMORT. Move the cell A101 and enter the macro title and name as it appears in Figure 10-12.

```
A103: [W5] 'PT                                                         READY

         A      B          C          D          E          F          G
101  Macro Entry      Macro to prompt user for principal, int rate and time
102
103  PT
104
105
```

Figure 10-12

The set of steps that must be included in your macro include:

1. Erasing the old values in cells B5 through B7

2. Setting the calculation mode to manual

3. Using the {getlabel} and {getnumber} commands to prompt the user to enter the information for loan purpose, principal, interest rate and time period

4. Calculating the monthly payment amount after all necessary information has been input

Before creating the macro instructions, create the range name DATA_AREA and include cells B5..B7 as the range of cells.

To include an instruction in the macro that erases the current entries for principal amount, interest rate and time period:

Move	the cell pointer to cell B103
Enter	{blank DATA_AREA}

To specify that manual recalculation mode is to be used:

Move	the cell pointer to cell B104
Enter	'/wgrm

To include a macro instruction that displays a message requesting the user to input the purpose of the loan and place the entry in cell C2:

Move	the cell pointer to cell B105
Enter	{getlabel "Enter Purpose of the Loan: ",C2}~

To include an instruction in the macro requesting the user to enter the principal amount:

Move	the cell pointer to cell B106
Enter	{getnumber "Enter Principal Amount: ",B5}~

To specify similar macro instructions for requesting the user to enter the interest rate and time period data:

Move	the cell pointer to cell B107
Enter	{getnumber "Enter Interest Rate in Decimal Form: ",B6}~
Move	the cell pointer to cell B108
Enter	{getnumber "Enter Time Period in Months: ",B7}~

To include an instruction to recalculate the worksheet:

Move the cell pointer to cell B109

Enter {calc}

After entering the macro instructions, your screen should look like Figure 10-13.

```
B109: [W11] '{calc}                                                    READY

       A         B          C         D          E         F          G
101 Macro Entry    Macro to prompt user for principal, int rate and time
102
103 PT     {blank DATA_AREA}
104        /wgrm
105        {getlabel "Enter Purpose of the Loan:  ",C2}~
106        {getnumber "Enter Principal Amount:  ",B5}~
107        {getnumber "Enter Interest Rate in Decimal Form:  ",B6}~
108        {getnumber "Enter Time Period in Months:  ",B7}~
109        {calc}
110
111
```

Figure 10-13

Create the macro name PT and include B103 as the cell in its range. Before executing the macro PT save the current worksheets on file PROMPTMC.

So you can see the execution of the macro, move the cell pointer to cell A1. Execute the macro PT. Notice that the cells B5 through B7 have been "blanked". A message appears at the top of the screen requesting you to "Enter the Purpose of the Loan:"

Enter Furniture Purchases

The label now appears in cell C2 and a new prompt requesting you to enter the principal amount of the loan appears at the top of the screen.

Enter 20000

The number $20,000 now appears in the worksheet in cell B5. A prompt indicating you need to enter the interest rate in decimal form now appears at the top of the screen.

Enter .12

The interest rate 12 percent now appears in cell B6 and you are requested to enter the time period in months for repaying the loan.

Enter 60

The time period of 60 months now appears in cell B7. The macro completes the calculation of the monthly payment amount, and your screen should look like Figure 10-14. Do not save the results of this exercise.

```
A1: [W5]                                                              READY


         A        B        C         D          E          F          G
1                          LOAN AMORTIZATION
2                          Furniture Purchases
3                 ASSUMPTIONS
4                 ===================================================
5                 $20,000.00          PRINCIPAL
6                     12.00%          INTEREST RATE PER YEAR
7                         60          TIME PERIOD IN MONTHS
8                      1.00%          MONTHLY INTEREST RATE
9                     444.89          CALCULATED PAYMENT AMOUNT
10                ===================================================
11
12       *********************************************************************
13                                                        PRINCIPAL   INTEREST
14       PMT      PAYMENT  PRINCIPAL INTEREST   PRINCIPAL     PAID       PAID
15       NUM      AMOUNT    AMOUNT    AMOUNT     BALANCE    TO DATE    TO DATE
16       *********************************************************************
17                                              20,000.00
18        1       444.89    244.89    200.00   19,755.11     244.89     200.00
19        2       444.89    247.34    197.55   19,507.77     492.23     397.55
20        3       444.89    249.81    195.08   19,257.96     742.04     592.63
                                     UNDO
```

Figure 10-14

Changing Program Flow and Looping

Sometimes you may want to change the flow of instructions when a macro is used. For example you may want to repeat a set of instructions a specific number of times or until a particular condition occurs. In this section, you will create macros that *loop* through a sequence of instruction when the number of iterations that need to be completed is either known or unknown.

Executing a Loop of Instructions When the Number of Iterations Is Known

The macro you will create in this section illustrates the use of the {for} command to loop through a set of instructions a specific number of times. For this exercise, you need to have a blank worksheet on your screen. Enter the numbers on the worksheet so that your screen looks like Figure 10-15.

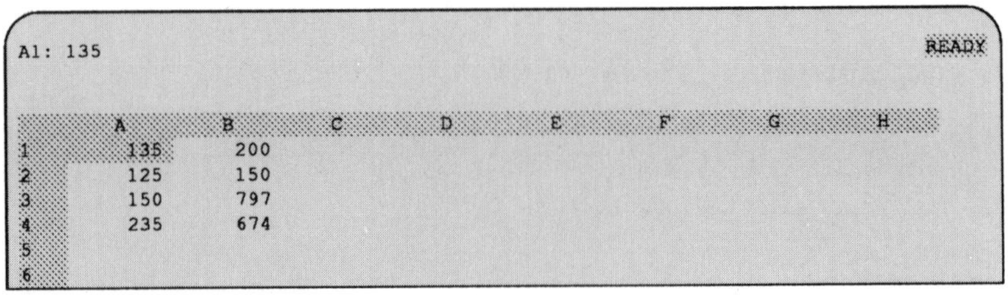

Figure 10-15

Suppose that you want to add the numbers in column A and column B for each row and place the sum in column C. You will now create a macro to accomplish this objective. Before entering the macro, enter the title and macro name information that appear in Figure 10-16.

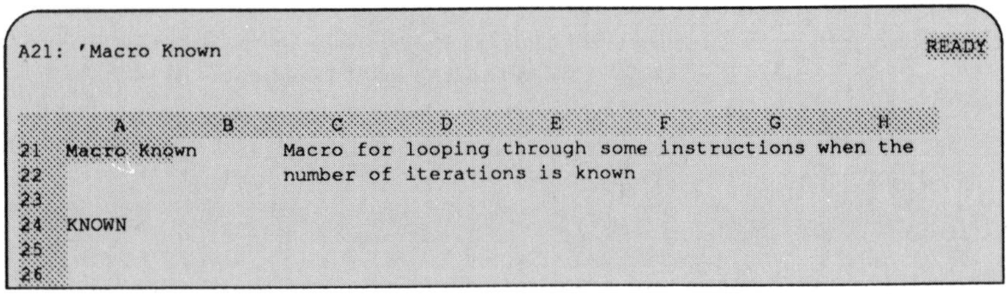

Figure 10-16

To place an instruction in the macro that will place the cell pointer in the proper starting cell position:

Move   the cell pointer to cell B24

Enter   {goto}C1~

To solve this problem, you need a macro command that will process a loop of instructions that adds the numbers in columns A and B for each row and places the cell pointer in the proper starting cell position for the next summation operation:

Move   the cell pointer to cell B25

Enter   {for COUNT,1,4,1,LOOP}

This macro command indicates that the set of macro instructions which starts with the initial cell in the range name LOOP is to be executed four times. The cell associated with the range name COUNT is initialized with a value of 1 and incremented by 1 each time the LOOP routine is executed. The first number after COUNT is the initialization value, the second number is the termination value and the third number is the value by which COUNT is to be incremented each time the set of instructions is executed. When the value of COUNT exceeds the termination value, the looping process is ended.

To specify that the cell pointer is to be moved to cell A1 after the macro is executed:

| **Move** | the cell pointer to cell B26 |
| **Enter** | {goto}A1~ |

To place the name of the LOOP routine on the worksheet:

| **Move** | the cell pointer to cell A28 |
| **Enter** | LOOP |

To include a macro instruction that adds the numbers in column A and B for a row and enters the sum in column C for the row.

| **Move** | the cell pointer to cell B28 |
| **Enter** | '+{left}{left}+{left}~ |

Assuming that the cell pointer is in C1 when the macro is executed, this macro instruction specifies that a formula is used that sums the value two columns to the left of C1 and the value one column to the left of C1. The ~ symbol represents the ⏎ key. When the macro processes this keystroke, the formula +A1+B1 is placed in C1.

To indicate that the cell pointer needs to be moved down one cell in column C before the routine is executed again:

| **Move** | the cell pointer to cell B29 |
| **Enter** | {down} |

To include the COUNT variable name on your screen:

| **Move** | the cell pointer to cell A32 |
| **Enter** | COUNT |

You must create a range name for LOOP and COUNT. The range name LOOP should only include cell B28 and the range name COUNT should only include cell B32.

After creating the range names LOOP and COUNT, your screen should look like Figure 10-17.

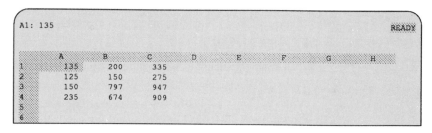

```
A32: 'COUNT                                                        READY

          A          B          C          D          E        F        G        H
21  Macro Known            Macro for looping through some instructions when the
22                         number of iterations is known
23
24  KNOWN       {goto}C1~
25              {for COUNT,1,4,1,LOOP}
26              {goto}A1~
27
28  LOOP        +{left}{left}+{left}~
29              {down}
30
31
32  COUNT
33
34
```

Figure 10-17

After comparing your macro instructions with those in Figure 10-17 and making any necessary modifications, create the range name KNOWN for the macro name and include cell B24 as its range. Save the worksheet file using the name KNOWNMAC.

After you execute the macro, your screen should look like Figure 10-18. Notice that the values for columns A and B for each row have been added and the resulting total placed in column C.

```
A1: 135                                                           READY

          A          B          C          D          E        F        G        H
1        135        200        335
2        125        150        275
3        150        797        947
4        235        674        909
5
6
```

Figure 10-18

To see what happened on the macro worksheet, press the (PgDn) key to display the macro on your screen. Refer to Figure 10-19.

```
A21: 'Macro Known                                                      READY

        A         B         C         D         E         F         G        H
 21  Macro Known            Macro for looping through some instructions when the
 22                         number of iterations is known
 23
 24  KNOWN     {goto}C1~
 25            {for COUNT,1,4,1,LOOP}
 26            {goto}A1~
 27
 28  LOOP      +{left}{left}+{left}~
 29            {down}
 30
 31
 32  COUNT          5
 33
 34
```

Figure 10-19

Notice that the number 5 appears in cell B32. The number 5 indicates that as the set of macro instructions associated with the range name LOOP were executed, the value of COUNT was incremented from an initial value of 1 by 1 each time the set of instructions was executed. The value of COUNT was compared to the termination value of 4. When the value of COUNT was less than or equal to 4, the set of instructions associated with the range name LOOP was again executed. When the value of COUNT became 5, it was greater than the termination value and the macro stopped executing.

Executing a Loop of Instructions When the Number of Iterations is Unknown

In the previous section, you created a macro that repeated a set of macro instructions a specific number of times based on the fact that you knew how many times the set of instructions needed to be executed. Sometimes you may not know how many times a set of macro instructions needs to be repeated.

You created a macro in the last section to add the numbers in column A and column B for a row and enter the sum in column C of the row. You knew the number of rows in which numbers appeared in columns A and B. In this section, you will create a macro for solving this problem that is general enough so that it will work properly whenever you do not know the exact number of rows that have values in column A and B.

The {if}, {quit} and {branch} commands will be used in the macro that you develop to solve the problem. These commands will allow you to loop through a set of instructions when the number of times they need to be repeated is not known prior to executing the macro. They also permit you to change the program flow within a macro.

For this exercise, you will need to erase the worksheet on your screen and create a worksheet so that your screen looks like Figure 10-20.

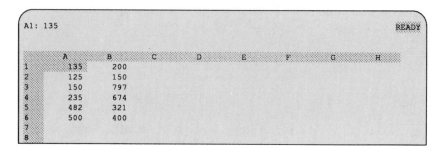

Figure 10-20

The steps necessary to solve this problem are:

1. Move the cell pointer to the proper starting position.

2. Add the two numbers in column A and B and enter the sum in column C.

3. Move the cell pointer down one cell in column C and then to the left once so the cell pointer is in column B.

4. Create a test range consisting of the cell in column B and immediately above it. Recall that the cell above the one in column B has a number in it.

5. Move the cell pointer to the right once so the cell pointer is in column C. Note that this cell is the cell in which you will place a sum if the cell immediately to the left of column B has a number in it.

6. Use the @COUNT function to determine the number of non-blank cells in the test range. If the count equals one, then the cell in column B is blank and, therefore, does not have a number in it. The macro then needs to stop executing. If the count is two, then the instructions for adding the cells in column A and B need to be repeated.

Before entering the macro instructions, enter the title of the macro and macro name information that appear in Figure 10-21.

```
A21: 'Macro Unknown                                                    READY

          A         B         C         D         E         F         G         H
21  Macro Unknown         Macro for looping through a set of instructions
22                        when the number of iterations is unknown
23
24  UNKNOWN
25
26
```

Figure 10-21

Assume that the values in columns A and B always begin with row 1 in the worksheet on which the macro is used. To specify C1 as the location for the first sum:

Move   the cell pointer to cell B24

Enter   {goto}C1~

To include a macro instruction for adding the numbers for the present row in columns A and B and entering the sum in column C for the row:

Move   the cell pointer to cell B25

Enter   '+{left}{left}+{left}~

To define a macro instruction that moves the cell pointer down one row and to the left one cell so the cell pointer will be in column B:

Move   the cell pointer to cell B26

Enter   {down}{left}

To enter a macro instruction that creates a test range consisting of the cell in column B and the one immediately above it:

Move   the cell pointer to cell B27

Enter   '/rncTEST~{up}~

To include a macro instruction for moving the cell pointer to the right once so it will be in column C again:

Move   the cell pointer to cell B28

Enter   {right}

At this point you need to specify a macro instruction that determines if the range name TEST has a count = 1.

Move   the cell pointer to cell B29

Enter   {if @count(TEST) =1}{branch END}

Note that if the count for the range name TEST equals 1, control will be transferred to the initial cell in the range name END. In this situation, the cell in column B is blank; and the macro needs to be terminated.

If the count for the range name TEST equals 2, then there are numbers in column A and B that need to be summed. You will also need to delete the range name TEST so that it can be created again to determine whether the macro needs to stop executing.

To include a macro instruction for deleting the range name TEST:

Move   the cell pointer to cell B30

Enter   '/rndTEST~

To specify a macro instruction that indicates control needs to be transferred to the macro instruction that sums the numbers in columns A and B:

Move   the cell pointer to cell B31

Enter   {branch ADD}

At this point you need to:

Move   the cell pointer to cell A25

Enter   ADD

Create the name range ADD and specify its range to be cell B25. Note that cell B25 includes the macro instruction for summing the numbers in columns A and B, and then entering the total in column C.

Here you need to place the macro instructions for ending the macro on the macro worksheet. You must define the location of the range name END so the {branch END} command specified earlier will execute properly, delete the range name TEST, move the cell pointer to cell A1 and quit. To define the location of the range name END and to delete the range name TEST:

Move   the cell pointer to cell A33

Enter   END

Move   the cell pointer to cell B33

Enter   '/rndTEST~

Now, create the range name END and specify its range as cell B33. Note that the identifiers ADD and END are not actually required, but the use of such labels enhances the clarity of the macro instruction execution flow.

To include the macro instruction that moves the cell pointer to cell A1 after all of the sets of numbers in columns A and B have been summed:

Move	the cell pointer to cell B34
Enter	{goto}A1~

You could have used {home} instead of {goto}A1~.

To define the macro instruction that stops the execution of the macro:

Move	the cell pointer to cell B35
Enter	{quit}

The {quit} command in this macro is not essential since the macro would end when a blank cell is encountered. However, the {quit} command clarifies the ending point for the macro.

Your screen should look like Figure 10-22.

```
B35: '{quit}                                                              READY


         A         B         C         D         E         F         G         H
21  Macro Unknown        Macro for looping through a set of instructions
22                       when the number of iterations is unknown
23
24  UNKNOWN   {goto}C1~
25  ADD       +{left}{left}+{left}~
26            {down}{left}
27            /rncTEST~{up}~
28            {right}
29            {if @count(TEST)=1}{branch END}
30            /rndTEST~
31            {branch ADD}
32
33  END       /rndTEST~
34            {goto}A1~
35            {quit}
36
37
```

Figure 10-22

After you compare your macro with Figure 10-22 and make any necessary modifications, name your macro using the name UNKNOWN and include cell B24 as the initial cell in the macro. Save the worksheets using the file name UNKNOMAC.

Move the cell pointer to cell A1. Notice that you have six sets of numbers to sum. Execute the macro UNKNOWN. Your screen should now look like Figure 10-23. You do not need to save the results after the macro is executed.

```
A1: 135                                                                    READY


         A          B          C        D        E        F        G        H
1       135        200        335
2       125        150        275
3       150        797        947
4       235        674        909
5       482        321        803
6       500        400        900
7
8
```

Figure 10-23

Using Subroutines

Subroutines are independent sets of instructions that can be called at any point in a macro. One advantage of using a subroutine is that the set of instructions can be easily called from any place in the macro so that the set of commands do not have to be duplicated. Another advantage of using a subroutine is that it can be called from several different locations within a macro.

Suppose you want to create a macro that permits you to input a code that designates whether or not you want to print the loan amortization schedule after the monthly payment amount is calculated.

Before you solve this problem, you will need to retrieve file AMORT and enter the macro title and name information so your screen looks like Figure 10-24.

```
A101: [W5] 'Macro Subrprt                                                  READY


         A      B        C          D          E          F          G
101 Macro Subrprt    Macro for illustrating the use of subroutine for
102                  testing a code to determine whether or not to print
103
104 SUBR
105
106
```

Figure 10-24

The steps that must be included in the macro to solve this problem are:

1. Set the worksheet to manual recalculation mode so you do not have to wait for 1-2-3 to calculate the worksheet each time you enter data.

2. Prompt the user to enter the data on principal, interest rate and time period.

3. Calculate the loan payment using the data input for principal, interest rate and time period.

4. Prompt the user to enter a code to indicate whether the person wants to print the loan amortization schedule.

5. Test the code and, if appropriate, print the loan amortization schedule.

To make sure the macro executes on the loan amortization schedule, you need to place an instruction in the macro to move the cell pointer to cell A1.

Move   the cell pointer to cell B104

Enter   {goto}A1~

To include an instruction in your macro to set the recalculation mode to manual:

Move   the cell pointer to cell B105

Enter   '/wgrm

At a later point in the macro, you enter a message prompting the user to input the code to determine whether to print the loan amortization schedule. To ensure that the range of cells used are blank when the macro executes:

Move   the cell pointer to cell B106

Enter   '/reI1.I5~

To place the instructions for prompting the user to enter the principal, interest rate and time period in your macro:

Move   the cell pointer to cell B107

Enter   {getnumber "Enter Principal Amount: ",B5}~

Move   the cell pointer to cell B108

Enter   {getnumber "Enter Interest Rate in Decimal Form: ",B6}~

Move   the cell pointer to cell B109

Enter   {getnumber "Enter Time Period in Months: ",B7}~

To include a macro command for calculating the loan amortization schedule after the principal, interest rate and time period have been input:

Move   the cell pointer to cell B110

Enter   {calc}

To call the subroutine that prompts the user to enter the code for printing, that tests the value of the code, and, if appropriate, prints the loan amortization schedule:

Move	the cell pointer to cell B111
Enter	{CKCD}

To include instructions that will remove the CALC symbol from your screen after the macro has executed and then move the cell pointer to cell A1:

Move	the cell pointer to cell B112
Enter	{calc}
Move	the cell pointer to cell B113
Enter	{goto}A1~

To place a command in the macro that terminates execution of the macro:

Move	the cell pointer to cell B114
Enter	{quit}

At this point, you need to create the set of instructions that are included in the CKCD subroutine.

To place the subroutine name on the macro worksheet, and to specify a location to enter the code:

Move	the cell pointer to cell A116
Enter	CKCD
Move	the cell pointer to cell B116
Enter	{goto}I1~

You now need to create the range name CKCD and include B116 as its range. When the macro instruction in B111 is executed, control will be transferred to cell B116.

To include the instructions for prompting the user to input the print code:

Move	the cell pointer to cell B117
Enter	If you wish to print the schedule: {down}
Move	the cell pointer to cell B118
Enter	type a 1 and press enter {down}

Move	the cell pointer to cell B119
Enter	If you do not wish to print the schedule: {down}
Move	the cell pointer to cell B120
Enter	type 2 and press enter {down}

To include a command that causes the macro to pause and wait for the user to enter the print code:

Move	the cell pointer to cell B121
Enter	{?}~

After the code is input, you need to include instructions to make sure a valid code is specified. If the code is invalid, the instructions for entering the code must be repeated. If the code is valid, then the code needs to be tested to see whether or not it is appropriate to print the loan amortization schedule.

To test whether the code that was input is valid:

Move	the cell pointer to B122
Enter	{if I5=1#or#I5=2}{branch TEST}

If cell I5 has a value of 1 or 2, control transfers to the initial cell in range name TEST to determine whether the loan amortization schedule needs to be printed.

When the code is not valid, the input range (I1..I5) needs to be erased and control needs to be transferred to the first instruction in the subroutine so the user can be prompted to enter the code again. To place these instructions in your macro:

Move	the cell pointer to cell B123
Enter	'/reI1.I5~
Move	the cell pointer to cell B124
Enter	{CKCD}

At this point, you need to enter the instructions for testing the code. If the code has a value of 1, then you do need to print the loan amortization schedule. If the code has a value of 2, you do not print the schedule.

To include the instructions for testing the code and printing:

Move	the cell pointer to cell A126
Enter	TEST

Move   the cell pointer to cell B126

Enter   {if I5=2}{return}

This {if} command tests the code value to see if it is 2. When the code has the value of 2, control is transferred to the first macro command after the subroutine was called using the {return} command. In such a situation, the loan amortization schedule will not be printed. At this point, create the range name TEST and include cell B126 in its range. If the value in I5 is a 1, then the loan amortization schedule needs to be printed.

To print the schedule and return to the macro command after the subroutine was called:

Move   the cell pointer to cell B127

Enter   '/pprA1.G77~

Move   the cell pointer to cell B128

Enter   agppq

To include an instruction to return to the command immediately following the command which called the subroutine:

Move   the cell pointer to cell B129

Enter   {return}

Your macro should look like the one illustrated in Parts 1 and 2 of Figure 10-25.

```
A101: [W5] 'Macro Subrprt                                         READY


        A       B           C         D         E         F         G
101 Macro Subrprt    Macro for illustrating the use of subroutine for
102                  testing a code to determine whether or not to print
103
104 SUBR {goto}A1~
105      /wgrm
106      /reI1.I5~
107      {getnumber "Enter Principal Amount:  ",B5}~
108      {getnumber "Enter Interest Rate in Decimal Form:  ",B6}~
109      {getnumber "Enter Time Period in Months:  ",B7}~
110      {calc}
111      {CKCD}
112      {calc}
113      {goto}A1~
114      {quit}
115
116 CKCD {goto}I1~
117      If you wish to print the schedule: {down}
118      type a 1 and press enter {down}
119      If you do not wish to print the schedule: {down}
120      type a 2 and press enter {down}
                          UNDO
```

Figure 10-25
Part 1

```
B129: [W11] '{return}                                              READY


     A        B         C         D         E         F         G
121        {?}~
122        {if I5=1#or#I5=2}{branch TEST}
123        /reI1.I5~
124        {CKCD}
125
126 TEST  {if I5=2}{return}
127        /pprA1.G77~
128        agppq
129        {return}
130
131
```

Figure 10-25
Part 2

After you compare your macro with the one appearing in Figure 10-25, Parts 1 and 2, and make any necessary changes, name your macro using the range name SUBR and include cell B104 as the cell in its range. Save the worksheet using the file name PRCHK.

Move the cell pointer to cell A1. Execute the macro SUBR using $10,000 for the principal amount, 9 percent for the interest rate, and 60 months for the time period. When you are prompted for the print code, enter the number 1. Your screen should look like Figure 10-26 after the macro executes properly. You also should have printed the loan amortization schedule.

```
A1: [W5]                                                          READY


     A        B         C         D         E         F         G
1                     LOAN AMORTIZATION
2
3          ASSUMPTIONS
4          ----------------------------------------------------------
5          $10,000.00          PRINCIPAL
6               9.00%          INTEREST RATE PER YEAR
7              60              TIME PERIOD IN MONTHS
8               0.75%          MONTHLY INTEREST RATE
9             207.58           CALCULATED PAYMENT AMOUNT
10         ----------------------------------------------------------
11
12         ****************************************************************
13                                                   PRINCIPAL  INTEREST
14         PMT   PAYMENT  PRINCIPAL  INTEREST  PRINCIPAL  PAID      PAID
15         NUM   AMOUNT   AMOUNT     AMOUNT    BALANCE    TO DATE   TO DATE
16         ****************************************************************
17                                             10,000.00
18          1    207.58   132.58     75.00     9,867.42   132.58    75.00
19          2    207.58   133.58     74.01     9,733.84   266.16   149.01
20          3    207.58   134.58     73.00     9,599.26   400.74   222.01
                                    UNDO
```

Figure 10-26

Execute the macro again, using a value of 2 for the print code. Finally execute the macro using 3 for the print code. Notice that you are prompted for a print code until you enter a 1 or a 2. Do not save the results after the macro is executed.

Creating User-Designed Menus

In some situations, you may want to design your own menus using the Lotus 1-2-3 command language. The process for preparing a menu includes the following:

1. Write a "menu-processing" macro that initiates the execution of the user-designed menu.

2. Determine the entries for the menu line and the description line.

3. Write the macro commands for each menu option.

The following guidelines can be used in a developing a user designed menu:

1. Find a portion of the spreadsheet that has at least as many blank columns as there are menu options.

2. The first row of the user designed menu contains the menu options as they will appear on the screen.

3. The row below the menu options includes a description of each menu option that will appear on the screen when a menu option is highlighted.

4. The macro commands for each menu option can be placed immediately below the menu item or in a range of cells at another location on the spreadsheet.

5. A menu processing macro must be placed on the macro worksheet that contains the menu.

Some cautionary guidelines for creating menus follow:

1. Do not place more than 8 menu options in the first row of the menu you are designing.

2. The cell immediately to the right of the last menu option must be blank.

3. The options on the menu line should be short enough to make sure they will appear on the screen.

4. Make sure the options on a menu do not start with the same first character so that a menu option can be selected by typing the first character of the menu option.

5. Do not leave blank entries between the menu options.

Single-Tiered Menu

Suppose that you desire to design a menu for the loan amortization schedule worksheet that permits you to calculate the monthly payment and print the appropriate schedule for a one- or a five-year time period. For this example, assume that the loan amount is $50,000 and the interest rate is 12 percent. When you finish this exercise, your screen will look like Figure 10-27 Part 1.

```
A104: [W5] 'SGL                                              READY

          A       B        C        D        E        F        G
101 Macro Single    Macro for illustrating the design and use of a one tier
102                 menu
103
104 SGL   {menubranch MAIN}
105
106 MAIN 1-year     Print-1  Five-year  5-Print      Stop
107      1 year term1 year sch5 year term5 year schedQuit process
108      {goto}B7~  /pprA1.G29{goto}B7~  /pprA1.G77~ /reB7~
109      12~        agppq    60~          agppq
110      {goto}A1~  {menubranc{goto}A1~   {menubranch MAIN}
111      {menubranch MAIN}    {menubranch MAIN}
112
113
```

Figure 10-27
Part 1

The complete contents of the cells are illustrated in Figure 10-27 Part 2.

Macro Single		Macro for illustrating the design and use of a one tier			
		menu			
SGL	{menubranch MAIN}				
MAIN	1-year	Print-1	Five-year	5-Print	Stop
	1 year term	1 year sched	5 year term	5 year sched	Quit process
	{goto}B7~	/pprA1.G29~	{goto}B7~	/pprA1.G77~	/reB7~
	12~	agppq	60~	agppq	
	{goto}A1~	{menubranch MAIN}	{goto}A1~	{menubranch MAIN}	
	{menubranch MAIN}		{menubranch MAIN}		

Figure 10-27
Part 2

To complete this exercise, retrieve the file AMORT. After placing the title and macro name on your worksheet, your screen should look like Figure 10-28.

```
A104: [W5] 'SGL                                                          READY


        A       B          C          D          E          F          G
101 Macro Single   Macro for illustrating the design and use
102                of a one tier menu
103
104 SGL
105
106
```

Figure 10-28

When you execute a user-designed menu macro, you must include a {menubranch} command to indicate to 1-2-3 on which menu you want to start. To include this command on the macro worksheet.

    Move   the cell pointer to cell B104

    Enter   {menubranch MAIN}

To enter the label MAIN in your macro:

    Move   the cell pointer to cell A106

    Enter   MAIN

The five menu options to be included are 1-year, Print-1, Five-year, 5-Print and Quit. If the 1-year menu option is selected, the loan amortization schedule will be computed using 12 months as the time period. When the Print-1 option is selected, the loan amortization schedule for a one year (12 months) time period will be printed.

If the Five-year menu option is chosen, the loan amortization schedule will be calculated using a 60-month time period. When the 5-Print is chosen, the loan amortization schedule for a five-year (60 months) time period will be printed. When the Quit menu option is selected, execution of the macro will stop.

To include the five menu options in your macro:

    Move   the cell pointer to cell B106

    Enter   '1-year

    Move   the cell pointer to cell C106

    Enter   Print-1

    Move   the cell pointer to cell D106

Enter	Five-year
Move	the cell pointer to cell E106
Enter	'5-Print
Move	the cell pointer to cell F106
Enter	Stop

At this point, you have placed the menu options on the macro worksheet. You now need to create the range name MAIN and include the location of the first menu option, B106, as its range.

The second row of your menu macro includes the description for each menu option that will appear in the control panel when the menu pointer is highlighting it. To enter the descriptive information for each of the menu options:

Move	the cell pointer to cell B107
Enter	'1 year term
Move	the cell pointer to cell C107
Enter	'1 year sched
Move	the cell pointer to cell D107
Enter	'5 year term
Move	the cell pointer to cell E107
Enter	'5 year sched
Move	the cell pointer to cell F107
Enter	Quit process

The macro instructions that are to be executed when a menu option is selected can appear immediately below the description of the menu option or in a range at another location on the macro worksheet. For this example you will place the macro instructions immediately below each menu option.

For the 1-year menu option you need to enter macro instructions that enter the number 12 for the time period in cell B7, place the menu pointer in cell A1 and branch to the main menu.

To include these instructions below the first menu option:

Move	the cell pointer to cell B108
Enter	{goto}B7~
Move	the cell pointer to cell B109
Enter	'12~
Move	the cell pointer to cell B110
Enter	{goto}A1~
Move	the cell pointer to cell B111
Enter	{menubranch MAIN}

When the Print-1 option is selected, you must include instructions that select the proper range of cells and print a 12-month loan amortization schedule. Then, you must specify that control is to be transferred to the main menu.

To place the appropriate macro instructions under the second menu option:

Move	the cell pointer to cell C108
Enter	'/pprA1.G29~
Move	the cell pointer to cell C109
Enter	agppq
Move	the cell pointer to cell C110
Enter	{menubranch MAIN}

The Five-year menu option requires the same set of instructions as the 1-year option, except the number 60 must be entered for the time period in cell B7.

To include the instructions that must appear below the Five-year menu option:

Move	the cell pointer to cell D108
Enter	{goto}B7~
Move	the cell pointer to cell D109
Enter	'60~
Move	the cell pointer to cell D110
Enter	{goto}A1~

Move	the cell pointer to cell D111
Enter	{menubranch MAIN}

The set of instructions that must be included below the 5-Print menu option are the same as the Print-1 menu option, except the print range must include 60 months of data instead of 12.

To place the appropriate instructions under the 5-Print menu option:

Move	the cell pointer to cell E108
Enter	'/pprA1.G77~
Move	the cell pointer to cell E109
Enter	agppq
Move	the cell pointer to cell E110
Enter	{menubranch MAIN}

The final menu option is Stop. For this menu option, you need to enter instructions to erase cell B7, where you placed the time period data, and end the execution of the macro.

To place these instructions below the Stop menu:

Move	the cell pointer to cell F108
Enter	'/reB7~
Move	the cell pointer to cell F109

Your screen should now look like Figure 10-29 Part 1.

```
F108: [W12] '/reB7~                                                    READY


         A        B           C          D          E          F          G
101 Macro Single      Macro for illustrating the design and use of a one tier
102                   menu
103
104 SGL   {menubranch MAIN}
105
106 MAIN 1-year      Print-1    Five-year  5-Print      Stop
107      1 year term1 year sch5 year term5 year schedQuit process
108      {goto}B7~   /pprA1.G29{goto}B7~   /pprA1.G77~ /reB7~
109      12~         agppq      60~        agppq
110      {goto}A1~   {menubranc{goto}A1~   {menubranch MAIN}
111      {menubranch MAIN}     {menubranch MAIN}
112
113
```

Figure 10-29
Part 1

```
  Macro Single                 Macro for illustrating the design and use of a one tier
                               menu

  SGL     {menubranch MAIN}

  MAIN    1-year               Print-1           Five-year         5-Print           Stop
          1 year term          1 year sched      5 year term       5 year sched      Quit process
          {goto}B7~            /pprA1.G29~       {goto}B7~         /pprA1.G77~       /reB7~
          12~                  agppq             60~               agppq
          {goto}A1~            {menubranch MAIN}  {goto}A1~        {menubranch MAIN}
          {menubranch MAIN}                      {menubranch MAIN}
```

Figure 10-29
Part 2

After you have compared the menu you designed with Figure 10-29 Part 1 and the information appearing in Figure 10-29 Part 2, make any necessary changes. Name your macro SGL. Include the cell B104 as the range for the macro SGL, and save the worksheet using the file name SINGLMAC.

Move the cell pointer to cell B7 and erase the contents of the cell. The ERR indicator will appear in some of the worksheet cells. When you execute the macro SGL, the ERR indicator will disappear from the cells. Make sure the principal amount is $50,000 and the interest rate is 12 percent. If necessary, change the values.

Execute the macro SGL and select the 1-year menu option. Figure 10-30 Part 1 includes the menu when it initially appears on the screen. Figure 10-30 Part 2 illustrates the appearance of the screen after the 1-year option is selected. Figure 10-30 Part 3 displays the screen after the Stop option is selected from the menu.

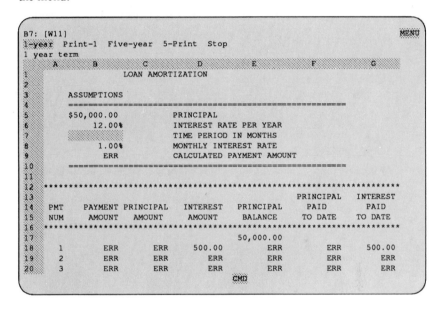

```
B7: [W11]                                                            MENU
1-year  Print-1  Five-year  5-Print  Stop
1 year term
       A       B          C          D          E          F          G
 1                   LOAN AMORTIZATION
 2
 3           ASSUMPTIONS
 4           ===========================================================
 5           $50,000.00           PRINCIPAL
 6               12.00%           INTEREST RATE PER YEAR
 7                                TIME PERIOD IN MONTHS
 8                1.00%           MONTHLY INTEREST RATE
 9                ERR             CALCULATED PAYMENT AMOUNT
10           ===========================================================
11
12  ***********************************************************************
13                                                   PRINCIPAL   INTEREST
14  PMT     PAYMENT PRINCIPAL    INTEREST  PRINCIPAL     PAID       PAID
15  NUM     AMOUNT  AMOUNT       AMOUNT    BALANCE    TO DATE    TO DATE
16  ***********************************************************************
17                                        50,000.00
18   1        ERR      ERR       500.00       ERR        ERR      500.00
19   2        ERR      ERR        ERR         ERR        ERR       ERR
20   3        ERR      ERR        ERR         ERR        ERR       ERR
                                       CMD
```

Figure 10-30
Part 1

```
A1: [W5]                                                            MENU
1-year  Print-1  Five-year  5-Print  Stop
1 year term
        A       B        C          D          E          F         G
1                       LOAN AMORTIZATION
2
3         ASSUMPTIONS
4         ==================================================================
5         $50,000.00           PRINCIPAL
6            12.00%            INTEREST RATE PER YEAR
7            12               TIME PERIOD IN MONTHS
8             1.00%           MONTHLY INTEREST RATE
9         4,442.44            CALCULATED PAYMENT AMOUNT
10        ==================================================================
11
12  ***********************************************************************
13                                                 PRINCIPAL   INTEREST
14  PMT     PAYMENT  PRINCIPAL   INTEREST  PRINCIPAL    PAID       PAID
15  NUM     AMOUNT    AMOUNT     AMOUNT    BALANCE    TO DATE    TO DATE
16  ***********************************************************************
17                                        50,000.00
18   1    4,442.44  3,942.44     500.00   46,057.56  3,942.44     500.00
19   2    4,442.44  3,981.86     460.58   42,075.70  7,924.30     960.58
20   3    4,442.44  4,021.68     420.76   38,054.01 11,945.99   1,381.33
                                              CMD
```

Figure 10-30
Part 2

```
A1: [W5]                                                            READY

        A       B        C          D          E          F         G
1                       LOAN AMORTIZATION
2
3         ASSUMPTIONS
4         ==================================================================
5         $50,000.00           PRINCIPAL
6            12.00%            INTEREST RATE PER YEAR
7                              TIME PERIOD IN MONTHS
8             1.00%           MONTHLY INTEREST RATE
9            ERR              CALCULATED PAYMENT AMOUNT
10        ==================================================================
11
12  ***********************************************************************
13                                                 PRINCIPAL   INTEREST
14  PMT     PAYMENT  PRINCIPAL   INTEREST  PRINCIPAL    PAID       PAID
15  NUM     AMOUNT    AMOUNT     AMOUNT    BALANCE    TO DATE    TO DATE
16  ***********************************************************************
17                                        50,000.00
18   1      ERR       ERR        500.00      ERR        ERR       500.00
19   2      ERR       ERR        ERR         ERR        ERR       ERR
20   3      ERR       ERR        ERR         ERR        ERR       ERR
                                UNDO
```

Figure 10-30
Part 3

Note that the macro is designed so the menu will continue to appear on the screen until you select the Stop menu option.

Multiple-Tiered Menus

User designed menus can be linked together to form a *tiered* menu structure. The example here is an extension of the single-tiered menu in the previous section that allowed you to select a one- or five-year time period and then print the amortization schedule for a loan with a principal amount of $50,000 and an interest rate of 12 percent.

Suppose you desire to allow a user of the loan amortization schedule worksheet the flexibility to specify the principal amount, interest rate and time period in one menu and then print the amortization schedule from a second menu. It is assumed for this example that you will be entering either 12 or 60 months for the time period; therefore, you will have the options to print a one- or a five-year loan amortization schedule.

Parts 1 and 2 of Figure 10-31 illustrate what the two-tier menu will look like when you finish this exercise. Notice in this example there are two menus: MENU1 and MENU2. The first menu includes options for entering the principal amount, interest rate, time period, transferring control to the second menu to print the appropriate loan amortization schedule and for stopping the execution of the macro. Figure 10-31 Part 3 includes the exact contents of each cell.

```
A101: [W5] 'Macro Mult-Menu                                          READY


      A         B         C         D         E         F         G
101 Macro Mult-Menu Macro for illustrating the use
102                of multiple tiered menus
103
104 MULT {menubranch MENU1}
105
106 MENU1Principal  Int-Rate   Time       Schedule    End
107      Loan amountInterest raLoan periodPrint-schedQuit process
108      {branch PRI{branch INT{branch TIM{branch SCH{branch END}
109
110      Principal  Int-Rate   Time       Schedule    End
111
112      /wgrm      /wgrm      /wgrm      {calc}      /reB5.B7~
113      {goto}B5~  {goto}B6~  {goto}B7~  {menubranch{calc}
114      {?}~       {?}~       {?}~                   {goto}A1~
115      {goto}A1~  {goto}A1~  {goto}A1~
116      {menubranch{menubranch{menubranch MENU1}
117
118
119
120

                        UNDO
```

Figure 10-31
Part 1

```
A121: [W5] 'MENU2                                                    READY


      A         B         C         D         E         F         G
121 MENU2Print-1    5-Print    Stop
122      1 year sche5 year scheQuit process
123      {branch PRI{branch 5-P{branch STOP}
124
125
126
127      Print-1    5-print    Stop
128
129      /pprA1.G29~/pprA1.G77~/reB5.B7~
130      agppq      agppq      {calc}
131      /reB5.B7~  /reB5.B7~  {goto}A1~
132      {calc}     {calc}
133      {menubranch{menubranch MENU1}
134
135
```

Figure 10-31
Part 2

```
Macro Mult-Menu            Macro for illustrating the use
                           of multiple tiered menus


MULT    {menubranch MENU1}

MENU1   Principal          Int-Rate           Time               Schedule           End
        Loan amount        Interest rate      Loan period        Print-sched        Quit process
        {branch PRINCIPAL} {branch INT-RATE}  {branch TIME}      {branch SCHEDULE}  {branch END}


        Principal          Int-Rate           Time               Schedule           End

        /wgrm              /wgrm              /wgrm              {calc}             /reB5.B7~
        {goto}B5~          {goto}B6~          {goto}B7~         {menubranch MENU2} {calc}
        {?}~               {?}~               {?}~                                  {goto}A1~
        {goto}A1~          {goto}A1~          {goto}A1~
        {menubranch MENU1} {menubranch MENU1} {menubranch MENU1}




MENU2   Print-1            5-Print            Stop
        1 year sched       5 year sched       Quit process
        {branch PRINT-1}   {branch 5-PRINT}   {branch STOP}



        Print-1            5-print            Stop

        /pprA1.G29~        /pprA1.G77~        /reB5.B7~
        agppq              agppq              {calc}
        /reB5.B7~          /reB5.B7~          {goto}A1~
        {calc}             {calc}
        {menubranch MENU1} {menubranch MENU1}
```

Figure 10-31
Part 3

To complete this exercise, retrieve the file AMORT. After placing the title and
macro name on your worksheet, your screen should look like Figure 10-32.

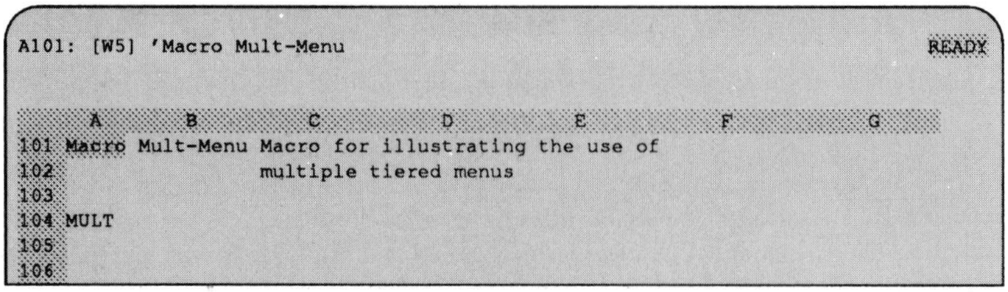

```
A101: [W5] 'Macro Mult-Menu                                    READY

      A        B         C         D         E         F        G
101 Macro Mult-Menu Macro for illustrating the use of
102                 multiple tiered menus
103
104 MULT
105
106
```

Figure 10-32

When you execute a user-designed menu macro, you must include a
{menubranch} command to indicate to 1-2-3 on which menu you want to start.

To include this command on the macro worksheet:

Move	the cell pointer to cell B104
Enter	{menubranch MENU1}

To place the MENU1 label in your macro:

Move	the cell pointer to cell A106
Enter	MENU1

To include the MENU1 menu options in your macro:

Move	the cell pointer to cell B106
Enter	Principal
Move	the cell pointer to cell C106
Enter	Int-Rate
Move	the cell pointer to cell D106
Enter	Time
Move	the cell pointer to cell E106
Enter	Schedule
Move	the cell pointer to cell F106
Enter	End

At this point, you have placed the menu options for MENU1 on the macro
worksheet. You now need to create the range name MENU1 and include the
location of the first menu option, B106, as its range.

To place the description for each menu option that will appear in the control panel when the menu option is highlighted by the menu pointer:

Move	the cell pointer to cell B107
Enter	Loan amount
Move	the cell pointer to cell C107
Enter	Interest rate
Move	the cell pointer to cell D107
Enter	Loan period
Move	the cell pointer to cell E107
Enter	Print-sched
Move	the cell pointer to cell F107
Enter	Quit process

In the single-tier menu example, you placed the macro instructions for each option immediately below the description of the menu option. For this exercise, you place the instructions several cells below the macro options to illustrate another approach for entering them.

To start the process for placing the instructions for the macro options:

Copy	the menu options in cells B106..F106 to cells B110..F110

You now need to define the range names for Principal, Int-Rate, Time, Schedule and End. Include the individual cell B112 through F112, respectively, as the range for each of the menu option range names. For example, the range name Principal should have cell B112 as its range and End should have F112 as its range.

Here you need to enter the instructions for the various menu options below the menu option identifiers that appear in row 110. The instructions for the Principal menu option must specify that the manual calculation mode is to be used, the cell pointer needs to be moved to cell B5 for the user to enter the principal amount B5, the macro must pause for the user to enter the principal value and control is to be transferred to MENU1 after the principal amount is entered.

To place the appropriate instructions on your macro worksheet:

Move	the cell pointer to cell B112

Enter	'/wgrm
Move	the cell pointer to cell B113
Enter	{goto}B5~
Move	the cell pointer to cell B114
Enter	{?}~
Move	the cell pointer to cell B115
Enter	{goto}A1~
Move	the cell pointer to cell B116
Enter	{menubranch MENU1}

The macro instructions for the Int-Rate and Time menu options are exactly the same as for the Principal menu option except for the cell in which the appropriate data is to be entered.

To place the instructions for the Int-Rate menu option on your macro worksheet:

Move	the cell pointer to cell C112
Enter	'/wgrm
Move	the cell pointer to cell C113
Enter	{goto}B6~
Move	the cell pointer to cell C114
Enter	{?}~
Move	the cell pointer to cell C115
Enter	{goto}A1~
Move	the cell pointer to cell C116
Enter	{menubranch MENU1}

To include the instructions for the Time menu option in your macro:

Move	the cell pointer to cell D112
Enter	'/wgrm
Move	the cell pointer to cell D113

Enter	{goto}B7~
Move	the cell pointer to cell D114
Enter	{?}~
Move	the cell pointer to cell D115
Enter	{goto}A1~
Move	the cell pointer to cell D116
Enter	{menubranch MENU1}

For the Schedule menu option you need instructions for calculating the loan amortization schedule and transferring control to the menu for printing the schedule.

To place these instructions on your macro worksheet:

Move	the cell pointer to cell E112
Enter	{calc}
Move	the cell pointer to cell E113
Enter	{menubranch MENU2}

The final menu option for MENU1 to consider is END. For this menu option, you must enter instructions for erasing the principal, interest rate and time period values, removing the CALC indicator from the screen, moving the cell pointer to cell A1 and stopping the execution of the macro. To incorporate these instructions on your macro worksheet:

Move	the cell pointer to cell F112
Enter	'/reB5.B7~
Move	the cell pointer to cell F113
Enter	{calc}
Move	the cell pointer to cell F114
Enter	{goto}A1~

Now you need to place {branch} commands in the cells immediately below the descriptions for the menu options so control will be transferred to the appropriate macro instructions for the various menu options.

To place these branch commands in the proper cells:

Move	the cell pointer to cell B108
Enter	{branch PRINCIPAL}
Move	the cell pointer to cell C108
Enter	{branch INT-RATE}
Move	the cell pointer to cell D108
Enter	{branch TIME}
Move	the cell pointer to cell E108
Enter	{branch SCHEDULE}
Move	the cell pointer to cell F108
Enter	{branch END}

Execution is transferred to MENU2 when you select the Schedule menu option on MENU1. The Print-1 and 5-Print menu options on MENU2 provide you with the ability to print a 1 year or 5 year amortization schedule.

You are now ready to place the macro instructions for MENU2 on your macro worksheet. Use the information in Figure 10-33 to enter the macro instructions for MENU2.

```
Macro Mult-Menu              Macro for illustrating the use
                             of multiple tiered menus

MULT   {menubranch MENU1}

MENU1  Principal             Int-Rate            Time               Schedule            End
       Loan amount           Interest rate       Loan period        Print-sched         Quit process
       {branch PRINCIPAL}    {branch INT-RATE}   {branch TIME}      {branch SCHEDULE}   {branch END}

       Principal             Int-Rate            Time               Schedule            End

       /wgrm                 /wgrm               /wgrm              {calc}              /reB5.B7~
       {goto}B5~             {goto}B6~           {goto}B7~          {menubranch MENU2}  {calc}
       {?}~                  {?}~                {?}~                                   {goto}A1~
       {goto}A1~             {goto}A1~           {goto}A1~
       {menubranch MENU1}    {menubranch MENU1}  {menubranch MENU1}




MENU2  Print-1               5-Print             Stop
       1 year sched          5 year sched        Quit process
       {branch PRINT-1}      {branch 5-PRINT}    {branch STOP}



       Print-1               5-print             Stop

       /pprA1.G29~           /pprA1.G77~         /reB5.B7~
       agppq                 agppq               {calc}
       /reB5.B7~             /reB5.B7~           {goto}A1~
       {calc}                {calc}
       {menubranch MENU1}    {menubranch MENU1}
```

Figure 10-33

After you have entered the information, be sure and create range names as follows:

Range Name	Cell to Include in the Range
MENU2	B121
PRINT-1	B129
5-PRINT	C129
STOP	D129

After you have compared the multi-tiered menu you designed with Figure 10-33, make any necessary changes. Name your macro MULT. Include the cell B104 as the range for the macro range name, MULT, and save the worksheet using the file name MULTIMAC.

Move the cell pointer to cell B5 and erase the cells B5 through B7. The ERR indicator will appear in some of the worksheet cells. When you execute the macro MULT, the ERR indicator will disappear from the cells. Execute the macro MULT. Figure 10-34 Part 1 includes the menu when it initially appears on the screen.

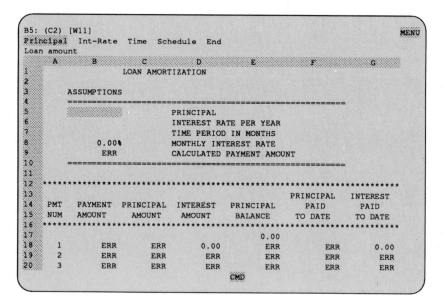

Figure 10-34
Part 1

To illustrate the use of the macro:

Select   Principal

Enter	50000
Select	Int-Rate
Enter	.10
Select	Time
Enter	12

To print the resulting amortization schedule:

Select	Schedule

Figure 10-34 Part 2 illustrates the screen after the Schedule option is selected.

```
A1: [W5]                                                                    MENU
Print-1  5-Print  Stop
1 year sched
       A       B          C          D          E          F          G
1                    LOAN AMORTIZATION
2
3      ASSUMPTIONS
4      ===================================================================
5      $50,000.00              PRINCIPAL
6         10.00%               INTEREST RATE PER YEAR
7            12                TIME PERIOD IN MONTHS
8          0.83%               MONTHLY INTEREST RATE
9       4,395.79               CALCULATED PAYMENT AMOUNT
10     ===================================================================
11
12     *************************************************************************
13                                                    PRINCIPAL    INTEREST
14     PMT     PAYMENT   PRINCIPAL   INTEREST  PRINCIPAL    PAID        PAID
15     NUM     AMOUNT     AMOUNT      AMOUNT    BALANCE    TO DATE     TO DATE
16     *************************************************************************
17                                            50,000.00
18      1     4,395.79   3,979.13    416.67   46,020.87   3,979.13     416.67
19      2     4,395.79   4,012.29    383.51   42,008.59   7,991.41     800.17
20      3     4,395.79   4,045.72    350.07   37,962.86  12,037.14   1,150.25
                                              CMD
```

Figure 10-34
Part 2

Select	Print-1

After the schedule is printed:

Select	End

Your screen should look like Figure 10-34 Part 3.

```
A1: [W5]                                                              READY

      A        B          C           D            E          F          G
 1                       LOAN AMORTIZATION
 2
 3           ASSUMPTIONS
 4           ================================================================
 5                                 PRINCIPAL
 6                                 INTEREST RATE PER YEAR
 7                                 TIME PERIOD IN MONTHS
 8           0.00%                 MONTHLY INTEREST RATE
 9           ERR                   CALCULATED PAYMENT AMOUNT
10           ================================================================
11
12    ****************************************************************************
13                                                    PRINCIPAL    INTEREST
14    PMT     PAYMENT    PRINCIPAL   INTEREST    PRINCIPAL   PAID       PAID
15    NUM     AMOUNT     AMOUNT      AMOUNT      BALANCE     TO DATE    TO DATE
16    ****************************************************************************
17                                               0.00
18    1       ERR        ERR         0.00        ERR         ERR        0.00
19    2       ERR        ERR         ERR         ERR         ERR        ERR
20    3       ERR        ERR         ERR         ERR         ERR        ERR
                                    UNDO
```

Figure 10-34
Part 3

■USING THE MACRO LIBRARY MANAGER

In some situations you may need to use the same macro on several worksheets. A macro that prints an entire worksheet is an example of such a macro. Rather than place the same macro on every worksheet, you can use the Macro Library Manager add-in capability available in Lotus 1-2-3. You create the macro for printing once and then save it on the Macro Library Manager. Whenever you need to use the macro for printing, you can use the Macro Library Manager to execute the macro.

In this section, you will first learn some basic terms about using an add-in with 1-2-3. Then you will create a macro for printing an entire worksheet and save it on the macro library manager. Finally, you will use the macro to print a worksheet.

There are some basic terms you need to learn regarding the use of the Macro Library Manager add-in. Attaching Macro Library means loading an add-in into the memory of your computer. Invoking the Macro Library Manager activates the use of the Macro Library Manager. Detaching relates to deleting the Macro Library Manager from your computer's memory.

Creating a Macro to Place in the Macro Library Manager

Suppose you need to create a macro that will print an entire worksheet that can be used with any worksheet you have prepared.

Before creating the print macro, make sure you have a blank worksheet on your screen. Enter the macro appearing in Figure 10-35 on your worksheet.

```
B3: '/wtc                                                               READY


             A           B           C          D          E          F          G
1    MACRO PRINT_SHEET        Macro for printing any worksheet
2
3    PRINT_SHEET   /wtc                            Clear any titles settings
4                  /ppcr                           Clear any print ranges
5                  r{home}.{end}{home}~            Specify print range
6                  agppq                           Print the worksheet
7                  {home}                          Move cell pointer to cell A1
8
```

Figure 10-35

Name the macro PRINT_SHEET and include cell B3 as its range. The first instruction clears any titles settings that you may have specified using the Worksheet Titles command sequence. The second macro instruction clears any previously set print ranges. The third macro command specifies the range of cells beginning with cell A1 and ending with the last cell in the worksheet. The fourth macro command instructs 1-2-3 to print the worksheet. The final macro instruction moves the cell pointer to cell A1.

Save the macro on a file using the name PRINT. Test the macro by running PRINT_SHEET and make any necessary corrections.

Attaching and Invoking the Macro Library Manager

To attach the Macro Library Manager (load it into your personal computer's memory):

Press   /

Select   Add-in

Select   Attach

To indicate you want to invoke the Macro Library Manager:

Select   MACROMAGR.ADN

To specify the key you want to use to invoke the Macro Library Manager:

Select   8

Note that you could have selected any of the numbers or No-Key.

The Macro Library Manager is loaded into the memory of your computer and the add-in menu again appears on your screen.

You can activate the use of the Macro Library Manager by invoking the add-in. To activate the Macro Library Manager, you can either select Invoke from the add-in menu or hold down the (Alt) key and then press the number of the key you designated as the key to invoke the use of the add-in. If you did not specify a key for invoking the add-in, you must use the Add-in Invoke command sequence.

To activate the use of the Macro Library Manager for this situation:

Select   Invoke

A list of available add-ins appears in the control panel. To specify that you want to use the Macro Library Manager:

Select   MACROMGR

The Macro Library Manager menu appears again and your screen should look like Figure 10-36.

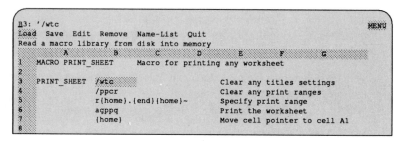

```
B3: '/wtc                                                              MENU
Load  Save  Edit  Remove  Name-List  Quit
Read a macro library from disk into memory
       A          B           C          D        E        F        G
1   MACRO PRINT_SHEET       Macro for printing any worksheet
2
3   PRINT_SHEET    /wtc                         Clear any titles settings
4                  /ppcr                        Clear any print ranges
5                  r{home}.{end}{home}~         Specify print range
6                  agppq                        Print the worksheet
7                  {home}                       Move cell pointer to cell A1
8
```

Figure 10-36

Placing a Macro in a Macro Library

To enter the print macro into a library:

Select   Save

When prompted for the name of the macro library to save:

Enter   PRTSHEET

To specify the range of cells containing the macro:

Move   the cell pointer to cell A1

Anchor   cell A1 and highlight cells A1..E7

Press   ⏎

To indicate you do not want to use a password to lock the library:

Select   No

The macro is now saved in a library named PRTSHEET. Notice the macro instructions no longer appear on your screen, as illustrated in Figure 10-37.

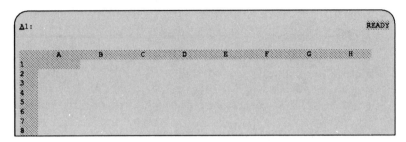

Figure 10-37

Using a Macro in a Macro Library

Suppose you want to print the file ABCSAL that you created in Chapter 7. Retrieve the file ABCSAL.

To print the ABCSAL worksheet using the macro that is in the macro library:

Press   (Alt-F3)

Select   PRINT_SHEET

The Macro Library Manager executes the macro in the library as though it was in the ABCSAL worksheet.

Detaching the Macro Library Manager

To delete the Macro Library Manager from your computer's memory:

Press   /

Select   Add-in

Select   Detach

To indicate you want to detach the Macro Library Manager add-in:

Select   MACROMGR

To exit the add-in menu:

Select   Quit

There are a number of specific rules related to using the Macro Library Manager. See the Lotus 1-2-3 reference manual for additional information.

■ /X COMMANDS

The /x commands were included in Lotus 1-2-3 Release 1A. These commands provided users with some programming ability. In Lotus 1-2-3 Release 2.2 there are equivalent commands available that are easier to understand. The /x commands are available in later releases of 1-2-3 to maintain compatibility with macros developed using Lotus 1-2-3 Release 1A.

/xg	goto programming command
/xm	menu processing command
/xi	if-then programming command
/xn	message command to prompt user to input a number
/xl	message command to prompt user to input a label
/xc	subroutine call command
/xr	return to macro from subroutine command
/xq	quit programming command

/xg

The /xg command transfers control to a specific cell in a macro sequence. Execution then continues at the specified location.

The /xg command has the following format:

```
/xg location~
```

The equivalent advanced macro command in later versions of 1-2-3 is {branch}.

/xm

The /xm command is used to direct control to a user-designed menu in a specified location.

The /xm command has the following format:

```
/xm location~
```

The equivalent advanced macro command in later versions of Lotus 1-2-3 is {menubranch}.

/xi

The /xi command is used to execute different steps in a macro depending on a specified condition.

The /xi command has the following format:

```
/xi condition~
```

If the condition is true, the macro commands to the right of the condition are executed. If the condition is false, the macro cell in the row immediately below the /xi command is executed. The equivalent advanced macro command in later versions of 1-2-3 is {if}.

/xn

The /xn command is used to prompt an individual to enter a number that will be placed in the cell specified by the location. The prompt appears at the top of the screen.

The /xn command has the following format:

```
/xn message~location~
```

The equivalent advanced macro command in later versions of 1-2-3 is {getnumber}.

/xl

The /xl command is similar to the /xn command, except a person is prompted to enter a string of characters. The characters are placed in the cell specified by the location. A maximum of 39 characters can be included in the message.

The /xl command has the following format:

```
/xl message~location~
```

The equivalent advanced macro command in later versions of Lotus 1-2-3 is {getlabel}.

/xc

The /xc command directs control to location where a subroutine appears. A subroutine is a set of macro steps located outside of the main macro. Subroutines are often used when a specific condition is satisfied within a macro. The /xc command is used within the main macro to indicate where the subroutine appears on the spreadsheet.

The /xc command has the following format:

```
/xc location~
```

The equivalent advanced macro command in later versions of 1-2-3 is {subroutine}.

/xr

The /xr command is used in conjunction with the /xc command. The /xr command is used to indicate that a subroutine operation has been completed and it is time to return to the main macro. When an /xr command is encountered in a subroutine, control is transferred to the macro cell immediately following the /xc command that called the subroutine. Execution of the main macro then continues.

The equivalent advanced macro command in later versions of Lotus 1-2-3 is {return}.

The /xr command has the following format:

```
/xr
```

/xq

The /xq command stops the execution of the macro.

The /xq command has the following format:

```
/xq
```

The equivalent advanced macro command in later versions is {quit}.

Another way to stop a macro is by holding the Ctrl key down and then pressing the Break key.

SUMMARY

Macros provide an efficient way of automating repetitive procedures. They can be used for operations such as combining files, printing a spreadsheet, completing a data query, sorting data and restricting input to specific cells. Advanced macro commands can be used to enter sequences of numbers, to execute a loop of instructions, to prompt users to enter labels and numeric data, to create subroutines and to develop user-designed menus. Macros provide users of Lotus 1-2-3 with immense flexibility in developing various applications.

KEY CONCEPTS

Advanced macro commands
Debugging a macro
Looping through a sequence
   of macro commands
Macro
Macro symbols

Multiple-tiered menus
Single-tiered menus
Subroutines
User-designed menus
/X Commands

CHAPTER TEN
EXERCISE 1

INSTRUCTIONS: Circle T if the statement is true and F is the statement is false.

T   F   1.   You cannot use macros to place a sequence of values on a worksheet.

T   F   2.   A macro can be automatically executed when a file is retrieved by naming the macro ZERO.

T   F   3.   A series of macro instructions can be repeated only if you know how many times the instructions need to be repeated.

T   F   4.   A maximum of 10 menu options can be included in any user-designed menu.

T   F   5.   The /X commands have equivalent macro commands available in later releases of Lotus 1-2-3 that are easier to understand.

T   F   6.   Macros can be used to restrict the input by a user of a worksheet to a specific set of cells.

T   F   7.   The only way to use an interactive macro is if you force the macro to execute when the file containing the macro is retrieved.

T   F   8.   Macros can be written that prompt a person to input information.

CHAPTER TEN
EXERCISE 2
Creating a Macro to Query a Database Table

INSTRUCTIONS: Retrieve the file PERSON you created as an exercise in Chapter 7.

Write a macro that extracts the last names and first names for the individuals living in New York or San Antonio with the last name Adams. Include a print macro that prints the database table and the extracted records. The macros should be properly documented.

Print the worksheet containing the database table and extracted records. Also, print the macros you created.

CHAPTER TEN
EXERCISE 3
Creating a Macro for Entering Numbers

INSTRUCTIONS: Make sure you have a blank worksheet on your screen.

Create a macro that permits you to enter numbers across a row of a worksheet so that you do not have to move to the next cell after you press the ⏎ key. Document the macro properly.

Enter the numbers 100, 25, 125, 200 in cells B10 through E10 using the macro.

Print the worksheet containing the numbers you input. Also, print the macro for entering the numbers.

CHAPTER TEN
EXERCISE 4
Executing a Loop of Instructions When the Number of Iterations is Known

INSTRUCTIONS: Make sure you have a blank worksheet on your screen.

Enter the following data on a worksheet.

Cell	Value
A1	10
B1	15
C1	5
A2	15
B2	20
C2	25
A3	30
B3	20
C3	10
A4	5
B4	15
C4	25
A5	15
B5	25
C5	10

Create a macro that for each row computes the sum of the cells in column A and column B and then multiplies the sum by the value in column C. Place the result in column D of each row. You can assume that you know that you need to repeat the calculation procedure five times.

Prepare a macro that prints the worksheet with the final results. Document the macros properly.

Print the worksheet containing the values you entered and the resulting computations. Also, print the macros.

CHAPTER TEN
EXERCISE 5
Executing a Loop of Instructions When the Number
of Iterations is Unknown

INSTRUCTIONS: Make sure you have a blank worksheet on your screen.

Enter the following data on a worksheet.

Cell	Value
A1	20
B1	25
C1	15
A2	25
B2	30
C2	35
A3	40
B3	30
C3	20
A4	15
B4	25
C4	35
A5	25
B5	35
C5	20

Create a macro that for each row subtracts the value in column B from the value in column A and then divides the difference by the value in column C. Place the results in column D of each row. Assume that you do not know the number of times you need to repeat the calculation procedure.

Prepare a macro that prints the worksheet with the final results. Document the macros properly.

Print the worksheet containing the values you entered and the resulting computations. Also, print the macros.

CHAPTER TEN
EXERCISE 6
Prompting a User to Enter Labels and Numeric Data

INSTRUCTIONS: Create an application of your own for prompting a user to enter labels and numeric data.

Print the worksheet containing the application you prepare and the macro you create. Document the macro properly.

CHAPTER TEN
EXERCISE 7
Creating a Single-Tier Menu

INSTRUCTIONS: Create an application of your own for using a single-tier menu.

Print the worksheet containing the application you prepare and the single-tier menu macro you create. Document the macro properly.

CHAPTER TEN
EXERCISE 8
Creating a Two-Tier Menu

INSTRUCTIONS: Create an application of your own for using a two-tier menu.

Print the worksheet containing the application you prepare and the two-tier menu macro you create. Document the macro properly.

CHAPTER TEN
EXERCISE 9
Creating a Three-Tier Menu

INSTRUCTIONS: Create an application of your own for using a three-tier menu.

Print the worksheet containing the application you prepare and the three-tier menu macro you create. Document the macro properly.

CHAPTER TEN
EXERCISE 10
Creating a Macro Library

INSTRUCTION: Create an application of your own for using a Macro Library.

Print the macro you create.

CHAPTER ELEVEN

IMPROVING THE APPEARANCE OF 1-2-3 DOCUMENTS USING ALLWAYS, THE SPREADSHEET PUBLISHER

OBJECTIVES

In this chapter, you will learn to:

- Understand basic terms related to publishing improved looking 1-2-3 documents
- Use Allways to improve the appearance of a worksheet
- Use Allways to improve the appearance of a graph

■CHAPTER OVERVIEW

In the previous chapters, you have used standard printing processes available in 1-2-3. Prior releases of 1-2-3 did not have the ability to prepare presentation quality documents. Lotus 1-2-3 Release 2.2 has the Allways spreadsheet publishing software included in the software as an add-in. This add-in product allows you to format and print presentation quality documents.

■INTRODUCTION TO ALLWAYS

Allways can be used only if you are using a personal computer that has at least 512 RAM memory and a hard disk. By using Allways, you can:

Include a maximum of eight fonts on any printed document
Bold text and numbers
Place double underlines on a worksheet
Add various degrees of shading to areas on a worksheet
Draw horizontal and vertical lines
Modify row height and column width
Place a box around one cell or outline a range of cells
Print a graph on the same printout with a worksheet
Print color documents when a color printer is available

With these capabilities you can enhance your reports and presentations with improved quality documents. Note that you should only use Allways if you have a printer that will allow you to select and print the various features allowed in Allways.

■SOME BASIC TERMS AND CONCEPTS

There are some basic terms and concepts that will be used in this chapter that you need to learn. Attaching Allways means loading Allways into the memory of your computer. Invoking Allways activates the use of Allways. Detaching relates to deleting Allways from your computer's memory.

There are several type styles that you can use. Typeface refers to the design of the characters on a printed document. Font is used to indicate a specific typeface with a particular size. A font set is a collection of fonts you select for a particular printout.

By using Allways you can change the format of a cell dramatically. Some of the additional format options available include changing the font and typeface, bolding characters, specifying colors for numbers and text, placing solid lines on the edges of a cell, placing double underlines on a cell and including various degrees of shading. When you use Allways, you can also modify the column width and row height.

■INVOKING ALLWAYS

In this section you will first attach and invoke Allways. Then you will examine the appearance of the Allways screen. Before attaching allways, disable Undo using the **Worksheet Global Default Other Undo Disable** command sequence.

To attach Allways (load the software into your personal computer's memory):

Press	/
Select	Add-In
Select	Attach

To indicate you want to invoke Allways:

Select	ALLWAYS.ADN

To specify the key you want to use to invoke Allways:

Select	7

A message appears on your screen indicating that Allways is being loaded into your personal computer's memory. The add-in menu appears on your screen after Allways is attached.

You can activate the use of Allways by invoking the add-in. To activate Allways, you can either select Invoke from the add-in menu or hold the (Alt)   key and then press the number of the key you designated as the key to invoke the use of the add-in. If you did not specify a key for invoking the add-in, you must use the **Add-in Invoke** command sequence.

To activate the Allways add-in in this situation:

Select	Invoke

A list of available add-ins appears in the control panel. To specify you want to use Allways:

Select	Allways

The Allways screen now appears on your monitor. Your screen should look similar to Figure 11-1.

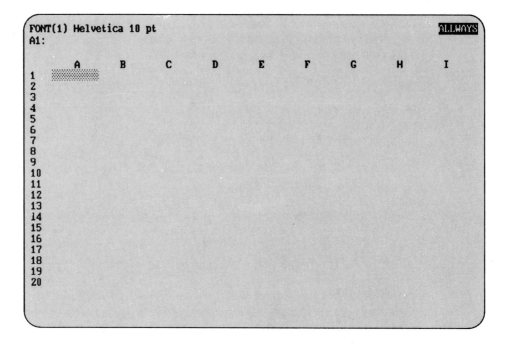

Figure 11-1

The Allways screen looks similar to the worksheet screen in 1-2-3. All of the format changes you make will be seen in the worksheet area that appears below the column letters and to the right of the row numbers. Notice the characters ALLWAYS appear in the mode indicator portion of the screen. Above the cell address position in the control panel appears the default font that is currently being used.

To exit ALLWAYS:

Press   /

Select   Quit

You returned to 1-2-3.

■USING ALLWAYS TO IMPROVE THE APPEARANCE OF A WORKSHEET

To illustrate the use of Allways, you first need to retrieve the file BUDGET from which you saved the graph BUDBAR in Chapter Four.

Suppose you want to change the appearance of the worksheet as follows:

Change the font of the worksheet titles

Bold the worksheet titles, column headings and row labels

Place solid underlines under the MISCELLANEOUS and TOTAL EXPENSES entries

Place solid double underlines below the GROSS PROFIT entries

Add shading to the column headings

Place an outline around the cells containing the assumptions

To invoke Allways:

Press   (Alt-F7)

To change the font to Times 14 point for the worksheet titles:

Move   the cell pointer to cell C1

Press   /

Select   Format

Select   Font

To indicate the appropriate typeface and size:

Move   the cell pointer to Times 14 point

Press   ⏎ to select Use

To specify the range of cells to format:

Move   the cell pointer to cell C2

Press   ⏎

Your screen should look like Figure 11-2.

```
FONT(1) Helvetica 10 pt                                        ALLWA
A1..H19:

            A         B       C       D       E       F      G       H
 1                          ABC COMPANY
 2                            BUDGET
 3
 4
 5                       QTR1    QTR2    QTR3    QTR4   YR TOTAL
 6
 7    SALES           $60,000 $61,200 $62,424 $63,672 $247,296
 8
 9    EXPENSES
10      SALARIES       35,000  35,500  36,200  37,000  143,700
11      RENT            9,000   9,000   9,000   9,000   36,000
12      TELEPHONE       1,000   1,050   1,103   1,158    4,311
13      OFFICE SUPPLIES   750     800     850     900    3,300
14      MISCELLANEOUS   1,000   1,030   1,061   1,093    4,184
15                    -------- -------- -------- -------- --------
16     TOTAL EXPENSES  46,750  47,380  48,214  49,151  191,495
17                    -------- -------- -------- -------- --------
18    GROSS PROFIT    $13,250 $13,820 $14,210 $14,521  $55,801
19                    ======= ======= ======= ======= =======
```

Figure 11-2

Notice the row height for rows 1 and 2 were automatically increased when the font size was changed.

To bold the worksheet titles:

Press   /

Select   Format

Select   Bold

To add boldface to the worksheet titles:

Select   Set

Move   the cell pointer to cell C2

Press   ⏎

Your screen should look like Figure 11-3.

```
FONT(1) Helvetica 10 pt                                              ALLWA
A1..H19:

              A         B        C        D        E        F        G        H
 1                              ABC COMPANY
 2                                BUDGET
 3
 4
 5                            QTR1     QTR2     QTR3     QTR4   YR TOTAL
 6
 7    SALES              $60,000  $61,200  $62,424  $63,672  $247,296
 8
 9    EXPENSES
10      SALARIES          35,000   35,500   36,200   37,000   143,700
11      RENT               9,000    9,000    9,000    9,000    36,000
12      TELEPHONE          1,000    1,050    1,103    1,158     4,311
13      OFFICE SUPPLIES      750      800      850      900     3,300
14      MISCELLANEOUS      1,000    1,030    1,061    1,093     4,184
15                       --------  --------  --------  --------  --------
16       TOTAL EXPENSES   46,750   47,380   48,214   49,151   191,495
17                       --------  --------  --------  --------  --------
18    GROSS PROFIT       $13,250  $13,820  $14,210  $14,521   $55,801
19                       ========  ========  ========  ========  ========
```

Figure 11-3

To bold the column headings:

Move	the cell pointer to cell B5
Press	/
Select	Format
Select	Bold
Select	Set
Move	the cell pointer to cell F5
Press	↵

Repeat the Format Bold Set command sequence to boldface the row labels in cells A7 through A32. After placing the cell pointer in cell A1, your screen should look like Figure 11-4.

```
FONT(1) Helvetica 10 pt                                          ALLWAYS
A1:

               A         B        C        D        E        F       G        H

1         ▓▓▓▓▓▓▓▓▓▓▓▓        ABC COMPANY
2                                 BUDGET
3
4
5                        QTR1     QTR2     QTR3     QTR4    YR TOTAL
6
7    SALES             $60,000  $61,200  $62,424  $63,672  $247,296
8
9    EXPENSES
10     SALARIES         35,000   35,500   36,200   37,000   143,700
11     RENT              9,000    9,000    9,000    9,000    36,000
12     TELEPHONE         1,000    1,050    1,103    1,158     4,311
13     OFFICE SUPPLIES     750      800      850      900     3,300
14     MISCELLANEOUS     1,000    1,030    1,061    1,093     4,184
15                     -------- -------- -------- -------- --------
16     TOTAL EXPENSES   46,750   47,380   48,214   49,151   191,495
17                     -------- -------- -------- -------- --------
18   GROSS PROFIT      $13,250  $13,820  $14,210  $14,521   $55,801
19                     ======== ======== ======== ======== ========      -
```

Figure 11-4

To place a solid underline under the MISCELLANEOUS expenses:

Move	the cell pointer to cell B14
Press	/
Select	Format
Select	Underline

To specify a single underline is to be used:

Select	Single

To indicate the range of cells to underline:

Move	the cell pointer to cell F14
Press	⏎

Your screen should look like Figure 11-5.

```
FONT(1) Helvetica 10 pt Underline                               ALLWAYS
B14: 1000

               A        B        C        D        E        F      G      H
   1                          ABC COMPANY
   2                            BUDGET
   3
   4
   5                        QTR1     QTR2     QTR3     QTR4    YR TOTAL
   6
   7     SALES           $60,000  $61,200  $62,424  $63,672  $247,296
   8
   9     EXPENSES
  10     SALARIES         35,000   35,500   36,200   37,000   143,700
  11     RENT              9,000    9,000    9,000    9,000    36,000
  12     TELEPHONE         1,000    1,050    1,103    1,158     4,311
  13     OFFICE SUPPLIES     750      800      850      900     3,300
  14     MISCELLANEOUS     1,000    1,030    1,061    1,093     4,184
  15                     --------  -------- -------- -------- --------
  16     TOTAL EXPENSES   46,750   47,380   48,214   49,151   191,495
  17                     --------  -------- -------- -------- --------
  18     GROSS PROFIT    $13,250  $13,820  $14,210  $14,521  $55,801
  19                     ========  ======== ======== ======== ========        -
```

Figure 11-5

To remove the previously specified sets of underlines and double underlines, you must first return to 1-2-3.

| **Press** | / |
| **Select** | Quit |

Notice the worksheet has returned to the standard appearance.

To remove the undesirable single underlines and double underline entries:

| **Delete** | rows containing single and double lines |

To activate Allways:

| **Press** | Alt-F7 |

The underlines you entered earlier appear on the screen again.

To place the remaining single underlines below the TOTAL EXPENSES entries:

| **Move** | the cell pointer to cell B15 |
| **Press** | / |

Select	Format
Select	Underline
Select	Single
Move	the cell pointer to cell F15
Press	⏎

To include a double underline below the GROSS PROFIT entries:

Move	the cell pointer to cell B16
Press	/
Select	Format
Select	Underline

To specify you want a double underline:

Select	Double

To indicate the range of double underlines:

Move	the cell pointer to cell F16
Press	⏎

Your screen should look like Figure 11-6.

```
FONT(1) Helvetica 10 pt Dbl-Underline                          ALLWAYS
B16: +B7-B15

           A         B         C         D         E         F      G      H
 1                             ABC COMPANY
 2                               BUDGET
 3
 4
 5                   QTR1      QTR2      QTR3      QTR4    YR TOTAL
 6
 7     SALES        $60,000   $61,200   $62,424   $63,672  $247,296
 8
 9     EXPENSES
10       SALARIES    35,000    35,500    36,200    37,000   143,700
11       RENT         9,000     9,000     9,000     9,000    36,000
12       TELEPHONE    1,000     1,050     1,103     1,158     4,311
13       OFFICE SUPPLIES 750     800       850       900     3,300
14       MISCELLANEOUS 1,000    1,030     1,061     1,093     4,184
15       TOTAL EXPENSES 46,750  47,380    48,214    49,151   191,495
16     GROSS PROFIT  $13,250   $13,820   $14,210   $14,521   $55,801
17
18
19     GROWTH RATE
```

Figure 11-6

To place a light shading on the cells containing the column headings:

Move	the cell pointer to cell B5
Press	/
Select	Format
Select	Shade

To indicate the use of a light shading:

Select	Light

To specify the range of cells for light shading:

Move	the cell pointer to cell F5
Press	⏎

Your screen should look like Figure 11-7.

```
FONT(1) Helvetica 10 pt Bold, SHADE:Light                    ALLWAYS
B5: ^QTR1
```

	A	B	C	D	E	F	G	H
1			ABC COMPANY					
2			BUDGET					
3								
4								
5		QTR1	QTR2	QTR3	QTR4	YR TOTAL		
6								
7	SALES	$60,000	$61,200	$62,424	$63,672	$247,296		
8								
9	EXPENSES							
10	SALARIES	35,000	35,500	36,200	37,000	143,700		
11	RENT	9,000	9,000	9,000	9,000	36,000		
12	TELEPHONE	1,000	1,050	1,103	1,158	4,311		
13	OFFICE SUPPLIES	750	800	850	900	3,300		
14	MISCELLANEOUS	1,000	1,030	1,061	1,093	4,184		
15	TOTAL EXPENSES	46,750	47,380	48,214	49,151	191,495		
16	GROSS PROFIT	$13,250	$13,820	$14,210	$14,521	$55,801		
17								
18								
19	GROWTH RATE							

Figure 11-7

To place an outline around the cells containing the values for the growth rate assumptions:

Move	the cell pointer to cell A22
Press	/
Select	Format
Select	Lines

To specify an outline of the cells is desired:

Select	Outline

To indicate the appropriate cells to be outlined:

Move	the cell pointer to cell E25
Press	⏎

After moving the cell pointer to cell A26, your screen should look like Figure 11-8.

```
FONT(1) Helvetica 10 pt Bold                                    ALLWAYS
A26:
```

	A	B	C	D	E	F	G	H
7	SALES	$60,000	$61,200	$62,424	$63,672	$247,296		
8								
9	EXPENSES							
10	SALARIES	35,000	35,500	36,200	37,000	143,700		
11	RENT	9,000	9,000	9,000	9,000	36,000		
12	TELEPHONE	1,000	1,050	1,103	1,158	4,311		
13	OFFICE SUPPLIES	750	800	850	900	3,300		
14	MISCELLANEOUS	1,000	1,030	1,061	1,093	4,184		
15	TOTAL EXPENSES	46,750	47,380	48,214	49,151	191,495		
16	GROSS PROFIT	$13,250	$13,820	$14,210	$14,521	$55,801		
17								
18								
19	GROWTH RATE							
20	ASSUMPTIONS							
21								
22	SALES		1.02	1.02	1.02			
23	TELEPHONE		1.05	1.05	1.05			
24	OFFICE SUPPLIES		50.00	50.00	50.00			
25	MISCELLANEOUS		1.03	1.03	1.03			
26								

Figure 11-8

To print the enhanced version of the BUDGET worksheet:

Move	the cell pointer to cell A1
Press	/
Select	Print
Select	Range

To specify the range of cells to print:

Select	Set
Move	the cell pointer to cell F29
Press	⏎

To print the worksheet:

Select	Go

Your printout should look like Figure 11-9.

ABC COMPANY
BUDGET

	QTR1	QTR2	QTR3	QTR4	YR TOTAL
SALES	$60,000	$61,200	$62,424	$63,672	$247,296
EXPENSES					
SALARIES	35,000	35,500	36,200	37,000	143,700
RENT	9,000	9,000	9,000	9,000	36,000
TELEPHONE	1,000	1,050	1,103	1,158	4,311
OFFICE SUPPLIES	750	800	850	900	3,300
MISCELLANEOUS	1,000	1,030	1,061	1,093	4,184
TOTAL EXPENSE	46,750	47,380	48,214	49,151	191,495
GROSS PROFIT	$13,250	$13,820	$14,210	$14,521	$55,801

GROWTH RATE
ASSUMPTIONS

		QTR2	QTR3	QTR4
SALES		1.02	1.02	1.02
TELEPHONE		1.05	1.05	1.05
OFFICE SUPPLIES		50.00	50.00	50.00
MISCELLANEOUS		1.03	1.03	1.03

Figure 11-9

Exit Allways and save the worksheet on a file using the name BUDGETAL. When you finish saving the file, invoke Allways again.

■USING ALLWAYS TO IMPROVE THE APPEARANCE OF A GRAPH

By using Allways you can enhance the appearance of a graph. In this section, you will improve the appearance of the BUDBAR graph you prepared in Chapter 4. It is assumed that you still have the BUDGETAL worksheet on your screen and Allways has been invoked.

Adding a Graph to a Worksheet

To add the graph BUDBAR to your worksheet:

Move	the cell pointer to cell A31
Press	/
Select	Graph
Select	Add

To specify that you want to use the BUDBAR graph from among the .PIC files available:

Select	BUDBAR

To indicate the range of cells on which to place the graph:

Type	.
Move	the cell pointer to cell F45
Press	⏎

Your screen should look like Figure 11-10. If the graph does not appear on your screen, quit from the Allways graph menu; then issue the **Display Graphs Yes Quit** command sequence. Before continuing, bring up the Allways graph menu again by selecting **Graph**.

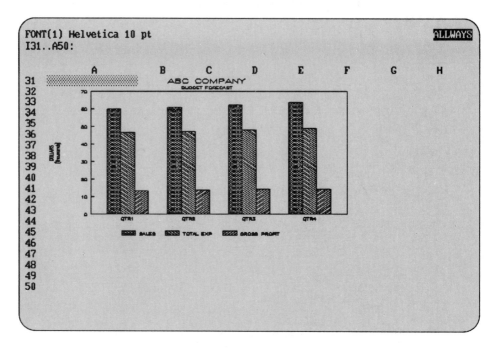

Figure 11-10

Note that Allways adjusts the size of your graph to fit in the graph range that you specified.

You can change the fonts for the first line of the graph title and the other text on the graph from the current settings to other settings. To change the fonts from the default BLOCK1 to ROMAN1:

Select   Settings

Select   Fonts

To indicate you want to change the font for the first line of the graph titles:

Select   1

To specify you want to use a ROMAN1 font:

Move   the cell pointer to ROMAN1 in the list

Press   ⏎

To use the ROMAN1 font for the remaining text characters on your graph:

Select	Fonts
Select	2
Select	ROMAN1
Press	⏎

To leave the settings menu and see your graph:

Select	Quit

The text on your graph now appears in the ROMAN1 font style.

Your screen should look like Figure 11-11.

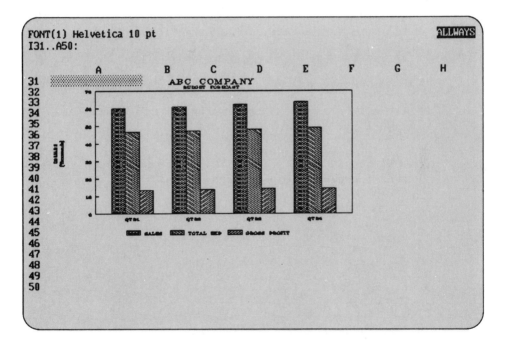

Figure 11-11

Note that the graph is superimposed on the worksheet. If desired, you can use any of the Allways format options available on any of the cells in the graph. For example, you can now bold the contents of a group of cells or place an outline on a range of cells or underline some of the information on the graph.

Suppose you want to bold the two graph title lines and place a light shading on the cells containing the title lines.

To bold the two graph title lines:

Move	the cell pointer to cell B31
Press	/
Select	Format
Select	Bold
Select	Set
Move	the cell pointer to cell D32
Press	⏎

Note that a portion of the top line of the graph frame is now bold. To make sure this segment of the graph is not bold when you print, you must change the row height of row 32.

Move	the cell pointer to cell B32

Notice that the bottom of the cell pointer includes a portion of the top line of the graph frame.

To change the row height so the portion of the graph frame is not included in the cells appearing in row 33:

Press	/
Select	Worksheet
Select	Row
Select	Set-Height

When you are prompted to enter the row height:

Type	6
Press	⏎

The default value for row height is 12 point. By specifying a smaller row height, you will not include any portion of the graph frame in the cells that will appear bold on the graph.

To place a light shading on the graph title lines:

Move	the cell pointer to cell B31
Press	/

Select	Format
Select	Shade
Select	Light
Move	the cell pointer to cell D32
Press	⏎

Your screen should look like Figure 11-12.

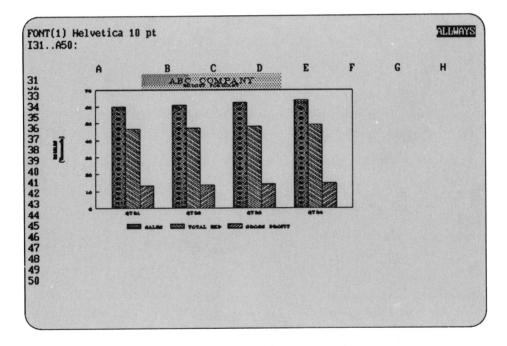

Figure 11-12

■PRINTING A WORKSHEET AND GRAPH

You can use Allways to print a worksheet and graph on the same page.

To print the worksheet and graph:

Press	/
Select	Print
Select	Range

To remove any previously set print ranges:

Select   Clear

To specify the worksheet print range:

Select   Range

Select   Set

Press   [Esc]

Move   the cell pointer to cell A1

Type   .

Move   the cell pointer to cell F45

Press   [↵]

To print the worksheet:

Select   Go

Your printout should look like Figure 11-13.

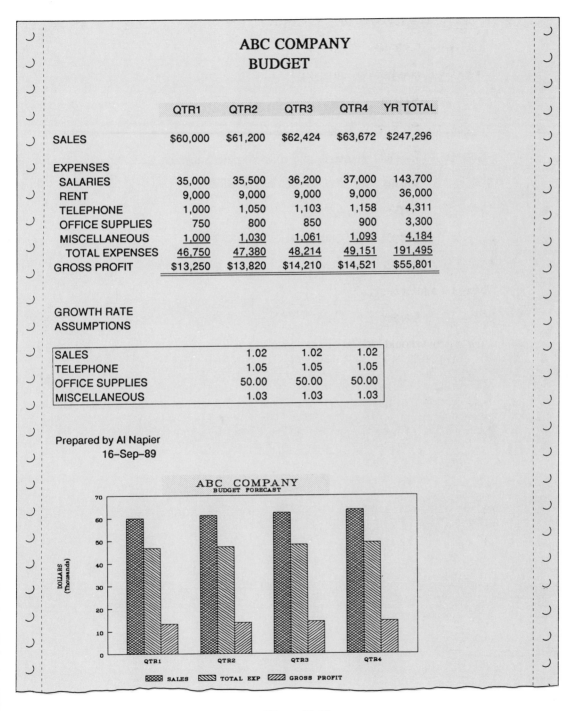

ABC COMPANY
BUDGET

	QTR1	QTR2	QTR3	QTR4	YR TOTAL
SALES	$60,000	$61,200	$62,424	$63,672	$247,296
EXPENSES					
SALARIES	35,000	35,500	36,200	37,000	143,700
RENT	9,000	9,000	9,000	9,000	36,000
TELEPHONE	1,000	1,050	1,103	1,158	4,311
OFFICE SUPPLIES	750	800	850	900	3,300
MISCELLANEOUS	1,000	1,030	1,061	1,093	4,184
TOTAL EXPENSES	46,750	47,380	48,214	49,151	191,495
GROSS PROFIT	$13,250	$13,820	$14,210	$14,521	$55,801

GROWTH RATE
ASSUMPTIONS

SALES		1.02	1.02	1.02
TELEPHONE		1.05	1.05	1.05
OFFICE SUPPLIES		50.00	50.00	50.00
MISCELLANEOUS		1.03	1.03	1.03

Prepared by Al Napier
16–Sep–89

Figure 11-13

■ EXITING AND DETACHING ALLWAYS

To exit Allways:

Press　　/

Select　　Quit

You can also exit Allways by pressing the [Esc] key.

To detach Allways and remove it from your computer's memory:

Press　　/

Select　　Add-in

Select　　Detach

Select　　Allways

To exit the add-in menu:

Select　　Quit

■ OTHER CAPABILITIES OF ALLWAYS

Allways allows you to improve the appearance of worksheets and graphs in ways other than those described in this chapter. The Lotus 1-2-3 reference manual contains additional information on using Allways.

SUMMARY

By using the Allways add-in that comes with the Lotus 1-2-3 Release 2.2 software, the format of 1-2-3 worksheets and graphs can be improved to the level of presentation quality documents. Allways can also be used to print a worksheet and graph on the same page.

KEY CONCEPTS

Add-in
Allways
Attach
Bold
Detach
Font
Invoke
Typeface
Type style

CHAPTER ELEVEN
EXERCISE 1

INSTRUCTIONS: Circle T if the statement is true and F if the statement is false.

T   F   1. By using Allways, the appearance of worksheets can be significantly improved.

T   F   2. At most 6 type styles can be used on a worksheet.

T   F   3. You cannot shade the background of a cell.

T   F   4. When the underline option is used, the underline covers the entire width of the cell.

T   F   5. You cannot use 1-2-3 without invoking Allways.

CHAPTER ELEVEN
EXERCISE 2

INSTRUCTIONS: Retrieve the file UNITPROD you created as an exercise in Chapter Two.

Change the font of the worksheet title to Times 20.

Bold the worksheet title, column headings and row labels.

Print the worksheet.

CHAPTER ELEVEN
EXERCISE 3

INSTRUCTIONS: Retrieve the file PRACTICE you created as an exercise in Chapter Two.

Change the font of the worksheet title to Times Italic 10.

Place a dark shade around the worksheet title.

Place solid underlines on the EXPENSES cell entries and the TAXES cell entries. The underlines should cover the entire bottom border of the cells.

Place solid double underlines on the PROFIT AFTER TAX cells.

Bold the column headings and row labels.

Print the worksheet.

Save the file for use in the next exercise.

CHAPTER ELEVEN
EXERCISE 4

INSTRUCTIONS: Use the file PRACTICE from the previous exercise.

Add the graph you created in Chapter Four to your worksheet.

Change the font for the graph title lines to FORUM.

Place an outline around the two graph title lines.

Print the worksheet and the graph using Allways.

CHAPTER TWELVE

SUMMARY

As mentioned in the Introduction, the design of this book is intended for individuals who need to learn the capabilities of Lotus 1-2-3. Each chapter could be lengthened to include additional 1-2-3 capabilities for the features being discussed and an endless variety of applications could be added. However, the chapters are deliberately limited to the essential, basic concepts. Stressing the basics allows you to concentrate on the main idea of each exercise without being distracted by a multitude of other issues. At the same time, the examples are comprehensive and thorough enough to provide you with the tools needed to create larger, more complex spreadsheets. The next logical step for you is to apply the skills learned in this book to your own applications.

APPENDIX A

LOTUS 1-2-3 COMMAND TREES

There are many Lotus 1-2-3 commands. The commands available in 1-2-3 are included on the command trees appearing in this appendix.

The menu below is the main menu that appears when the menu structure is entered. The pages following include the menu structure for the various menu options.

Worksheet Range Copy Move File Print Graph Data System Add-In Quit

Worksheet Commands

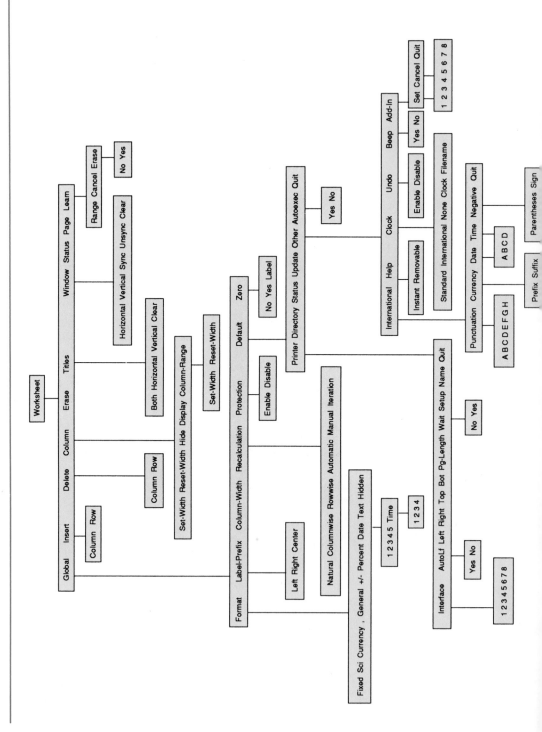

Range Commands

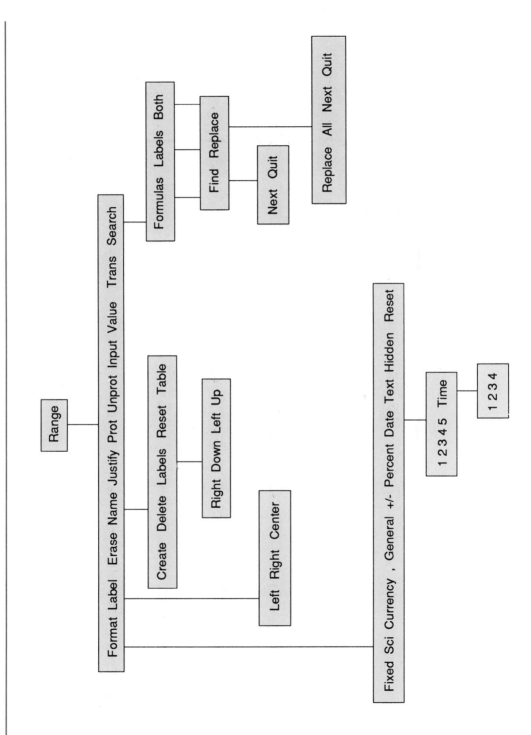

File Commands

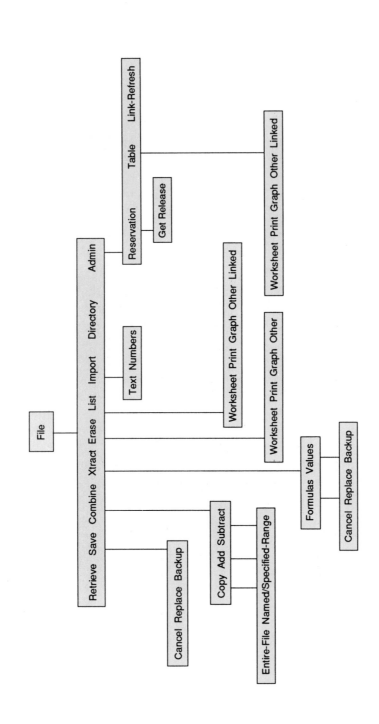

Print Commands

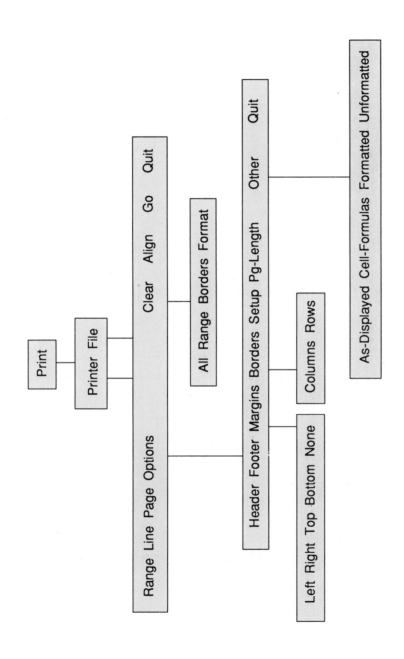

Graph Commands

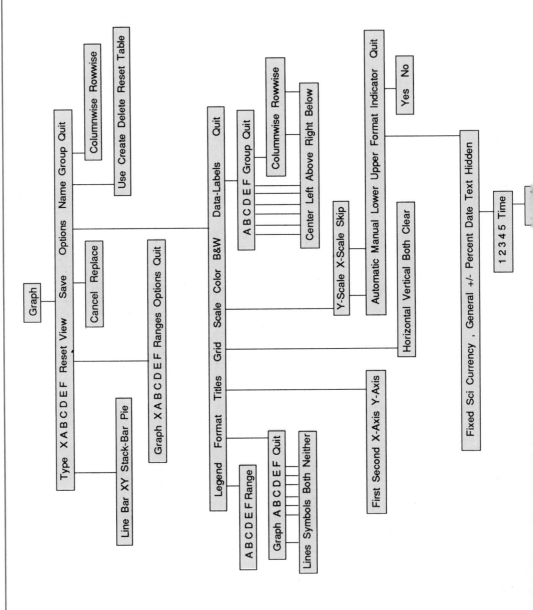

Data Commands

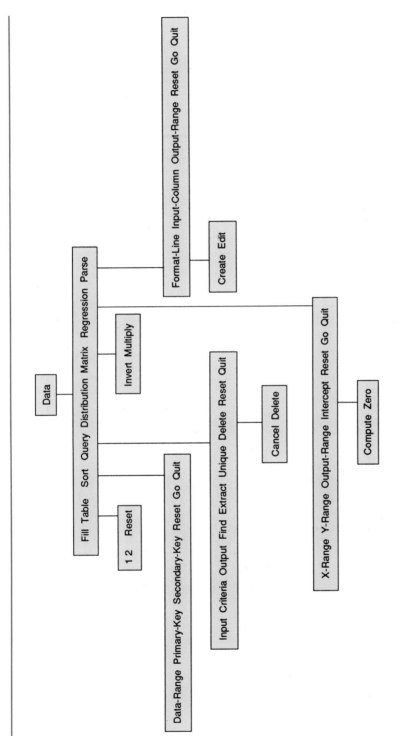

Add-In Commands

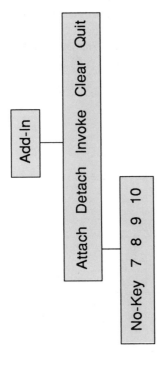

APPENDIX B

SUMMARY OF COMMANDS COVERED IN THIS BOOK

As indicated by the previous diagrams, there are many types of commands available in Lotus 1-2-3. Below is a summary of the functionality of the commands covered in this book. This summary is useful when a person knows what needs to be done but does not know what command to use. A complete list of the functionality of the 1-2-3 commands can be found in the Lotus 1-2-3 reference manual that comes with the software.

The keystrokes required for each command sequence are in bold and a description of the command sequence is included.

Data Analysis

Determine a frequency distribution for some data in a range of cells

/DD /Data Distribution

Change formulas into values

/RV /Range Value

Create graphs from data in a spreadsheet

/G /Graph

Sort data in a spreadsheet

/DS /Data Sort

Modifying the Appearance of the Spreadsheet

Change the format of a specific cell or group of cells in the spreadsheet

/RF   /Range Format

Restore the format for a range of cells to the original format

/RFR   /Range Format Reset

Change the default format for numeric values in the spreadsheet

/WGF   /Worksheet Global Format

Change the width for a specific column in the spreadsheet

/WCS   /Worksheet Column Set-Width

Return a column to its original width

/WCR   /Worksheet Column Reset-Width

Widen multiple columns

/WCCS   /Worksheet Column Column-Range Set-Width

Change the column default width

/WGC   /Worksheet Global Column-Width

Copy information from one portion of the spreadsheet to another section of the spreadsheet

/C   /Copy

Show formulas instead of numbers

/RFT   /Range Format Text

Erase a specific cell or range of cells in the spreadsheet

/RE   /Range Erase

Erase the entire spreadsheet

/WEY   /Worksheet Erase Yes

Hide a column or group of columns in the spreadsheet

/WCH   /Worksheet Column Hide

Hide a range of cells

/RFH   /Range Format Hidden

Insert a blank row or rows in a spreadsheet

/WIR   /Worksheet Insert Row

Insert a blank column or columns in a spreadsheet

/WIC   /Worksheet Insert Column

Keep row labels or column headings on the monitor

/WT   /Worksheet Titles

Move information from one section on the spreadsheet to another section on the spreadsheet

/M   /Move

To clear windows

/WWC   /Worksheet Window Clear

Modify the arrangement of text in a spreadsheet

/RJ   /Range Justify

Change the alignment of a label or group of labels

/RL   /Range Label

Display previously hidden column

/WCD   /Worksheet Column Display

Delete a row or rows from a spreadsheet

/WDR   /Worksheet Delete Row

Delete a column or columns from a spreadsheet

/WDC   /Worksheet Delete Column

Divide the spreadsheet on the screen into two parts or windows

/WW   /Worksheet Window

Suppress from view all cells that have a value of exactly 0

/WGZ   /Worksheet Global Zero

Copying Data

Copy information from one portion of the spreadsheet to another section of the spreadsheet

/C   /Copy

Change formulas into values

/RV   /Range Value

Include data from another spreadsheet file into the spreadsheet in the memory

/FC   /File Combine

Erasing Data

Delete a row or rows from a spreadsheet

/WDR   /Worksheet Delete Row

Delete a column or columns from a spreadsheet

/WDC   /Worksheet Delete Column

Erase the contents of one or more specific cells

/RE   /Range Erase

Erase the spreadsheet presently being used if no changes have been made since the last time the worksheet was saved

/WEY   /Worksheet Erase Yes

Graphing Data

Indicate the type of graph desired

/GT   /Graph Type

Specify the data to appear on the X-axis in a graph

/GX   /Graph X

Specify the data to be graphed (six variables can be graphed at a time)

/GA	/Graph **A**
/GB	/Graph **B**
/GC	/Graph **C**
/GD	/Graph **D**
/GE	/Graph **E**
/GF	/Graph **F**

Create a graph using a group

/GG	/Graph **Group**

Display the graph on the monitor screen

/GV	/Graph **View**

Indicate various graphic settings

/GO	/Graph **Options**

Specify legend labels for variables being graphed

/GOL	/Graph **Options Legend**

Specify title lines for the graph

/GOTF	/Graph **Options Titles First**
/GOTS	/Graph **Options Titles Second**

Specify labels for X-Axis and Y-Axis

/GOTX	/Graph **Options Titles X**-Axis
/GOTY	/Graph **Options Titles Y**-Axis

Place labels on data points

/GOD	/Graph **Options Data-Labels**

Place horizontal, vertical or both horizontal and vertical lines on the graph

/GOG	/Graph **Options Grid**

Name a graph

/GN	/Graph **Name**

Save a graph on a file for later printing

/GS	/Graph **Save**

Reset or cancel some or all of the graph settings

/GR   /Graph Reset

List the graph files

/FLG   /File List Graph

Hiding Data

Restrict the display of a column or columns

/WCH   /Worksheet **Column Hide**

Display a column or columns that have previously been hidden

/WCD   /Worksheet **Column Display**

Suppress from view all cells that have a value of exactly 0

/WGZ   /Worksheet **Global Zero**

Loading Data

Load a spreadsheet file into the memory of the microcomputer

/FR   /File **Retrieve**

Include data from another spreadsheet file into the spreadsheet in the memory

/FC   /File **Combine**

Moving Data

Move information from one section on the spreadsheet to another section on the spreadsheet

/M   /Move

Insert a blank row or rows in a spreadsheet

/WIR   /Worksheet **Insert Row**

Insert a blank column or columns in a spreadsheet

/WIC   /Worksheet **Insert Column**

Delete a row or rows from a spreadsheet

/WDR   /Worksheet **Delete Row**

Delete a column or columns from a spreadsheet

/WDC   /Worksheet **Delete Column**

Printing a Portion or an Entire Spreadsheet

Specify the range of data to print

/PPR   /Print Printer **Range**

Indicate top of page setting

/PPA   /Print Printer **Align**

Initiate printing

/PPG   /Print Printer **Go**

Advance printer paper to top of next page

/PPP   /Print Printer **Page**

Place spreadsheet on a text (ASCII) file

/PF   /Print File

Alter present printing settings

/PPO   /Print Printer **Options**

Put a column border on each page

/PPOBC   /Print Printer **Options Border Columns**

Place a footer at the bottom of each page

/PPOF   /Print Printer **Options Footer**

Place a header at the top of each page

/PPOH   /Print Printer **Options Header**

Specify margins for printing page

/PPOM   /Print Printer **Options Margins**

Print cell formulas instead of numeric values

/PPOOC   **/Print Printer Options Other Cell**-Formulas

Print what appears on the screen if cell formulas were previously used

/PPOOA   **/Print Printer Options Other As**-Displayed

Insert a page break

/WP   **/Worksheet Page**

Saving a Spreadsheet or Graph

Save a spreadsheet on a file

/FS   **/File Save**

Save a graph

/GS   **Graph Save**

Database Commands

Indicate input range of the database

/DQI   **/Data Query Input**

Indicate the criterion to be used

/DQC   **/Data Query Criterion**

Indicate the information to be output if the criterion is satisfied

/DQO   **/Data Query Output**

Find and highlight records in the database that satisfy the criterion

/DQF   **/Data Query Find**

Copy the data from the records that satisfy the criterion to the output range

/DQE   **/Data Query Extract**

Copy the data from the records that satisfy the criterion to the output range and eliminate duplicate data

/DQU   **/Data Query Unique**

Delete records from the database that satisfy the criterion

/DQD   /Data **Query Delete**

Enter a sequence of values, dates or times on a worksheet or multiple worksheets

/DF   /Data **Fill**

Sort records in a database

/DS   /Data **Sort**

Specify data range to be sorted

/DSD   /Data **Sort Data**-Range

Specify the primary sort key

/DSP   /Data **Sort Primary**-Key

Specify the secondary sort key

/DSS   /Data **Sort Secondary**-Key

Initiate sorting process

/DSG   /Data **Sort Go**

Reset data sort settings

/DSR   /Data **Sort Reset**

Initiate data table options

/DT   /Data **Table**

File Operations

Retrieve or load a file

/FR   /File **Retrieve**

Save a spreadsheet on a file

/FS   /File **Save**

Change the drive or path from which files are retrieved and saved

/FD   /File **Directory**

Change the default drive or path from which files are retrieved and saved

/WGDD   **/Worksheet Global Default Directory**

Save a spreadsheet in a text (ASCII) file

/PF   **/Print File**

Include data from another spreadsheet file into the spreadsheet in the memory

/FC   **/File Combine**

Create a table of file names

/FAT   **/File Admin Table**

Display names of files in current directory

/FL   **/File List**

Remove or erase a file

/FE   **/File Erase**

Save a graph for printing at a later time

/GS   **/Graph Save**

Saving a file or a graph to make a backup (BAK) file

/FSB   **/File Save Backup**

Using Named Ranges

Create a named range for a cell or group of cells

/RNC   **/Range Name Create**

Delete a named range

/RND   **/Range Name Delete**

Remove or delete all range names

/RNR   **/Range Name Reset**

Working with Numeric Values

Modify the default format of all numbers

/WGF   /Worksheet Global Format

Modify the format of a cell or group of cells

/RF   /Range Format

Check the recalculation settings

/WS   /Worksheet Status

Indicate how and when recalculation of formulas occurs

/WGR   /Worksheet Global Recalculation

Suppress from view all cells that have a value of exactly 0

/WGZ   /Worksheet Global Zero

Modify the column width when asterisks appear in a cell

/WCS   /Worksheet Column Set-Width

Associate a range name with a number or set of numbers

/RNC   /Range Name Create

Convert a cell or group of cells with a formula(s) to a value(s)

/RV   /Range Value

Determine a frequency distribution for some data in a range of cells

/DD   /Data Distribution

Protecting Cells in a Worksheet

Protecting all cells in a worksheet

/WGPE   /Worksheet Global Protection Enable

Unprotect a worksheet

/WGPD   /Worksheet Global Protection Disable

Protect a range of cells

/RP   /Range Prot

Unprotect a range of cells

/RU /Range Unprot

Add-in Commands

Load an add-in into memory

/AA /Add-in Attach

Remove an add-in from memory

/AD /Add-in Detach

Activate an attached add-in

/AI /Add-in Invoke

Remove all attached add-ins

/AC /Add-in Clear

Miscellaneous Commands

Display amount of memory available and current default settings for format, column width, cell protection, zero suppression and so on

/WS /Worksheet Status

Display current configuration for the printer, directory, margins and so on

/WGDS /Worksheet Global Default Status

Change configuration settings for the printer, directory, margins and so on

/WGD /Worksheet Global Default

Change spreadsheet settings for format, column width, recalculation, protection and so on

/WG /Worksheet Global

Indicate how and when recalculation of formulas occurs

/WGR /Worksheet Global Recalculation

Exit to the operating system

/S /System

Quit using 1-2-3

/Q   /Quit

Search and Replace

/RS   /Range Search

Turn the UNDO feature on

/WGDOUE /Worksheet **G**lobal **D**efault **O**ther **U**ndo **E**nable

UNDO a change

[Alt-F4]

Turn the UNDO feature off

/WGDOUD /Worksheet **G**lobal **D**efault **O**ther **U**ndo **D**isable

APPENDIX C

ANSWERS TO
ODD-NUMBERED EXERCISES

INSTRUCTIONS: Answer the following questions in the space provided.

1. Define the following terms:

   a. Row Numbers—the row of numbers on the left border of the worksheet screen.
   b. Column Letters—the letters that appear across the top border of the worksheet screen.
   c. Cell—the area on a worksheet that occurs at the intersection of a column and a row.
   d. Cell Pointer—rectangular item that is used to highlight a cell.
   e. Current Cell—the cell that is highlighted by the cell pointer. When information is entered into a worksheet, it is placed in the cell highlighted by the cell pointer.
   f. Cell Address—the location of a cell. It is defined by a column letter followed by a row number.
   g. Control Panel—the area above the column letter section of the worksheet.
   h. Mode Indicator—appears in the top right corner of the control panel of the worksheet.
   i. Status Indicator—specifies the condition of certain keys or of the program.

j. Time Indicator—current time being used by Lotus 1-2-3 that appears in the lower left-hand corner of the worksheet screen.

k. Date Indicator—current date being used by Lotus 1-2-3 that appears in the lower left-hand corner of the worksheet screen.

2. Describe the standard way of using the 1-2-3 menu structure.

The first action is to press the / key (sometimes called the command key). The menu pointer is then moved to whatever menu option is desired and the ⊖ (return or enter) key is pressed. The process is continued until the command sequence desired by the user is completed.

3. Describe the alternative method of using the 1-2-3 menu structure.

The only difference in using the alternative method instead of the standard method is that the first letter of the menu option can be typed rather than moving the menu pointer to the desired menu option and pressing the ⊖ key.

4. Describe the purpose of using the function keys F1 through F10.

The function keys have been "programmed" to perform specific operations. These keys let the user perform specific actions such as going to a particular cell without having to use the arrow (directional) keys.

Note: Exercise 3 does not require an answer key.

CHAPTER TWO/EXERCISE 1 ANSWERS

INSTRUCTIONS: Circle T if the statement is true and F if the statement is false.

T F   1. One way to correct incorrect data is to move to the incorrect data's cell, retype the data correctly, and press the ⊖ to enter the correction.

T **F**   2. The formula SUM(A..A7) will add the data in cells A1 through A7.

T **F**   3. To round a number to two decimal places, you use the **Range Format** command.

T F   4. The **Worksheet Erase Yes** command sequence erases the worksheet currently in use from memory.

T F   5. A print range must be specified before a spreadsheet can be printed.

T F   6. The "@" character must precede special functions such as the SUM and ROUND functions.

T **F**   7. Lotus 1-2-3 will automatically save changes that are made to a spreadsheet file.

T F   8. The **File Retrieve** command is used to look at a previously saved file.

T   **F**   9. "BUDGET 1" is an acceptable file name.

T   **F**   10. The letter "X" is the symbol for multiplication when using Lotus 1-2-3.

T   **F**   11. Fonts cannot be changed.

CHAPTER TWO/EXERCISE 3 ANSWERS

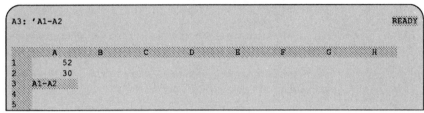

Exercise 2-3

1. What caused the error in cell A3?

    Because A1-A2 begins with an alphabetic character, the formula was read by Lotus as a label.

2. How can the error be corrected?

    Retype or edit the formula to be +A1-A2. Since the formula now begins with an arithmetic operator, the formula will calculate correctly.

CHAPTER TWO/EXERCISE 5 ANSWERS

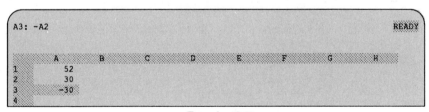

Exercise 2-5

1. What caused the error in computing A1-A2?

    +A1 was typed in and ⏎ was pressed before the formula was completely typed in; at this point, +A1 was entered as the complete formula. -A2 was typed and the ⏎ was pressed again, which resulted in -A2 being entered in cell A3. -A2 results in the answer -30, since 30 is the number in cell A2.

2. How can the error be corrected?

Do not press ↵ before the entire formula is written.

Note: Exercises 7 and 9 do not require answer keys.

CHAPTER THREE/EXERCISE 1 ANSWERS

INSTRUCTIONS: Circle T if the statement is true and F if the statement is false.

T   F
1. An absolute cell reference means that the reference is kept constant, even when copied.

T   F
2. The [F2] key allows you to correct a cell entry without having to retype the entire entry.

T   **F**
3. Worksheet **T**itles allows you to center titles on a spreadsheet.

T   F
4. Worksheet **W**indow allows you to view two different areas of a spreadsheet at the same time.

T   F
5. Worksheet **P**age creates a page break in a spreadsheet.

T   F
6. If column D is hidden on a worksheet using Worksheet **C**olumn Hide, column D will not appear if the worksheet is printed.

T   F
7. Worksheet **G**lobal **R**ecalculation **M**anual is activated so that data can be entered without the worksheet recalculating after each new entry.

T   F
8. Changing the **F**ile **D**irectory changes the drive designation or path to which 1-2-3 saves and retrieves files.

T   **F**
9. **F**ile **E**rase erases a file from memory.

T   **F**
10. The System command permanently returns you to the operating system.

T   **F**
11. Only one cell at a time can be erased.

T   F
12. The width for multiple contiguous columns can be changed to the same width at the same time.

CHAPTER THREE/EXERCISE 3 ANSWERS

1. How can the formula in cell C1 be changed so that cells D1 and E1 also refer to cell B2 for the projected revenue rate?

Change the formula +B1*B2 in cell C1 to +B1*$B$2 so that B2 is an absolute cell reference. This can be accomplished by editing the formula to add the dollar signs to B2. Another method is to reenter the formula and, after highlighting cell

B2 (or typing B2), press the (Abs) key to add the dollar signs. After changing the formula in cell C1, copy the formula to cells D1 and E1. Your screen should look like the one below.

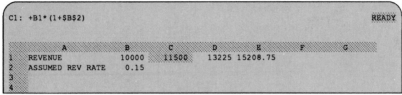

Exercise 3-3

CHAPTER THREE/EXERCISE 7 ANSWERS

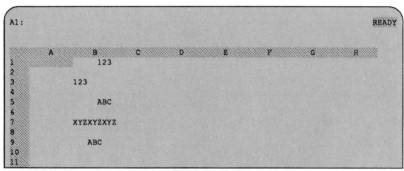

Exercise 3-7

Note: Exercises 5, 9, 11 and 13 do not require an answer key.

CHAPTER FOUR/EXERCISE 1 ANSWERS

INSTRUCTIONS: Circle T if the statement is true and F if the statement is false.

T   F   1. A Lotus 1-2-3 graph can contain up to six different data ranges.

T   F   2. To change a bar graph into a line graph, change the **G**raph **T**ype from **B**ar to **L**ine.

T   F   3. If numbers are changed on the spreadsheet, the graph will reflect the changes when the graph is viewed again on the screen.

T   **F**   4. If numbers are changed on the spreadsheet, the changes will be automatically reflected on any graph file that was previously created from the worksheet.

T   F   5. It is possible to create three completely different graphs with data from one worksheet.

I   F   6. If **File Save** is not executed after a graph is made, the graph settings will not be saved.

T   **F**   7. If a computer is not configured to show graphics on the screen, it is not possible to create and print a Lotus 1-2-3 graph.

T   **F**   8. A color graph on the screen displays the colors in which the graph will be printed on a color printer or plotter.

I   F   9. A pie graph displays the data in data range A.

I   F   10. An XY graph is different from other Lotus graphs because it includes data for variable X.

I   F   11. The scale indicator can be deleted.

CHAPTER FOUR/EXERCISES 3 and 5 ANSWERS

ABC COMPANY

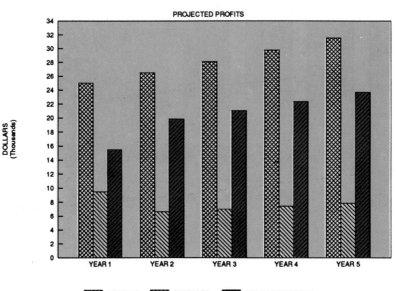

Exercise 4-3

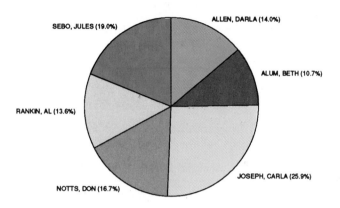

Exercise 4-5

CHAPTER FIVE/EXERCISE 1 ANSWERS

INSTRUCTIONS: Circle T if the statement is true and F if the statement is false.

T   **F**   1.   In Lotus 1-2-3, a template file must be combined with another file containing data to generate a new spreadsheet.

T   F   2.   A template is a good way to keep spreadsheets standardized.

T   **F**   3.   When data is added to a template in memory, it is automatically added to the template file on the disk.

T   F   4.   A template can be used to create multiple worksheets.

T   F   5.   After adding data to a template in order to create a new spreadsheet, the worksheet should be saved using a name other than the template file name.

Note: Exercise 3 does not require an answer key.

CHAPTER SIX/EXERCISE 1 ANSWERS

INSTRUCTIONS: Circle T if the statement is true and F if the statement is false.

T   **F**   1. The range name for a range of cells must be taken from a label already existing on the worksheet.

T   F   2. A template is a good way to keep range names standardized for several worksheets.

T   **F**   3. A detail worksheet is used for summarizing data from several worksheets.

T   **F**   4. The **File Combine Copy** command sequence is used to add numbers together from various worksheets.

T   F   5. If desired, the exact range location rather than a range name can be specified when using the **Named/Specified-Range** command to combine data between worksheets.

T   **F**   6. **File Combine Add** can add numbers to existing cells containing values or formulas.

T   **F**   7. The **Range Value** command can change values into formulas.

T   F   8. The **File Combine Copy** command sequence can be used to copy formulas from one worksheet to another worksheet.

T   **F**   9. When files are combined, the original detail worksheet and summary worksheet are automatically changed.

T   **F**   10. Cells on separate worksheet files cannot be linked.

CHAPTER SIX/EXERCISE 3 ANSWERS

```
B10: 18600                                                              READY

                A           B        C        D        E        F        G
  1                                ABC COMPANY
  2                                  BUDGET
  3
  4
  5                            QTR1     QTR2     QTR3     QTR4   YR TOTAL
  6
  7   SALES                 $60,000  $61,200  $62,424  $63,672 $247,296
  8
  9   EXPENSES
 10     SALARIES            18,600   18,600   19,500   20,200   76,900
 11     RENT                 9,000    9,000    9,000    9,000   36,000
 12     TELEPHONE            1,000    1,050    1,103    1,158    4,311
 13     OFFICE SUPPLIES        750      800      850      900    3,300
 14     MISCELLANEOUS        1,000    1,030    1,061    1,093    4,184
 15                       ------------------------------------------
 16        TOTAL EXPENSES  30,350   30,480   31,514   32,351  124,695
 17                       ------------------------------------------
 18   GROSS PROFIT         $29,650  $30,720  $30,910  $31,321 $122,601
 19                       ==========================================
 20
                                   UNDO                         CAPS
```

Exercise 6-3

CHAPTER SIX/EXERCISE 5 ANSWERS

1. The command sequence **File Combine Add** will not add values from the detail worksheet to cells in the summary worksheet that contain formulas. Therefore, the first value was added to cell A1 and it was used to evaluate the other cell formulas.

2. Use the **Range Value** command sequence to change the cell contents from formulas to their evaluated values. Then execute the **File Combine Add** command sequence.

CHAPTER SEVEN/EXERCISE 1 ANSWERS

INSTRUCTIONS: Circle T if the statement is true and F if the statement is false.

T **F**   1. When sorting a database in Lotus 1-2-3, the data-range must include the field titles.

T F   2. The field titles must be located in the line directly above the first record of the database for the **Data Query** command sequence to work properly.

T **F**   3. It is appropriate to have more than one line consisting of field titles designated in the input range.

<u>T</u>   F   4. Each criteria consists of two cells.

<u>T</u>   F   5. The input range, criteria, and output range must be manually set up on the worksheet and then identified through the menu options.

<u>T</u>   F   6. The output range allows you to copy the desired fields that match the criteria to another area on the worksheet.

T   <u>F</u>   7. When designating the output range, you may highlight only the field names that are desired; the records will appear directly below the field names on the worksheet in the output range when the **Q**uery **F**ind is executed.

<u>T</u>   F   8. The QUERY key allows you to perform a query based upon previously set ranges.

T   <u>F</u>   9. The criteria for a worksheet can be set by setting the bin range.

T   <u>F</u>   10. The **Q**uery **U**nique command deletes multiple records in a database.

<u>T</u>   F   11. The **D**ata **T**able option makes it possible to analyze changes in variables that impact decision-making situations.

CHAPTER SEVEN/EXERCISES 3, 5, 7, 9 AND 11 ANSWERS

```
A1: [W18]                                                    READY

            A            B           C          D       E        F
1                   ABC COMPANY
2
3
4
5        LAST NAME    FIRST NAME     CITY       STATE
6   CERNOSKY         ELENA         MIAMI        FL
7   FERNANDEZ        JOE           MIAMI        FL
8   ADAMS            JOSEPH        NEW YORK     NY
9   ADAMS            JENNIFER      NEW YORK     NY
10  NOLAN            RYAN          NEW YORK     NY
11  ADAMS            CHARLES       SAN ANTONIO  TX
12  ARRON            SANDRA        SAN ANTONIO  TX
13  NGUYEN           ALFRED        SAN ANTONIO  TX
14
15
```

Exercise 7-3

```
E6:  (T) +C6="NEW YORK"#OR#C6="SAN ANTONIO"                              READY


          B               C          D      E          F           G            H
 1    ABC COMPANY
 2
 3
 4
 5    FIRST NAME        CITY       STATE  CITY     LAST NAME    FIRST NAME
 6    JOSEPH          NEW YORK     NY    +C6="NEW ADAMS        JOSEPH
 7    SANDRA          SAN ANTONIO  TX             ARRON        SANDRA
 8    JENNIFER        NEW YORK     NY             ADAMS        JENNIFER
 9    JOE             MIAMI        FL             NGUYEN       ALFRED
10    ALFRED          SAN ANTONIO  TX             ADAMS        CHARLES
11    CHARLES         SAN ANTONIO  TX             NOLAN        RYAN
12    ELENA           MIAMI        FL
13    RYAN            NEW YORK     NY
14
15
```

Exercise 7-5

```
A1:                                                                      READY


          A        B        C        D        E        F        G            H
 1
 2        1        4        7       10       13       16       19
 3
 4
 5
 6       0.1
 7       0.2
 8       0.3
 9       0.4
10       0.5
11       0.6
12
13
```

Exercise 7-7

```
A1: [W11]                                                          READY


           A          B          C          D          E          F          G
 1                  HOUSE LOAN
 2
 3    ASSUMPTIONS
 4       $75,000              PRINCIPAL
 5        11.00%              ANNUAL INTEREST RATE
 6          240               LOAN PERIOD IN MONTHS
 7         0.92%              MONTHLY INTEREST RATE
 8       $774.14              CALCULATED PAYMENT AMOUNT
 9
10                  PAYMENT
11    PRINCIPAL      AMOUNT
12                   774.14
13       75,000      774.14
14       80,000      825.75
15       85,000      877.36
16       90,000      928.97
17       95,000      980.58
18
19
20
                               UNDO                              CAPS
```

Exercise 7-9

```
B17: [W10] 'BIN RANGE                                             READY


        A        B        C        D      E        F        G        H        I
 1                                      ABC COMPANY
 2                                      SALARY BUDGET
 3
 4
 5   EMP NO LAST NAME FIRST NAME DIV   QTR1     QTR2     QTR3     QTR4    TOTAL
 6     568  SPROUT    AL          3   5,950    5,950    6,450    6,450   24,800
 7     123  LYLIE     SUSAN       1   7,800    7,800    7,800    8,580   31,980
 8     390  CHIN      TOMMY       2   5,000    5,000    5,200    5,200   20,400
 9     972  JOHNSON   SANDRA      1   8,200    8,200    9,000    9,000   34,400
10     898  VALETTI   GEORGE      3   5,900    5,900    6,300    6,300   24,400
11     239  ARMOUR    CYNTHIA     2   5,200    5,200    5,400    5,400   21,200
12     576  JOHNSON   ERNEST      1   8,000    8,000    8,800    8,800   33,600
13     833  JONES     NINA        3   6,750    6,750    6,750    7,450   27,700
14                                    ------------------------------------------
15          TOTAL                    52,800   52,800   55,700   57,180  218,480
16
17          BIN RANGE FREQUENCY
18                1         3
19                2         2
20                3         3
                               UNDO                              CAPS
```

Exercise 7-11

CHAPTER EIGHT/EXERCISE 1 ANSWERS

INSTRUCTIONS: Circle T if the statement is true and F if the statement is false.

T **F**   1. @MIN determines the minute for a given serial number.

I F   2. Multiple items in a range may be listed individually (e.g., the syntax in the formula @COUNT(B1,B3,B4) is correct).

T **F**   3. Arguments within an @ function may be placed in any order desired by the user.

I F   4. Extra spaces are not acceptable within @ functions.

I F   5. A label has a value of 0 and will be counted as such if included in a range for an @ function.

I F   6. It is possible to alter an @ function with arithmetic operations to get the desired results (e.g., the formula @PMT(B1,B2/12,B3*12) is syntactically correct).

I F   7. If a worksheet file containing the @NOW function (formatted to show the date) is retrieved from a file and actively recalculates, the @NOW function will display the *current* system date.

T **F**   8. A single-cell item in an argument may not be entered directly into the formula (e.g., the formula @NPV(A1,B1..B6) cannot be entered as @NPV(.1,B1..B6).

I F   9. More than one @ function may be used in a formula.

I F   10. The @IF statement allows you to test one or more conditions in a worksheet and provide appropriate responses for either a true result or a false result.

I F   11. Date and time special functions are available in 1-2-3.

T **F**   12. XLOOKUP allows you to look up values in a row or a table.

I F   13. You can modify the appearance of a series of characters using the string functions.

T **F**   14. Data queries cannot be accomplished using special functions.

CHAPTER EIGHT/EXERCISE 3 ANSWERS

INSTRUCTIONS: Use the Financial Analysis Functions available in Lotus 1-2-3 to solve the following exercises.

1. Compute the internal rate of return for the following cash flow stream using .15 as the guess rate:

   -1000, -500, 900, 800, 700, 600, 400, 200, 100
   The answer is .313959 or 31.4%.

2. Compute the net present value for the following cash flow stream using .10 as the discount rate:

   -1500, 900, 800, 700, 600, 400, 200, 100
   The answer is 1327.646 or 1206.951 depending upon whether the initial investment of $1,500 is discounted.

3. Compute the future value if the payment per period is 500, the interest rate is 10%, and the term is 15 years.
   The answer is 15886.24.

4. Compute the present value using the arguments previously given in problem 3.
   The answer is 3803.039.

5. Compute the payment amount for a $100,000 loan that has an interest rate of 10 percent and is to be paid on an annual basis for a period of 12 years.
   The answer is 14676.33.

6. Compute the *monthly* payment amount assuming all arguments in problem 5 stay the same except the time period is 30 years.
   The answer is 877.5715.

7. Compute the straight-line depreciation for an office machine having an initial cost of $13,000, an estimated useful life of 8 years and a salvage value of $200.
   The answer is 1600.

8. Using the data given in problem 7, compute the depreciation of the office machine for the sixth year using the double-declining balance method.
   The answer is 771.2402.

9. Using the data given in problem 7, compute the depreciation of the office machine for the sixth year using the sum-of-the-years'-digits method.
   The answer is 1066.666.

10. Suppose $10,000 has been invested in an account that pays an annual interest rate of 10%, compounded monthly. Determine how long it will take to get $30,000 in the account.
   The answer is 132.3820 months or about 11 years.

11. Suppose that $5,000 is deposited at the end of each year into a bank account. If 8% interest is earned per year, compute how long it will take to earn $20,000.
The answer is 3.607432 or about 3 1/2 years.

12. Suppose $15,000 has been invested in a bond which matures in 9 years to $25,000. Interest is compounded monthly. Determine the monthly interest rate.
The answer is .004741.

CHAPTER EIGHT/EXERCISES 5, 7, 9 AND 11 ANSWERS

```
B3: (T) [W38] @IF(A3>60,@TRUE,@FALSE)                          READY

         A                    B                    C        D
1        20  @IF(A1>=30#AND#A1<=40,"True","False")
2        30  @IF(A2>25,@TRUE,@FALSE)
3        50  @IF(A3>60,@TRUE,@FALSE)
4
5
6
7
8
9
10       NA  @ISNA(A10)
11       10  @ISNUMBER(A11)
12  Worksheet@ISSTRING(A12)
13
14
```

Exercise 8-5
Part 1

```
B3: @IF(A3>60,@TRUE,@FALSE)                                    READY

         A     B     C     D     E     F     G     H
1        20 False
2        30     1
3        50     0
4
5
6
7
8
9
10       NA
11       10
12  Worksheet
13
14
```

Exercise 8-5
Part 2

```
B3: @IF(A3>60,@TRUE,@FALSE)                                         READY


        A        B        C        D        E        F        G        H
1            35 True
2            10        0
3            75                 1
4
5
6
7
8
9
10        NA
11        10
12  Worksheet
13
14
```

Exercise 8-5
Part 3

```
C10: @SQRT(B10)                                                     READY


        A        B        C        D        E        F        G        H
1              -45       45
2               45       45
3                2 7.389056
4          52.9876       52
5              1.5 0.405465
6               10        1
7               20        8
8               12 0.636568
9          67.3468   67.347
10             225       15
11
12
```

Exercise 8-7
Part 1

```
C10: (T) [W13] @SQRT(B10)                                           READY


        A        B        C        D        E        F        G
1              -45 @ABS(B1)
2               45 @ABS(B2)
3                2 @EXP(B3)
4          52.9876 @INT(B4)
5              1.5 @LN(B5)
6               10 @LOG(B6)
7               20 @MOD(B7,B8)
8               12 @RAND
9          67.3468 @ROUND(B9,3)
10             225 @SQRT(B10)
11
12
```

Exercise 8-7
Part 2

```
D3: (F2) [W10] @CHOOSE(C3,@ERR,$D$11,$D$12,@ERR)*B3                    READY
```

	A	B	C	D	E	F	G
1			Sales Tax	Sales			
2	Product	Price	Rate Code	Tax			
3	Beans	0.79	1	0.00			
4	Hammer	2.59	2	0.21			
5	Nail	0.25	2	0.02			
6	Cake	1.25	1	0.00			
7							
8							
9			Sales Tax				
10			Rate Code	Tax Rate			
11			1	0%			
12			2	8%			
13							
14							

Exercise 8-9
Part 1

```
D10: [W12] @HLOOKUP(B10,$B$3..$E$6,C10)                               READY
```

	A	B	C	D	E	F
1						
2	COMMISSION		SALES AMOUNT			
3	CODE	$2,000	$3,000	$4,000	$5,000	
4	1	200	300	400	500	
5	2	100	150	200	250	
6	3	40	60	80	100	
7						
8		SALES	COMISSION	COMISSION		
9	EMPLOYEE	AMOUNT	CODE	AMOUNT		
10	ABRAMS	$2,500	3	40		
11	CHEN	$3,500	1	300		
12	MARTINEZ	$3,100	1	300		
13	SMITH	$4,900	2	200		
14	ZACHARY	$3,000	3	60		
15						
16						

Exercise 8-9
Part 2

```
C10: (P0) @VLOOKUP(B10,$A$4..$B$6,1)                                  READY
```

	A	B	C	D	E	F	G
1							
2		TAX					
3	SALARY	RATE					
4	$25,000	2%					
5	$50,000	7%					
6	$75,000	15%					
7							
8							
9	EMPLOYEE	SALARY	TAX RATE	TAXES			
10	ABBOTT	$78,000	15%	$11,700.00			
11	GARCIA	$52,000	7%	$3,640.00			
12	MONTEGUET	$60,000	7%	$4,200.00			
13	SMITH	$48,000	2%	$960.00			
14							
15							

Exercise 8-9
Part 3

```
A13: @N(NUMBERS)                                                    READY

          A        B         C         D        E        F        G        H
1    592.783 592.783
2
3     Lotus 1-2-3  is  fun  to  use
4    Lotus 1-2-3 is fun to use
5
6    123.456    123.456
7
8    Northeast
9    Northeat
10          0
11
12          1        2         3
13          1
14
15
```

Exercise 8-11
Part 1

```
A13: @N(NUMBERS)                                                    READY

          A              B              C         D        E
1        592.783    @STRING(A1,3)
2
3     Lotus 1-2-3  is  fun  to  use
4    @TRIM(A3)
5
6    123.456        @VALUE(A6)
7
8    Northeast
9    Northeat
10   @EXACT(A8,A9)
11
12              1              2         3
13   @N(NUMBERS)
14
15
```

Exercise 8-11
Part 2

CHAPTER NINE/EXERCISE 1 ANSWERS

INSTRUCTIONS: Circle T if the statement is true and F if the statement is false.

T   **F**   1. The range name for a macro must be taken from a label already existing on the worksheet.

T   **F**   2. The range name for a macro must begin with a forward slash and a letter of the alphabet.

T   F   3. A macro is a way to automate a repetitive procedure.

T   F   4. Certain keystrokes in a macro must be enclosed in braces (the { and } characters).

T	**F**	5.	In a macro, the tilde (the ~ symbol) represents pressing the forward slash (the command key /).
T	**F**	6.	To execute the macro named \ Z, you must hold down the Ctrl key and tap the letter Z.
T	F	7.	A named range for a macro must contain the first macro step as the first line in the range.
T	**F**	8.	When entering data on a worksheet manually, the tilde can be used instead of pressing ⏎.
T	**F**	9.	Either apostrophe (the ' or the ') can be used to preface a macro step.
T	**F**	10.	Documentation must be included in a macro.
T	F	11.	You can automatically record macro keystrokes.
T	**F**	12.	Macro instructions can be executed one step at a time by using Alt-F1.
T	**F**	13.	It does not matter where you place macros on a worksheet.

CHAPTER NINE EXERCISES 3 AND 5 ANSWERS

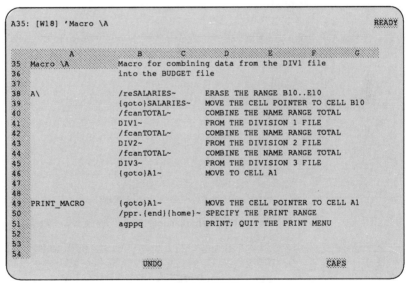

Exercise 9-3

```
A18: [W18]                                                          READY

              A                 B           C           D          E          F
18
19  MACRO \G            Macro for creating a bar graph
20
21  \G                  {goto}A1~              MOVE TO CELL A1
22                      /grg                   RESET PREVIOUS GRAPH SETTINGS
23                      tb                     SELECT BAR AS GRAPH TYPE
24                      xYEARS~                SELECT YEARS FOR X AXIS
25                      aREVENUE~              SELECT REVENUE FOR A RANGE
26                      bPBT~                  SELECT PBT FOR B RANGE
27                      cPAT~                  SELECT PAT FOR C RANGE
28                      olaREVENUE~            ENTER LEGEND FOR A RANGE
29                      lbPROFIT BEFORE TAX~   ENTER LEGEND FOR B RANGE
30                      lcPROFIT AFTER TAX~    ENTER LEGEND FOR C RANGE
31                      tfABC COMPANY~         ENTER FIRST TITLE
32                      tsPROJECTED PRIFITS~   ENTER SECOND TITLE
33                      tyDOLLARS~             ENTER Y AXIS TITLE
34                      qvq                    QUIT OPTIONS, VIEW, QUIT GRAPH
35
36
37
                            UNDO                                    CAPS
```

Exercise 9-5

CHAPTER TEN/EXERCISE 1 ANSWERS

INSTRUCTIONS: Circle T if the statement is true and F is the statement is false.

T   **F**   1. You cannot use macros to place a sequence of values on a worksheet.

T   **F**   2. A macro can be automatically executed when a file is retrieved by naming the macro ZERO.

T   **F**   3. A series of macro instructions can be repeated only if you know how many times the instructions need to be repeated.

T   **F**   4. A maximum of 10 menu options can be included in any user-designed menu.

T   F   5. The /X commands have equivalent macro commands available in later releases of Lotus 1-2-3 that are easier to understand.

T   F   6. Macros can be used to restrict the input by a user of a worksheet to a specific set of cells.

T   **F**   7. The only way to use an interactive macro is if you force the macro to execute when the file containing the macro is retrieved.

T   F   8. Macros can be written that prompt the user to input information.

CHAPTER TEN/EXERCISES 3 AND 5 ANSWERS

```
A1: 'Macro \E                                                              READY


        A         B         C         D         E         F         G         H
1   Macro \E Macro for entering numbers across a row of a worksheet
2
3   \E        {goto}B15~
4   ENTER     {?}{right}
5             {branch ENTER}
6
7
8
9
10
11
12
13
14
15            100       25        125       200
16
17
```

Exercise 10-3

```
A1: 20                                                                     READY


        A         B         C         D         E         F         G         H
1       20        25        15 -0.33333
2       25        30        35 -0.14285
3       40        30        20    0.5
4       15        25        35 -0.28571
5       25        35        20   -0.5
6
7   Macro \C Macro for calculation
8
9   \C        {goto}D1~                              Move to cell D1
10  COMPUTE   +({left 3}-{left 2})/{left}~           Enter the formula
11            {down}{left}                           Move to column C
12            /rncTEST~{up}~                         Create test range
13            {right}                                Move to column D
14            {if @COUNT(TEST)=1}{branch END}        Branch to end if through
15            /rndTEST~                              Delete range name TEST
16            {branch COMPUTE}                       Enter next formula
17
18  END       /rndTEST~                              Delete range name TEST
19            {goto}A1~                              Move to cell A1
20            {quit}                                 End of macro
                        UNDO                                    CAPS
```

Exercise 10-5
Part 1

```
A23: 'Macro \P                                                    READY

         A         B         C         D         E         F         G         H
 21
 22
 23  Macro \P  Macro to print the results
 24
 25  \P        {goto}A1~            Move to cell A1
 26            /pprA1.D5~           Define the print range
 27            agppq                Print the worksheet and quit
 28
 29
```

Exercise 10-5
Part 2

Note: Exercises 7 and 9 do not require an answer key.

CHAPTER ELEVEN/EXERCISE 1 ANSWERS

INSTRUCTIONS: Circle T if the statement is true and F if the statement is false.

<u>T</u>   F   1. By using Allways, the appearance of worksheets can be significantly improved.

T   <u>F</u>   2. At most 6 type styles can be used on a worksheet.

T   <u>F</u>   3. You cannot shade the background of a cell.

T   <u>F</u>   4. When the underline option is used, the underline covers the entire width of the cell.

T   <u>F</u>   5. You cannot use 1-2-3 without invoking Allways.

Note: Exercise 3 does not require an answer key.

INDEX

1-2-3 COMMANDS

1-2-3 FUNCTIONS

1-2-3 ADVANCED MACRO COMMANDS
